Adventuring in the Caribbean

The Sierra Club Adventure Travel Guides

*A*dventuring in the Caribbean

COMPLETELY
REVISED
AND
UPDATED

CARROL B. FLEMING

SIERRA CLUB BOOKS · SAN FRANCISCO

The Sierra Club, founded in 1892 by John Muir, has devoted itself to the study and protection of the earth's scenic and ecological resources—mountains, wetlands, woodlands, wild shores and rivers, deserts and plains. The publishing program of the Sierra Club offers books to the public as a nonprofit educational service in the hope that they may enlarge the public's understanding of the Club's basic concerns. The point of view expressed in each book, however, does not necessarily represent that of the Club. The Sierra Club has some sixty chapters coast to coast, in Canada, Hawaii, and Alaska. For information about how you may participate in its programs to preserve wilderness and the quality of life, please address inquiries to Sierra Club, 85 Second Street, San Francisco, CA 94105.

LIBRARY OF CONGRESS CATALOGING-IN-PUBLICATION DATA
Fleming, Carrol Bernard.
 Adventuring in the Caribbean : the Sierra Club travel guide to forty islands of the Caribbean Sea including the Bahamas, Jamaica, the Dominican Republic, Puerto Rico, Antigua, Barbados, Grenada, Trinidad, and the Virgin Islands / Carrol Fleming.
 p. cm.
 ISBN 0-87156-393-2
 1. Caribbean Area—Description and travel—1981– — Guide-books.
 I. Sierra Club. II. Title.
 F2165.F58 1989
 917.2904'52—dc20   89-6143

Production by Robin Rockey • Cover design by Bonnie Smetts • Book design by Amy Evans • Maps by Ellen Milan • Composition by Wilsted & Taylor

Printed in the United States of America on acid-free paper containing a minimum of 50% recovered waste paper, of which at least 10% of the fiber content is post-consumer waste

10 9 8 7 6 5 4 3 2 1

To my Mom and Dad

who gave me my tropical blood and so much else.

I wish my Dad had lived to see this finished.

Contents

List of Maps

Acknowledgments

The first thank-you goes to my editor, Jim Cohee, whose advice, patience, and support have made this book a reality at last. Jim has seen this project through its long life of ups and downs.

Ellen-Marie Milan has also been involved from early on and has provided the original maps that highlight the text.

Erika Smilowitz, Ph.D., of the University of the Virgin Islands and the founding editor of *The Caribbean Writer,* has contributed greatly toward the completion of this work. She wrote the section on Caribbean literature. Her critical advice and encouragement were essential to the completion of the manuscript.

This book would have taken considerably longer without the help of two able typists: Ruth Cherkas of ABC Secretarial Services in Santa Monica, California, and Christene Henry of St. Croix.

A number of people—named and unnamed—contributed technical and local information in the course of my travels and research. They include Maria Grech of St. Lucia; Lowell and Cloyd Laporte; and Joy Michaud, Walter Knausenberger, and Rudy O'Reilly of the University of the Virgin Islands Cooperative Extension Service, who readily provided background material.

The tourist boards of Jamaica, Barbados, Bonaire, and St. Lucia and the Clement-Petrocik Company for the French West Indies Tourist Board were particularly helpful.

My sisters Colleen and Pattie, my nephew Dalton, and my friends Pat and David, Bonnie, Julia, and Angie all provided tremendous moral support—everything from letters and jokes to child care and chocolate. My daughter, Arietta, who has grown up Caribbean, has shared her adaptable sense of adventure, insights, smiles, and erasers. She is delighted that we have finally finished.

Revised Edition: Special thanks to Patricia Castillo for her timely and efficient research and to Richard D., Kathy McCallum, Ann and Lowell Laporte, Erika and Francis Waters, Marjorie Bishop, and my mother for continuing support.

PART ONE

Islands and Sea—
Geography and
Natural History

"Time is longer than rope."

Caribbean proverb

Islands in the Sun: Name, Place, and Size

The ease of air travel and the association between the Hawaiian shirt and the palm tree have so homogenized the world's islands that lots of people don't really know where the islands are. In the Caribbean, the problem is compounded by various names and subdivisions. It may be that the very romance of the words Antilles, Caribees, and West Indies carries too much historical freight for the islands to sit firmly in their own latitudes. So, let's start with a few geographical basics.

When Columbus discovered these islands on his second voyage, he called them Antillia. He thought he might have found Atlantis, but, hedging his guess, he named them for the lesser-known legendary island. The Indians he found there—the Caribs—called their sea the Caribbean and its islands the Caribees. "Antillia" was shuffled slightly by the mapmakers and came back as "Antilles." Other mapmakers preferred the term "Western Islands," which soon evolved to the more romantic "West Indies."

The West Indies is a ridge of islands that separates the Atlantic Ocean from the Caribbean Sea. This archipelago stretches some 1,500 miles in length, arcing northward from the Venezuelan shoulder of South America as gracefully as a dancer's arm pointing the way to Florida. The northern end of this crescent is formed by Cuba, ninety miles off Key West, Florida; the southern tip is Trinidad, just nine miles from Venezuela.

Of the hundreds of islands in the West Indies, only fifty or so are inhabited. Cuba is the largest land mass of the island chain; at 44,218 square miles, it is about twice the size of Ireland. The West Indies include other bits of land that are hardly large enough to accommodate a resting seabird. Some of these islands are sea mountains newly emerged from the ocean, with the sharp peaks of their volcanoes still smouldering. Others, barely above sea level, are composed of corals built upon centuries' accumulation of their own dead. Whole nations may be contained in a few square miles.

The entire land mass of West Indies is about 91,000 square miles, somewhat smaller than the state of Oregon. The relative smallness does not seem possible, so greatly does the visual space exceed the reality. Places embraced by the ocean seem to be inherently large. And such an ocean . . .

The Caribbean (usually pronounced Car-ib-BE-an, although Ca-RIB-be-an is still a dictionary second) is a blue, blue offshoot of the Atlantic Ocean that fills a sea basin of about a million square miles. The Caribbean lies between 9° and 22° north latitude and 60° and 89° west longitude. On the south, it washes the northern coast of South America, where Colombia and Venezuela were once called the Spanish Main; it also brushes Panama. On the west, the Caribbean touches the shores of Costa Rica, Nicaragua, Honduras, Guatemala, Belize, and Mexico's Yucatan Peninsula. To the north, the sea is bounded by the larger West Indian islands, called the Greater Antilles—Cuba, Hispaniola (shared by Haiti and the Dominican Republic), Jamaica, and Puerto Rico. On the east it is bounded by a chain of islands called the Lesser Antilles, which arc from the Virgin Islands in the north to Trinidad in the southeast.

All of the West Indies lie within the tropics. This means that even the northern boundary of Cuba is south of the Tropic of Cancer. If you're one of those people, as I am, who has always thought of the Tropic of Cancer as a literary event, this is a good time to look at the map. Geographically, the Tropic of Cancer marks the northern boundary of the tropical belt, the latitude 23°27' north, at which the sun can be directly overhead. This imaginary line is projected through Little Exuma Island, just south of Georgetown, Bahamas. (All of the Bahama Islands lie completely in the Atlantic Ocean; we'll pinpoint them later.)

Now, back to the Greater and Lesser Antilles. A few more confusing subdivisions will make you far better informed than the average tourist (even if you wear a Hawaiian shirt). The Lesser Antilles—Guadeloupe is the largest with 680 square miles—are divided again into the Windward Islands and the Leeward Islands.

Sailors long have called windward the direction from which the wind blows, and leeward the direction it blows toward. Think of it this way: If the wind is blowing your hair straight back from your face, you're looking to windward; if the wind's at your back, you're looking to lee.

St. Lucia, St. Vincent, Grenada, and the Grenadines make up the Windwards; the islands from Martinique north to the Virgins make up the Leewards. Story has it that the Leewards were originally named be-

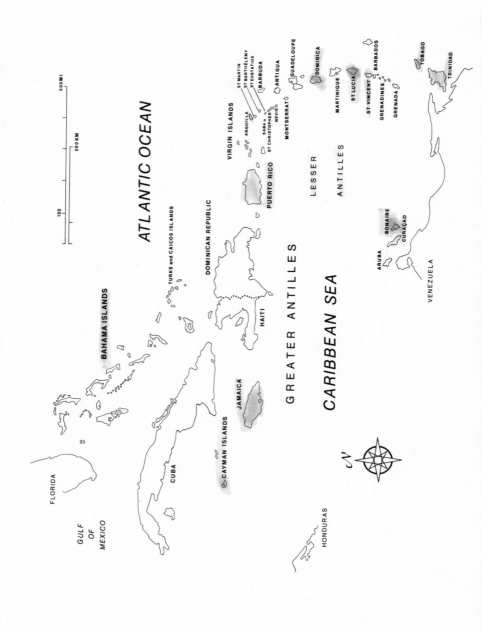

cause they lie to the lee of the important British colony of Barbados. A quick glance at the map shows that the Windwards also lie to the lee; so, who knows. I've heard islanders say the Windwards are so named simply because the wind blows harder there.

Each of the islands, regardless of its name, has both a windward and a leeward side. Don't give up; this is the final confusion for the moment. The Caribbean trade winds are easterlies, which means they come off the Atlantic and blow over these islands. The Atlantic side is the windward side of every island, the side where the sea swells crash landward after running the Atlantic, often bringing Portuguese glass balls and corks, sometimes bottles or Styrofoam full of barnacles from Africa. The windward.

The other side of each island—the Caribbean Sea side—is where the wind heads. It is the soft side, the leeward, where most of the sheltered harbors and big settlements have grown up.

Once Upon Paleozoic Times—Geology

So many millions of years ago that it is absurd to consider, story has it that the continents of the world were one. One land mass called Pangaea or "all lands" was washed by a common sea called Panthalassa. Then the land began to move apart. Ever so slowly, with the passage of unfathomable geologic time, it separated into the continents we know, dividing the ocean waters.

While this may read like well-dreamed legend, it is readily explained by the currently accepted theory of plate tectonics. Start by thinking of this 4.5 billion-year-old planet from the inside. The earth's central core is surrounded by a hot, viscous mantle. On top of this is the thin shell of the earth's crust. Plate tectonics proposes that this crusty shell, which seems solid ground to us, is composed of twenty or so great chunks or plates that actually move.

These plates, somewhat like great rafts thirty to a hundred miles thick, freight the continents and oceans as they grind, bump, sink, and well up, much like crackers in slowly stirred soup. The plates' movements result in the formation of new land and the loss of old. The jostling of these plates produces earthquakes and volcanic eruptions. The edges of the plates are destroyed as they fold downward, or subduct, under opposing plates, and disappear into the earth's mantle along the ocean's deep sea trenches.

In the ocean basins where the earth's crust is thinnest, the plates may crack and spread apart. Molten rock may well up through these cracks, solidifying and expanding the ocean floor. The Atlantic Ocean continues to widen in area an inch or two a year. This is pivotal to the geological story of the Caribbean Sea.

While the exact age of the Caribbean Sea has not been pin-pointed, theory holds with a certain chain of events. Long ago, the Caribbean Sea and the Mediterranean Sea were joined. About 200 million years ago, these seas slowly separated, and the intermediary—and geologically young—Atlantic Ocean was formed.

At present, the Caribbean Sea encompasses an area of more than a million square miles of tropical blueness. Considered a suboceanic basin of the Atlantic, the Caribbean seabed is ridged, buckled, and divided into five basins of its own. Oddly enough, considering the expanse of the Caribbean, subsurface water enters from the Atlantic in only two places, or sills. One sill is more than 6,000 feet below Anegada Passage; the other sill is about 5,000 feet below the Windward Passage between Cuba and Haiti. This flow of water, while not always understood, has always been important to mariners who have long respected the wily currents of these passages.

Another significant landmark of this sea basin is the Cayman Trench (or Bartlett Deep), which lies just north of Jamaica and stretches horizontally most of the way from the Cayman Islands to Cuba. Plunging 25,216 feet, it is the Caribbean's deepest point.

The eastern shores of most of the Caribbean islands form the official boundary line between the Atlantic Ocean and the Caribbean Sea. In fact, the volcanic islands that fringe the eastern Caribbean mark the meeting of the Atlantic and Caribbean plates. Active volcanoes give visible evidence of the great heat generated as the Atlantic plate is being driven slowly under the Caribbean plate. In the north, the Greater Antilles have a marked east-west fault system where the North American plate and the Caribbean plate grind together. Puerto Rico and the Virgin Islands lie along this fault system.

As one might expect, earthquakes are common where there is so much geological stress. Actually, the greatest number of earthquakes occur in the sea depths, especially in the Cayman and Puerto Rican trenches. (The Puerto Rican Trench, not far off the island's shore, lies in the Atlantic.) Earthquakes vary in intensity from the barely perceptible to the very destructive. One noteworthy disaster occurred along a Jamaican fault in 1692, when an intense quake toppled the thriving town of Port Royal into what is now Kingston Harbour. Recent underwater excavations have yielded a wealth of information and relics, which can be seen in the Kingston Archaeological Museum.

At times, earthquakes occur independently, but they also may accompany volcanic activity, often preceding eruptions. This century has seen several volcanic eruptions that caused considerable loss of life and property. The most dramatic was the 1902 eruption of Mount Pelée on Martinique, which completely destroyed wealthy, cultured St. Pierre—"Little Paris of the West Indies"—and all but one of its 30,000 inhabitants. Mount Pelée's Musée Volcanologique documents the eruption with pictures and relics, including clocks that melted to a stop at 8 A.M.

These are only two very visible examples of geological change in this active section of the earth's crust, where volcanism, faulting, and major uplift help explain the geology of both the seabed and the islands themselves.

The West Indian islands are the remnants of several different mountain chains. The remnants are suited with lavish costumes—hillsides of smooth, green satin; coral sands of soft, white velvet; and coastlines of nubbly brocade. Some places wear coats and colors unquestionably volcanic: black beaches and yellow sulfur springs.

Most of the islands are high, cresting in a central mountain range or a single peak visible for miles. How dramatic and mysterious their sudden heights must have appeared to the early explorers long confined to sea level. The higher peaks, which often seem continually capped with clouds or misted with light rain, appear snow-covered from out at sea. The sight of one cloud-wrapped volcano so struck Columbus on his second voyage that he named the island Señora de las Nieves (Our Lady of the Snows). The island still bears the Anglicized version of that name—Nevis.

The dramatic contours of the islands are accented by deep valleys; short, twisting rivers that flow rapidly to the sea; and narrow coastal plains. The coasts are marked by lagoons and mangrove thickets as well as sandy beaches (both white coral and black lava). Coasts are often ringed with coral reefs, so that while there are deep natural harbors, many have treacherous entrances.

Before you get the idea that this central mountain geography strings the islands together like well-matched pearls, let me point out obvious differences that reflect different origins. Both Antigua and Barbados, with their limestone bases, are low and undulating. The larger islands of Hispaniola, Jamaica, and Puerto Rico have more flat areas and wider coastal plains, although Cuba is the only island with what might be called extensive lowlands. Anguilla, Anegada, the Turks and Caicos, and the Bahamas barely rise above sea level.

The mountainous islands have varying geologies. In the north, three very old mountain ranges arc over, and under, the Caribbean and tend to form the islands' central spines. The northernmost range is the lowest and may be the oldest. (The oldest rocks in the West Indies are found on Cuba and Trinidad.) This range starts in the low hills of Belize in Central America, runs along the eastern Yucatan Peninsula, and surfaces again in northwestern Cuba.

The second mountain chain buckled upward some 100 million years ago and forms the highest mountains in the West Indies. It begins in southwest Mexico and runs northeast to form the Cayman Ridge in the Caribbean Sea; the Sierra Maestra range in Cuba; and the Cordillera Central of Hispaniola where Pico Duarte in the Dominican Republic reaches 10,417 feet. This old loop of high mountains also forms a central ridge in Puerto Rico.

The most southerly of these ancient mountain ranges also starts in southern Mexico, sweeps out into the Caribbean Sea (Swan Island may be one of its peaks), and surfaces again in Jamaica. There the ridge reaches 7,500 feet in the Blue Mountains (of coffee-bean fame) that form Jamaica's lovely backbone. The range then winds on through southern Haiti, where it rises to a misty 9,000 feet.

Let's follow the geologic record of St. John, in the U.S. Virgin Islands, as an example of the geological history of the West Indies. Deep earth-drilling projects on the island have given a fairly accurate account of the stages of its formation.

Some 100 million years ago in the late Cretaceous period (when dinosaurs became extinct), volcanoes erupted deep in the Caribbean seabed. Their outward flows solidified layer upon layer. These ancient lava flows can still be seen and are still separately recognizable; on St. John they're called the Water Island formation.

These volcanic rocks probably were exuded at a great depth, because there are few signs of explosive fragmentation and very little pumice in them. It would take the pressure of at least 15,000 feet of water to dampen the explosive cooling of this molten rock.

A few million years of undersea volcanic activity passed like this. The slow thickening of lava flows coincided with an overall decrease in water depth and an uplift of the entire Caribbean area.

The next phase of island building on St. John was violent. It is the period of earth building favored by moviemakers, with a fiery horizon and boulders flying sky high. One house-sized piece of the old underwater flow called Easter Rock still sits high on a hill on St. John.

During the passage of thousands of years of hellfire and brimstone land building—a period politely called subaerial volcanism—the slopes of the explosive cone weathered and the sediments were deposited in the surrounding seas. During another submergence, the dramatic cone lost its fiery impulse and sharp peak and began to weather round. A long, quiet underwater period followed, during which marine sediments—the skeletons of coral and plankton—filtered down and built up on the old shell. The first layer over the volcanic base was a layer of limestone about 100 feet thick. Over this was a much thicker layer of impure sediments—mostly debris from the older volcanic periods—probably dumped over the limestone during submarine earthquakes. The earthquakes caused underwater landslides and watery mud slides called turbidity currents.

One more important geologic event gave St. John its present structure. This was the rather late intrusion of molten rock that cooled slowly before it reached the surface. The intrusion resulted in a fine-grained black rock called diorite.

All of this island building—volcanism, uplift, sedimentary deposition—was pretty much completed some 60 million years ago. Of course, the earth's shaping forces didn't stop then. Continuing changes, due to active earth movements along faults, resulted in the Caribbean's valley systems and deep bays.

The islands probably were never completely underwater again, although there were considerable worldwide variations in sea level during the ice ages. At one point, the sea level was 200 to 400 feet lower than it is today, leaving much of the Great Bahama Bank exposed and revealing considerably different land configurations in the northern Caribbean as well. The Puerto Rican plateau—the shelf that now includes Puerto Rico, the Virgin Islands, and numerous cays and islets—was probably a single land mass at that time. In addition, Cuba may have formed part of a land bridge to Florida, and Jamaica may have been joined to Nicaragua.

Apparently, the ocean temperature in the northern Caribbean during glacial times was not warm enough for much coral growth. Extensive coral reef development coincided with increasing sea temperatures and rising sea levels caused by melting glaciers.

The narrow coastal plains on islands like St. Thomas, St. John, and Tortola are also tied to the continuing rise in sea level. Eroded material from the uplands has had little time to accumulate, and many lower valleys have been filled by the rising seas. This phenomenon is referred to as the "drowned coastline." There are many classic examples in the northern islands, where picturesque ridges reach directly to the sea, separating a series of small bays with their steep headlands.

As for the remaining more southerly islands, their younger geology fits more easily the image of islands born overnight from the sea. Many of them look newly emerged, with sharp crags and valleys, boiling lakes, and steaming sulfur springs. The outer arc of the Lesser Antilles is a series of young limestone islands. Antigua is the classic example. The inner arc —Dutch Saba south to Grenada—is volcanic, with at least one active or semiactive volcano on every island.

This inner sweep of still-smoldering islands probably lifted up about 75 million years after the older mountains of the Greater Antilles. These rugged islands rise from a submarine ridge that starts 3,000 to 5,000 feet below sea level. Underwater and aerial volcanism and subsequent uplift are responsible for the islands' present shapes.

Barbados, which sits considerably to the east of these volcanic islands, has different origins. It's a young, uplifted island, where the flat, fertile fields cover a coral crust laid down over folded shales and sandstone.

Trinidad, Tobago, Aruba, Bonaire, and Curaçao are all of sedimentary origin. They are also structurally associated with South America; Trinidad seems to fit into the Gulf of Paria like a puzzle piece. Geologically, Trinidad evolved in much the same way as the Greater Antilles, except that limestone is rare; the sandy quality of its sedimentation reflects deposits from the nearby delta of Venezuela's great Orinoco River. Trinidad's mountains are thought to be extensions of the coastal Andes.

This dry scenario with its ancient convolutions and vague connections seems far removed from the actualities of island forest and farmland, far from the vibrant colors of tree-borne bromeliads over the black soil of a rain forest or the stooped women tending the terraced red clay of Haitian hills. But ancient earth-boiled origins are binding. Histories and, consequently, cultures in this part of the world have balanced on the inability of land to bear cane, the height of mountains, the position of harbors, and the wiles of the prevailing winds.

The Green Flash

Some say the green flash brings money or luck to its beholders. The flash is a very narrow ribbon of color that streaks horizontally across the horizon as the last bit of the sun's disk slips away for the night.

One needs a clear view of the horizon and air free of dust or haze—conditions that are most likely to be found on mountains, in deserts (the Egyptian desert is famous for its sunset displays), and on tropical seas. Most Caribbean islands have favorite green-flash viewing sites, usually a mountaintop bar.

I'm not suggesting that you complicate your evening rum punch with the laws of physics, but this capricious, momentary flash of color has a real, physical explanation. Once considered fantasy, optical illusion, or a result of retinal fatigue, the green flash is now known to be a purely atmospheric phenomenon that can be rather lightly (so to speak) explained. Think of the way white light is bent and spread out into a visible spectrum as it passes through a glass prism. The same thing happens to sunlight as it slows upon entering the earth's atmosphere. The sunlight is bent, or refracted, and spread out—dispersed, if you will—into a rainbow of colors of different wavelengths, with red—the longest—at one end of the spectrum and violet—the shortest—at the other.

When the sun's disk is fully visible, the light rays overlap so that the spectrum cannot be seen. As the sun slips below the horizon, the colors of the spectrum disappear one at a time, the longest first, just as the children's song recounts—red, orange, yellow, green, blue, purple.

However, we don't see this orderly passing of rainbow colors into twilight, and we only rarely see a flash of green because the earth's atmosphere filters out the other colors. Light, as well as being dispersed in air, is also absorbed and scattered by it. Absorption, which is mostly due to water vapor, ozone, and oxygen, mainly affects the orange and yellow bands of light. Scattering has the strongest effect on the short wavelengths of blue and violet. The scattering of blue light colors the sky.

So when the sun nears disappearing, the red rays slide first below the horizon. The orange and yellow light rays are caught and absorbed by the thick cushion of air they must travel before we see them. Blue and violet are scattered to invisibility. That leaves green—bright, pure green—the wavelength least affected. That is what one sees or hopes to see—the green flash. (Sometimes at high altitudes with particularly clear air, the shorter light rays may make it through, and the flash will be blue or violet.)

If you're eager to see a green flash, you can use binoculars or a small telescope to help widen the band of color. It is very narrow, appearing about as wide as a one-inch ribbon looks from a distance of about 600 yards. The duration of the flash depends on the rate at which the sun slips below the horizon, a rate that varies with the time of year. I've found the word "momentary" to be a valid description of its passage in the tropics: The sun sets more slowly from the equator toward the poles (a summer's eve flash in Norway at 79° north latitude might linger as long as ten to fourteen minutes). To avoid eye damage, turn your binoculars toward the horizon only when the sun is nearly gone. With a telescope, be sure to use a filter or solar eyepiece.

Don't be discouraged if you don't see the green flash on your first sunset; it takes a bit of practice. Once you've seen it (or have seen photographs), you're more likely to see it again. Usually, only about a third of the people in a group will see it on a given evening.

If your vacation is short (and your obsession strong), you might want to try to see a sunrise green flash. It's about as common as the sunset variety, although it may be more difficult to observe because the viewer must judge the exact position of sunrise. Capricious and momentary are the bywords. After all, if everyone saw the green flash every time, it would lose its allure.

Tropical Days and Tropical Nights—Climate

In the West Indies, tropical days tend to slide into tropical nights almost every day, all year. The annual temperature for the entire island chain averages a balmy 80°F (27°C). That is a fact, although it doesn't exactly answer every potential traveler's first question: "Is it really hot?" Oddly enough, that question is answered more accurately with tourist brochure evasion: "Well, yes, no, maybe, sometimes, and take a light wrap for nights."

Let me elaborate. We all know that 80°F is warmer than room temperature by a few degrees. We may not all know at this point that these islands—or most of these islands, most of the time—are cooled by the fresh, easterly trade winds. Eighty degrees on Tortola or St. Lucia, for example, just doesn't feel like 80° in, say, Washington, DC, or Los Angeles. On a Caribbean island, simply stepping into the shadow of a building or climbing a few feet above sea level, not to mention slipping into the surrounding waters, will be immediately cooling. The Caribbean Sea's steady temperatures (80° to 82°F) also help keep the islands pleasant.

Altitude also affects temperature. When staying in the mountains or planning to hike there, be aware that temperatures drop 1°F for every 300-foot gain in altitude. This also means that the city heat of, say, San Juan or Port-au-Prince can be escaped with a short drive up a nearby mountain.

Island temperatures may drop as much as 12° to 19°F at night (prompting the advice to take a wrap for evenings). This means day-to-night (diurnal) variations are far greater than those between the seasons, which are divided simply into wet and dry. The wet season generally lasts from May or June until October or November. Most of this summer moisture is associated with weather called easterly waves, a disturbance in the trade winds that brings cloudy skies and rain. The average annual rainfall for the West Indies is about 65 inches. However, this varies considerably with latitude, altitude, and the configuration of the land. Since much of this rain is carried by winds forced to rise over the mountains, most islands have wet windward slopes and dry leeward ones. Jamaica, for example, has windward slopes that get 150 inches of annual rainfall, while nearby leeward slopes get only 60 inches. These great differences are clearly reflected in both the natural vegetation and agriculture.

Generally, low islands have less rainfall; flat Antigua receives an annual 44 inches while Dominica's high mountains receive more than 120 inches per year. Latitude also makes a difference: The more northern islands tend to get less rain. Cuba, which sits barely south of the Tropic of Cancer, receives about 54 inches of rain a year; most of the low, dry Bahamas lie north of the line and receive even less. These islands do, however, get occasional winter storms. These northers, or "nortes," which blow down from North America and are often responsible for lots of rain and low temperatures, are most likely in December, January, and early February.

What this means to you as a vacationer is, basically, once you're south of the Tropic of Cancer, rainfall will relate more to local topography than

The Caribbean's balmy temperatures add to the enticements of tropical nights. (Photo courtesy of Jamaica Tourist Board.)

anything else. Remember also that, for the most part, these are *warm* rain showers. While most occur at night, the short bursts that may moisten a day are neither long nor unpleasant. You can usually see them coming, and rain clouds or squalls are often so localized that it will be raining on one side of the road and not on the other. These conditions also give rise to spectacular rainbows.

If all this seems too perfect, you're right. Enter the hurricane. Hurricanes are tremendous low-pressure storms with counterclockwise winds circulating around a calm center, or eye. When cyclonic winds exceed 75 miles per hour, a storm receives hurricane status. Winds may continue to intensify, sometimes reaching speeds of 100 to 200 miles per hour. Passing hurricane clouds may drop as much as ten to fifteen inches of rain, often averaging an inch per hour. Extremely low barometric pressure and violent seas are also characteristic. Long storm swells often reach out for a thousand miles beyond a hurricane and are often the first noticeable sign of its approach.

Hurricanes can occur any time of year, but they tend to form in the

late summer and fall. An often-repeated bit of island folklore sums up hurricane season:

> June too soon
> July pass by
> August we must
> Remember September
> October all over.

While we don't know exactly what causes hurricanes to form, a great deal
is known about their behavior after they develop. The average Caribbean
hurricane is 400 to 500 miles in diameter, with a calm, often-blue-sky eye
of perhaps ten to fifteen miles in diameter. The entire system travels at
fifteen miles per hour or less and has an average life span of nine days.
The Caribbean Sea, the western North Atlantic, and the Gulf of Mexico
combined average about six hurricanes per year, with considerable variation. Some years won't have even a scare. Other years have many: 1933
had twenty-one named hurricanes! A number of hurricanes never actually
come ashore in the West Indies. They merely spend their youth at sea and
continue to intensify as they move toward the large land mass of North
America. The Virgin Islands actually have fewer hurricanes than Providence, Rhode Island.

While the exact paths of hurricanes are still somewhat unpredictable,
weather satellites have taken much of the anxiety out of hurricane season.
Now, residents can usually depend on at least forty-eight hours' notice.
All of the islands have active civil defense units and hurricane shelters. If
you plan to camp in an out-of-the-way place, keep in touch once a day by
listening to the news on the local AM radio station. In the unlikely event
that the island you are visiting is put on hurricane alert, simply follow
directions. Tourists are included in safety plans. You might spend some
time really getting acquainted with other tourists and islanders in a snug
cinderblock school or church.

Hurricanes continue to be viewed with great respect. Some of the
islands—the Virgin Islands and Puerto Rico—still take a holiday called
Hurricane Supplication Day on the fourth Monday in July to pray for
safety during the coming hurricane season. Another holiday, Hurricane
Thanksgiving Day, on the third Monday in October, ends the vigil.

Be assured, the odds are in favor of perfect vacation weather; hurricanes are rare. This information is not to scare you but rather to enlarge
your understanding of a climate that on the surface may appear to be all
ripe fruit, warm sand, and calm seas.

Living with the threat of natural catastrophe, including volcanoes,
earthquakes, and hurricanes, has had a profound effect on the West Indian

view of the world, the powers of Providence, the wiles of fate. Old-timers who remember the days of do-it-yourself weather prediction, when hurricanes arrived without notice, tell harrowing tales of those caught out in small boats, of forests without a tree left standing, or of whole towns flattened. Someone might point out an old boat that sits up a mountain where it was carried by a storm still dangerous in memory.

One old woman dramatically recalled being spared when she was six years old and so frightened by the screaming winds and buckets of gray rain that she hid under the dining room table. When the hurricane had passed, she was under that old table shivering in her light summer dress and the whole house was gone.

Uniqueness and Balance—How Plants and Animals Get to Islands

Islands are special places. There are no two exactly alike anywhere. Isolated by the encompassing sea, they are finite, complete. Space is precious. Each island develops a finely tuned ecosystem—a mini-world of delicate balances that is easily jostled.

Essentially, there are two types of islands—oceanic and continental. Oceanic islands, through the marvels of evolution, tend to nurture unusual species—from flightless birds to swimming iguanas—perfectly suited for niches not found elsewhere. So-called continental islands were once connected to major continents with land bridges that probably disappeared when sea levels rose after the ice ages. These islands have flora and fauna akin to that on their parent continents. Trinidad, which was part of South America as recently as 8,000 years ago, is the only continental island in the West Indies and, as such, has a far greater number of plant and animal species than the rest of the islands.

The oceanic islands tell a different story. Their original plants and animals somehow must have migrated from other places. In this century, scientists who have watched new volcanic islands slowly become colonized by plants and animals have a number of theories concerning the ways life got there, a study usually referred to as "island dispersal."

The intrepid Charles Darwin was the first to consider how islands get their original flora and fauna. He thought that ocean currents might have carried plant seeds to the Galápagos Islands and experimented to see if certain seeds would still sprout after being soaked in saltwater. Darwin found a number of species that would; further studies have found the red mangrove, with its long bean seed, to be the hardiest of all. This sturdy, floating seed, from six to twelve inches long, can ride the ocean currents for months and still sprout when it comes ashore. This no doubt accounts for the presence of mangroves on most of the world's tropical islands. The red mangrove is a true colonizer; its arching root system stabilizes the coastline and provides food and shelter for a great number of other species. (See The Mangroves for more information.)

The subtle wash of seed flotation is not the only way ocean currents bring species to islands. The most dramatic method is called rafting. Insects and larger animals may ride to islands on floating debris, anything from a single leaf to a branch or a whole tree. In the Caribbean, hurricanes in particular are responsible for uprooting entire trees that may pick up dozens of hitchhikers as they careen down a swollen river on the way to the sea.

One raft story tells of a large boa constrictor that arrived on St. Vincent wrapped around the trunk of a cedar tree. Tree and snake probably drifted up from Trinidad, some 200 miles south. In this case, the snake lived only long enough to kill a few sheep and did not establish a new species. Scientists presume this is probably the same way the deadly fer-de-lance viper arrived on Martinique, since the snake isn't found on any of the other Caribbean islands.

Most reptiles are fairly successful raft riders: Lizards, especially geckos, fare better than snakes, but snakes do better than amphibians and mammals that need fresh water. Perhaps for this reason, mammals and even amphibians are rare in the Caribbean. The only indigenous mammals are a few varieties of insectivores, rodents, and a diverse group of bats. Bats are expert travelers and are found on nearly every island in the world. The West Indies has bats of all descriptions. Some eat fruit or insects; others eat fish. Trinidad alone supports sixty-two different species, including the real version of the fabled vampire bat.

As for the Caribbean's amphibian population, only one type of frog is common to all the islands; only thirty species of frogs and toads are found throughout the entire chain. Many of them—from the tiny, singing tree frog to the plump freshwater frog that is cooked into a delicacy called mountain chicken—are found only in limited areas. The endangered frog that becomes mountain chicken is found only on Dominica and Montserrat; Dominica has recently established a hunting season to help protect the huge frog's dwindling numbers.

Like ocean currents, air currents are also responsible for adding to island populations. Airborne insects can drift on the wind for weeks. Islands, especially high ones, attract wind-carried organisms simply by the moisture in their atmosphere. When the air currents they ride bring them into the damp air around an island, the insects absorb moisture, become heavier, and drop to the ground.

Birds are numerous and varied in the West Indies. Like insects, they also may arrive on swift air currents or be blown to a new place by a storm. Birds often carry seeds, and they may have small animals, even snails or their eggs, stuck to them. In one experiment, Darwin fed the seeds of freshwater plants to fish and then fed the fish to birds. He found that the seeds still sprouted after they had passed through the birds, apparently unharmed by the digestive processes.

Most of the Caribbean islands have their own indigenous bird species. Of the 340 bird species on the large island of Cuba, fifty-four are indigenous. These numbers tend to drop in direct relation to the size of an island. But most of these islands, especially the geologically younger and more isolated Windwards, have at least one "nowhere-else" species of bird. Several types of rare parrots live on only one mountain on one island.

Of course, arriving on an island carries no guarantees for a new species. Obviously, on a new island the simplest forms of life—lichens, fungi, algae—must gain the first foothold to help create a base for more advanced forms. Carnivores must have prey; herbivores or insectivores must be able to find plenty of plants or insects in order to survive. Anything that arrives out of sequence will perish.

Even plants and animals that arrive in an order that makes survival possible must adapt quickly to their new environment. They must adjust to the climate, find shelter and food, and perhaps stave off predators. On top of that, in order to establish a new species, the migrants must be either pregnant females or a mating pair. Once these problems are overcome, an island species will evolve more rapidly than one on the mainland. It's also possible for the descendants of a pioneering species to evolve in different ways, much as Darwin's celebrated Galápagos finches.

Over millions of years, chance arrivals to the Caribbean developed in diverse ways, and each island came to support a unique, exquisitely balanced web of interactions. Without large predators or food competition with foragers, numbers of unusual birds and lizards thrived.

But these finely tuned ecosystems were easily put awry by the great transporters and users of plants and animals—people. In the West Indies, as on islands everywhere, people have greatly altered the delicate natural systems.

The first pre-Columbians, whose dugout canoes rode the currents north from South America in much the same way as the islands' original flora and fauna, led simple lives. They planted a few crops, starting the island tradition of slash-and-burn agriculture. They hunted the docile iguana and agouti, and they fished nearby. Later, the Arawaks brought their barkless dogs with them (eaten to rapid extinction by Spanish explorers) and kept parrots as pets. Theirs was an era of simple interaction with a pristine landscape. Yet they fished out some shallow-water sites; their massive shell piles of time-blackened conchs and tritons still dot certain coasts.

Early explorers hunted animals unused to predators. Many early accounts of the islands mention how tame the animals were as they were slaughtered. The Bahamian monk seal was completely exterminated early on, as were most of the iguanas along the trade routes. Several species of parrots and doves were hunted to extinction, or nearly so. The ranks of the great lumbering sea turtles were decimated by sailors who stacked them helpless on their backs on board ship to provide fresh meat at sea.

These changes to island flora and fauna did not stop with the early explorers. Colonists brought cows and goats to forage on island plants that had fed only birds in the past. The importation of one plant—sugarcane—dramatically altered entire islands, ecologically as well as historically. Each new group of people came to the Caribbean with plants and animals from other places. Slaves brought plants from Africa, Captain Bligh brought the breadfruit tree from the South Pacific, hoteliers landscaped with Hawaiian ornamentals. The list continues to the present.

The Caribbean is no longer ecologically Edenic. Very little vegetation still resembles pre-Columbian growth. It is said that Dominica, with its wild, inaccessible heights, is the only island that Columbus would still recognize. Today, sea turtles and a number of other species remain endangered. Great tracts of once-fertile land have been deforested and leached by erosion and overfarming. Fishermen must venture farther and farther from population centers to find conch, lobster, and fish that once flourished off nearby coasts.

Widespread respect for island plants and animals is slow in coming, and new conservation laws often remain unenforced. Yet in the last few years, island governments have become more appreciative of natural assets they once took for granted. National trusts have been activated; national parks, sanctuaries, and reserves protecting animals and areas, from rain forests to coral reefs, are on the increase. A number of islands have legislation protecting habitats and endangered species; some places have seasonal restrictions on hunting and lobster fishing, for example. Many islands conduct ecology-oriented public awareness campaigns.

But conservation simply lacks practical logic on many islands. These are poor places where people need the fruits and animals of the earth to survive. It's very hard to explain to a Haitian fisherman, for example, that he must not kill sea turtles when his own children are starving. Even on islands with better standards of living—where there is great poverty but not the destitution seen in Haiti—no police officer is going to rebuff a man who is providing for his family by killing an iguana in a sanctuary.

People are not willing to believe that destroying mangrove trees ruins the fishing. Many people live from meal to meal, scratch by scratch; things come and go, time passes. It's hard to worry over the vague future when today is burden enough.

These problems and attitudes make it extra hard to institute effective, long-term conservation programs to protect the unique ecologies of these islands. But daily life—whether the bulldozer of "progress" or the snare of a peasant—cannot indefinitely continue to ignore the slow process of the islands' original greening.

The Mangroves

In the shore world of blatant blues and bright corals, only the mangroves have a dress of quiet that surrounds them like a stage costume in a show noted for its sense of impeccable line. Their every reach seaward is a presentable arch as their aerial roots weave land and sea together in one of the most complex, productive, and underrated ecosystems of the tropics. While the mangroves' primeval aura seems to evoke a certain casual curiosity (and lots of literary references), few people actually explore the mangrove thickets and observe the amazing array of organisms that find food and shelter there.

Nearly 25 percent of the Caribbean coastline belongs to the mangroves. The quiet places—the still waters of the estuary or lagoon that attract more herons and pelicans than people—are where the graceful prop roots of the mangrove trees arch seaward into the shallows.

As the mangroves grow outward from the shore, they gradually stabilize and build the coastline. Leaves drop, silt gathers, the shells of sea animals and coral rubble compound. Almost imperceptibly the space beneath the roots fills and the shore bows outward.

The activity is more visible in the canopy of branches overhead and in the interlacing roots of the trees. Flocks of storks, herons, egrets, cormorants, kingfishers, and ibises may roost on branches where lizards sun, snails cling, and crabs scuttle down toward the water. At the waterline, the mangrove roots are thick with flat, dull clusters of mangrove oysters. When Sir Walter Raleigh returned to England after visiting Barbados in 1595, he was nearly laughed out of court for his description of these oysters that grow on trees.

The mangrove ecosystem is just as unique beneath the water, where the looping roots interlace along the sea bottom. The newest roots land short and wave with the currents. Often they are covered with coral, sponges, algae, and mollusks. Grunt, snapper, grouper, tarpon, and sea trout either breed or do much of their growing in mangrove areas. The trees also provide natural buffer zones that absorb the shock of hurricane waves and filter pollutants from freshwater runoff.

Mangroves are common throughout the tropics in both hemispheres, and there are about fifty-five species worldwide. They reach north well into the temperate zone, although the mangroves of Florida and Baja California are somewhat smaller than those of warmer areas. The trees are markedly similar throughout the world and indeed may have colonized from a primary source. West African mangroves, for instance, are the same type as those in the Caribbean.

Under the ideal growing conditions of lagoon or estuary, mangroves may grow into impenetrable thickets. On more rigorous coasts they may occur in patches or as solitary trees. Wherever it roots, the mangrove tree must deal with stringent conditions to survive. It is essentially a large, woody salt-marsh plant that has evolved unique ways of obtaining fresh water and oxygen from its salty, water-logged environment.

Most plants extract oxygen from air spaces between soil particles. But in the sodden mud of the mangrove swamp, the soil is compacted and lacks air spaces. Mangroves solve this problem by extracting oxygen directly from the air.

The prop roots of the red mangrove have tiny holes in their bark. The mangrove breathes through these pores, called lenticels. If the pores are blocked in any way by algae, silt, or oil spills, the tree literally smothers.

Only the red mangrove can tolerate the harsh conditions at the water's edge. Although the tree may be wholly or partially rooted in saltwater, it cannot use the water as is. The red mangrove solves this difficulty by being saltier inside than the seawater outside, so the less dense fresh water can enter. It has also developed cutin-thick leaves like many drought-resistant plants.

Farther inland where the land is more stable, conditions become suitable for other types of mangrove trees. The colonies of black mangroves that grow directly behind the red mangroves lack dramatic aerial roots and have solved the oxygen dilemma another way. The black mangrove obtains its oxygen with odd woody roots that grow upward through the soil in low clusters, like soda straws protruding through the mud. The black mangrove is most easily recognized by these characteristic strawlike pneumatophores.

Behind the marshy zone of the black mangroves there are sometimes strips of white or buttonwood mangroves. They can be identified by their small white blossoms or tiny brown pineconelike buttons. These trees grow on the landward fringes of the swamp where life is somewhat easier.

Although life may be tough for this pioneer plant, once the mangrove is established, the tree makes things a lot easier for the diverse interdependent group of organisms that gather around it. The food web of the nearby community actually starts with the mangrove leaf.

When mangrove leaves drop to the mud or into the water, they begin to decay through the actions of bacteria and fungi. The leaves are gradually broken down into smaller and smaller pieces, forming a rich layer of organic matter, or detritus, which feeds shrimps, crabs, worms, shellfish, insect larvae, and small fish.

Six months after a leaf settles to the bottom, about a third of it will have been grazed by scavengers. There are mangrove areas where the leaf detritus exceeds three tons per acre per year. It can form up to 90 percent of the diet of detritus feeders, which in turn become prey for larger invertebrates and the juvenile fish that find the mangroves an ideal environment in which to grow. These organisms feed many commercially sought fishes that eventually feed people.

Not all mangrove debris—leaves, twigs, flowers, fruit—remains in the immediate area. It is often washed from the mangrove ecosystem and transported by currents into other habitats, where it may form the base of food chains. Much of the impact of the mangroves on the local ecology is not apparent in the immediate swamp. But so important is their contribution, for instance, as a fish nursery, that research in the U.S. Virgin Islands has directly linked the decline in red mangrove acreage to the decline of valuable offshore fishes. This is especially true with regard to game fish, such as snook, tarpon, and spotted sea trout.

In earlier times, mangroves were considered useful in more basic ways.

Mangrove bark is rich in tannin, which was once extracted for commercial use. The wood was used for making charcoal, fish traps, and ropes and halters for cattle.

Increasing population pressures in tropical areas have resulted in the decimation of countless numbers of mangrove areas. Not only have thriving mangrove lagoons been bulldozed and filled, but remaining stands near population centers have suffered slower deaths through pollution, which can result in fatal algal blooms.

The conditions that threaten mangroves with algal growth are often subtle. Sometimes it's as simple as the development of the waterfront bordering a mangrove lagoon. When the land is cleared and either developed or paved, the increased rainwater runoff washes more nutrients and sediment into the lagoon. The extra nutrients, which can also come from untreated sewage, result in increased algal growth that can clog the mangroves' breathing pores. It can also block sunlight, causing a slower change in the biotic balance. In addition, sediment can build up from runoff and eventually form a blanket of black mud that kills the trees in much the same way an oil spill does.

Fortunately, public awareness of these problems, and of the mangroves' ecological importance, is growing. Many places now require some type of official sanction for the cutting of even one mangrove tree. Puerto Rico was one of the first places to institute severe fines for destruction of mangroves. A court case on that island awarded the Environmental Quality Board $6.1 million following an oil spill that destroyed twenty-three acres of mangroves. This compensation—about six cents per organism killed—was the first time that a ship's owners have been held responsible for more than the oil cleanup. While the penalty can't replace the complex life chain of a formerly thriving lagoon, it may encourage shippers to be more careful in the future.

It is almost certain that only continued public support and appreciation for these quiet areas, where such a dense array of life clusters to spawn and grow, can save the mangroves and their dependent fisheries.

The mangrove begins life as an elongate seed that drops from its parent plant when ready to root or float. It can tolerate months in saltwater riding the currents and still sprout on some distant coast. How ironic that a tree with such a survival capacity is unable to cope with the modern stress of pollution.

If You Explore . . .

Be ready for mud and mosquitoes. Mangrove areas are usually marked on local boating charts. If not, ask around; almost all West Indian islands have patches of mangroves. If you can't find a fully developed labyrinth of trees, you may be able to observe the mini-environment of one or two; even in developed harbors, there are often a few mangroves sprouting up near the docks.

The red mangrove (*Rhizophora mangle*) likes sheltered coasts, deep bays, estuaries, and lagoons; so check these quiet areas first, especially on the southern shores of larger islands.

Rich mangrove stands may be found along the southern coasts of Cuba, Puerto Rico, and Jamaica; the North Sound off Grand Cayman; the Samaná area of the Dominican Republic; and the Gulf of Paria coast of Trinidad. Ensenada Honda Bay, Culebra, Puerto Rico; and Hurricane Hole, St. John, U.S.V.I., have extensive mangrove stands. And some of their winding bayous, best reached by small boat, have water clear enough for good snorkeling.

A few other relatively accessible mangrove areas may be found on Martinique (Park Presqu'Île de la Caravelle on Trinité Peninsula), Montserrat (Fox's Bay Bird Sanctuary; the north end has very large trees, in mud with paths); Puerto Rico (Boquerón); and St. Thomas, U.S.V.I. (Red Hook).

The most comfortable (and sometimes the only) way to explore the mangroves is by boat. Be sure to shut down the outboard and drift, row, or tie to a tree on a long painter to really observe this quiet area.

Most mangroves are in tidal zones. Low tide will reveal a little more intertidal life, like tree oysters. However, the tidal flux is rarely more than a foot or so in most of the West Indies and is sometimes considerably less in these protected spots.

Tides *are* important in the Bahamas where the water flow is considerable and the currents may be strong. Nobody wants to get stuck in a tiny bayou with a small outboard and a three- to four-knot current running against them, or to be left high and dry with six hours or a half mile of mud in front of them.

Always ask for local knowledge before venturing out. If you're still in doubt or unsure of handling a small boat, take a guide. Sometimes you can get a fisherman with a boat to guide you for less than the price of a boat rental alone. It goes without saying: Agree beforehand on price (don't be afraid to bargain, especially if you feel you're getting hustled) and time (which is generally "around and about").

Bird activity in the mangroves is likely to relate more to time of day than tide. Most of the large birds feed or roost in the mangroves during the early morning or evening, although I've seen great blue herons and pelicans at all times of day.

Unfortunately, these cooler early and late hours also coincide with the height of insect activity; that is, mosquitoes, sand flies (also called no-see-ums and, in Puerto Rico, mi-mis—pronounced me-me's), and sometimes big green-headed flies as well. Wear repellent. It's a good idea to wear a hat or put a good dose of repellent in your hair; the no-see-ums love the scalp and face. Long sleeves are also a good idea.

During the midday hours there are fewer bugs, but the heat may shorten a trip unless you plan to snorkel among the mangrove roots to observe underwater life. Check with locals first, since the water in some mangrove swamps is too murky to see much. There's exceptionally clear water in several places in Hurricane Hole, St. John, U.S.V.I., and also in Leinster Bay, St. John, where the water is quite shallow and provides an easy view for even nonswimmers. I've seen bonefish tailing (feeding nose down with their tails breaking the surface) in Leinster's warm waters and also found the old, worn-down teeth of manatees on the rocks along the shore. The teeth of these huge sea mammals come conveyor belt–style, with fresh ones popping up as the old ones are worn down by the constant grazing on sea grasses and are discarded.

Things You May Notice

BLOOMS AND SEEDLINGS: the red mangroves' small, yellow star-shaped flowers that lengthen into brown-green pods (like smooth, thick string beans). These pods, called propagules, may be hanging on the adult plant or floating nearby; they are often found on beaches.

CORALS: usually the encrusting type; sometimes they find space on the mangrove roots.

FIDDLER CRABS: active little crabs often found among the pneumato-phore straws. They live in the mud in burrows about an inch in diameter. They are most easily recognized by one flashy, enlarged claw that the males fling and fiddle in their battles and mating dances. These claws are so much for show that the crabs can't feed with them; they must depend on their single small claw for such activity. The females have two of the smaller claws. Approach quietly; fiddler crabs startle easily.

HERMIT CRABS: found just about anywhere in any old shell; both land and marine varieties.

LENTICELS: the breathing pores (little holes) on the prop roots of the red mangroves.

LITTORINA: gray-turbaned snails about one-quarter inch to one inch in size. Found from the high-water line to well up in tree branches, they need moisture but don't like to get wet. A species in transition, they leave silver silk trails.

NUDIBRANCHS: shell-less snails that often resemble the ruffled leaves of sea lettuce; most commonly pale green here. Look closely; they move.

OYSTERS: the flat, dull clumps found on the roots near the tide line are mangrove oysters; those with serrated edges are coon oysters. Both are filter feeders that are preyed upon by birds as well as marine predators such as oyster drills and the carnivorous murex snails.

PNEUMATOPHORES: soda-straw breathing tubes of black mangroves; look on the shoreward side of the red mangroves where the land is more stable.

SEA ANEMONES: soft animals that look like tentacled flowers. They grow on or near mangrove roots in colonies or singly; colors vary.

SEA SQUIRTS (TUNICATES): soft finger tubes, often yellowish.

SEA URCHINS: familiar black pincushions, generally in evidence or tucked back in the mangrove roots.

SPONGES: usually the most brightly colored growth clinging to the mangrove roots below the water.

This list merely scratches the surface. Look well back in the shadows of the mangrove roots for lobsters and young fish; you can often see pencil-sized barracuda developing their uncanny stares. Stay as still as you can; these juveniles are quite timid, with good right.

Look in the bottom mud among the leaves. You may see worms; crabs; murex snails; plump sea cucumbers; and that strange, upside-down jelly-fish, *Cassiopeia*. They look like fat brown pancakes, tiered with a fringe of tentacles reaching upward to catch food particles. Typical of mangrove areas and quiet bays, *Cassiopeia* of all sizes sometimes absolutely blanket the seafloor. They grow to a foot or so in diameter, pulsate in the mud, and occasionally are stirred up by storms or prop wash. They're harmless bottom dwellers with little or no sting.

Apparel and Accoutrement

Bathing suits with long-sleeved shirts and pants (or you can wrap your legs in a towel to foil sun and bugs); a hat and mud shoes; sunscreen;

insect repellent; sunglasses; towels; binoculars; bird and fish guides; cameras; snorkeling gear; lunch.

If you can't find a place where the water is clear enough to snorkel comfortably, you can wade or lean out of the boat and hold your mask (or glass-bottom bucket) in the water for a small glimpse of this underwater community.

Coral Reefs

Long before the ocean inspired tales of mermaids and sea monsters, it nurtured a genuine and amazing community—the coral reef. It is not an individual creature but a balanced marine habitat where plants and animals live among the sculptures of corals.

The coral reef rises from the sea bottom like an underwater garden. The blue sparkle and quick shadow of sea light glints over coral shaped like lettuce, like lace, like fingers, like cactus. The flat branches of elkhorn coral reach toward the surface light like great trees. Staghorn coral extends pointed sprigs, and brain coral grows in convoluted lumps.

Bright yellows, reds, and purples color the thickets and grottoes that drop into crevasses sheltering lobster, eels, and fish of every conceivable color and variation. Wildly crayoned inventions of modern art swim in the sea—mock black eyes for the four-eyed butterfly fish and turquoise stripes for the queen triggerfish.

Crabs, sponges, worms, and mollusks cling and burrow; calcareous algae cement the gaps. Extravagant plumes and netted sea fans wave like a visible pulse. The rules are simple here: Eat and be eaten, and spawn in between.

Because of their branched shapes and vibrant colors, corals were once thought to be exotic sea plants. But these underwater gardens are the work of a simple animal, the coral polyp. The polyp is little more than a double-walled cylinder with a tentacled mouth for trapping its planktonic food. Tiny symbiotic algae live within the polyps, both coloring them and providing them with nutrients the algae produce by photosynthesis.

In form, the coral polyp is similar to its flowerlike relative the sea anemone, except that the coral polyp secretes a limy, cuplike skeleton for its own support. By filtering and processing seawater within its soft animal body (a protoplasm not unlike your own), the coral polyp can produce a ruffled cup of calcium carbonate as hard as rock.

Each species of coral forms its own distinctive shape. Polyps can reproduce by asexual budding as well as by eggs and sperm. Each successive generation makes its home on the skeletal remains of its ancestors. In this way, by cementing a living layer on top of a dead one, extensive reefs are built from billions upon billions of tiny castings.

The sculptural superstructure of a mature coral reef is the result of thousands of years of slow growth. Branches of staghorn or elkhorn corals may lengthen from three to eight inches a year. The dense boulders of brain coral grow even more slowly; a fifty-year-old brain coral may be only a foot in diameter.

In order to grow, the coral polyp requires consistent conditions, beginning with uncontaminated water of average salinity and water temperatures of 75 to 85°F. It needs sunlight and enough water movement to supply food and remove silt and sand from the reef area. Even as coral grows, natural forces such as burrowing worms and browsing parrot fish work to break it into sand. If this sedimentation is not washed away, the polyps can be buried and smothered.

Such specific requirements limit the coral reef to tropical waters less than 250 feet deep and to the eastern shores of continents where warm equatorial currents flow landward. Western shores, with their cold currents and upwellings of cold water, are not conducive to reef formation.

Unchanged for hundreds of millions of years, the world of the coral reef is now struggling to survive new man-made stresses. Increasing pollution, dredging, filling, and other alterations that change the natural flow of the water threaten the survival of the coral reef.

The reef's fragile surface of living polyps is probably more vulnerable to wounds and infection than a child's skin. Merely brushing against living coral damages its delicate protoplasm. If it does not die outright, it becomes a prime target for disease and algae that ordinarily would not harm it. And when the coral of a reef dies, the bustling community that lives there must move or starve, leaving only the eroding white skeletons of dead coral.

If You Explore . . .

No Caribbean vacation is complete without a glimpse of a living coral reef. If you leave the beach only once, do it for a snorkeling trip, or even a glass-bottom boat ride.

Every island has a reef; some are easier to reach than others. Many interesting reef communities are right off the beach; others require short boat rides. Check boating charts of the area if you're unable to get directions locally.

If you haven't done much snorkeling, arrange for instruction from locals or a dive shop. Most dive operations provide inexpensive equipment rental and on-the-spot snorkeling instruction for beginners. Some hotels, as well as the National Park Service on St. John, U.S.V.I., also provide this service.

The Caribbean has a number of underwater parks in places especially suited to novice snorkelers. Most have self-directed underwater trail markers to point out the sights. Among them are Buck Island Reef National Monument off St. Croix, U.S.V.I.; St. John National Park, U.S.V.I.; Great Exuma Island, Bahamas; and the Cayman Islands.

Avoid snorkeling in busy harbors *anywhere* in the Caribbean, regardless of what tourist brochures suggest; they are all polluted (Sandy Cay in Port-au-Prince, Haiti, is one example). The general consensus among islanders (although it is gradually changing) is that sewage belongs in the ocean and should arrive there by the shortest possible route (that is, raw). If you simply avoid swimming and diving near large population centers, you'll be fine.

The only other general precaution is not to go snorkeling on days with a heavy ground swell running (as there often is on unprotected coasts during the winter northers) or when or where you can see waves breaking on the reef. Some rise and fall is okay; it's crashing waves you want to avoid. Sometimes a reef that breaks at low tide is fine at high tide.

The midday hours from about 10 A.M. to 2 P.M. when the sun is high are usually the best for underwater visibility. Unfortunately, this is the worst time for sun exposure. If you don't have a good waterproof sunscreen, wear a shirt and/or pants, depending on your skin; water does *not* shield you from the sun's rays.

Know that the shadowy early morning and evening hours are fish feeding times. Don't wear any jewelry; its glint in the sun may look like the flash of food in water with poor visibility or to fish with poor eyesight. Don't swim at night, except with organized dives in well-known areas, like the night dives run by the National Park Service in Cinnamon Bay, St. John, U.S.V.I. And avoid snorkeling (or swimming) where people are spearfishing or line fishing.

Now for a few "do's." The best way to see the most is to move slowly. Float. Let the animals forget you. Noises and sudden movements startle timid reef creatures. Many a first-time snorkeler thrashes clear around a reef only to report not seeing a single fish. I'll bet. If you are quiet enough and keep your fins just below the surface so they don't smack the water, you may see the secretive octopus, eel, or lobster. Take time to look closely. A good picture guide will help identify much of what you see.

Things You May Notice

Fish are probably the flashiest members of the reef community, from darting schools of silver fry to the huge parrot fish. Two of the most interesting things about reef fish are their territorialness and their odd proclivity for changing sex (a behavior often related to territory as well as reproductive opportunity). Most of the groupers, parrot fish, and wrasses start out life as females (of one color) and change into males (of another color) when they are old and large. This makes for some confusion in identification, since the opposite sexes of the same species often look very different—red instead of blue and green, for example; try to concentrate on the fishes' general outline rather than their color and size.

ANGELFISH: in the familiar shape of the popular aquarium fish, but larger and in many colors.

BALLYHOO (NEEDLEFISH): elongate little fish, similar to a baby swordfish that can skim considerable distances over the surface.

BARRACUDAS: long, gray, and ominous looking; a curious fish that may grow to six feet. Every reef seems to have one, hovering and watching. While barracudas make many divers nervous and occasionally have bitten people when visibility was poor, the biggest danger from barracuda comes from eating it.

DAMSELFISH: small rounded tropical fish that vary in color from yellow to blue to black. The sergeant major, with dark, vertical bands, is one of the more common. The damselfish are very territorial and will nip at larger fish or even a diver's hand if their space is violated. The males guard the eggs.

GROUPERS: in several patterns, which lighten and darken to match the environment. The popular Nassau grouper is a mottled gray-green. They retire to their holes and are often timid, especially in areas where they've been hunted for food.

PARROT FISH: look, indeed, like fish pretending to be parrots. Their wild colors, great size (the blue are said to reach a length of four feet), and strong, beaked mouths make them unmistakable. Their names—stoplight, midnight, rainbow—describe their variable appearance. Rarely hunted, these slow-moving algae grazers are important members of the reef community. As they feed (you can sometimes hear the rasping sound), they turn coral and rock into fine sand.

WRASSES: small, cigar-shaped fish often seen nuzzling in the sand with their buck teeth, sifting for small invertebrates to eat. The young females are blue and black (horizontal halftones); the larger males are blue and green. Other species exhibit similar variations.

GORGONIANS (SOFT CORALS): including sea fans, sea whips, sea plumes, sea pens, and sea feathers; it's relatively easy to fit the animal to its descriptive name. They come in an array of colors. Their skeletons can often be found on the beach after storms (the only conscientious way to acquire them). The dried frames of sea fans were once used as flour sifters by island cooks.

SEA SQUIRTS (TUNICATES): elongate or blanket form, often yellowish or tan. The blanket form looks somewhat like a flattened mass of melted marshmallows with a hole in each puff.

SPONGES: forming soft blankets over coral and rocks or growing free-form in characteristic vases, tubes, barrels, fingers, et cetera. These soft shapes are the simplest multicelled animals; they are neither colonies nor well-defined individuals. They form the dominate biomass—sometimes as much as 80 percent—of the reef and help control its climate as they move large quantities of water through their bodies.

Precautions

SEA URCHINS: dark, spiny pincushions with brittle, sharp spines that can easily puncture skin and break off beneath it.

BRISTLE WORMS: like fat, hairy centipedes; they are often pretty, sometimes green and red, and always deliver a fiery sting.

FIRE CORAL OR FIRE SPONGES: not always the classic red or orange color, the encrusting fire coral is often a yellow-tan; all sting.

Note: Remember, it's best for the reef and for you if you don't touch *anything*. That way you won't get hurt or damage any delicate organisms (coral is particularly vulnerable to contact damage). As a general rule, if anything bothers you, get out of the water.

Apparel and Accoutrement

Bathing suits, sunscreen, and cover-up if need be (don't be embarrassed to swim in a tight-fitting shirt; your health is more important than appearances and a tight-fitting garment won't be too encumbering in the water); snorkel, mask, and fins; underwater camera; fish guide. One of my favorites is the waterproof version (you actually can take it underwater) of the *Guide to Corals and Fishes of Florida, the Bahamas, and the Caribbean* by Idaz and Jerry Greenberg, Seahawk Press, 6840 SW 92nd Street, Miami, FL 33156. Clear drawings and fish in family groupings make it easy to use.

Wear a personal flotation device if you are unsure of your swimming skills. For more hints and a list of underwater parks, also see Snorkeling and Scuba Diving in Exploring by Water in Part 4.

The Rocky Shore

Sit some afternoon on the warm rocks of a quiet cove. Face seaward with your back to the hot shore, where the cactus and runners of purslane are taking hold in the sandy crevasses or the dry, gray needles of the casuarina trees curve in the trade winds. Let the warm water soothe your feet. Stare, simply stare into the clear shallows. Your mind will drift; that is to be expected. But what calls it back will be unexpected. It might be the snaking dart of a moray eel the size of a Tootsie Roll; the waving antennae of lobsters that look like oversized crickets; or the slow, spiky walk of a sea urchin. Watch closely; you won't be disappointed. These warm nooks and crannies of the Caribbean's rocky shores provide niches and nurseries for a rich variety of marine life.

While the white coral sand beaches tend to get top tourist billing, there's invariably a dramatic rocky backdrop just around the next point. These islands are ringed with various types of rocky shores. They vary from wave-tangled cliffs—the eastern and northern shores tend toward steep headlands and pounding surf—to quiet cobblestone coves, with all sorts of volcanic variations in between. The shore may be lined with slabs of limestone or dark, smooth boulders of fine-grained rock called diorite or have the rough, porous surface of solidified ash—the tough-on-the-hands-and-feet rocks that seem to have come straight from a volcano. Appropriately enough, they're called tuff. The more sheltered areas tend to bring together the best of the rock and reef worlds. They are inset with deep bays that have patch reefs along the shore; corals often grow on top of rocks and rubble in very shallow waters.

Since tides are minimal in the West Indies—often less than a foot, usually not more than two feet—the dramatic intertidal zones that are apparent farther north are subtle here. Still, there is usually a certain zonation running in horizontal stripes along the shore.

The most shoreward rocks receive little moisture and are sparsely populated. They are characterized by a littoral snail or periwinkle (called prickly winkle on some islands) that is slowly evolving into a land dweller and needs only high-flung spray to moisten its gills. This small snail, with its knobby gray tent of shell, may be found at surprising distances from the water. Periwinkles, of different species throughout the world, mark this area of the rocky shore, which is usually called the littoral or splash zone. Below it is the low-tide zone, which harbors animals that belong quite clearly to the ocean.

These intertidal extremes—the splash zone on the dry side and the low-tide zone on the wet—are linked by the high- and middle-tide zones that also run horizontally along the shore. These zones are usually popcorned with barnacles (though not as heavily as most more northern areas). Often growing here also are dark clusters of tiny mussels, segmented chitons with their armored plates, limpets, black- and white-domed nerites, and whelks with their pointed checkerboard shells. Hermit crabs and the reddish tidepool crabs, *Grapsis grapsis,* scurry about near the waterline.

Plants and animals have distributed themselves in these bands in relation to the amount of water, air, sun, and wind they can tolerate. Life on the whole shore, then, is striped horizontally in relation to the tides and water level in much the same way as forest growth on a mountain changes with altitude.

While these zones are subtle in the tropics (you must look carefully to find the thin line of dry wrack at the storm-tide line) and intertidal areas are often sparsely populated, the shallows of the low-tide zone are almost always accessible. The areas that would be observable elsewhere only on minus tides are rarely ever more than ankle deep here. Small rocky basins that support the predictable tidepool dwellers—chitons, urchins, anemones—also shelter a variety of juvenile forms, from eels and lobsters to colorful reef fish. In sheltered areas, corals and gorgonians grow on top of the rocks, adding color and a number of reef species to the rocky shore.

Although each zone has characteristic limits and animal life, there is some overlapping. Hermit crabs, mussels, and barnacles can appear from the high- to the low-tide zone. Regardless of their placement, all of these animals must survive certain stresses. Some of them must deal with alternative exposure to air and water; all of them must feed and elude predators.

Some animals have claws or teeth; others have food traps or filters. There are predators like the crabs, starfish, and dog whelks that kill and eat animals of similar size. Some predators are messy eaters. The small bits of food they leave are picked up by scavengers like the hermit crabs and shrimp that characterize the middle-tide zone.

There are also filter feeders, usually stationary animals that sieve the passing water with various devices. Barnacles have six shrimplike legs bristling with tiny hairs that net bits of food. Sea anemones have stinging tentacles; mussels simply wait with open shells. Filter feeders eat plants, small animals, bacteria, or decaying scraps that happen to wash by.

These animals often need protection from the pounding surf and from their natural enemies. In every zone, animals hide under rocks, burrow in sand, and cling where they can. Some simply hide within their own shells or depend on spines, claws, camouflage, stinging cells, or a bad flavor to discourage predators. All are keenly adapted to their special niches.

One of the most dramatic adaptations is the ability of crabs and brittle stars to voluntarily sever a claw or ray and later regenerate a replacement. This process, called autonomy, is a distinct advantage for an animal pinned beneath a loose rock that has been overturned by the surf.

If You Explore . . .

Be ready for rough rocks, water, sun, and maybe insects and cactus or thorn-riddled beach drift as well. To really see the intricacies of the rocky shallows, find a relatively quiet area—a shore in the lee of a headland or protected by an outer reef, or, best of all, a deep-set, rock-lined cove such as Norman Island in the British Virgin Islands. A rocky shore with lapping waters rather than actual waves is the most pleasant and has the most abundant sea life.

There are many such places throughout the Turks and Caicos, the northern islands, and the Bahamas (it's possible to find interesting rocky areas right in Nassau). When you reach the Leewards and Windwards, the rocky shores usually become steeper and rougher. But it's still possible to find a cluster of rocks in a sheltered corner of a beach where you can observe in microcosm.

The best way to discover a rocky shore is just to happen on it—to wander down the beach and around the headland and find you are no longer wandering on sand, or to snorkel shoreward and find rocky shallows at the water's edge. If you wish to trust less to happenstance, check boating charts, on which the shore and even bottom types are marked, or ask one of the locals. (To avoid stares and sarcasm, ask where people go for whelks, not for beach rocks.)

The best times of day for rock-pool watching—to avoid insects and high sun yet still catch part of the shadowy feeding hours—are from 8 to 10 A.M. and from 2 to 3 or 4 P.M., depending on the direction the shore faces and the ferocity of the insects. Sometimes the rare overcast day will offer the best viewing, since animals wary of sunlight venture out at midday.

Give yourself time to wander and to sit and stare. Be patient; move slowly. Keep your shadow away from the area you're watching, or let it slowly cover the entire pool like a cloud over the sun. Many sea animals are very sensitive to movement, light, and shadow. Your shadow or quick movement seems no different from that of a predator. Approach carefully or you'll be watching an empty pool.

If you turn over rocks to glimpse the life beneath (wiry little brittle stars are fond of this niche), do it carefully. Children need close supervision here; rocks are often heavier, slimier, or pricklier than they look. Be sure to replace the rocks *exactly* as they were. Under-rock life perishes quickly when exposed to upper-rock stresses.

Remember all of these living creatures are important interacting members of a unique ecosystem. Please don't harass them or take them for souvenirs. Take pictures; make memories. Look higher on the shore for keepsakes; there you'll find shells, corals, even sea fans, already dead (and cleaned!). On cobbled shores, sift among the smooth stones for treasures.

As you sit and stare at life on the rocky shore, you may feel intricately connected to some warm, timeless time, anchored to the moment only by the rippled winging of the bright yellow and brown sea hares in clear waters cradled by the rocks. There is something hypnotic about these slow, graceful creatures that can exude an astonishing magenta ink when startled. Nudibranchs, the shell-less advance in mollusk evolution, graze the shallows like great, surreal garden slugs, amazing and elaborate as dream.

As you sit, glance up occasionally, if only to feel the sea wind and root yourself on the horizon. If you've found a relatively out-of-the-way shore, you may notice some bird activity. Isolated areas like high, rocky outcrops provide favorite nesting sites for the osprey or fish hawk (also called sea eagle in some places). The osprey is a large bird of prey that builds a massive pile-of-sticks nest five or six feet in height and width, which is refurbished and reused year after year. From a distance it may look like a rounded pile of debris flung high by a storm. Up close, the sticks are often augmented with dried sea fans or seaweeds, even old rubber flipflops. Both male and female osprey are involved in nest building, and they seem to use whatever they find on nearby beaches. *Never* approach a nest in use or one where birds are in the area.

The osprey's white head, soaring flight, and fish-nabbing plummet (talons first) are characteristic. An unusual, reversible outer toe helps the bird grasp its slippery prey. The osprey feeds almost exclusively on surface fish that it catches in this manner. These birds, different species of which have keenly adapted to the rigors of shore life on oceanic islands throughout the world, tend to avoid areas of intense human activity and frequently nest in the southern Bahamas, on Turks and Caicos, and on the cays of Cuba. On Provo, Turks, and Caicos, however, they've grown somewhat accustomed to humans and often perch on the masts of boats anchored in Third Turtle Cove.

Apparel and Accoutrement

Bathing suits, cover-up, sunscreen, insect repellent, plastic bag for (dead) beach treasures, camera, lunch, snorkeling gear (at least a mask is always a good idea; you just may want to hold it in a tidepool to clarify your view); some type of shoe—flipflops if you're sure-footed, otherwise tennis shoes that can get wet. Rubber-soled cotton Chinese slippers, sometimes sold as kung-fu shoes, also are good for climbing over rocks.

The Sand Flats, Grass Beds, and Sandy Beach

There is something undeniably idyllic about a palm-fringed shore of coral sand. The warmth, colors, texture, and sparkling surfaces are transfixing.

Thoughts fall where they may. It's easy to forget that this sand and water is a viable ecosystem of interacting dynamics.

Sandy beaches tend to be geologically older than rocky shores. It takes time as well as certain conditions—shore slope, currents, waves, material for sand—to build and maintain an irresistible crescent of coral talc. This powder-fine sand is made up of calcium carbonate particles, mostly finely ground bits of coral that were once parts of living reefs offshore. Some coral sand beaches in the Bahamas actually have a pink cast that matches the living organisms nearby.

Coral beaches accumulate sand from a number of sources other than rock-grinding wave action. Broken mollusk shells, sea urchin spines, even fish bones all can become sand particles in time. One of the most efficient sand producers is the parrot fish. As these large fish graze for algae on the corals, their strong beaks also rasp off bits of the corals' stony structure. These sand-sized coral scrappings become new beach material as soon as they pass through the digestive tracts of the fish.

The skeletons of calcareous algae can add appreciable amounts of sand material to the beach. Once you know what these odd marine plants are, they're unmistakable. They are like stony seaweeds. The tiny cups called mermaid's wine glass, the bristly stalk of merman's shaving brush, and the beaded links of Halimeda can often be seen growing in grass beds or on pilings; uprooted pieces frequently wash ashore.

This continuous accumulation of new sand does not end up on the beach immediately. Waves or currents wash it from the reef area into a nearby sand reserve. These sandy areas, which support their own inhabitants, are still well below the tide line. Storms and currents gradually shift sands between the beach and shallow water.

It takes a living reef to maintain a coral sand beach. Most of the islands don't have huge rivers to bring sand and gravel shoreward to their beaches. On the larger islands where rivers do occur, beaches are likely to have gray or golden sands. Many of the younger islands have bold, black sand beaches, their fine particles etched from volcanic rocks.

Whatever the type or color of their sand, all beaches are subject to storm stresses. Heavy storm swells can shift bottom sediments that are as much as twenty-five feet deep and move sand reserves to deep water. Very fine sand particles can hang suspended in turbulent water long enough to ride currents offshore, or they can be blown inland by storm winds. Seasonal winter storms often wash out entire beaches. The long-term effects of hurricanes can be devastating; not only do they move large quantities of sand, they may also damage the beach-maintaining reefs offshore.

As well as being the source of sand material, the living coral reefs also act as the beaches' protective barrier. Obviously, the reefs absorb lots of wave energy outright. They also, by their direction of growth, may affect the angle at which waves actually hit the beach and the strength of currents that move beach sands along the shore. This sideways or lateral sand travel is also moderated by the Caribbean's typically twisting coastline. Rugged headlands tend to keep the sand pockets isolated, so that each cove or bay along with its sand reserve is a relatively closed system.

The soft, warm sands of many island beaches provide essential nesting sites for the dwindling ranks of great sea turtles. The hawksbills, green turtles, and leatherbacks (called trunkbacks on some islands) that nest on Caribbean beaches are all on the endangered species list. The females return seasonally, each to the exact beach of her birth, lumbering ashore and laying their leathery eggs in shallow sand nests above the tide line. But only a few females now nest where turtles once came ashore in great numbers. Although many islands have some type of law protecting sea turtles and their eggs, respect and enforcement are not widespread.

Full-time inhabitants of the beach must deal with its great stresses— moving water, shifting sands, and tropical sun. In this stringent environment, the safest existence for beach animals is to breathe, eat, and reproduce under a cover of sand. It takes a highly specialized organism to do this. Most of them fall into the clam category—the multitudes of bivalve mollusks that can burrow rapidly, close tightly, and filter feed in the turbulent waters of surf zone and inshore sands.

The shells of these tropical species tend to be thinner and more vibrantly colored than those of cold-water varieties. Double-shelled clams in a variety of sizes, shapes, and colors occur on island beaches. Combinations include white and brown, and orange and purple. There are rose-pink clams the size of a baby's fingernail, the yellow clam rounds of buttercup lucinas, and even the delicately ridged lavender shells of the royal comb Venus clam with its exotic spines.

The crabs have also adapted to the stresses of the sandy beach. Just above the surf line you may see whitish ghost crabs peeking from a sand burrow or scampering in the foam after some decaying tidbit, or perhaps shy hermit crabs hiding under their borrowed seashell hats. Hermit crabs are night feeders and usually spend their days under debris on the upper beach or hunkered down in the cool sand.

Beyond the surf zone, the sands reach seaward under quieter waters. This underwater continuation of the beach—the interacting areas of sand reserves—provides another niche for specialized organisms. The inhabitants of the sand flats, like those of the more rough-and-tumble tide line, are, for the most part, burrowers and hiders.

It's entrancing to drift over the rolling dunes of the sand flats face down in a mask and snorkel. The white sand, bright through the sparkling water, is rippled and piled into hillocks, hummocks, mounds, and hollows; each animal creates it own variation. The sand is bright enough to hurt the eyes; it is wavy enough to bring on vertigo. It also is completely hypnotic, if one does not pause to gather the china bone skeletons of sand dollars or the pink-, yellow-, and orange-streaked butterfly shells of sunrise tellins. Life is private here. Living sand dollars and tellins keep themselves well hidden under the sand; only the dead reach the surface.

Sand trails, burrow holes, protruding antennae, and breathing siphons hint of living occupants. In this realm of shifting sands, plants and animals have nothing to attach to or to hide under—no secure rocks, coral crevices, or sheltering mangrove roots. Since little plant life is available for food, most of the animals are either filter feeders (their unique food traps sieve food particles from the water itself) or those who eat filter feeders. Other animals consume the sand and digest the organic bits it contains, like earthworms consume soil. As well as numbers of clam-type mollusks, certain starfish, worms, sand dollars, and little leggy burrowing shrimp are at home on the sand flats. They have all found ways to survive beneath the sands.

One seldom-seen inhabitant of the sand flats is the heart urchin, or sea biscuit, as it is more often called in the West Indies. This large, puffy version of the sand dollar makes itself a mucus-lined cave of sand about a foot below the surface. Yet the king helmet, a large carnivorous snail much prized for its tawny shell, still ferrets it out. The king helmet slowly pulls the sea biscuit to the surface of the sandy bottom and, with its special rasping mouthpiece called a radula, bores a small hole in the sea biscuit's thin, fur-covered shell. It doesn't take long for the giant snail to suck the soft animal from its shell. Nor does it take long for the dark spiny fur to fall off the dead animal. Soon, the suck and draw of the currents roll the sea biscuit's puffed hollow to an etched whiteness that showcases the five-petaled flower on its upper surface. The bottom side of this simple animal—an echinoderm, a relative of the starfishes and urchins—has only two pores or holes, an "in" and an "out." The basics. Pure and simple, like the sand flats themselves.

The stark openness of the sand flats may darken into an underwater meadow of sea grasses. The flat, sturdy blades of turtle grass and the darker, wispier manatee grasses provide a nutrient-rich habitat, and their root systems stabilize the substrate. These sea grasses are true plants, not algae like the seaweeds. Like land plants, they flower; produce oxygen during photosynthesis; and have leaves, stems, and roots woven together with a network of rhizomes.

These rhizomes are like fibrous pipe cleaners extending in all directions and rooted down at intervals. Above the underwater bottom, the rhizomes support tufts of grass blades. Below the surface of the sand, their crisscrossing actually weaves together, in a wave-resistant mat, sand-grass-coral rubble; grasses prefer a mixed substrate.

Although considerably more stable than the beach or sand flats, grass beds can be uprooted by storms. Sometimes nearby beaches will be littered with grass fragments in barely discernible form. Rhizomes may be rubbed and bleached to smooth, Styrofoam-like sticks; grass blades may be frayed to feathery tassels or dried flat, their veined strips as white and papery as parchment. While large-scale washouts can be destructive, uprooting and fragmentation by storms, fish, and currents also help propagate grass beds. These sea grasses rarely flower, with male and female plants often flowering at different times, but new plants start easily from broken pieces.

As well as establishing a more stable environment than that of the sand flats, the grass beds provide rich nutrients. Many animals feed directly on the grasses, and, as always, others feed on those animals. Small plants and animals grow on the grass blades themselves. And diverse colonies of molds and bacteria blossom when the grasses decay.

This wealth of plant material supports an interesting variety of inhabitants, including some dramatic forms like turtles and sea horses—those unusual little pipefish that swim poorly and often cling to sea grasses with their prehensile tails. Grass beds provide niches for many worms, small crustaceans, and mollusks that burrow among the grasses' roots or hide among their waving blades. Grass beds are a favorite habitat of the fat, brown cylinders of sea cucumbers and shy octopuses, which ring their lairs with the shells of mollusks they've eaten. The spiky rounds of white sea urchins are common in the grass beds. These short-spined urchins don't inflict painful stabs like their long-spired black relatives. (In Barbados, the white sea urchins are called sea eggs and are cooked and served as a special delicacy.)

The queen conch, another grass bed familiar, is even more widely sought after for food than the white sea urchin. Its sweet, white meat—similar in taste to a scallop—has been a primary protein source in the Caribbean since primitive times. The conch (pronounced KONK) is a large marine snail known in most places for its extravagant pink fan shell. Ever useful, these hard, thick shells have provided tools, horns, cameos, and curios; the pulverized shell is still used as an ingredient in fine porcelain. The living conch looks like a mossy rock that moves. It grazes these undersea meadows with its pearly pink aperture pressed to the sea bottom and its visible spires blunted with sea growth. There's no mistaking the conch's characteristic hopping movement. Unlike most snails that glide from place to place, the conch uses its large, muscular foot, which ends in a fingernail-like operculum, to hop along the sea floor. The front of the conch—the end opposite the spires—has two stalked eyes and a simple snout-mouth in between them. To eat, conchs simply extend this foraging tube over a convenient morsel. Grass blades up to a foot in length have been found in their stomachs.

Conchs usually spawn in the warmer months. After internal fertilization (the male conch has a regenerative penis, or verge, which is frequently nibbled off by eels), females deposit an egg cluster in a sandy area near the grass beds. Eggs hatch into free-swimming larvae called veligers in about five days. These tiny ciliated creatures, or protoconchs, with their minute and future shells, drift with the currents for about three weeks. Then the veliger settles to the bottom and starts to develop its foot and snout-mouth.

Juvenile conchs, which lack the adult's dramatic flared lip, spend most of their days buried in sand or gravel. They feed at night to avoid predators (a number of fish as well as hermit crabs, lobsters, stingrays, and loggerhead turtles make meals of them). In two years, the young conchs will have shells about six inches long. They reach sexual maturity in about three years, when they will have eight-inch shells and yield about a half pound of meat.

When conchs reach six inches or so in size, people become their major predators in a rather direct-link example of grass-bed productivity. Island cooks prepare them in any number of dishes, from chowder and fritters to salad. (The solid foot muscle is eaten, after having been pounded tender.)

As the tourist and local populations have increased, so has the demand for conch. The growing market has also increased the price and led to overfishing and the gathering of more and more immature conch (those without the fan lip). While conch is not officially endangered, Caribbean supplies have been sufficiently depleted to cause concern. Many grass beds, especially near population centers, that once had conch in knee-deep water are now marked only by piles of empty shells. Closed seasons, fishing limits, and mariculture are all being considered to help repopulate the shallow-water grass beds with this once-plentiful mollusk.

Soufrière to Thorn Forest—Flora and Fauna

As one might imagine, it is impossible to make generalizations about the flora and fauna found on islands extending from the northern Bahamas just off the coast of Florida to Trinidad just off Venezuela. Most sources refer vaguely to the neotropical or West Indian; others divide island flora and fauna into Bahamian and Antillian, grouping Trinidad's more numerous species as South American. However, all the islands have differences as well as similarities. Oceanic islands, by their very nature, support unique ecosystems that often include plants and animals found nowhere else.

Names complicate discovery even further. Most Caribbean plants and animals seem to have names of a sort. Of all sorts, actually. Not only are names different in the Spanish, French, and English languages, they also differ between islands in the same language groups, sometimes even between different villages on the same island.

What I am saying is that some West Indian plant and animal names may be too local to be of anything but personal use. Anyone serious about naming the elements of an island universe will need books that give formal Latin names. Most books separate the fruit bearers from the introduced ornamentals such as the bright, papery-blossomed bougainvillea and the fragrant frangipani; most ignore the more commonplace varieties altogether. The few animals that are native to these islands have received scant mention. Consider this overview a first brush with island flora and fauna.

The upper reaches of the rocky shores and beaches, whether coral or volcanic, are often fringed with specialized drought-resistant, salt-tolerant plants. Seaside sweet pea or seaside morning glory, among other names, is easy to recognize as it winds along the sand with its purple trumpet-shaped blooms blazing at intervals. Purslane (or verdolagas) is a low, clinging succulent with runners that help stabilize the upper shore. Its crisp, salty leaves make an interesting ingredient in salad.

Farther above the shore may grow the poisonous manchineel (or manzanillo) tree or a fringe of sea grapes, with their rustling pancake-shaped leaves. Sea almonds and coconut palms can also lend an elegant border to the beach. These moist, upper-beach areas with their leafy debris are often home to land hermit crabs and the big, hard-shelled land crabs that spend their days in mud-packed burrows. Sometimes after a heavy rain, tiny brown toads hatch in the upper shore vegetation.

Farther inland, the salt-tolerant plants of the upper shore give way to the trees and brambles of thorn forest, or evergreen bushland, as it is sometimes called. Thorns, however, is the definitive word; everything has them. The undergrowth in this area is likely to support prickly grasses; sticker weeds; the thorny brambles of various acacia species called casha or coosha; and probably an easy-to-recognize kalanchoe, the mother-of-a-thousand or leaf-of-life that is sold in the States as a hothouse plant. This hardy succulent shuns pampering here and may grow to several feet in height and produce a flower stalk with papery mauve bells. The plant's scalloped leaves will sprout new plants between each loop if the leaves fall to the ground or are picked.

If this bushland area is very dry, you're likely to see a variety of cactuses, from prickly pears, Turk's heads, and yuccas to branched tree forms. The huge, spike-leaved florets of agaves, or century plants, often dominate dry, rocky hillsides. The century plant adds to its stark beauty with an occasional bloom spike that may shoot up twenty or thirty feet from the center of a leaf cluster. Golden yellow flowers bloom at intervals, moving up the spike. In spite of its name, a century plant takes about ten years, not a century as once thought, to bloom. After its magnificent, long-lasting flower display, both the bloom spike and the plant slowly die. New plants bud from the old plant as well as from the fallen stalk.

These areas of dry thorn forest once covered great portions of the islands. But much of the forest, being at such accessible elevations, was cleared for cultivation, especially for growing sugarcane. Since this once-great industry has dwindled, the land has been planted in sea island cotton or pineapples or simply abandoned, left to grazing animals.

Grazing animals are the fauna you're most likely to see in these culture-abandoned areas. Often the ruins of sugar mills or plantation houses will overlook grasslands returning to bush. The huge iron caldrons that once held sugar for boiling now often hold water for grazing cattle. You'll probably see sheep and goats tethered in grassy areas or along roadsides. Island sheep and goats are an unusual lot; they look quite similar, to the uninitiated. A foolproof identification guide, once given to me in passing as patiently and simply as one might instruct a child, quips, "Sheep tail down, goat tail up." It never fails.

In wetter places in culture-abandoned areas, the bushland supports trees like the indigenous guava or perhaps mangoes or limes. On Montserrat and Dominica, a careful observer might glimpse a rabbit-sized rodent called an agouti; they often come down to feed on fruit in the dry season. These shy creatures—sleek, short-eared relatives of the guinea pig—sit up like squirrels to eat fruit and seeds.

Dense tropical forest, the vegetation one imagines for these warm islands, needs rain to support it, about seventy inches a year. This tropical forest, which grows only at altitudes below about 3,000 feet, is characterized by thick, bushy undergrowth and many deciduous trees that bloom seasonally, such as bay rum, locust, and balsa. The vines, air plants, and great buttressed trees of the rain forest are scarce. Agriculture, charcoal-making, urbanization, and the lumber industry have practically eliminated these dense stands.

The tropical forest, with its rich bird and plant life, remains only in small bands surrounding the rain forest and in so-called "gallery" forests along riverbanks. Here, native species are often joined by numbers of transplants, especially the breadfruit tree. Now widely distributed, the breadfruit tree was actually introduced to Jamaica in 1793 by Captain Bligh, of *Bounty* fame, who sailed from the South Seas with his deck carpeted by small trees. The breadfruit is a striking tree, large and spreading with green globe-shaped fruits and huge leaves with multifingered loops reaching out from a central vein. Giant bamboo, mango, and rose apple trees may also be found here.

While similarities may appear in the shore, dune, and scrub species of the Bahama Islands, Turks and Caicos, and some of the low coral islands of the West Indies, the forests, or coppices, as they are called in the Bahamas, have different components. The areas that Bahamians often refer to as whiteland coppice are sparsely populated, with rugged trees and shrubs, some acacia, and cactus scrub—essentially a dry bushland–thorn forest habitat. The wetter, more densely forested lands, called blackland coppice, support larger trees than does the whiteland coppice, including mahogany, horseflesh, mastic, and cedar; and more birds, lizards, spiders, orchids, and bromeliads.

The Caribbean pine, a sturdy, fast-growing species that needs little in the way of soil and rainfall, forms another unique type of island forest. Although these fast-growing pines thrive almost anywhere, by some twist of dispersal and evolution they occur only in the northern Bahamas—on Andros, the Abacos, New Providence—and then appear again well to the south on the Turks and Caicos, the Caymans, and Jamaica. Although they are quite resistant to fire, Caribbean pines in low areas are easily killed by standing water. Scientists speculate that the sea-level changes of the last ice age may account for the trees' scattered distribution. The tall, straight pines, long sought by shipbuilders, are not to be confused with the supple casuarina (or filao). The casuarina, an import from Australia, has limp gray needles and tiny cones. It has become a familiar seaside tree on many dry islands, often to the detriment of native species.

Rain forest is the habitat most likely to fit the image of lush jungle. With its tiered niches and constant warmth and wetness (these areas need at least 120 inches of rain per year, about equally divided by month), the rain forest is a seasonless, self-contained system with a continuous flowering and fruiting of different species.

Along with suitable climatic conditions, time is also necessary for the complex interdependencies of a true rain forest to become established. The giant ceiba trees, which were seedlings when Columbus arrived nearly 500 years ago, now may be 200 feet tall and 40 feet in diameter. Their great buttresses help anchor them in the thin soil. (Most large rain forest trees have buttresses, or a network of prop roots, to help support them.) Huge philodendrons often encircle the tree trunks, and there seem to be hanging vines (called lianas), air plants, orchids, ferns, and bromeliads everywhere. These soilless plants, especially bromeliads (sometimes called old man beard) and orchids, have many varieties; several islands have a number of endemic species. The vanilla bean is hand-gathered from one species of orchid.

The rain forest has unique tiered strata, from the fungi, molds, worms, termites, and other insects that thrive under fallen leaves on the forest floor to plants and animals that never leave the overhead canopy. With each tier having its own miniclimate and specific flora and fauna, the rain forest harbors the densest array of organisms of any habitat on earth. It is a magical place where ferns and exotic blossoms seem imaginary in the filtered light, a place where bird song seems at times as dense as the misty forest itself. (On Puerto Rico, the dominant song is often that of a small tree frog, the coqui, which sings its own name.)

Another specialized version of the dense tropical forest grows at altitudes over 3,000 feet or on lower slopes exposed to harsh prevailing winds. This type of growth, where tropical forest species are dwarfed by local conditions, is called elfin woodland or simply altitudinal vegetation. While the number of species is much smaller here, there are many odd indigenous plants. A curious white ground orchid and the dwarf sierra palm, some of which never exceed a foot in height, may be found in these areas.

As is obvious from these brief descriptions, West Indian terrain is varied, rich, and unique on each island. Naturally, the islands are not all undisturbed tracts of arid hills or dense forests. Limestone caves are numerous: there are said to be more than 2,000 on Puerto Rico alone. There are rivers, waterfalls, lakes, expanses of rolling meadows, palm groves, banana plantations, and piles of bare rock. Areas overlap or are broken by settlements or by great ravines, known as *ghuts,* that fill with runoff from the mountains during the rainy season.

Some of the geologically younger islands have semiactive volcanic areas, or *soufrières,* that still let off steam. Deep calderas, with boiling lakes, sulfur hot springs, and fumaroles, have a look all their own. Pastel-colored rocks—some powdery, some with flaky crystals, and many with hazy striations—may line rivulets of steaming gray water. The bold yellow of sulfur rocks provides a distinguishable touchstone. In places, the air is so heavy with the rotten-egg fumes of sulfur that it blackens coins in your pocket; the water is often hot enough to boil eggs. The landscape is, above all, primeval. Visitors tend to be quiet when confronted with such a glimpse back in time. Few seem to notice the mosses, lichens, and occasional clumps of dark grass or ferns that manage to be green in these stark, treeless regions. It is enough to sense amazing process revealed.

There is a wealth of diversity on these islands. Plant colonies vary considerably in relation to their *very* local climates, with differing altitude, rain, humidity, wind, and soil conditions. Exploring the bare bones of a volcano or the lavish greenness of a rain forest, or simply looking at the truncated woodlands, wind-bent and twisted, that struggle along under the mountain clouds, it is easy to imagine island geology, the gradual arrival of life forms, the ways that new arrivals evolved to fit special niches. The sensibility of evolution is especially apparent on an island. It is as simple as birds feeding by day on the same seeds and fruits sought by the bats at night.

One of the most unique things about an island is this self-containment. Although you can learn and see a good deal in a short time, do remember there is nuance and layered meaning that may not be immediately apparent. Ask names, take pictures, compare habitats, but don't make assumptions or take any answer as absolute. Some time ago, after a trip to Dominica, I was talking with the well-known poet Derek Walcott from St. Lucia about language—local usage and what's called what here and there. Eager to appear knowledgeable, I told him that on Dominica, large guavas are called apricots.

"I never heard that," he said. "How do you know?"

"A guide told me," I said.

He laughed. "Ohh. No, you mean one guide on Dominica in that village. What was the boy's name?"

"Peter." [i]

"Well, on Dominica, a guide named Peter calls large guavas apricots. *That's* what you mean."

I am sharing this lesson. Islands are small places, with every distance.

If You Explore . . .

Botanical gardens are good places to see tropical plants, sometimes with names attached. Most islands have one such garden. The Hope Botanical Gardens on Jamaica, with about 200 acres and a renowned orchid house, is one of the largest; it also has qualified guides. Don't overlook gardens around governors' houses and government buildings and in national park areas. Each island has a ministry of agriculture; many have experimental stations and interesting plantings of native flora. The Mayagüez Institute of Tropical Agriculture on Puerto Rico is also a good source of information.

As for actually exploring different habitats, see the following list for suggestions of where things are; then check the individual island listing for specifics. Part 4, Exploring, may also be useful.

RAIN FORESTS: Caribbean rain forests, although they lack the diversity of the true Amazonian rain forest (with the possible exception of Trinidad), are nevertheless special. It is startling to see tree ferns as high as two-story houses, or an entire mountainside dotted with colorful impatiens, or a bromeliad blooming in the wild. Best bets for islands with rain forests include Puerto Rico, St. Lucia, Dominica, Guadeloupe, Martinique, Jamaica, Domincan Republic, St. Vincent, Grenada, and Trinidad.

Other islands have remnants of ancient rain forests or dense forests they call rain forests. These interesting areas may be seen on Haiti, Antigua, Tortola, St. Croix, and Montserrat.

VOLCANOES: Most of the eastern Caribbean islands have a volcano. If you'd like to explore one, look for the word "soufrière" on the map. It's not always pronounced the same, but it always means the same thing; it's French for "endure" or "suffer" as well as "sulfur" and "brimstone." Interesting areas of semiactive volcanism can be found on Grenada, Dominica, St. Lucia, St. Vincent, Martinique, and Montserrat. See the individual island listings for details.

WATERFALLS: Best bets include St. Lucia, Dominica, Guadeloupe, and Jamaica. Haiti, Grenada, Montserrat, and Puerto Rico each have at least one waterfall. All are more spectacular in the rainy season.

Birds and Bird Sanctuaries

While parrots don't screech from every tree or flamingos wade on every shore, the Caribbean islands do have an accessible population of interesting birds. Most of the common species are widespread and can be found in the mountains or lowlands or along the coasts at any time of year. Most of the land birds can be seen near roadsides or in gardens, especially on the larger islands.

If you're serious about bird-watching, make James Bond's classic field guide *Birds of the West Indies* (Houghton Mifflin, Boston) your companion. As well as describing the birds and their behavior, Bond lists local names (there are many variations) for each bird, which may be an invaluable time-saver. It's also a good idea to take along a standard field guide to North American birds, since many of the birds you'll see are transients from the mainland.

Even if you're not an avid birder, you undoubtedly will notice some bird life here. Large flocks of brown pelicans, which are endangered elsewhere, feed and nest on many islands; there's a large breeding colony on St. John, U.S.V.I., and the nearby islets. Watching the pelicans' spectacular plunges into the water after fish (some zoom from heights of 50 feet) can easily occupy an afternoon, whether you view them from shore or through a mask while snorkeling.

Brown boobies, which are often seen with pelicans, and large frigate birds (look for their scissor tail) may fly overhead. Most of the sea gulls you see will be laughing gulls, with handsome black heads and jeering cries.

Little brown and yellow bananaquits, or sugar birds, as they're sometimes called, may hop right onto outdoor tables and dine uninvited at the sugar bowl. Delicate hummingbirds, flashing their iridescence in shades of green, yellow, blue, and black—some even have dashes of pink and purple—buzz almost like bees at nectar-filled flowers. The smallest species of hummingbird, which lives on Cuba, is actually called the bee hummingbird and is only two-and-a-half inches long. Although the colors and sizes of hummingbirds vary from island to island, their whirring wings and nectar-sucking bills are characteristic.

The smooth-billed ani, or black witch, with its exotic appearance and high visibility, seems to be a favorite among bird-watchers. These large birds are long-tailed cuckoos, shiny black with oversized parrotlike beaks. They prefer fields, pastures, and even gardens. Several females layer their eggs, randomly separated with leaves, into a common nest; as many as twenty-nine eggs have been counted in a single nest. The bottom layers of eggs, fertile or not, simply do not hatch.

The oystercatchers (also called sea-pies, whelk-crackers, and osteros) are easy to recognize. Their vermilion blade-shaped bills, ideal for opening shellfish, are distinctive even when seen from a distance and complement their pink feet and peculiar red eyelids. Oystercatchers are found on most of the southern Bahama Islands and in the Virgin Islands. If you can't see them and they're nearby, there's no mistaking the plaintive wheep, wheep, wheep they utter along the shore.

The more exotic tropical pink birds, such as the scarlet ibis, roseate spoonbill, and flamingos, seem to favor more specific locales. Roseate spoonbills nest in the mangroves on Cuba, Hispaniola, and Great Inagua, Bahamas; you may come across solitary birds in many locations. There's a large colony of scarlet ibis in the Caroni Bird Sanctuary on Trinidad. The shy, stilt-legged flamingo (also called fillymingo and flamenco) still has large breeding colonies on Great Inagua, Bahamas; and on Bonaire.

Bonaire, Aruba, Curaçao, Trinidad, and Tobago are really not within the area of Antillean avifauna. These islands are so close to the mainland of South America that, while their bird life does have an Antillean component, it is more typically neotropical. The rest of the West Indies is divided into two general sections with regard to bird populations. The birds of the more northern islands, which run from the Bahamas to the Virgin Islands, fall into the Greater Antillean group. The area of Lesser Antillean aviafauna runs from the Virgin Islands south to Barbados and Grenada. Of course, there is considerable overlap. Also, remember these islands have isolated areas, and some species, especially parrots, have very small and specific locales.

The parrots of the West Indies live in remote, mountainous areas, a species or two per island. St. Lucia, St. Vincent, Dominica, Cuba, and Jamaica all have dwindling numbers of indigenous parrots. The native Puerto Rican parrot now survives solely in the Luquillo National Forest Preserve.

Bird Sanctuaries and Bird-Watching Areas

Antigua

Bird-watching boat tours to observe migratory, sea, and indigenous species.

Barbuda

Sanctuary for frigate birds.

Bonaire

WASHINGTON/SLAGBAAI NATIONAL PARK: about 135 bird species; major flamingo nesting sites at Goto Meer and Pekel Meer.

Dominican Republic

The national park on Isla Saona (off the coast to the southeast) is a nesting site for white-crowned doves.

Great Inagua, Bahamas

Flamingo sanctuary.

Grenada

GRAND ÉTANG LAKE BIRD SANCTUARY AREA: various species in dense, tropical forest at an elevation of 1,800 feet.

Jamaica

ROCKLANDS FEEDING STATION: in Anchovy: sanctuary for about 100 species, fed daily; public admission afternoons only; admission fee (minimum age, four years).

Montserrat

FOX'S BAY BIRD SANCTUARY: Montserrat oriole, egrets.

Puerto Rico

LUQUILLO NATIONAL FOREST PRESERVE: Puerto Rican parrot.

LUIS PEÑOS BIRD PRESERVE: seabirds, brown pelicans (islet off Culebra Island).

Trinidad

ASA WRIGHT NATURE CENTER, SPRING HILL ESTATE (about 20 miles from Port-of-Spain): exotic birds including toucans, cuckoos, and a breeding colony of guacharos (nocturnal oilbirds).

CARONI BIRD SANCTUARY (about seven miles south of Port-of-Spain): boat tours through mangroves reveal hundreds of scarlet ibis. The inner nesting sanctuary is open only from May to October; the rest of the sanctuary is open all year.

Turks and Caicos

Many species—laughing gulls, osprey, migratory species—in and out of rather nebulous protected areas.

All national parks listed in Part 4 provide good bird-watching areas. See the individual island listings for more information.

PART TWO

People and Culture— Social History

"Tis hurrystance ar kill yo."

Caribbean proverb

History/Time Frames

The Pre-Columbian Era—Arawaks and Caribs

We know very little of the Caribbean's first inhabitants except that they were a Stone Age people, without permanent settlements, who lived on the islands nearly 4,000 years ago. They were wanderers and gatherers who made stone and flint tools but not pottery. These first islanders disappeared some 1,000 years before the arrival of the next wave of Amerindians—the Arawaks. The Arawaks found—and apparently reused—the primitive implements of the former residents, a people they called the Ciboney (after the Arawak word *ciba*, for stone). We know little else about the Ciboney. Like the Arawaks, who first found their traces, we still do not know where the mysterious Ciboney came from or where they went.

Considerably more is known about the Arawaks, the peaceful Amerindians that Columbus met when he arrived in this New World. Their major subgroups were called Lucayans in the Bahamas and Tainos on Hispaniola, Puerto Rico, and Cuba. Although the Arawaks were rapidly annihilated by their "discoverers," we do have a number of relics and some firsthand observations of their simple ways.

The Arawaks were originally from the Rio Orinoco region of Venezuela. Paddling and riding the currents in their large dugout canoes, they arrived on the Windward Islands about 2,000 years ago and gradually migrated up the island chain. They lived in villages headed by *caciques*, or chiefs, who also served as priests for religious rituals. The Arawaks lived simple lives on the warm Edenic islands. They gathered fruit, roots, and shellfish; hunted birds, iguana, and agouti with bows and arrows; and fished using hooks, nets, traps, and herbal poisons. They also farmed, cutting and burning the bush to clear the land—an early version of the slash-and-burn method still popular—and planted crops like sweet potatoes, yams, and cassava. The roots of the cassava plant were ground and used to prepare cassava bread, the Arawaks' starchy staple.

Cassava, or manioc, was such an important part of the Arawak diet that their supreme male god was called Yocahu, the giver of cassava. The head female deity was Atabeyra, a fertility goddess of moon and moving waters. Opiyel Cruabiran (or Wa'obrian), a dog deity, protected the dead. In some places, images of these deities were carved on cave walls or rock formations, where they can still be seen. More often, though, small images, called *zemies,* were carved into a spiritual talisman of stone or shell.

Yocahu, the cassava god, always had a pointed head or body; his spirit resided in a volcano—a symbol, perhaps, of the island land that produced cassava. The earliest Yocahu *zemies* were simply conch shells—sometimes a single large spire or a complete conch with all the spires chipped away, revealing the volcanic shape of the shell. Later artifacts, especially those from the northern islands, where the culture was more advanced, show the lean lines and pure understatement that marked Arawak art, from their elegant pottery to their imaginative animal-shaped stools, or *duhos,* the ceremonial seats of their chiefs. Arawak religious ceremony involved inhaling a narcotic mixed with tobacco. This required a ritual purge beforehand, and some of the most elaborate Amerindian artifacts are smooth, decorated vomit spatulas.

When Columbus first arrived on Hispaniola in 1492, the Arawak population probably numbered between 200,000 and 300,000. By 1496, one-third of them were dead, either killed outright or victims of disease and overwork; many Arawaks poisoned themselves to avoid enslavement by the Spaniards. Few survived the sixteenth century, and the Caribbean Arawaks were soon a vanished race.

The warlike Caribs, the only other group of Amerindians living on the islands when Columbus arrived, fared slightly better; there is still one colony of them on the remote windward coast of Dominica. The Caribs were later migrants to the West Indies who had begun conquering the Arawaks and settling the islands only some 200 years before Columbus arrived. Also originally from the Orinoco River area of Venezuela, the Caribs were as fierce as the Arawaks were peaceful, and they often ate their prisoners of war after roasting them on a spit. The Spaniards, who called them *Caribales,* the word that became cannibal, tended to avoid colonizing Carib strongholds. This they left to the English and the French, who managed to involve the Caribs in several of their own wars.

It was the Caribs' custom to go on war raids in their long dugout canoes (from the Carib word *canoua*), which they rigged with sails. The Caribs were expert sailors (the Arawaks only paddled their canoes) and fierce warriors, who fought with arrows dipped in manchineel poison. When a war party returned with captives, they ate the men and boys and married the women. These captured women retained their own ways, including the Arawak language. Only the men of the Carib tribe spoke Carib, so that over the years these Amerindian cultures intermingled. Much information about these people was preserved by an observant missionary on Guadeloupe, Father Breton, who published a Carib-French dictionary in 1665.

By 1700, most of the Caribs had been wiped out by the side effects of colonization—war, disease, and enslavement. It is said that enslaved Caribs simply ate dirt until they died. At that time, an estimated 400 Caribs remained on Dominica, the last Indian stronghold; today they number perhaps a hundred. The last Carib to speak the language died in the early 1900s. Many Indians have married local blacks, so that the pure Carib with the classic almond eyes and straight ebony hair is increasingly rare.

The Caribs' unique ways have fascinated many ever since some early adventurer reported with wonder (and a certain incredulity) that the Caribs considered the French the best meal, followed by the English and Dutch; the Spaniards were said to be so tough and gristly that they were hardly worth eating. Today, the Caribs are a little-remembered force behind the words cannibal and Caribbean. The Caribs who now live in Salybia and the nearby villages in the Carib Reserve on Dominica's rugged Atlantic coast still farm small plots, fish from dugout canoes, and weave watertight baskets. They are a proud, insular people with their own elected chief. It's hard to believe that the quiet couple strolling down the road with a portable radio, or the cluster of children in school uniforms clammering for pencils, are descendants of the warriors who terrorized the Caribbean for centuries.

Discovery and the Spanish Indies

It is generally believed that the inconspicuous island of San Salvador in the mid-Bahamas was the site of Christopher Columbus's first landfall in 1492, although new evidence presented by a recent National Geographic expedition makes a better case for nearby Samaná Cay. At any rate, there is no dispute over the central Bahamas location and the fact that the Amerindians in residence—Lucayans, an Arawak subgroup—called their island Guanahani. The Indians were in awe of these first Europeans in their fancy Spanish battle dress and called them "men from the sky." (The Arawaks generally went naked except for cotton bands tied around their elbows and knees and an allover coating of red roucou plant dye to repel insects.) Columbus and the Indians exchanged pleasantries via sign language and gifts. The Arawaks, by most accounts, gave Columbus live parrots, spun cotton, and wooden spears tipped with stingray tails. He gave them hawk's bells, red caps, and glass beads and sailed on to discover Cuba and the large island of Hispaniola (first called Española, for Spain).

Columbus landed on Hispaniola on 5 December 1492, and after some serious boating troubles built a fort from the wreckage of the *Santa Maria*. He left thirty-eight men there who would never be seen again. After exploring a bit and trading with Indians wearing small gold ornaments, Columbus returned to Spain to announce the discovery of "The Indies."

One hears a lot about Columbus in the Caribbean. Every island makes a point of noting on which voyage he discovered it, what he called it, if he passed by or came ashore. Basically, Columbus's four voyages of discovery followed this pattern:

1492–1493	San Salvador (or Samaná Cay) and the lower Bahamas, Turks and Caicos, eastern Cuba, north coast of Hispaniola.
1493–1496	Dominica and north up the islands to the south coasts of Puerto Rico, Hispaniola, Cuba, and Jamaica.
1498–1500	Trinidad, Gulf of Paria, Margarita.

On this last voyage, he came to Martinique and skirted up the islands and down to Central America looking for a westward route to India. Columbus died poor and officially disgraced in 1506, just seven years before Balboa found the Pacific Ocean, the long-sought path to the Indies.

There has always been a certain enumeration of the "gifts" from the New World—tobacco, coffee, cocoa beans, pineapples, tomatoes, and such. Two items with lasting historical impact are usually omitted—hammocks and syphilis. Columbus and company returned with both, if not from the first voyage, surely the second. The Amerindians slept in hammocks (from the Arawak *hamaca*) of hand-spun sea island cotton. The idea had immediate appeal to sailors used to sleeping on hard decks, and this soft, hanging cradle soon became a shipboard standard. And the syphilis is, well, still making history.

The Spanish had the Caribbean largely to themselves until the mid-1500s. They colonized, held mass, converted, enslaved, killed, and in general tormented the docile Arawaks, fought the Caribs, and above all looked for gold. Santo Domingo in the Dominican Republic was the center of this early Spanish era. It was a remarkable time, marked by hardship, determination, stamina, bravery, religious zeal, greed, hypocrisy, and injustice. Here are a few dates to refresh your memory and mark the era:

12 October 1492	Columbus discovers Guanahani in the mid-Bahamas and claims it for Spain.
5 December 1492	Columbus lands on Española (Hispaniola) and builds the Acul Bay Fort from the wreckage of the *Santa Maria;* leaves thirty-eight men.
6 January 1496	First Spanish colony in the New World is established at Isabella, Dominican Republic, with more than 1,000 colonists; Columbus leaves his brother Bartholomew in charge to deal with the Indians and to acquire gold from them. His leadership leaves much to be desired.
1507	First time the word "America" is used on a map in a book.
1508	Sebastian de Ocampo sails around Cuba.
1509	Ponce de León arrives in Puerto Rico with Spanish settlers.
1511	Queen Isabella sets up a tribunal in Santo Domingo, Dominican Republic, for appeals to the crown, establishing a precedent for colonial government with a local mayor.
25 September 1513	Balboa discovers the Pacific Ocean from a peak in Panama.
1513	Ponce de León discovers Florida for Spain while looking for the fountain of youth. He also explores the Bahamas.
1515	Havana, Cuba, founded.
1517	Coffee introduced to Europe.

1518	Spanish crown licenses private traders to import African slaves into the West Indies.
1521	Cortez captures Mexico City.
1522	Magellan's ship returns from circumnavigating the globe.
1528	Cocoa beans first imported to Europe.

In 1521, when Cortez captured the Aztec stronghold in Mexico City with its great accumulation of wealth, power began to slip away from Santo Domingo. The Caribbean settlements gradually became way stations and guardians for the transport of Spanish gold and silver. Their inhabitants supplied passing ships with hides, tallow, and sugar. These early Spanish settlers managed their own estates but remained essentially town dwellers with churches (Catholic), shops, schools, and hospitals centered around useful harbors. This was a very different life-style from that of the later English colonists who actually lived on their estates and raised small crops of food and tobacco.

The Privateers

As the Caribbean developed as a sea-lane for the Spanish treasure fleet carrying the gold and silver of Mexico and Peru back to Spain, it entered a new historic phase—the oft-romanticized era of gentlemen pirates, the privateers. Jack Hawkins and Francis Drake typified these state-sanctioned plunderers willing to endure for God (in this case, Protestant), queen, and country (in this case, England).

This time frame also anticipated the later slave traffic, which reached its height in the eighteenth century and gave the islands their major ethnological input. Although the Spanish had imported small numbers of Africans to work in their mines on Hispaniola (which were quickly depleted) and then their cattle ranches, it was Hawkins's voyage in 1562 that is generally considered the beginning of the great influx of African slaves.

The mid-1500s to the early 1600s in the Caribbean mark a time of increasing European interest in smuggling and sparring, carried out between privateers (not to be confused with later pirates and buccaneers) and Spanish ships and towns. Since these privateers, although state-sanctioned, were not members of an official navy, peacetime in Europe had little bearing on rampage and plunder in the islands. To help protect herself, Spain shipped in convoys and fortified her cities—especially strategic ports like San Juan, Cartagena, and Havana—and settlements on the Spanish Main (a term that refers to the mainland bordering the Caribbean, *not* the sea itself).

While the Spanish tried to maintain their initial Caribbean monopoly, continual attacks on Spanish shipping and the plundering of her ports weakened her hold. By the early 1800s, colonists from other countries were staking claims. In the seventeenth century, the British, Dutch, French, and Danish all established colonies in the Lesser Antilles. This period marks the blossoming of the Dutch trade abroad—the powerful Dutch West India Company was formed in 1621—and of culture at home, where Rembrandt, Hals, and Vermeer painted.

1553	The French pirate François Le Clerc, known as Timberleg (Pie de Palo) to the Spanish, plunders and burns several West Indian ports.
1562	Jack Hawkins's first voyage anticipates the triangle trade—rum and sugar, slaves, and European goods and textiles.
1565	Hawkins introduces sweet potatoes to England.
1567	Hawkins's third voyage; he is accompanied by a twenty-six-year-old redhead, Francis Drake.
1568	Hawkins's flotilla is attacked by Spaniards while on a slave run.
1570	Drake's first Caribbean voyage.
1585	Drake's Caribbean romp—he sacks Santo Domingo and Cartagena with the blessings of another powerful redhead, Queen Elizabeth I.
1588	English defeat Spanish Armada.
1595–1596	Hawkins and Drake at sea in the West Indies.
1596	Tomatoes are introduced to Europe.
1605	French found Port Royal, Jamaica.
1621	Foundation of Dutch West India Company.
1624	First permanent English settlement in West Indies is started on St. Kitts.
1625	Settlement on Barbados.

1635	French settle on Guadeloupe and Martinique.
1637	First sugarcane planted on Barbados.
1646	Bahamas first colonized.
1648	Treaty of Munster confirms Dutch possession of St. Martin, St. Eustatius, and Curaçao.
1649	First serious slave mutiny, on Barbados.

The Buccaneers

By the early 1600s, Spain's harsh colonial policies and the lure of mainland riches left Hispaniola pretty much deserted except for great herds of wild cattle and pigs. Thus endowed with a small population and plentiful game, the island became a provision stop and a hideaway for smugglers. Remember that Spain at this time did not recognize any other nation's right to trade in the West Indies. This situation set the scene in the seventeenth century, which was a swashbuckler's heyday—the time of the buccaneers.

These wild adventurers—a group of English, Dutch, French, and Portuguese who all detested the Spanish—were pirates ungarnished with knighthood (God or country). Keep in mind that these renegades were a completely different group from the earlier privateers, as well as from the outlawed pirates of the eighteenth century. Their very name came as a label of their livelihood—the practice of saltless meat preservation learned from local Indians. The meat (a mainstay in the illicit provision trade) was cut into strips, sun-dried, and then smoked over a greenwood fire—a method of meat preservation called buccanning.

As buccaneering became profitable around the 1630s, the buccaneers seized the small island of Tortuga to establish a stronghold and to secure their smuggled goods from the Spanish. In 1641, the Spaniards attacked Tortuga and massacred everyone they could find. Their actions intensified hostilities somewhat, and the few buccaneers who escaped were joined by new members from all the trading nations. The rising ranks of buccaneers considered it extremely good fortune when the British joined them to capture Jamaica from Spain in 1655.

Roving from place to place, often living mainly at sea, the buccaneers were the scourge of Spanish trade for three-quarters of a century. Two of the big names in their story were Edward Mansfield and Henry Morgan. In 1664, Mansfield decided that the buccaneers should settle New Providence Island in the Bahamas, and Morgan concurred. However, both

Mansfield and the idea died young, so the band of hunter-sailors fell back on the leadership of Morgan and continued to rove. The ruthless Morgan plagued the entire Caribbean from his lair on Jamaica, even attacking the heavily fortified town of Porto Bello, Panama. In 1672, the wily Welshman was called to England and imprisoned in the Tower of London. But as fate (or politics) would have it, he was returned to Jamaica in 1674 as lieutenant-governor. During the later phase of his life there, he worked actively in suppressing his former cronies; the gallows silenced many inconvenient memories.

Even though the buccaneers had defeated the Spanish fleet in 1685, their epoch rally against the decaying Spanish empire was nearly over. In 1689, when war broke out between England and France, repercussions reached the New World, interrupting buccaneer loyalties. Without a united front against Spain, the buccaneers dwindled to a few small-time marauders. By the eighteenth century, Caribbean skirmishes were fought by royal navies.

1655	England captures Jamaica from Spain.
1664	French West Indies Trading Company founded by Jean Baptiste Colbert.
1666	France declares war on England, captures Montserrat, and raids Antigua.
1670	British colonies set up in the Bahamas.
1685	Defeat of Spanish fleet by Caribbean buccaneers.
1685	France under Louis XIV establishes *Code Noir*, hoping to prevent slave uprisings resulting from mistreatment by owners.
1692	Port Royal, Jamaica, earthquake topples buccaneer paradise into the harbor.
1693	Kingston, Jamaica, founded.
1697	Treaty of Ryswick cedes western Hispaniola—Saint Domingue, now Haiti—to France.
1697	Buccaneers help the French capture Cartagena, the final event in their story.

Colonialism and Cane

The next hundred years in the West Indies mark a period of international musical chairs. Islands changed hands regularly. Some were passed back and forth between the British and French so often that many of today's islanders still speak a patois blend of both languages. Other islands had a more diverse string of rulers. The U.S. Virgin Islands, for instance, were ruled by Spain, England, France, Holland, the Knights of Malta, and Denmark before they became American possessions. Britain's superior eighteenth-century sea strength aided her ascendancy in the islands. By 1815, only Guadeloupe and Martinique were still French, and even they had been captured by the British for a time. The Caribbean islands, with the prosperity of their new sugar economy, had become desirable colonies.

Originally, sugarcane from the Canary Islands was taken to Brazil and from there to Barbados, where it thrived in the fertile soil and tropical warmth. Sugar was a high-profit, labor-intensive crop that required large tracts of land and a substantial financial investment. The need for cheap labor was met by the expanding slave trade. Dutch entrepreneurs—the Dutch at this time were the world's sugar experts—supplied technical and financial support. They often supplied sugar-making equipment against future crops, and Dutch-style windmills for grinding cane began to dot the islands.

Sugar was money, no doubt about it. Never had empires had such rich colonies. And never has so much been said about the cost: The sugar era changed forever the face of the West Indies, both environmentally (native vegetation was stripped for planting anywhere cane might prosper) and ethnologically. The eighteenth-century slave trade brought masses of Africans from many tribes who soon formed the soul and backbone of Caribbean culture. Blacks who had been captured or sold into slavery in Africa were chained in the holds of ships like so many matchsticks—side by side and end to end—to endure the unfathomable rigors of the Atlantic crossing. Arrival in the West Indies meant the auction block of a slave market and another journey that led to the harsh yoke of some sugar plantation.

Negro slaves very quickly outnumbered the white planters, overseers, and merchants. But cheap labor was essential to the sugar industry, and the plantocracy instituted a system of strict routine, severe discipline, and racial separation in hopes of maintaining control. Slave uprisings and mutinies were violently quelled, and, as the century progressed, subjugating the proud, resilient blacks became critical to the survival of plantation life. The concept of the free individual expounded by the French Revolution in 1792—an ideology that crossed the Atlantic—fired more frequent uprisings. A full-scale slave revolt in Haiti led by Toussaint L'Ouverture resulted in the country's 1804 declaration of independence.

Eventually, slavery was outlawed—in 1833 in the British colonies, 1848 in the French colonies, and not until 1886 on Spanish-held Cuba. The plantocracy was obsolete. The masses of relatively new West Indians were freed into the quiet, bewildering poverty of colonialism—which didn't pay like the once-rich economy nourished by sugar and slaves.

Often, former slaves stayed on at now-struggling plantations as low-paid laborers. On Trinidad, this cheap labor niche was generally filled by new immigrants—the great influx of East Indians. In other places, the sugar land, its soil depleted by cane, was divided into small parcels, and many islanders took up agrarian traditions and became subsistence farmers. The years between 1860 and 1920 especially were quiet ones, time for a deep breath and a revamp before new nationalism and the slow road to twentieth-century independence.

1733	Molasses Act forbids American trade with West Indies.
1794	British capture St. Lucia from French.
1797	British capture Trinidad from Spain.
1801	Haiti declares itself a republic.
1803	British capture Tobago.
1804	Haiti declares its independence.
1807	British slave trade outlawed.
1833	Abolition of slavery in British colonies.
1844	Dominican Republic declares its independence.
1846	Beginning of East Indian migration into Trinidad.
1848	Abolition of slavery in French West Indies.
1886	End of slavery on Cuba.
1898	USS *Maine* blown up in Havana Harbor; Puerto Rico ceded to the U.S. after the Spanish-American War.

The Twentieth Century

The balance of trade and power in the Caribbean shifted toward the Western Hemisphere after the Spanish-American War in 1898, in which the U.S. obtained Puerto Rico from Spain. As the United States became a world power, the American presence in the Caribbean—both in terms of commercial and military force—had been in clear evidence. Ever since Theodore Roosevelt added his 1904 "corollary" to the Monroe Doctrine, U.S. presidents have not hesitated to intervene in Caribbean politics.

World War I helped the islands economically. The French discovered minerals on their islands, the price of sugar went up about fivefold, and many farms diversified into profitable crops like bananas, spices, coffee, and cocoa. In the years after World War II, the islands began to enjoy the rewards (and problems) of tourism. The Caribbean's natural assets— balmy weather, clear waters, and dazzling beaches—began to mean money.

By the 1950s, the rising tide of West Indian nationalism steered a number of islands toward independence. However, Guadeloupe, Martinique, and St. Martin chose to remain overseas departments of France, while the Dutch islands gave up colonial status to become self-governing partners of the Netherlands. Jamaica, Trinidad, and Tobago became independent from Britain in the early 1960s, and many islands have followed suit, most recently St. Kitts and Nevis in 1983. Other places like the Cayman Islands, Turks and Caicos, and Montserrat have chosen to remain British with local governing bodies.

Political independence has not guaranteed economic independence. Some of the inequities in the slave era have been slow to balance. Haiti, eighteenth-century France's wealthiest colony, is now the poorest nation in the Western Hemisphere.

The twentieth century has been one of political turmoil on many islands. Cuba and the Dominican Republic have had a series of dictators and revolutions. Jamaica had a period of political violence in the early 1980s. Oil-rich Trinidad is still suffering growing pains. The 1980s also have seen the invasion of Grenada and the abdication of the Duvalier regime in Haiti. Barbados remains the prime example of independent stability and success; Antigua also appears to be heading in that direction.

The initial years of independence for some of these countries represented a struggle to stabilize local affairs and shrug off the vestiges of colonialism. The Caribbean's paradisaical image has often hidden real problems from outsiders. Most of these emerging nations have had to deal with product shortages, power outages, overburdened public works departments, unemployment, crime, illiteracy, and inadequate health care all bundled together with poverty and the restlessness of those eager for more opportunity. On top of these internal affairs, new governments have had to deal with foreign trade, national debt, and, above all, an image change.

This striking photo is from a postcard labeled "lumps of coal—St. Thomas, Danish West Indies, 1912." St. Thomas, now a major cruise-ship port in the U.S.V.I., was once a trans-shipment point for coal. (Photo courtesy of St. Thomas Historical Society.)

The Caribbean has had to assert its new status over a diehard stereotype. A few years back, Jamaica had a tourist slogan that proclaimed: "We're not just a beach, we're a country!" Whole nations, some the size of Texas ranches, that had long been viewed as the world's sandboxes, shaded by palms and bordered by never-empty glasses of rum punch, had to establish a new aura of seriousness. This effort often evidenced itself as a tight circle of black nationalism that didn't offer tourists a very friendly welcome. Now, with local pride and know-how and their international position more firmly established, most islands have learned to enjoy the economics of the tourist dollar and are trying to make visitors feel more welcome.

1902	Mount Pelée erupts on Martinique, destroying St. Pierre.
1902	Cuba gains independence from Spain.
1906–1909	U.S. occupies Cuba.
1915–1934	U.S. occupies Haiti.
1916–1934	U.S. occupies Santo Domingo, Dominican Republic.
1917	U.S. buys the Virgin Islands from Denmark.
1930	General Rafael Trujillo comes to power in the Dominican Republic.
1933	Batista overthrows Cuban dictator Machado and rises to power.
1940	"Operation Bootstrap" begins on Puerto Rico.
1949	Charter granted to University of the West Indies.
1952	Puerto Rico becomes a U.S. commonwealth.
1954	Aruba, Bonaire, and Curaçao become self-governing partners (rather than colonies) in the Kingdom of the Netherlands.
1957	"Papa Doc" Duvalier comes to power in Haiti.
1958	West Indies Federation is formed.
1959	Jamaica becomes self-governing within the federation.

1959	Castro comes to power on Cuba after the fall of the Batista regime.
1961	Bay of Pigs fiasco on Cuba.
1962	Jamaica, Trinidad, and Tobago gain independence from Britain.
1965	U.S. troops are sent to the Dominican Republic in response to a revolt.
1966	Barbados gains independence from Britain.
1973	The Bahamas gain independence from Britain.
1974	Grenada gains independence from Britain.
1978	Dominica gains independence from Britain.
1979	St. Lucia and St. Vincent become independent from Britain.
1979	Mount Soufrière erupts on St. Vincent.
1981	Antigua gains independence from Britain.
1983	St. Kitts and Nevis gain independence from Britain.
1983	U.S. troops invade Grenada.
1986	Young Duvalier ("Baby Doc") flees Haiti in a U.S. plane.
1986	Aruba becomes a separate entity within the Kingdom of the Netherlands.
1992	St. Lucian poet Derek Walcott wins the Nobel Prize for Literature.
1994	U.S. troops land in Haiti to return Aristide to power.
1996	Galway's Soufrière erupts on Montserrat.

Sites, Ruins, and Museums

The Caribbean has many archaeological sites, from extensive excavations like Port Royal, Jamaica, to unmarked shell piles and petroglyphs. One such pre-Columbian shell pile on a remote island in the southern Bahamas looks like no more than a mass of gray shells lining the high shore above the storm line. The shells have irregular round holes where the Indians had drilled the animals' muscle loose by pounding shell upon shell, the stony spire of one conch easily boring into the next. Only after the arrival of the Europeans did the holes in the shells take on the elongated slit of a steel implement.

Every island on which sugarcane was raised is dotted with plantation ruins—windmills, houses, and sugar factories. Unmarked ruins of stone forts or fortifications still guard many harbors and beaches. The point is that history is everywhere, although these islands simply don't have the resources to restore and signpost every landmark. So great are the present problems that there is a certain local disregard for the historic. If you really want to see ruins or petroglyphs, for example, make sure you *insist;* otherwise you could be denied a view of Indian drawings by a cabdriver determined to show you a batik factory.

The many small island museums are an odd mix by American standards, but intriguing because you can never tell what you'll find. Although the museum in the fort at St. Thomas, U.S.V.I., has a very small collection of oddities, it is housed in the massive seventeenth-century Old Fort Christian, where pirates were hanged, governors lived, and church services were held; it still served as a jail in recent times. The small museum on Montserrat has a well-displayed selection of local artifacts. An old wood and wrought iron donkey saddle with side loops for a carrying cane was recently acquired by buying its owner a new saddle.

The colonial cities of Santo Domingo, San Juan, and Havana deserve particular mention. Between them, they contain just about the oldest "everything" in the New World. As well as restored sixteenth- and seventeenth-century buildings, museums, shops, and galleries abound. For more information on these old cities with their cobbled byways and romantic aura of Old Spain, see the individual island listings for the Dominican Republic, Puerto Rico, and Cuba.

Here are a few suggestions of what's where to help you plan. You may want to join the historical society or the National Trust on your favorite island; many accept yearly memberships for as little as U.S. $20. Or you might even want to volunteer for an archaeological dig; addresses are given so you can write for more information.

Archaeological Sites, Parks, and Museums

Antigua and Barbuda

INDIAN POINT CREEK, ANTIGUA: Arawak village excavation.

NELSON'S DOCKYARD, ENGLISH HARBOUR, ANTIGUA: completely restored version of eighteenth-century naval life and ruins associated with fortifications at Shirley Heights.

ARAWAK MUSEUM AND ARCHAEOLOGICAL SITE: near English Harbour, Antigua.

AMERINDIAN CAVES WITH PETROGLYPHS, BARBUDA.

Aruba

CAVES WITH AMERINDIAN HIEROGLYPHICS.

Bahama Islands

PIGEON CREEK, SAN SALVADOR: large Arawak site under excavation since 1973 by College Center of the Finger Lakes, NY.

COLUMBUS LANDING SITE, SAN SALVADOR: site of multiple activities by pre-Columbian people on the west coast. For information about admission to the site and requirements for volunteers, write to: Donald T. Gerace, Director, CCFL Bahamian Field Station, 270 SW 34th Street, Ft. Lauderdale, FL 33315.

Barbados

BARBADOS MUSEUM, GARRISON SAVANNAH: Amerindian artifacts, old maps, coins, furniture; small admission charge.

ST. JAMES CHURCH: built in 1684.

ST. NICHOLAS ABBEY: a Jacobean great house built in the 1650s, completely furnished; open 10 A.M. to 3 P.M. Monday to Friday; admission charge.

Bonaire

PETROGLYPHS.

Cuba

The old colonial city of Havana is full of historic landmarks, some converted, some restored.

MUSEUM OF THE CITY OF HAVANA: Amerindian artifacts, antiques, and memorabilia; open 2:30 to 10 P.M. Tuesday through Sunday; free.

CASTILLO DE LA PUNTA AND EL MORRO, HAVANA: sixteenth-century fortification and castle, parts still in military use.

Dominican Republic

MUSEUM OF DOMINICAN MAN, SANTO DOMINGO: major collection of pre-Columbian artifacts.

MUSEO DE LAS CASAS REALES, SANTO DOMINGO: In the old city, this museum houses Taino Indian artifacts, ancient navigational instruments, eighteenth-century sugar-making paraphernalia, and more. (See the individual island listings for more details on the historical buildings in the old section of Santo Domingo, the first city in the New World.)

MUSEO PANTÉON Y YACIMIENTO ARQUELÓGICO DE LA CALETA: thirty-three Taino Indian skeletons preserved as they were buried. Located at Caleta Point, just east of Santo Domingo on the road to the airport.

Guadeloupe

PARC ARCHEOLOGIQUE DES ROCHES GRAVÉES: rocks incised with pre-Columbian drawings.

Haiti

THE CITADELLE AND SANS SOUCI PALACE: monumental nineteenth-century structures from King Christophe's day; located outside of Cap-Haitïen on the north coast.

Jamaica

PORT ROYAL: ongoing underwater excavations of the city of Port Royal, near Kingston, which was toppled into the bay by an earthquake in 1692. There are many important sites and museums in this area—see the individual island listings for more details. Port Royal can be reached by bus, ferry, or taxi from Kingston. No appointment necessary; guides available. Volunteers normally not accepted, but experienced professionals and academics may apply; participation is usually through a graduate course given by the Nautical Archaeology Program. For details, write D. L. Hamilton, Texas A&M University, Nautical Archaeology Program, College Station, TX 77843, or Carey Robinson, Jamaica National Heritage Trust, 79 Duke Street, Kingston, Jamaica.

COLUMBUS CARAVEL SURVEY, NEW SEVILLE: continuing underwater work on two caravels abandoned by Columbus on his last voyage in 1504. Located on St. Ann's Bay, seven miles from Ocho Rios, sixty- three miles from Kingston; appointments necessary. Volunteers accepted; write Carey Robinson, Jamaica National Heritage Trust, 79 Duke Street, Kingston, Jamaica.

SEVILLA LA NUEVA: various sites in a national park. Three Arawak villages, first Spanish settlement on Jamaica, Anglo-Jamaican plantation ruins. Columbus Caravel Survey, Runaway Bay Museum, and more nearby. No appointment necessary for admission. Located near St. Ann's Bay on the north coast, seven miles from Ocho Rios and sixty-three miles from Kingston. Volunteers with advanced degrees in archaeology or American history and Spanish proficiency required; write Lorenzo Lopez, Esquilache 12, Madrid, Spain 28003.

Martinique

FORT-DE-FRANCE MUSÉE DÉPARTMENTAL DE LA MARTINIQUE: Arawak relics and skeleton. Located on Rue de la Liberté (near Hotel Lafayette), Fort-de-France. Closed Saturday afternoons and Sundays.

Montserrat

MONTSERRAT MUSEUM, PLYMOUTH: small collection housed in an old windmill; well-displayed Arawak and plantation artifacts.

GALWAY'S SUGAR PLANTATION: picturesque ruins of sugar works active from 1660 to 1860. Directions: south from Plymouth to St. Patrick's village, take Galway's Road up the mountain to 1,100 feet. Volunteers accepted for summer excavations; contact Lydia M. Pulsipher, Department of Geography, University of Tennessee, Knoxville, TN 37996-1420. Currently on hold due to volcanic activity.

Puerto Rico

With its long history and rich Spanish heritage, Puerto Rico is dotted with sixteenth- and seventeenth-century buildings, and is rich in artifacts left by a well-developed Taino Indian culture. Here are a few highlights to get you started in Old San Juan, a Spanish colonial city beautifully restored and full of intriguing exhibits, galleries, shops, and restaurants. (See Puerto Rico in the individual island listings for a more complete description of Old San Juan.)

EL MORRO: the harbor's guardian fortress built by the Spaniards between 1539 and 1586 on more than 200 acres 145 feet above the tempestuous Atlantic. Administered by the U.S. National Park Service; tours available; especially appealing to children.

SAN JOSÉ CHURCH: oldest place of worship still in use in the Western Hemisphere; started in 1523.

For Amerindian buffs, visit the Taino ceremonial ball parks in the midwestern mountains; a cave with pre-Columbian drawings and carvings, four miles east of the town of Arecibo; or a shell midden at Loiza Aldea, on Route 187. There are several small museums with Indian relics in towns throughout the island.

St. Eustatius (Statia)

Sometimes called the "historical gem of the Caribbean." Walking tour designed by Statia's Historical Foundation (maps free) will take visitors by examples of seventeenth-, eighteenth-, and nineteenth-century buildings, including Fort Oranje, built in 1636 and recently restored.

DUTCH REFORMED CHURCH: built in 1775 and newly restored; on the coast at the edge of the capital.

ORANJESTAD MUSEUM: memorabilia from Statia's past, housed in a nineteenth-century clapboard building.
   Several sites under excavation, including an eighteenth-century government guest house and an eighteenth-century Jewish ceremonial complex. No appointment necessary for admission; sites accessible by taxi, foot, wheelchair. Volunteers accepted; write Norman F. Barka, Director of Excavations, Office of International Studies, College of William and Mary, Williamsburg, VA 23185.

St. Kitts

BRIMSTONE HILL FORT: "the Gibraltar of the West Indies," an impressive fort 700 feet above the sea with a fantastic view; good for picnics, too.

AMERINDIAN PETROLGYPHS: Wingfield Estate and West Farm.

Turks and Caicos

Middle or Grand Caicos has limestone caves with Arawak relics.

U.S. Virgin Islands

ST. CROIX: CHRISTIANSTED NATIONAL HISTORIC SITE: includes well-preserved examples of seventeenth- to eighteenth-century Danish architecture—Fort Christiansvaern, the Old Danish Customs House, the Danish West India and Guinea Company Warehouse, the Steeple Building, and more. Pick up the park service pamphlet at the visitors' station downtown.

WHIM PLANTATION GREAT HOUSE: restored sugar planter's house of the prosperous late 1700s, now a museum, complete with rebuilt windmill; near Frederiksted, admission charge.

FORD FREDERIK, FREDERIKSTED: built by the Danish in 1760, completely restored, with a small museum.

ST. JOHN: AMERINDIAN PETROGLYPHS: at Reef Bay in the U.S. National Park. Stop at the visitors' center in Cruz Bay for a trail map.

ST. THOMAS: The Old Danish free port of Charlotte Amalie has many buildings of historic interest, from the Government House to the open-air market, where slaves once were sold.

Old Fort Christian, with its massive stone walls painted bright red, dominates the waterfront. Built by early Danish settlers, it is more than 300 years old. Get a glimpse inside by visiting the Museum at the Fort.

⌐ People, Gods, and Time

Visualize a Haitian mask carved of thick, dark mahogany with the sinuous ridge of a palm tree running up the center of the face. Its trunk, curled to one side to give the hint of a mouth, goes on to form the nose ridge and then feathers into a topknot of fronds. The face is painted to resemble a pineapple, and the tree, of course, is mahogany and green. Two deep eyeholes imply something elusive behind the mask, adding seriousness to the artist's tropical whimsy.

Like the mask, the Caribbean hides a complex culture behind its tourist facade. The West Indies has long been a crossroads settled by transplanted peoples—treasure seekers, traders, and a great number of the traded themselves. Three-quarters of the population is of African descent; the rest is a mix of Europeans and East Indians. This rich mélange has produced a vibrant blended cultural heritage sometimes collectively called "Creole." The European heritage includes Danish, Spanish, English, Dutch, and French. All of these languages are still spoken, giving the islands built-in linguistic divisions and accompanying cultural ones, as well.

The Spanish-speaking islands still seem more Spanish than West Indian. The same is true of the French, with the exception of Haiti, which revolves in its own sphere.

These divisions may be due, in part, to religious practices. The early Spaniards felt that converting locals to their brand of Catholicism was the next step after claiming the lands; the French had similar proclivities. Today, the Spanish- and French-speaking islands still tend to be predominantly Catholic.

Religion came later and less centrally to the British possessions, so that today's sects on those islands are more varied. Whereas the Africans that fueled the sugar era brought their own tribal beliefs and practices, English plantation lords soon found that slaves converted to Christianity were easier to manage; imported religion made economic sense. A number of forms of Christianity took hold. English-speaking islands still tend to be Protestant, with a strong Anglican following plus a variety of other churches, including Moravian, African Methodist, Evangelical, and Seventh Day Adventist. Baptist sects, with local variations like the "shouters" and the "jumpers," long have been popular on many islands.

The East Indian immigration to Trinidad in the late 1880s provided still more religious diversity as Hindus and Muslims brought and continued to practice their faiths. Spanish and Portuguese Jews relocated on French, Dutch, and Danish islands during the Spanish Inquisition, establishing important synogogues on a number of islands, including St. Thomas. The synagogue built in 1732 on Curaçao remains the oldest in use in the Western Hemisphere.

Often, modern religious practices in the West Indies represent an amalgam of old and new, of Africa and the West. Nowhere is this more evident than in Haiti, where the practice of voodoo has taken on the Saints' Days for its own drum-pulsed rituals, despite long-term disapproval from the official Catholic church.

Voodoo, from the African *vodun,* or "spirit," has formal practices that involve ritualized symbols, singing, dancing, and chanting led by a voodoo priest (*ougan*) or priestess (*mambo*). Afro-Haitian practitioners of voodoo see God, or "Gran Met," as the remote creator of heaven and earth and, as such, too distant to become involved with daily life. So spirits, or *lo'as,* which often reside in trees, ponds, or waterfalls, serve as intermediaries. *Lo'as,* traditionally associated with vital forces like love, death, fire, and water, must be kept in harmony. The Virgin Mary, for instance, is still associated with Ezili Freda, *lo'a* of love. Voodooists frequently consult the *lo'as* for advice in life. These ceremonial consultations are led by a priest or priestess in a ritual pattern that involves intensifying drumming to which participants dance themselves into a trancelike frenzy. When this point of "possession" is reached, many believe the behavior of the possessed helps identify the *lo'a* and its message. The voodoo priest or priestess holds an esteemed position in the Haitian community and is often sought for guidance in medical and personal matters, as well as religious ones.

Religious dance is also prevalent in a number of other religions practiced in the Caribbean. It is an integral part of the Shango sect, originally from Nigeria, which has a strong following on Trinidad.

The rather recent Rastafarian movement, which began on Jamaica in 1930, now has followers on most islands. The followers, usually youngish males, often wear their long hair in minispirals or braids known as dreadlocks and worship the late Haile Selassie (known as Ras Tafari before he became emperor of Ethiopia).

Another African carryover in the Caribbean is the belief in *obeah,* a sort of witchcraft that believers claim can be used for good or ill. Although no longer prevalent, this type of magic goes back to Ashanti practices. The *obi* (priest), or more commonly obeahman or obeahwoman, usually places some type of spell or curse on a person at the behest of another. Obeah also includes a belief in *jumbies,* the spirits of the recent dead. *Jumbies* account for certain mischiefs and instill fear in their beholders, apparently due to their unresolved states of suspension between this world and the next.

Mocko (or make-believe) *jumbies* on stilts are a traditional part of carnival in the U.S. Virgin Islands. They lead the carnival parade in wildly colored costumes covered with mirrors, which protect their legendary invisibility and show only the face of the beholder.

Even in modern times, many curious things have been and are still attributed to *jumbies* or *obeah.* This excerpt from a letter written in 1946 provides a vivid example:

11 Duke Street
Kingston, Jamaica, BWI
10 June 1946

My dear Herbie,
. . . And now about the stones falling on and in the house. I spoke to our friend Hazelwood. . . . He said send away the girl at once, and get some camphor cakes not the balls, and burn one in each room of the house the very night she leaves. Of course you know that Hazelwood is an Obeah-man himself. . . . Hazelwood says that this stone-falling appears to be an old African cult brought by the people of Africa to the West Indies and it usually happens in the case of girls. It appears that someone gives the girl as an offering to the unknown, and if that promise is not kept when the

child becomes a certain age, then stones appear to fall wherever the child is and they appear to fall for sometime. . . . You need not mention this to anyone, but send the child home.

(From a letter in the Montserrat Museum, reproduced with permission of the Montserrat National Trust.)

While incidents like this are rare these days, *jumbies* still elicit respect. Odd occurrences are likely to be attributed to *jumbies* in much the same way that Americans cite Murphy's Law. Blended views are simply part of the Caribbean life: It would not be at all odd for a West Indian farmer to use a sophisticated irrigation system, plant by the moon, attend mass on Sunday, and do a little *obeah* on the side using hex rings mail-ordered from Chicago.

Religious beliefs and practices, whether mixed with folklore, superstition, and magic, or not, hold a firm position in the social life of small islands. Many islands are still geographically divided into parishes. On most islands, churches of every sect, with their traditional festivals, bazaars, weddings, and funerals, continue to provide the central focus of daily life.

Caribbean social life, whether church- or community-centered, tends toward a certain stratification that separates the foreign-educated, the professional, the landed, and the moneyed elite—whether black or white—from the greater population of lower classes. It is mainly this large group of rural or urban workers, and the unemployed, who cling to strong peasant traditions. Generally, there is still a relatively small middle class, except perhaps on Puerto Rico, where it predominates. Social division tends to be political and economic rather than racial.

Low-income islanders, especially, tend to live in extended-family groupings, with a mother and her mother heading the household. Out-of-wedlock children are common and accepted. In many places, marriageable West Indian men are in short supply, since they must leave the islands to find work. Children provide women with security for old age where there is little or no outside help. Most of these islands, away from the glitter of tourist hotels and quaint downtowns, are poor, poor places.

Old-fashioned grocery store credit is still the key to subsistence for many. Credit is a fact of life, and many small village stores have prominent signs proclaiming their views. They range from the simple "No Credit" to explanations like this one from a small bakery in Kinsale, Montserrat:

You ask for trust.
Me no give.
You get vex.

You ask for trust.
Me give.
You no pay.
Me get vex.

Better you get vex.
Me no trust.

Despite the limitations of small islands and the hardships associated with poverty, most Caribbean people have an energetic sense of life. Ingenuity and creative solutions appear in every facet of island life, from architecture to fish traps to the stew pot. Along with the ability to make something from nothing (or something from the wrong thing), West Indians also seem to possess time itself, as a personal commodity, for one's own use. Much has been said about the island sense of time or lack thereof. Things do move slowly; appointments are no more than vague gestures, much to the irritation of local professionals. But it's more complex than the tropical laissez-faire of "what de rush mon?" Think of the inner clock, of time being personal and individually regulated—the literal interpretation of "make your own time." Like little else in the world, time is equally distributed. Its use is an individual matter.

The Caribbean sense of time has become a stereotypic touchstone, providing a love-hate relationship for visitors, an easily noticed detail. The point is, there's a much greater Caribbean behind the tourist mask. These are island nations in transition, with distinct geographies and national histories and a varied, distinct group of peoples. Assuming the Caribbean is only sunshine and unending rounds of rum punch and calypso shows is like spending a week in Las Vegas and thinking you've had an inside look at America.

Talking Story—
Language and Literature

To say "walk with it" instead of "bring it with you" is quintessentially Caribbean. From lilting expressions like this of the English-speaking islands to the Spanish of Puerto Rico where spoken words lose their final "s'es," the language of these islands remains lively and fresh.

It is impossible to either categorize or sum up these often very regional dialects. The Irish brogue of Montserrat, the complex Creole of Martinique, the patois of Dominica, the Spanglish of Puerto Rico, the papiamento of Bonaire all remain unique. Any island you visit is likely to have some type of publication elucidating local speech styles, proverbs, or expressions. Creole, in its various forms, is now recognized and frequently studied and written about by linguistic scholars. A number of studies relate the speech patterns of local proverbs, for instance, to certain African languages.

In recent years, language and its use have become political, the need to preserve Caribbean culture and language closely tied. In this modern context, Caribbean language is probably best described by Barbadian writer Edward Kamau Brathwaite, who terms it "nation language." The melting-pot dialect of papiamento spoken on Aruba, Bonaire, and Curaçao is a living example of the international heritage present in Caribbean speech. In papiamento, derived from Spanish, Dutch, English, Portuguese, African, and Amerind. dialects, *mi ta bon* means "I am fine" and *bon nochi* means "good night."

Wherever you visit, listen carefully. You may begin to notice French words that have remained standard even on English-speaking islands. Words like fête, jalousie, and jouvay (from *jour overt,* which is spelled many ways but always refers to the same thing—the opening day of carnival) have been incorporated into many dialects. You may begin to notice differences in native speakers from different islands; a Jamaican, for example, will not sound the same as a St. Lucian. It is simply a matter of polite questioning and of tuning your ear. It won't be long before phrases like "a wha dis?" make perfect sense.

Folktales and Proverbs

The vitality, creativity, and historic traditions of Caribbean language are readily evident in the islands' rich folklore. An active oral tradition has helped pass stories, proverbs, and even bush medicine from generation to generation. The most prevalent stories are probably those of Anansi, the spider man (from the African *ananse,* or spider). He may be Ananse or Annancy, depending on locale, just as he may be illustrated as anything from quite tarantulalike to an ordinary person. Since he is always described as half man, half spider (and occasionally too clever for his own good), he is sometimes pictured as a rotund man with four arms and four legs spidering out from his prominent midsection. In Anansi stories, animals and half-creatures intermingle and talk with grasses and gods alike in adventures that engage in witty trickery or teach listeners a lesson of cunning. Often, small, weak animals are able to triumph over strong, threatening ones like tigers or pythons by outwitting them with clever ploys.

On some islands, Crick Crack and Tim Tim stories serve the same purpose in tales where Mosquito, Iguana, Tiger, and Tortoise walk and talk. Traditionally, a Crick Crack story must open with the storyteller saying, "Crick Crack," to which listeners reply, "Break my back." The storyteller finishes with, "Wire bend." Listeners have the last word by answering, "Story end." A friend from Barbados reports this variation, "Snip snap snout. This tale's told out. Step on the wire. The wire doesn't bend. That's the way the story ends."

Island-to-island variations are also evident in Caribbean proverbs. It seems that even the most commonplace situation has a proverb to exemplify it. Other proverbs make social statements. Many homilies are reworked from biblical, European, and African sources. A proverb may announce that "Only the knife knows the heart of the pumpkin" or warn against wearing starched shirts in the rain. From Dominica comes "Si ou plante casave, m'pas ke fe fig," which translates, "If you plant cassava, you won't get bananas." While the implications are many, this is probably a regionalization of "You reap what you sow." You will find that most proverbs are in dialect, although translations and informal publications of them are often readily available. Many proverbs are recorded in versions that will help tune your ear to Caribbean sounds, like the observant, "Daag wag im tail fe suit im size."

Literature and Performance Poetry
by Erika J. Smilowitz

Like the coconut husk, the mango peel, and the almond shell, which drop away to reveal the substance within, the superficial similarities of the Caribbean islands drop away on close examination. These islands differ not only in the French, English, Spanish, and Dutch colonial powers, which defined their economic and cultural development, but also in their languages, religions, and myths. The best way to know the islands and to appreciate their differences, to really understand them for what they are, is to read their literature.

The literature of the English-speaking islands—a literature written by Caribbean peoples—is considered to have grown out of the rise of nationalism in the 1930s and 1940s. In fact, St. Lucian-born Derek Walcott's first book of poems, which he published himself in 1948, is often hailed as the beginning of island literature.

Walcott has gone on to become the preeminent poet of the region, winning the Nobel Prize in 1992. The work of Barbadian Edward Kumau Brathwaite, who was born in 1930, is heavily linked to his African heritage and often employs musical rhythms.

The best-known novelist of the region is V. S. Naipaul, whose early novels focus on life on the multicultural island of Trinidad. More recently, with his move to England, he has written incisive travel books. Dominican-born Jean Rhys (1894–1979), who has developed a cult following throughout the world, wrote novels and short stories about Caribbean life in the nineteenth and early twentieth centuries.

Fiction gives a picture of life on the islands, both past and present. George Lamming's classic *In the Castle of My Skin* (1953) tells of a young boy's life on Barbados, and Merle Hodge's *Crick Crack Monkey* (1970) records a girl's adolescence on Trinidad. The work of Jamaica Kincaid, well known to *The New Yorker* readers, reveals her Antiguan childhood. Olive Senior's stories offer a realistic picture of Jamaican rural life.

Despite strong colonial rule and the lack of independence, Guadeloupe and Martinique have produced some of the region's most influential writers. In the 1930s, with the formation of the negritude movement in Paris, French Antillean poets found their own voice. Then a student in Paris, Aimé Césaire, who was born on Martinique in 1913, preached the unity of all black people. Césaire's beautiful seventy-page poem, *Return to My Native Land* (1939), remains a landmark statement of outrage against white supremacy as well as a call for black pride.

A tiny island off Guadeloupe was the birthplace of St. John Perse (1887–1975), who won the Nobel Prize in 1960. Simone Schwarz-Bart, born on Guadeloupe in 1938, has written of her island's women.

Haiti's many writers and poets have worked and published both in French and the local Creole. The rise of the Indigenist movement, led by Jacques Roumain (1907–1944), created an appreciation of the folk elements, myths, and proverbs that characterize the literature of Haiti. Whereas politics have always played a role in Haitian literature, after "Papa Doc" Duvalier came to power in the late 1940s, and even now after his son's depose, most Haitian writers are in exile.

A recent development in the literature of all the French islands is that the vernacular is now being written. Fiction and poetry are being published in books and magazines such as *Antilla Kreyol,* thus broadening the audience and signaling a newfound Caribbean pride.

Cuba was the birthplace of Nicholás Guillén, a major figure in twentieth-century Hispanic literature. Born in 1902, Guillén was an early exponent, with novelist Alejo Carpentier (born in 1904), of Afro-

Cuban culture, and he urged the inclusion of all Cuba's people in the literature.

The Cuban revolution in the 1960s has dominated all writing since, creating a strong body of poetry, prose, and short fiction. Heberto Padilla, born in 1932, writes dramatic, counterrevolutionary poems of life in contemporary Cuba. Lourdes Casal (born in 1938), who won the prestigious Casa Las Americas Poetry Prize, describes her place in the modern world.

Like Haitian and Cuban writers, the writers of the Dominican Republic have also been influenced by their country's political events. From 1930 to 1961, writers wrote under the threat of the Trujillo dictatorship; others lived in exile. Novelist and short story writer Juan Bosch (born in 1909), who was briefly president after Trujillo's fall, is the country's most famous writer.

Puerto Rico still maintains a strong sense of Spanish heritage despite its Americanization. Rosario Ferré, an important new writer, is the author of several collections of short stories and poems.

A strong oral tradition, evidenced by storytelling and calypso, has always been present on the English-speaking islands of the Caribbean. Louise Bennett, born in 1919, has long entertained audiences with her topical, witty performance poetry, as have Bruce St. John (born in 1923) and Paul Keens-Douglas (born in 1942).

Dub poetry is a recent development. Dub poets perform to music, and their poetry is topical, influenced by Rastafarianism and written from the perspective of oppression.

Errol Hill (born in 1921) has portrayed typical Trinidadian yard life. In his plays, Derek Walcott has revealed contemporary Caribbean life with the battling allegiances of different generations, and has also chronicled its past. Poet Dennis Scott (born in 1939) has written innovative plays with the National Dance Theatre of Jamaica, and the Sistren Theatre Group has dramatized events in Jamaican women's lives.

Music and Dance

Caribbean music ranges from the voodoo drums of Haiti to the Spanish guitar of Puerto Rico, with reggae, scratch bands, steel drums, calypso, and folk music to round out the beat. Whatever its motif and politics, it is music that radiates rhythm as dependably as the tropical sun radiates warmth. Like everything else in the Caribbean, the music and dance reflect the traditions of a multiethnic heritage—African drums, French ballads, Spanish love songs. The French islands are credited with beginning the beguine; the plena is said to be Puerto Rican; Santo Domingo claims the merengue; Cuba, the congo, the rumba, and the bolero. Jamaica has become synonymous with reggae, and Trinidad sets first claim as the birthplace of steel drums and calypso.

Calypso, with its traditional 2/4 or 4/4 time, is the beat of carnival, love, and politics. Its roots are usually traced back to the slave era, when workers were not allowed to talk to one another; song became a way to communicate. Calypso has remained a lyrical repository of social and political commentary and witty stories, frequently with sexual innuendo. Calypsonians with bigger-than-life names such as the Mighty Sparrow, Attila the Hun, Growler, King Fanto, and Lord Iere write their own lyrics and often rely on showmanship and improvisation to capture an audience. Early Calypsonians made it their business to know "everybody business" and to let everybody hear about it. Calypso contests are a big part of every carnival on every island with traditional contest tents. The winning song receives a cash prize and becomes that year's road march, or theme song.

More recently, reggae as well as calypso has become a well-heard arena for political commentary. Its popularity became widespread in the early 1970s, probably as a result of the Jamaican movie *The Harder They Come,* starring singer Jimmy Cliff. The word "reggae" comes from the Latin *regis, regina,* or the king. The king's music, or redemption music, has become the podium of the Rastafarian movement. It usually portrays social and economic struggle, often juxtaposed with messages of brotherhood and love, as in the popular songs of the late Bob Marley. The impact of reggae is such that Bob Marley is considered a national hero in Jamaica. Jamaica's commitment to both Marley and reggae is underlined with the annual "Sunsplash" festival, which is held in Montego Bay every June and attracts the best reggae artists in the world.

Steel drums represent another ingenious musical form of the Caribbean with a tradition that stems from colonial suppression. While the drums' exact origins are a bit clouded, many people trace them to Trinidad and Tobago in the late 1800s, when drum-playing was forbidden in an effort to stifle local festivals. Consequently, to make legal music, revelers formed bamboo bands by playing on the stems of giant bamboo, as is sometimes done in Africa. These bands had a "boom" bamboo for bass, a "cutter" to play the lead, and a "buller" to harmonize the two.

This musical style lasted into the 1930s (not without police confrontations, however), when musicians found bamboo too limiting and began to bang on metal containers. It took about two years before the pans were arranged for their sounds. A "kittle" played harmony, "ping-pong" the tenor, and "boom" the bass, much as in the old bamboo bands. In a few more years, the pans were tempered and tuned to play the notes of the scale. Gradually, as the tempering, hammering, and skill of the musicians became more sophisticated, the motley array of tins was replaced with fifty-five-gallon oil drums, a by-product of Trinidad's oil wealth. Fortunately, long before the authorities recognized steel drum bands as music, a group of prominent citizens helped establish their right to practice. Experimentation and the standardization of the instruments led to greater musical sophistication. Many visitors are amazed to hear the wealth of popular and classical music that a good steel band can coax from fifty-five-gallon drums.

As with music, dance is culturally rich and varied, from intricate Afro-Cuban dances performed to a single drum to classical ballet with a complete orchestra. The national ballet companies of both Cuba and Puerto Rico enjoy international reputations, as do folkloric groups on Jamaica, Martinique, and a number of other islands. Many hotels, as well as local cultural centers, offer performances by guest artists, as well. Check the individual island listings for details on events on the island of your choice.

Food

Ingenuity and seasonings are binding ingredients of Caribbean cooking. Any variety of stews, sauces, pepper pots, chowders, *asopaos*, fritters, johnnycakes, and puddings make up the spicy, inventive food that is labeled "Caribbean." Local fruits and vegetables, seafood, chicken, goat, and, of course, a combination of peas or beans and rice are prepared in ways as varied as the islands themselves.

The regular fare on any island is influenced by the availability of ingredients. The vagaries of the growing season, irregular food shipments, rapid spoilage in the tropical heat, and the lack of fresh milk all conspire against standard treatments, but they give rise to experimental dishes and local specialties not found elsewhere. On Barbados, local specialties might include flying fish and sea eggs; on Jamaica, salt fish, ackee, and rice; on Montserrat, goat water; in the Virgin Islands, callaloo and fungi; and in the Bahamas, conch chowder and grouper fingers.

Wherever you eat and whatever is served, chances are that some type of hot-pepper sauce will be available to go with it. You may be offered "pepper" from an old rum bottle that has been packed with tiny "bird" peppers and filled with sherry, or "pepper" from a labeled product that contains one of the elaborate family recipes that have become cottage industries. This offering continues an ancient tradition: The Amerindians of these islands were making hot sauces of homegrown chili peppers long before Columbus arrived and tasted them.

Early explorers probably found a number of edible plants growing on the islands. There is some contention about whether coconuts and bananas were actually here at that time or introduced soon after. About guavas, pineapples, cashews, cassava, soursop, papayas, avocados, sweet potatoes, mamey apples, allspice, achiote, and corn, there is little argument. To these native plants the Europeans quickly added the now-widespread oranges, limes, mangoes, and rice. It wasn't long before another introduced species—sugarcane—changed the Caribbean forever.

With sugarcane came slavery, and with the African slaves came other imported food plants like okra, ackee, taro, pigeon peas, and pungent spices. It was during this era that Captain William Bligh, of *Bounty* fame, was dispatched to the South Seas to bring breadfruit trees back to the Caribbean, where planters were eager for cheap, easy-to-grow foods for their slaves. After his better-known intervening adventure, Bligh returned to the South Seas on another voyage, and sans mutiny, did arrive in Port Royal, Jamaica, in 1793 with his ship covered with breadfruit trees. While breadfruit, which looks like a green cantaloupe and tastes a bit like potato, is still eaten in many forms throughout the Caribbean, it is rarely served in restaurants; occasionally, breadfruit soup is offered as an apéritif.

Caribbean food and its preparation on different islands have also been influenced by the traditions (and demands) of the colonizing country. Afternoon tea is still a standard on many islands with British heritage, where it's not extraordinary to find Devon cream, Cheshire cheese, or Twinings teas in island shops. In the smallest villages on French islands, you'll find baguettes, croissants, and thick fruit preserves. Puerto Rican and Dominican stores stock Spanish olives and carmelos on a regular basis.

Trying new foods, especially the highly perishable fruits like soursops and sugar apples that are rarely exported, is part of the complete vacation experience. The Saturday morning fruit and vegetable market that is held in some form on almost every island is a good place to start. Take plenty of change and small bills and don't be afraid to bargain a little if the prices seem out of line. Certain prices are standard. Early in mango season (June through September in most places), mangoes are usually three for a dollar; by midsummer, it's possible to buy a whole bagful for a dollar. Then again, particularly large mangoes might run a dollar apiece anytime. The best bet is to look and listen before you buy. Remember to inquire about ripeness if a fruit is new to you. A papaya that won't ripen for a week can't be enjoyed if you're leaving the next morning. It's best to avoid picking wild fruit along the road or in the forest. There are inedible as well as poisonous fruits in the Caribbean, and most edible-fruit trees have owners. Buy from roadside stands or ask the locals if they know someone who will sell some fruit.

Local agriculture fairs are a great place to taste a variety of local specialties. These are usually not publicized as tourist events, so you may have to do some advance asking. The annual Virgin Islands Agriculture and Food Fair, held each year on St. Croix over the long President's Day weekend in February, features local entertainment, cooking contests, and livestock and produce competitions, as well as educational exhibits by the University of the Virgin Islands. It's worth a trip.

Dining where the locals eat rather than in tourist hotels and big city restaurants is another way to sample local specialties. On the more out-of-the-way islands, you may have no other choice. Since many local eateries cook only one or two dishes each evening and serve only until they run out, it's often best to stop by in the early afternoon, show interest in the menu, and make an informal reservation. The same is true if you have your heart set on trying a particular dish. If coo-coo and goat water are served only on Thursdays, it's better to find this out early in the week. If you're unsure about the menu or have dietary restrictions, talk it over in advance with the cook. You're not dealing with an anonymous kitchen; often, your waitress and cook head the restaurant household and your table may be on a converted porch or in the living room. Wherever you choose to eat, be patient and adventurous and you'll be in for a totally new experience.

Endangered Species

The only two endangered species that are served in restaurants with any regularity are sea turtle and mountain chicken (the large freshwater frog of Dominica and Montserrat, sometimes available on neighboring islands as well).

Mountain chicken is currently considered "threatened." Regulated hunting seasons have been instituted on Dominica but not Montserrat. Only the animal's muscular legs, which are usually described as either chickenlike or tasteless, are fried and served. You're on your own here.

Sea turtles are magnificent, harmless, ancient creatures that are highly endangered. Please do not even consider eating turtle. As a visitor to the Caribbean, you can help maintain the species by not ordering anything made with turtle, even if the waiter tells you it came from the Cayman turtle farms, the only legal source in many places. Turtle steak is usually described as tough and of unremarkable flavor, anyway. Since the animals themselves *are* remarkable, try for an underwater photo or sign up for an Earthwatch turtle patrol (see Part 4, Exploring, for more details) if you'd like an intimate turtle encounter.

Economic demand (that is, tourists who order turtle or turtle eggs) encourages poaching and confuses emerging environmental consciousness. You can emphasize your awareness and concern by politely telling a restaurant owner or manager that you are shocked and disappointed to see turtle on the menu. Some people feel that actually explaining your reasons and refusing to eat in such places make a more dramatic statement. Use your own judgment and try to understand that environmental concerns are sometimes slammed up against the wall of poverty that many islanders subsist behind. You, as an educated visitor, however, have no excuse.

Recipes

Some cold, bleak day when you are dreaming of Caribbean islands, you may want to cook a regional treat. Here are several recipes that contain readily available ingredients.

BAKED JOHNNYCAKES

   1 1/2 cups sifted flour
   2 tablespoons shortening
   1 tablespoon margarine
   1/2 teaspoon salt
   2 teaspoons baking powder
   1/2 cup milk or water
   2 tablespoons sugar
   1 teaspoon vanilla

Combine all the ingredients, adding liquid gradually to form a soft, pliable dough that does not stick to the sides of the bowl. Knead about 5 minutes. Shape into biscuit-sized balls, flatten, and bake at 350°F on a greased cookie sheet until golden brown.

COCONUT BREAD

   4 cups flour
   3 teaspoons baking powder
   3/4 cup sugar

$^1/_2$ teaspoon salt
2 cups grated coconut
6 ounces raisins
$^3/_4$ cup milk
$^1/_4$ cup margarine, melted
1 teaspoon vanilla extract
1 egg, lightly beaten

Sift dry ingredients together in a bowl. Stir in grated coconut and raisins. In another bowl combine milk, melted shortening, and vanilla; add beaten egg. Add milk mixture to flour mixture and blend well. Knead gently on floured board. Shape into loaves and place in greased loaf pans, filling only two-thirds of each pan.

Bake at 400°F until golden brown. When almost done, brush with a mixture of sugar and water.

For heavier coconut bread, use only 1 teaspoon baking powder and $^1/_2$ cup milk.

adapted from recipes by the
University of the Virgin Islands Cooperative Extension Service

LUCY'S BANANA FRITTERS

4 small ripe bananas, peeled and mashed
3 tablespoons sugar
A few drops of canned milk
2 teaspoons baking powder
Dash of cinnamon
About a capful of vanilla extract
4 heaping tablespoons all-purpose flour

Combine bananas and sugar and beat well. Add enough canned milk to make mixture smooth. Add remaining ingredients and mix thoroughly; batter should fall from the mixing spoon in a ball. If it's too soft, add more flour.

Cover bottom of a skillet with oil and heat the oil in the skillet. Test it with a little piece of batter; when it bubbles around the edges, start fritters by adding batter in spoonfuls. Cook until both sides are brown, turning down heat when fritters start to puff and brown. And more oil if necessary to prevent sticking.

Drain fritters on paper towel. Cool a little and eat, but not too many. They make you fat!

With typical Caribbean practicality, Lucy adds that pumpkin fritters can be made the same way, substituting mashed pumpkin for bananas, or "you could make a good cake by just adding a little butter and eggs."

from Lucy Reed of Trials, Montserrat

PART THREE

Going—Choosing an Island

"Take care is better than don't care."

Caribbean proverb

Hints for Choosing an Island

Choosing a destination or an itinerary may be the most difficult part of your preparation. You aren't the first visitor faced with this dilemma. As Columbus once commented, "I saw so many islands that I hardly knew to which I should go first."

It's a difficult choice, so forget where you should go for the moment and think about how long you have, how much you can afford to spend, and, most importantly, what exactly you want (or don't want) to do.

If you want serenity, warmth, and soft sand by the sea, you'll probably be happy on any island; even the busiest have quiet getaways. If you need to go golfing, shopping, sight-seeing, diving, mountain climbing, or night clubbing to have a satisfying vacation, your choices have automatically been narrowed. With the exception of a few islands with developed tourist facilities, the Caribbean is most treasured by visitors for its simplicity. There are places where having absolutely nothing to do *is* the big attraction.

There's one more thing to consider early on: If speaking a foreign language or using foreign money inhibits your pleasure, choose islands where you can speak the language and you know the currency.

If you're not really sure what you want to do, or you want to do a little bit of everything, or you're interested mainly in a low-cost vacation, choose one of the larger, more developed islands with a variety of tourist options. Puerto Rico would probably head the list. You can camp, gamble in casinos, dine in gourmet restaurants, or eat from roadside stands; airfares are relatively low and package deals abound. Jamaica is another good choice for economy and options. Visitors can explore the lush countryside or enjoy a resort. Package deals and the fluctuating Jamaican dollar can make U.S. money stretch.

Smaller islands with the most options include Barbados, St. Thomas and St. John in the U.S. Virgin Islands, and nearby British Tortola (in the off-season). The Dominican Republic (large but not particularly developed outside of Santo Domingo) is especially popular with Spanish-speaking visitors; it's possible to find a good weekend package from San Juan, Puerto Rico, and enjoy the two oldest Spanish cities in the Caribbean in one trip. The Cayman Islands offer bargain fly-hotel-dive packages. Nassau and Freeport, Bahamas, have year-round packages (although the summer Goombay season is considerably cheaper).

When planning a five- to seven-day visit, it is probably best to stay on one island and explore from there. Even for two-week stays, moving between related island groups and avoiding great cultural shifts is recommended; changing languages, for instance, takes most visitors several days of adjustment. Some island groupings that offer contrast rather than shock include St. Martin-St. Barts, Martinique-Guadeloupe-St. Barts, St. Maarten-Saba, U.S. Virgin Islands-British Virgin Islands, and Trinidad-Tobago. Puerto Rico-Dominican Republic and Puerto Rico-U.S. Virgin Islands are also relatively easy shifts. English is spoken often on Puerto Rico, and traveling between Puerto Rico and the U.S. Virgin Islands is eased by the lack of customs formalities, the number of frequent flights (usually on time), and the same monetary system.

For the most part, these combinations include a faster-paced island with a small-town, beach-oriented one (except Saba, where steep slopes drop directly into the sea and give the island other attributes). This gives travelers a chance to combine sight-seeing and shopping with sand and sun.

If you'd like to highlight your visit with a carnival, a music festival, a marathon run, or a cooking contest, check the Festivals and Holidays section for each island. Scan Exploring if you're more interested in a particular activity like fishing, diving, or mountain climbing. If true sand-and-sea seclusion is your dream, consider islands described as undeveloped, undiscovered, pristine, and secret, or look for short hotel lists.

If golf and tennis are high on your list, the best bet is a resort complex. This doesn't necessarily exclude quiet and a great beach; there are several small resorts in the pristine Turks and Caicos Islands with good tennis courts. Lots of the newer (albeit fancier) resorts are out of town, built bungalow-style right on the ocean.

Camping is limited almost entirely to Puerto Rico; St. John, U.S.V.I.; Jamaica; and Cuba (if a camping group can be arranged); facilities vary considerably. Camping, especially on the beach, is forbidden on many islands. This is one activity for which reservations and permissions must be arranged in advance. See Camping in Part 4 for more information.

One last thought about selecting your getaway: If you want small, picturesque lodgings but you're interested in creature comforts, ask a few basic questions first. Is there running water? How many hours a day? Are there hot showers? Are the rooms screened? Is there electricity? If you want a double bed, be sure to ask if it's possible; the "double" rooms in one charming getaway all have bunk beds. While these considerations may sound fussbudget, a six-day coating of salt on a sunburn might make you wish you had planned ahead.

If these suggestions seem more confusing than helpful, simply choose three things you'd like to do or see and three islands that offer all of them. Send for color brochures. Then choose at random. The Caribbean is exotic and breathtakingly beautiful—a very hard place not to like no matter where you are. The descriptions that follow will help you get started.

The Islands in a Nutshell

Anguilla (U.K.)

Its name means eel and, at sixteen miles long and about four miles wide, the island resembles one. The only island that has been under one power—British—since it was colonized, Anguilla is flat and quiet, ringed by white-sand beaches and coral reefs. Diving (bring your own scuba gear), beachcombing, bird-watching.

Antigua

Independent and English speaking. A relatively flat, dry island with lovely stretches of white sand, lagoons, reefs, and harbors. A major crossroads with well-developed tourist facilities, all water sports, beachcombing, bird-watching, shopping, some historical architecture, restaurants, entertainment, and more.

Aruba

White-coral beaches and oil refineries (it's just fifteen miles off the coast of Venezuela). Called "a little bit of Holland in the Caribbean," Aruba offers all tourist amenities, water sports, shopping, caves with Arawak Indian drawings, some old churches, and lots of unusual rock formations.

Bahamas

A low, sandy, English-speaking archipelago in the North Atlantic. Visitors have a wide range of choices, from the casinos and bustle of Nassau and Freeport with all the tourist amenities to out-island settlements, where a fresh head of lettuce on the weekly mail boat is an event. No clearer waters or finer beaches anywhere in the Caribbean. Renowned for sportfishing. Winter northers can bring temperatures down into the fifties.

Barbados

Often called "Little England"; cricket is the national sport and pubs and tea are part of island life. A well-developed tourist industry with all ranges of offerings. Parks, museums, galleries, historical buildings, antique shops, tennis, golf, beaches, all water sports, caves, and an underwater park.

Bonaire (Netherlands Antilles)

Most of the island is a nature preserve. Sometimes called "the land of flamingos," Bonaire has spectacular flamingo sanctuaries. The island also has 126 other species of birds, clear waters, beaches, water sports, tennis, and casinos.

British Virgin Islands

Tourist oriented but still quiet enough for restaurants to run out of food and close early. Exceptional beaches and a remnant of rain forest. Lots of yachting—Road Town, Tortola, the capital, is headquarters for the Moorings bare boats. Scattered resorts; good diving; lots of natural areas, such as the caves at Norman Island, and the spectacular rock formations at the Baths, Virgin Gorda. Tortola is the major island in the group and is an easy day trip by ferry from either St. John or St. Thomas, U.S.V.I.

Cayman Islands

The offshore activities of banking and diving sum up the tourist-oriented Caymans. White sand beaches, sea turtle farm, pirate caves, many shallow-water shipwrecks, and the Cayman Trench (for experienced divers). All water sports, tennis, some duty-free shopping; larger hotels offer some entertainment.

Cuba

Large, fertile island wrapped in a colorful history and the recently acquired allure of the forbidden for American travelers. Spanish-speaking Cuba has forests, beaches, parks, museums, theater, and camping, but it is not tourist oriented at present. Individual visitors are not encouraged. Most come as part of a tour group with a prearranged itinerary reflecting special interests (visitors on a cultural tour won't be camping, and there's little room for overlap).

Curaçao (Netherlands Antilles)

The strong Dutch influence is especially evident in the waterway of Willemstad, which resembles an Amsterdam canal. Old World flavor with casinos, a museum, floating schooner markets, botanical gardens, a zoo, tennis, golf, and water sports.

Dominica

Sometimes described as the only island Columbus would still recognize. Called "Nature Island," English-speaking Dominica is a naturalist's dream—a seemingly other world where mists cloud the tops of volcanic mountains. Black sand beaches, simple life-styles. Roseau, the capital, still has open sewers but it rains so much it's hard to notice. Scattered accommodations, rough roads. Carib Indian reservation, Boiling Lake, Emerald Pool, rain forest, and mountains. Good guides available.

Dominican Republic

Spanish speaking and bustling, the Dominican Republic shares the island of Hispaniola with Haiti, but the two countries are worlds apart. The city of Santo Domingo has high fashion, casinos, theater, museums, galleries, and a restored old sector with an awe-inspiring cathedral housing Columbus's bones. Many ancient Indian sites and a large expanse of *país* (countryside) where people fish and farm. Amber is mined in the mountains

Jamaica's lush Blue Mountains are popular with hikers, campers, and coffee lovers. (Photo courtesy of Jamaica Tourist Board.)

and is for sale everywhere. Scattered resorts with all amenities; scattered guest houses with few; it's the visitor's choice—from the high life to camping.

Grenada

A small, beautiful English-speaking "Spice Island," Grenada is becoming more interested in tourism. Water sports, spice plantations, lush flora and fauna, rain forest, and Grand Étang Lake.

Guadeloupe (French West Indies)

Guadeloupe is a bustling, industrial island with discos, casinos, and big hotels with entertainment. But it's easy to get out of town, and there are five small islands nearby for complete quiet. Beaches are the main attraction; also tennis, golf, hiking, diving, fishing, sailing, a rain forest, a volcano, and an archaeological park.

Haiti

French, Creole, and English are spoken here. Not in this century, barely in this hemisphere, Haiti is poor and rich in diverse ways. Not tourist oriented (and not for the faint of heart or stomach), but some rather complete facilities.

Jamaica

A large, fertile, English-speaking island with lush countryside, the famous Blue Mountains (and their coffee), waterfalls, rivers, beaches, historic sites, the University of the West Indies, bustling cities, dance, music, and culture. Many options, from simple to lavish resort complexes, from discos to rafting. Some political volatility but eager for tourists.

Martinique (French West Indies)

And very French it is. One of the islands with something for everyone (Columbus thought it the most beautiful country in the world). Casinos, French wine, topless beaches, folk dancers, most sports, varied terrain—from mangroves to forested, volcanic mountains. Don't miss the ruins on Mount Pelée and the volcanological museum.

Montserrat (U.K.)

A green, mountainous island, once colonized by the Irish and often called the "other Emerald Isle." Quiet, picturesque, still relatively undiscovered. Golf, tennis, and some water sports at one resort, but you're mostly on your own here. Hiking, mountain-climbing, bird-watching, black sand beaches, plantation ruins, museum. Waterfall and Galway's Soufrière, a steaming (sulfurous) volcano, are highlights.

Puerto Rico (U.S.)

Large, lush island of contrasts, from frantic San Juan to dreamy Fajardo, from deserts of tree cactus to rain forest; a generally underrated place with everything if you know where to look for it. Resorts have complete facilities; guest houses in outlying areas have complete quiet. Mostly Spanish speaking but English is spoken often; for instance, the legal system is American and conducted in English. Casinos and nightlife are centered around San Juan. On the outskirts, camping, hiking, and boating are available. El Yunque Forest, Phosphorescent Lake, Ponce Art Museum, Mayagüez Institute of Tropical Agriculture. Don't miss the coconut palm-lined beaches, mangroves, and the beautifully restored Spanish colonial city of San Juan—from the wave-dashed fort (which children love) to cobblestone streets lined with galleries and shops.

St. Barthélemy, or St. Barts (a dependency of Guadeloupe, French West Indies)

A quiet, 8-square-mile island, settled by Norman and Breton fishermen, that has maintained a French provincial quality. A few hotels; mainly mountains and spectacular beaches.

St. Eustatius, or Statia (Netherlands Antilles)

A quiet, Dutch island of about 8 square miles, a short flight from St. Maarten; many visitors come only for lunch and a donkey tour. Few places to stay—a true retreat. Flat, central plain rises to a volcanic crater with a forested interior.

St. Kitts and Nevis

English speaking and still green with cane, these quiet, friendly islands make a great getaway. Resorts offer golf, tennis, horseback riding, and water sports. Landmark fort; Amerindian sites. Walking and hiking on lush mountains.

St. Lucia

An English-speaking island known for its craggy, volcanic beauty, waterfalls, rare parrots, and ambience. Black sand beaches, some freeport shopping, water sports, horseback riding, historic sites, banana plantations. Hiking and walking are very rewarding; don't miss the rain forest and the sulfur springs.

St. Martin/St. Maarten and Saba

St. Martin is part of the French West Indies, a dependency of Guadeloupe; St. Maarten is the Dutch half of the same island. Both are pronounced the same, whatever the other differences. A major crossroads and free port, the island has about eighty restaurants, thirty-six beaches, and all amenities. Nightclubs, casinos, and water sports of all description. Busy, but there are quiet spots out of town, and most natives speak some English. Saba, part of the Netherlands Antilles and a short flight from St. Martin, is actually a single, breathtaking volcanic peak rising directly from the sea;

no beaches, nevertheless some dive operations. Very limited accommodations, so most visitors make this a day trip. A true retreat with dramatic mountains to explore.

St. Vincent and the Grenadines

These English-speaking islands are a marvelous getaway. Quiet and pristine with small inns that offer golf, tennis, and all water sports. Hiking, a volcano, waterfalls, nature trails, historic sites, a museum with pre-Columbian artifacts, traditional boat-building on Bequia. Quiet and simple.

Trinidad and Tobago

English speaking but a true melting pot with strong East Indian influences. Located right off the coast of Venezuela, these two islands have unspoiled beaches, bird sanctuaries (Tobago), and the chaotic commercial city of Port-of-Spain (Trinidad). With its oil and gas industry, Trinidad is becoming the wealthiest island in the Caribbean. Some of this relatively newfound money has gone toward establishing protected natural areas such as the Caroni Swamp Bird Sanctuary and the Asa Wright Nature Center (both musts for bird-watchers). Both islands have rich flora and fauna with many South American species; some natural curiosities like Pitch Lake. Venture beyond Port-of-Spain to really see the country. Most visitors say you must not visit Trinidad without seeing Tobago.

Turks and Caicos Islands (U.K.)

Actually a group of scattered cays at the bottom of the Bahamas. Still relatively unspoiled dunes, beaches, reefs, and crystal waters. Several large resort complexes on the island of Prova. Caves, birds, salt works, beaches, swimming, diving (in general, bring your own gear; check ahead), beachcombing, walking.

U.S. Virgin Islands (U.S.)

An island grouping including the large islands of St. Thomas, St. Croix, and St. John. St. Thomas is one of the major cruise-ship ports in the Caribbean. A free-port shoppers' paradise. St. Croix, the largest island in the U.S.V.I., offers the greatest variety of terrain, from arid hills to the remnants of a rain forest. Most of the island's industry is on the outskirts of historic Danish Christiansted. Lots of water sports, diving, beaches, an underwater trail at Buck Island Reef National Monument. St. John, easily reached by ferry from St. Thomas and Tortola, is mostly national park, with programs and trails, including an underwater trail at Trunk Bay. Accommodations on St. John range from camping to the understated luxury of Caneel Bay.

Money—How Much? What Kind?

How much money to bring is always the first question. Unfortunately, the answer is usually plenty, but less off-season. High season for tourism in the Caribbean is from 15 December to 15 April (unless Easter is unusually late, in which case the rates change the week after Easter). Hotel rates drop from 30 to 60 percent on most islands in the off-season. Food and interisland transportation stay the same, with the convenience of a smaller crowd. Sometimes, in-season airfare-hotel-car (or tennis, golf, or dive) packages offer considerable savings.

It's a good idea to take travelers' checks; make sure you have plenty of $20 checks—change is a problem in many places (but not large hotels). Although credit cards are accepted on the larger, more developed islands, some places are not equipped to deal with them. If you're going on a credit-card vacation, be sure to check in advance (see individual island listings).

A word of warning: There is *nowhere, anywhere* (is that strong enough?) to cash a personal check. It can take ten days or more for a mainland check to clear, and you'll be on your own until it does. Wiring money or bank transfers can take from a few hours to three days. Prepare to be self-sufficient. See individual island entries for more information.

How to Get There

Air

Most visitors to the Caribbean find that air travel is the quickest, easiest, cheapest means of transportation. Most of the larger islands have good air connections with North America, many via Miami or San Juan. It's a good idea for you or your travel agent to check several routings for the best possible connections; sometimes what appears to be a roundabout approach is faster. Keep a bathing suit in your carry-on bag just in case.

LIAT (Leeward Island Air Transport) based at V. C. Bird (formerly Coolidge) International Airport on Antigua (telephone: 20700) is the standard interisland air carrier. It stops at most out-of-the-way islands and is a good place to start if you aren't sure of your route. It also offers a Caribbean Explorer pass good for thirty days of unlimited travel on the LIAT network.

Cruise Ship

Traveling in the floating hotel of a cruise ship is a journey in itself. Many cruise ships dock at a number of Caribbean islands. Cruises vary in length from weekends to the Bahamas to two-week swings around the Caribbean. Over 300 cruise ships sail the Caribbean. Check with your travel agent for details.

Charter Boat

There are a number of boats available for crewed or bare-boat charters— an exciting vacation option. See Boating for details.

If you plan to sail your own boat to the Bahamas or the Caribbean, or take an extended cruise, there are several cruising guides available. You'll find them listed in Part 4 under Boating.

Customs

Customs requirements and visas vary from island to island; check individual island listings for details. In general, most islands do not require passports from U.S. and Canadian citizens. Passports sometimes make things easier, but often proof of citizenship—a birth certificate or voter's card—will do. Most islands do require either a return or an ongoing ticket. (Take note: If you appear too "counterculture," you may be asked to prove that you can sustain yourself financially during your visit.)

If you are planning to carry foreign-made cameras, binoculars, and such, take some documentation of purchase—a receipt if you bought the item at home or a customs receipt if you paid duty on the item on a previous trip. Or you may register the item with customs before you leave the country.

Most Caribbean countries allow you to bring along anything for your personal use. A few countries limit alcohol and the number of cigarettes; see individual island listings for specifics. Drugs—marijuana, opiates, barbiturates, and hallucinogens—are illegal throughout the area, and the quantity involved is of little consequence. The penalties for possession range from fines to deportation to jail, or a combination; smuggling is an even more serious offense. You are subject to the laws of the countries you visit; U.S. consulates and embassies cannot get Americans out of jail.

Returning

U.S. residents returning to the U.S. from any island except the U.S. Virgin Islands, who have been out of the country for forty-eight hours and haven't claimed an exemption within thirty days, may return from the French islands with U.S. $400 worth of merchandise for gifts or personal use without paying duty; from many other islands the amount is $600. Puerto Rico is considered U.S. soil, but the U.S. Virgin Islands aren't; however, it's a generous U.S. $1,200 exemption from the U.S. Virgin Islands. Families may pool their exemptions. Otherwise, the amount is the same for everyone, regardless of age. However, travelers must be over the age of twenty-one to return with the allowed one liter of alcohol (one gallon from the U.S. Virgin Islands), two hundred cigarettes, and one hundred cigars (non-Cuban). One bottle of perfume is allowed. Artwork—and it must be labeled as such when you buy it—is duty free.

What to Expect

Weather: Tropical Seasons and Seasonal Rates

The West Indies are tropical, with an average annual temperature of 80°F (27°C). The daytime temperature lingers between 78° and 85°F year-round. The Bahamas, which are semitropical or subtropical, have slightly cooler winters and a greater temperature variation.

The seasons are divided into wet and dry. The wet season (which coincides with hurricane season) lasts from May or June until October or November. September is considered the most likely month for these tropical storms, but they may occur anytime. Late summer and early fall have little wind and tend to be the warmest and most humid times of the year. (See Tropical Days in Part 1 for more details.) In short, the weather is consistent and pleasant enough not to be a consideration for most travelers.

What can be a consideration is the great difference in off- and on-season prices. High season in the Caribbean runs from 14 December to mid-April (usually about 15 April, depending on Easter). Most rates change right after the traditional Easter vacation. The rest of the year is considered off-season, when most hotel rates drop from 40 to 60 percent and many packages include sporting activities that would cost extra during the season. Check with individual hotels for details.

Time Zones

Most of the islands from the Dominican Republic east are on Atlantic standard time, which is an hour ahead of eastern standard time during the winter months and during daylight saving time. There are a few exceptions: the Bahamas, Cayman Islands, Turks and Caicos, Haiti, and Jamaica all operate on eastern standard time/daylight saving time all year. Cuba has daylight saving time only from May until the third week of September.

Electricity

Here's another island enigma. Although 110–120 volts AC (which operates U.S.-made appliances) tends to predominate, there are a number of variations. The islands of St. Kitts, St. Lucia, St. Vincent, and Grenada have 230 volts AC. Antigua and Montserrat have 220 volts DC (although many large hotels on Antigua also have 110 volts AC). The French West Indies have 110 volts AC; however, they have European plugs that require adaptors in order to use U.S.-made appliances. In addition, some beach hotels and mountain retreats generate their own power, and even more variations, including 12 volts DC. So if electrical devices are crucial to your vacation well-being, ask *specific* questions beforehand: What type of electrical current do you have? How many hours per day? Do all guest rooms have working outlets? Do you have convertors or adaptors available for such-and-such an appliance? Also keep in mind energy surcharges; many hotels bill extra for converters, adapters, and, perhaps more surprisingly, for air-conditioning.

Health

Travel in the Caribbean will not be hazardous to your health if you are aware of the potential problems, travel only when your general health is good, and take suitable precautions.

Visitors' most common afflictions—sunburn and diarrhea—can either be prevented or treated with over-the-counter remedies. No immunizations are required for travel in the Caribbean, although you may want to take malaria prophylaxis (chloroquine) if you visit Haiti or if you plan to rough it in the countryside. Chloroquine tablets are acquired by prescription; the dosage usually starts two weeks before you depart and is continued for six weeks after your return. A tetanus booster is also a good idea. Make sure that children's immunizations are up-to-date.

Other serious diseases that occur in the islands include tuberculosis and infectious hepatitis (jaundice). Tuberculosis can be transmitted by cows; drink only boiled, canned, pasteurized, or reconstituted milk and avoid eating unwashed mushrooms from cow fields.

Hepatitis is best avoided by taking extra care in hygiene and abiding by the tropical basics: Peel fruit, drink only pure water, stay in clean surroundings, and wash your hands. Soap and water hand washing is one of the best defenses against germs when traveling in unsanitary areas. Ironically, water to wash with is often scarce. Public restrooms, even on touristy islands like St. Thomas, rarely have running water; so premoistened towelettes are a must.

Many of the islands have trustworthy drinking water. Local people, and tourist brochures, are very forthright where general health is concerned. If you are told to drink only bottled water, believe it. Otherwise, the tap water is probably safe.

If you have a particularly nervous stomach or know you're prone to travelers' diarrhea, you may want to carry water purification tablets like Halazone. A few drops of tincture of iodine also work; buy the 2 percent solution in a dropper bottle at the pharmacy before leaving home. Use about eight drops per quart or liter of water and wait twenty minutes before drinking. Be sure to try whichever method you choose before you travel; both methods make water taste odd, and most people use them only when bottled water is unavailable. Other options include canned juice, soda, beer, and eating only in better restaurants.

If you're prone to travelers' constipation—and if you're heading for a charter boat, you probably will be—you may want to carry dried fruit, bran, or your favorite remedy.

Remember, sometimes travelers' diarrhea can be brought on simply by the change in environment, drinking water, and food, and the stress and excitement of packing and traveling, rather than something you ate or drank. A little moderation at the start of your vacation will often help. Four rum punches and a lobster in butter after flying eight hours are likely to upset the steadiest stomach. If you have a bout of intestinal flutters, simply take it easy and use your regular remedy (Kaopectate, Pepto-Bismol, and such). A diet of clear liquids, boiled rice, and bananas for a day or two will often speed your recovery. However you deal with your malady, be sure to drink plenty of nonalcoholic liquids. Club soda is a favorite stomach settler.

Polluted seawater may also pose a health hazard. Sewage treatment in the Caribbean is still based on downhill flow and the shortest route to the sea. There aren't going to be any signs announcing "Polluted," and local children will swim anywhere, so use common sense. Avoid swimming near population centers: Caribbean seawater can be clear in the worst of places, and you can't always see or smell pollution. The larger the settlement, the farther away you must go to swim in clean water (except in the Bahamas, where the strong tidal flow makes pollution less of a problem; even parts of Nassau Harbour are okay). You wouldn't hop into a busy harbor at home, so don't do it here either just because it's picturesque.

Food

In addition to lavish hotel buffets, the Caribbean is full of street vendors and marketplaces offering tempting tastes of the land. Sampling street food is a great way to become acquainted with a place, and on most islands (not Haiti) it is perfectly safe; but be conservative and try to be sensible before yielding to enticing aromas. Use discretion. Look at the vendor (don't buy from those who appear unhealthy, have rheumy eyes, sores on their hands, and so forth) and the stand (does it look well cared for?). As well as this first-glance, common-sense approach, watch for a few minutes: If a stand is busy, the food is probably fresh; if no one buys too often, find another place. Breads, pastries, and deep-fried fritters and pastillos are always safer bets than meats. Street-vendor ice cream is best avoided.

Outside of resorts catering to North Americans, you're better off eating local dishes made with fish, goat, and chicken than ordering hamburgers. Hot dogs should be avoided, period. Be leery of outdoor buffets with un-iced salads and mayonnaise or anything that looks a shade off-fresh; food spoils rapidly in the tropics.

Fish Poisoning

In the Caribbean, fish is a gift with a hook—ciguatera fish poisoning. It is caused by ciguatoxin that originates in single-celled plants called dino-flagellates. These microscopic organisms grow on scattered coral reefs, especially in environmentally disturbed areas. The toxin enters the food chain at the base level and accumulates as small fish are eaten by larger reef fish like barracuda, jacks, kingfish, and snappers. When a person eats these reef fish, dangerous levels of the toxin come part and parcel.

Symptoms of fish poisoning usually occur within six to eight hours after eating a fish with ciguatoxin. Symptoms often include tingling, itching, or numbness of the lips, fingers, or extremities accompanied by nausea, intestinal cramping, and diarrhea. Joint and muscle pain and a flulike weakness may also ensue.

Little can be done to alleviate the discomfort. Rest and drinking plenty of liquids is recommended. This is one time it's better not to take an anti-diarrheal; your body needs to rid itself of the fish. If the symptoms are severe and include dehydration, seek medical help. Fish poisoning is often serious and occasionally fatal. The toxin builds up in your system over time, just as in the fishes', so the poisoning is also a long-term threat. Extra caution is in order after your first bout.

Ciguatoxin has no taste or color or anything to indicate its presence. Researchers have been long at work trying to devise a detection test, but at present the best they can offer is a set of guidelines compiled from statistics. Barracuda is the most common culprit; avoid eating it no matter what convincing little homily is quoted. The islands are full of fish-poisoning folklore. "Long as your arm, it'll do you no harm" is often the barracuda rule, which may or may not be true.

Also avoid jacks and large reef fish in general; kingfish is chancy in some areas. Unethical restaurants sometimes pass off barracuda as kingfish, since they're both long, slim fish served in sections steaked through the backbone. When unfamiliar with a restaurant, stick to pan-fried fish served with the head and tail on for surefire identification.

Other safe and delicious fish are the fast-moving varieties of the open ocean—pelagic species like wahoo, tuna, and dolphin (called *el dorado* in Spanish and mahi-mahi in the western U.S. and Hawaii). Fresh Caribbean fish is a luxury to be savored: Don't avoid it; just be choosy.

As a final note, if you plan to do your own fishing, check with the local fisherman to find out what species are safest and best.

Flora and Fauna

Visitors should be forewarned about the manchineel tree, with its poisonous little crab apple–like fruit. The manchineel has nearly heart-shaped leaves and grows to a large shade tree on protected coasts; in dry areas it is often the only shrubbery untouched by goats. Its woody fruit (about the size of a flattened jacks ball) was the demise of many Spanish explorers overeager to taste the fruits of paradise. Perhaps because of these early mishaps, the manchineel gained a somewhat overblown reputation that includes dropping a blistering sap in the rain. The apples are definitely lethal; their rain-of-poison sap is questionable. On Puerto Rico, where some manchineel trees have benches under them, many islanders take their shade and shelter with nonchalance.

Suffice it to say, don't touch or eat any strange fruits or leaves. Many tropical plants contain irritating or poisonous substances. As a rule, avoid skin contact with anything that exudes milky sap. Some people have allergic reactions even to plants that are edible. Contact with mango skin or even the bark of the tree causes hives or a rash in some people. As for eating, proceed with caution. When you are served a fruit you haven't had before, sample it in moderation until you're sure it agrees with you.

One of nature's warnings comes in the form of coloration. Anything bright red and black seems to flash a warning. The islands have a number of insects (although all nonaggressive) that should be avoided—jack spaniels, several varieties of stinging bees, black widow spiders, hawk wasps, stinging caterpillars, and scorpions. Most stings occur when someone inadvertently lays a hand on an insect resting on a tree trunk or steps on one in the grass. Small red ants, called fire ants (their bites do burn), may also catch bare feet or legs unaware.

The best pain reliever for nonpoisonous stings is papaya enzyme, the same ingredient found in Adolph's meat tenderizer. Insect venom is a protein; the papaya enzyme breaks it down so it no longer stings. Fresh papaya is readily available on most islands, but just to be sure you may want to pack a bit of meat tenderizer, a few papaya tea bags, or the capsules of powdered papaya enzyme available in health-food stores.

If you are sensitive to insect bites or are allergic to bee stings, carry your usual medication or the emergency bee-sting kit available with a prescription. This is a must for boating, camping, hiking, and for small islands without accessible medical care.

If you are bitten by an insect or snake you suspect is dangerous (only Martinique, St. Lucia, and Trinidad have poisonous species), or if you have shortness of breath, hives, excessive swelling, numbness, convulsions, or hemorrhaging, go to the nearest hospital or clinic. If you can, bring the culprit for identification. If you cannot easily and safely bring it, unless you are absolutely sure what bit you and the local name for it, it's best to describe it in detail rather than call it by a name that may not be correct.

All of the local lizards, from the great iguana to the tiny chameleon, are harmless. This includes the shy wood slave that is wrongly maligned on some islands. Most lizards eat incredible numbers of insects and are welcomed indoors, which takes some people a while to accept.

Although most of the insects you come in contact with are annoying rather than dangerous, mosquitoes can carry dengue fever and malaria. Haiti and, from time to time, Trinidad have most of the cases. If you aren't taking malaria prophylaxis, apply insect repellent liberally and continually, especially in high-risk areas.

The most annoying insects are those little dust specks of solid jaw, the sand flies. They're also called midges, no-see-ums, and, on the Spanish-speaking islands, mi-mis (pronounced me-me's), which leads one to a probable explanation of the origin of the screaming me-me's. They are a fact of life in the tropics. They're worse at dawn and twilight and after rain and prefer to plague scalp, arms, and ankles. Insect repellent helps but is no miracle; clothing provides a better barrier. Concentrate on the sunset and pretend the sand flies don't bother you. And remember, infected insect bites respond well when regularly cleaned with hydrogen peroxide and dabbed with antibiotic salve.

In the rare-rare event you are bitten by a wild animal, especially a bat, seek medical care *immediately;* the Caribbean is not rabies free.

Sun

Although the sun is not be taken lightly anywhere because of skin cancer and premature aging, at these latitudes, the sun is intense and can be dangerous.

Limit your exposure: Thirty minutes on the beach is enough for the first day. Wear sunscreen and a cover-up. Remember that water time equals beach time, so don't be embarrassed to swim or snorkel with your clothes on. You'll tan right through them. A tight, long-sleeved cotton turtleneck and, if your legs aren't tan, tights or long pants work fine. Looking a little odd is a lot better than staying in bed with a can of Solarcaine. Another good way to limit your sun exposure is to avoid the beach from 10 A.M. to 2 or 3 P.M., when the sun is most intense.

Sunscreens are now rated with a sun protection factor (SPF) number. The higher the SPF number, the greater the protection; choose accordingly. Most active visitors prefer a waterproof formula. Remember to re-apply sunscreen as directed, paying extra attention to your ears, nose, the tops of your feet, and especially your lips. Lips burn easily and the sun may cause painful herpes simplex blisters to erupt.

Hats, cover-ups, trees, and umbrellas provide some shade, but they aren't impenetrable sun shields. Let your body adjust slowly to the heat, and especially the sun. The danger signals of sunstroke and sun poisoning include headache, vertigo, chills, fever, nausea, and blisters. Get out of the heat and the sun immediately. If symptoms are not severe and don't persist, you may get by with self-treatment—rest, cool showers, aspirin, Solarcaine (or such), and extra liquids (fruit juice, soda, or Gatorade to help replaced lost electrolytes). If you have any doubts, see a doctor.

Which brings us to another problem—doctors. Health care in the Caribbean varies greatly. Some islands have many qualified doctors and hospitals comparable to those in the U.S. (Lists are available through consulates and tourist boards.) On other islands, the locals know how to find an experienced pharmacist or the nearest nurse. Even the most remote islands have an air or boat ambulance for serious cases. Consider these factors before you leave home. Your choice of vacation islands should take into account your health needs. If you are particularly frail or nervous about your health, your best bet may be a cruise ship (each sails with its own doctor) or a big resort, with a house or consulting doctor, on a more developed island.

Above all, staying healthy while you travel means staying in touch with yourself. Know your needs and limits. If you're overtired from hiking or hung over from rum punch, don't rush out to go parasailing and sightseeing and have lobster for lunch. It might be better to dream away the afternoon in a shady spot on a nearby beach and eat lightly until your body catches up with the festivities.

In summary: Peel fruit, boil milk, and drink pure water. Wash your hands often. Wear insect repellent. Don't eat barracuda or large reef fish. Go easy with the sun. Drink plenty of (nonalcoholic) liquids. And, above all else (or when all else fails), use common sense.

P.S. Have fun!

Packing for Fun
and Security

The trick to successful packing is to take as little as possible and still have everything you need to wear and to feel secure. It's a delicate balance. Be assured, the Caribbean is warm and informal: Less is best.

Basically, you'll need a few changes of lightweight clothing. Natural fabrics—cotton heads the list—have greater breathability and are cooler than synthetics. Avoid 100 percent polyester, especially knits; they retain body heat. If you prefer the easy care of mixed fabrics, try the 50 percent cotton blends; they'll still be wrinkle free.

Women can't go wrong with short-sleeved summer dresses or skirts and tops; take at least one conservative style (with cap sleeves and a complete back) for sight-seeing, especially in churches and marketplaces. On most islands, locals frown at too much skin exposure, although the more touristed a place, the less this holds true. Men can go almost anywhere in walking shorts. Cut-off jeans (or any counterculture vestige) are best avoided.

You'll need appropriate sports clothes for activities like tennis, golf, hiking, and riding. Most visitors will want plenty of beach clothes; be sure to include hats, sunglasses, and cover-ups. Bring walking shoes, a light wrap for evenings, and something to wear out to dinner if dining out is in your plans. Evening clothes vary considerably from island to island; there are vacation styles and places where evening clothes are totally irrelevant. For casinos and razzle-dazzle, men will need jackets and ties, women, floor-length tropical dresses or cocktail dresses. In general, people dress with more pizzazz in the Dominican Republic, on Puerto Rico, and in casino towns. In the main town on a small island, visitors may dine comfortably (and often well) in slacks or sundresses.

If you're going to an out-of-the-way place via another island (Antigua and St. Martin are the usual transfer airports), be sure to carry on a few essentials, such as a change of clothes, swimwear, and cosmetics. It often takes a few days for luggage to catch up. If you must have all your luggage the moment you arrive, travel light; you're allowed one under-the-seat bag.

You are also allowed two pieces of checked luggage per person on most international flights. This may or may not include sports equipment, depending on the airline. If you plan to travel with golf clubs, surfboards, or scuba gear, check the policies of each airline you will be flying. There may be extra charges or procedures. If you're taking diving gear, even just masks and fins, be aware that it's hard to get in the islands and therefore worth plenty. Lock the gear in your suitcase, carry it on, or pack it in a cardboard box. The box (which is real island luggage) should be strong but ratty looking and clearly marked with your name and destination (town and island, not hotel or resort). Make sure the box is peppered with checked-baggage stickers. It goes without saying that all scuba tanks should be properly padded and depressurized. Tennis rackets are usually hand carried.

Relating your wardrobe to the activities you plan is the easiest way to pack what you'll need. Unless you are going to a major shopping area, it's a good idea to bring everything you want. These are generally poor islands, with supply problems and limited choices.

How much to pack depends on you—basically, how much you need to have with you to feel secure, how often you need to change clothes, and how you feel about doing hand laundry. You can have a great time in the wilds of Dominica in the skirt set and flipflops you arrive in, a versatile swatch of yardage from the general store, and a pair of borrowed shorts.

The point is, sometimes it doesn't matter how well you pack. Throw in something wild with pineapples, and carry your toothbrush.

Some suggestions:

BEACH GEAR: bathing suit, water clothes (a long-sleeved shirt and tights or pants—a must for children, the very pale, and the intrepid snorkeler), a cover-up, sunglasses, sunscreen, a hat (or visor for windy days). You may want some kind of beach bag and a beach towel; few resorts provide them. Snorkeling and other sports gear.

DAY–PLAY CLOTHES: shorts, sarongs, rompers, sundresses, slacks, sports clothes.

EVENING WEAR: for women, anything from white slacks to cocktail dresses and long tropical creations; for men, sports shirts to the classic tropic *guayaberra* to jackets and ties. Even shorts are okay in informal situations. Both men and women will want some type of light wrap for breezy evenings—cotton shawls, sweaters, summer jackets; you may need more than one in the mountains.

UNDERWEAR AND SLEEPWEAR: cotton is best; most women will need bras outside of resort areas and in Latin countries.

SHOES: some type of beach shoe and walking shoe—sandals, espadrilles, and boating shoes are all popular. You might also want tennis or golf shoes and something for evenings out as well (boating shoes or sandals can do double duty). Most people agree that socks and stockings are superfluous unless you need a pair of socks for sports.

COSMETICS: remember all your regulars, from dental floss to shampoo to aftershave and tampons. If you use it, bring it. If you're heading for a boat or camping in an area where fresh water is at a premium, a bottle of Joy dishwashing detergent is a good idea. It lathers well in saltwater and can be used for dishes, laundry, and shampoo. Just wash your hair as usual, rinse well (seawater is fine), and use a creme rinse. You won't be able to tell the difference—no saltwater buildup! It goes without saying, don't do this in a delicate marine environment. Corals are particularly sensitive to pollution. Find a sandy spot with good tidal flow or take a bucket of water ashore.

MINIPHARMACY: sunscreen, lots of it, and zinc oxide or Noskote for lips, et cetera; Solarcaine, Bactine, or such; aspirin, Tylenol, et cetera; insect repellent; Band-Aids; antibiotic salve; hydrogen peroxide, in a small plastic bottle (great for cleaning infected mosquito bites); vinegar, for jellyfish stings and such; Benadryl; hydrocortisone salve (for insect bites, itching); papaya enzyme for nonvenemous insect stings (Adolph's meat tenderizer, tea bags, or capsules—open to use, apply externally); antacid; antidiarrheal product (tablets pack easily); fever scan strip or thermometer (for children); chlorine bleach, iodine solution, or Halazone tablets to purify your own drinking water; seasickness remedies (Dramamine, ginger tablets, skin patches); any regular medications or vitamins (in their original bottles to avoid customs problems).

EXTRAS: flashlight (the power fails in the best of places; the small disposable lights tuck in anywhere and are good make-do book lights); camera, film, et cetera (bring what you need; film is expensive where available); books (novels, magazines, guidebooks, maps, language dictionaries, nature field guides, even notebooks are not readily available); radio (small AM, a must for keeping in touch in rural areas; we're talking hurricanes, volcanoes, insurrection, and your general safety); binoculars; miscellaneous (needle, thread, extra buttons, safety pins, pocketknife, et cetera).

PART FOUR

Exploring

"Put your ear to mango root, yo can hear crab laugh."

Caribbean proverb

Exploring on Foot

Exploring the Caribbean is meant to be done at the speed of discovery—the pace of a boat under sail or a person on foot. Both modes provide a sense of history and time. The speed of discovery is the natural speed for taking in this new environment—the bird and thorn byways where the colors hurt your eyes and the air may be scented with sage and grazing animals or with dark-soiled forest moisture and unseen blossoms. There is time to see, hear, and smell, and to experience the awe of first discovery that is shared by every new person to set foot on these islands.

Obviously, it's best to approach different habitats in different ways; you don't need city shoes for beachcombing. Other things are less obvious; it's not a good idea to walk after sunset on any of the islands. Most country people live dawn-to-dusk lives, and meandering around after dark is highly suspect. In some places, it's downright risky.

Here's a summary of a few good choices for exploring on foot. The National Parks chapter has more specific suggestions.

BEACHCOMBING (on long stretches of coral sand; for other types of shore environments, see Part 1, Islands and Sea):

Anguilla
Antigua and Barbuda
Bahamas
British Virgin Islands
Grenadines

Puerto Rico, especially Culebra and
Vieques
Tobago
Turks and Caicos

WALKING OR HIKING ON MARKED TRAILS (guides may be required):

Barbados
British Virgin Islands,
especially Tortola
and Virgin Gorda

Dominica
Guadeloupe
Jamaica
Martinique

Montserrat	St. Lucia
Puerto Rico	Trinidad and Tobago
Saba	U.S. Virgin Islands, especially
St. Kitts and Nevis	St. John

MOUNTAIN CLIMBING (guides required; see Islands and Sea for specific natural features such as volcanoes and waterfalls):

Dominica	Jamaica
Dominican Republic	Martinique
Grenada	Montserrat
Guadeloupe	Trinidad and Tobago

City Walking

Most visitors are experienced city walkers. It's the kind of vacation mode that goes unnoticed while shopping or sight-seeing, until you can't take another step.

Many islands have mapped walking tours that highlight important streets and structures. Check with the tourist board, landmark society, or historical society for details.

Remember that you will be out of your element if you wander too far off the beaten path. If you choose to do so, however, hire a guide or move in a group. Be realistic. All cities have unsavory areas, and many Caribbean islands have housing projects where an outsider is unsafe day or night. In fact, it is best to limit night walking in all large cities. Be as careful in Nassau or San Juan as you would in Manhattan or Chicago. Sunshine and palm trees do not prevent crime.

Apparel and Accoutrement

Be sensitive to local standards and dress as a guest. Some tourist boards have had to set mandatory dress codes because oblivious visitors have so offended locals by wearing bathing suits and scanty outfits in shops and churches. Conservative shorts for women are acceptable in tourist areas (if you are not visiting churches), but knee-length pants and sundresses are more acceptable; men can get by in walking shorts almost everywhere.

Footwear needs to be comfortable and have enough of a sole to cushion you on cobblestones and uneven pavement. Flipflops are okay everywhere; some people prefer the extra support provided by tennis or walking shoes. Thin-soled leather sandals are best avoided for long days on your feet.

Bring a hat, a cover-up with sleeves, and sunscreen if you'll be doing lots of walking. A small shoulder strap–style shopping bag is best if you must carry a purse. (Consider pockets or toss a wallet into a canvas shoulder bag for a hands-free alternative; you will also look less appealing to purse snatchers.) Don't forget a camera.

Do take time to drink plenty of liquids and to enjoy all the new sights, sounds, smells, and tastes.

Hiking and Mountain Climbing

Traveling on foot gives you contact with the landscape. There is time for intimacy, for the *feel* of a place rather than just a postcard view of it. An island can become real when your own sweat merges with the dry, dusty smells of the thorn forest that scratches your ankles and an iguana rustles toward the shadows as you approach. No vehicle tour can give you the feel of a thick rain forest in a cloud, where the ferns may be as tall as you are and the chatter of bird song alternates with the hush that falls like a light mist. The sounds, the silence, the smell of the wet earth as you disturb it—these are memories that keep. Once you've walked into a volcanic crevasse, you'll never look at another postcard of a smoldering soufrière without remembering the smell, crunch, and slide of the sulfurous rocks.

Take a short jaunt along a country road, through the secret paths of mangroves, along a beach, through a bamboo forest or a high pasture. Whether you spend a week on an extended hike or a half hour wandering along a road picking up bits of old pottery, walking will enrich your trip.

Choosing a Walk or Hike

Be aware of your own abilities and physical condition, and choose your walks or hikes accordingly. A number of the parks in the region have formal trails that are rated from "easy walk" to "rough hike." Also consider the time that will be involved; an easy walk becomes harder after an hour. Look at a detailed map and try to estimate the distance. If there is no published information on a hike or walk, try to ask other visitors, rather than the locals or a guide, about the distance and difficulty. Walking is still a form of transportation on many islands where local people may walk miles over rough terrain as a matter of course. As for guides, remember that the Caribbean is a poor area. In a place where a guide can make the average weekly wage in a day, to tell a visitor that a destination is "not far" is only economically sensible.

"Rough hiking" can often mean hands-on hiking that involves sliding down mud banks and even swinging down or at least clinging to lianas. Often your guide may have to open the path with a machete, or cutlass, as they are sometimes called. Not many trails have arrows and built-in steps for steep places, as many visitors from the U.S. mainland have come to expect.

Even short trails may be too rigorous to be pleasant for some. Visitors, especially seniors, have been encouraged by cabdrivers eager for a fare to take unsuitable trails. Check a map; differences in altitude indicate unevenness and incline. A hike that covers a thousand feet of altitude in three miles will require much more energy than the same-distance hike that wanders up a gentle slope. Also, ask specifically if a trail is rocky, muddy, et cetera. And don't forget your personal motivation. Is this just another activity in the tourist brochure, or is the hike to a landform you are genuinely interested in?

Taking a vehicle tour of an island, looking at a good survey map, reading any available publications, and talking to other walkers will help you choose a suitable and, perhaps, memorable hike.

Guides

In most places, guides are recommended for long excursions. In some places—the streets of Port-au-Prince and the wilds of Dominica, for instance—guides are essential. A registered guide is required for St. Lucia's rain forest walk (which is described as "a real hike, not a stroll"), and no one would consider taking on the Pitons of St. Lucia without a guide. Martinique as well asks that guides be engaged for the hike up Mount Pelée, which is often shrouded in mists and clouds that may be disorienting. Follow local regulations and recommendations; they are for your safety.

Although some hikers resent sharing their experience with a stranger, most Caribbean hikers agree that the added insights into culture and flora contributed by a guide more than make up for the intrusion. In areas where trails are unmarked, or are marked by faded machete notches in trees, it is more than a comfort to be accompanied by someone at home in the terrain. A guide can cut you a walking stick, point out edible berries, carry your camera, find potable water, improve your patois, and give you time with a Caribbean person. He will also, no doubt, point out where victims of poisonous gases died or where the last white man was found after straying from the trail without a guide. These islands have only informal rescue procedures, which in most places mean volunteers with no equipment. In the primeval landscape of the Valley of Desolation on Dominica, the idea of helicopter rescue is as far from reality as science fiction. You're on your own here—the importance of a guide cannot be overemphasized.

Qualified, mature guides are often registered by the tourist board, which may also govern prices. If your hotel or guest house cannot recommend a guide, check with the tourist board. Ask for several names and for the price, which may be set by the hike or by the day (usually about U.S. $20 a day and up). It is best to meet your prospective guide before the day you plan to hike. Get acquainted; there is no need to spend a day with someone you are uneasy about. The young and restless and the painfully hip types (who may also be charming) are best avoided; they are frequently more interested in collecting their money and being seen with "rich" Americans than in the environment. Ask your prospective guide a few questions (how long the hike usually takes, for one) and pass some time in talk. If you like him, set a meeting time and place. Fees are paid *after* the hike.

In the unlikely event that your guide behaves in an unacceptable way (throws rocks at the iguanas, tries to charge you double, gets lost, or walks you back to the wrong place), don't pay. Go—all of you—right to the tourist board or police station and slowly explain the problem. Or if you don't want a commotion, get his full name and village, pay him, and complain the next day or write the tourist board, the national trust of the island, and the local newspaper, giving all details. You probably won't hear from them, but chances are the guide will—and you'll feel better.

Apparel and Accoutrement

Consider mud, moisture, thorns, and insects when choosing clothing for a walk or hike, especially if you're trying to decide between long and short pants. If you're walking in a rain forest, shorts are probably the better choice; they'll dry quickly and they won't slap around your calves when wet. For a dry or thorn forest, long pants will help protect your legs from stickers (which you will later have to pick out of your pants). Generally, loose-fitting, fast-drying cottons or cotton blends are best. A shirt with sleeves is better than one without; some people like sleeves that can be rolled down for warmth and sun protection. There is no need, with the moderate conditions in the Caribbean, to make a big deal out of hiking or walking dress. Anything comfortable will do.

Footwear should also be selected for comfort. Rubber soles are good; tennis shoes will take you anywhere.

Bring something to eat and drink no matter how long your guide says a hike will take. Dried fruit, candy, or cookies might come in very handy.

As always, the fewer extras that are carried, the better. You may want a camera, binoculars, and a substantial lunch. On hikes to waterfalls and natural pools, wear or tote your bathing suit. A hat, visor, sunglasses, and a bandana are especially good in the hot, dry forest areas. Some people like a waterproof hat for rain forests.

Gear for Overnights

Many Caribbean campgrounds provide semipermanent tents or canvas shelters. Those that don't, usually rent tents of some sort. In fair weather, many overnighters sleep in the open. Camping at sea level is not much different from staying in a rustic guest house. In the mountains, where temperatures can be in the fifties, and lower at night, you will need clothing and bedding to help you stay warm. Wherever you camp, consider taking maps, a compass, a rain cape or poncho (which can function as an umbrella or a ground cover), a sweater or windbreaker, spare socks, a sleeping bag or blanket, a flashlight with spare batteries, a small first-aid kit, a water bottle, food, cooking utensils (knife, fork, spoon, bowl, mug, and saucepan), and matches. A portable radio is a must for tuning in to weather forecasts on extended jaunts. Custom pack to fit your own needs and comfort level.

Hiking Safety and Courtesy

Walk only from dawn until dusk. (The hike to Blue Mountain Peak on Jamaica, which is traditionally done at night by moonlight and flashlight, is the only exception.)

Always check the weather report before you set out. Carry a portable radio if you will be out long.

Stay on the trail. This keeps you safer and limits impact on the environment.

Carry a map. When in doubt, hire a guide.

Hike in groups of people with equal ability, preferably, three or more.

Tell someone where you are going and when you expect to return. (In the Blue Mountains of Jamaica, village police stations are geared to this practice; on other islands, your hotel or guest-house concierge is fine.)

If you plan an extended stay or an overnight, carry everything you will need, including a blanket or sleeping bag and a sweater.

Carry some high-energy food and water, regardless of the length of the hike.

Respect private property; don't hop fences or take fruit from planted areas without permission.

Use extra care with matches and cigarettes to avoid accidental fires.

Respect the environment. You are a guest; leave as little trace of yourself as possible. Carry away all debris, including cigarette butts, and use only a biodegradable soap. As the motto goes: Take only photographs. Leave only footprints.

Easy Walks

There are some good ones on every island. Try beaches, historical areas, national parks, and botanical gardens. If you have transportation, it's fun to drive out in the country, then park and wander on foot. Avoid the hottest midday hours. There are lots of old footpaths and donkey trails that can be explored this way. Do respect private property. The national park on Guadeloupe has a number of easy-to-moderate excursions; walks to Carbet and Vauchelet Falls are all rated as easy. Write for the park's excellent trail guide.

Moderate Hikes

There are lots of marked or mapped trails (no guides) over different types of terrains, usually with some incline. The most pleasant are through lush moist forests or rain forests. Try Sage Mountain on Tortola, British Virgin Islands; El Yunque on Puerto Rico; Emerald Pool Trail on Dominica; and Barre de L'Isle and Viewpoint (a quarter-mile loop) on St. Lucia.

Check local environmental groups and national trusts for hike suggestions. The St. Croix Environmental Association offers regularly scheduled field trips to different habitats for a small fee.

The Outdoor Club of Barbados has daylong walking excursions on Wednesdays and Sundays year-round. Saba, Statia, and Trinidad and Tobago all offer interesting nature and/or historical walks. See individual island section for details.

Difficult and Extended Hikes

Dominica

MORNE TROIS PITONS: at 4,400 feet, the highest peak in Morne Trois Pitons National Park. There are a number of trails throughout the park, many of which involve crossing 2,000- to 3,000-foot ridges. Boeri Lake is on Morne Trois Pitons; Freshwater Lake is near Morne Macaque. Hikers must scale Morne Nicholls to reach the Boiling Lake.

Dominica is very mountainous, rugged, and moist; many forests here receive more than 150 inches of rain per year. Rain and the local economy present negatives for campers, but there are a number of well-located guest houses that can provide an inexpensive (and dry!) base. A number of the more extensive trails start in the village of Laudat, which can be reached by car. Guides are essential for longer treks and may cost from U.S. $20 to $40 a day. Superb rain forest, waterfalls, breathtaking scenery. The Dominica National Parks Service prints a series of information sheets on major hikes that includes a simple map (not to venture forth on!) and some educational materials on forest species.

THE BOILING LAKE: rugged, all-day hike, a twelve-mile round trip from Laudat. The route passes through the sulfurous Valley of Desolation (be careful to stay on the trail; the soil crust is very thin in other places), as well as through rain forests, montane forests, and elfin woodland as it winds up and down several ridges, often via mud banks and lianas. The lake itself is the world's second largest boiling lake; its gray bubbling surface is about seventy yards across. This hike adds a new dimension to Dante's *Inferno*. Take your camera and your lunch. (See Dominica in the individual island listings for more information.)

Dominican Republic

CORDILLERA CENTRAL: topped by Pico Duarte, which at some 10,000 feet is the highest peak in the Caribbean. Treks into these mountains can be planned from nearby villages. You will need a guide (usually about D.R. $10 to $20 a day), and possibly mules, and a jeep to get to a takeoff point. There are no facilities in these lush mountains. Take *everything* you'll need, and prepare for damp and possibly altitudinal cold. This is rugged, poorly mapped terrain, not for the inexperienced. Speaking Spanish is helpful.

Guadeloupe

SOUFRIÈRE: 4,813-foot peak of a dormant but still-smouldering volcano with fumaroles and hot springs. The Soufrière is part of the Parc Naturel, with a number of well-marked trails of varying difficulty and from different takeoff points. The park's publication "Walks and Hikes" describes the Red Trail, which leads directly to the summit in less than an hour, as an "excursion" or easy "hike" (as opposed to "walk"). All trails in the park are mapped and described; there are also notes on the flora and fauna of each type of forest. It is possible to see a variety of habitats—from rain forest to Soufrière—on an easy walk. Opportunities for what is categorized as a "rough hike" (ten hours on the Victor Hughes trail up the 4,000-foot Morne Boutemps) are also listed. This pamphlet is a must and may be obtained at the park or in advance from the tourist board.

Jamaica

BLUE MOUNTAIN PEAK: 7,402-foot pinnacle of Jamaica's famous Blue Mountains that dominate eastern Jamaica as well as the coffee industry. The climb to the peak, usually described as "strenuous," is seven miles up from Whitefield Hall, a Forest Department post that can be reached by jeep. The hike is often done at night by the light of the full moon or flashlight to avoid rain showers and to enjoy the sunrise from the summit. December through March is considered the best time of year to make the climb.

There are several regular outfitters that arrange tours of the Blue Mountains as well as climbs to the peak, or you may make your own arrangements through Jamaica's Forest Department in Kingston. If you decide to venture out on your own (groups of three or more are recommended), you will need *A Hikers' Guide to the Blue Mountains* by Peace Corps volunteer Bill Wilcox. This twenty-eight-page pamphlet has all you will need to know about hiking and camping in the Blue Mountains. It contains times, approximate distances, and practical directions like "At the frame house with coffee plants, banana trees, turn sharp left." Wilcox has divided hikes into those starting from Jack's Hill, Gordon Town, and various upland villages, as well as from Blue Mountain Peak itself.

Jamaica's Forestry Department maintains a number of hostel-type guest houses and campsites in the Blue Mountains. Advance reservations are required. Apply in person at the forestry office, 173 Constant Spring

Road, Kingshill; telephone: (809) 924-2667. There are also several other places to stay; see Jamaica in the individual island listings for more details.

HIKING GUIDES AND INFORMATION

MAYA Hiking Centre
P.O. Box 216
Kingston 7, Jamaica
telephone: (809) 927-8282. (They have accommodations at the 2,000-foot level on Jack's Hill.)

Pine Grove Chalet
31½ Oliver Place
Kingston, Jamaica
telephone: (809) 922-7654. (They run a small guest house on a coffee plantation and will arrange for Land Rover drop-offs and mules.)

Jamaica Alternative Tourism
Camping & Hiking Association
c/o Arthur's Golden Sunset
Negril Beach, Jamaica
telephone: (809) 957-4241.

Note: Don't be too optimistic about receiving information by mail from Jamaica. You might want to give yourself extra time in Kingston to arrange for your trip, or work through one of Jamaica's mainland-based tourist boards.

Martinique

MOUNT PELÉE: 4,428-foot now-dormant volcano; its destructive 1902 eruption is now history. It is one of the forested peaks of the central Carbet mountains in the north. Contact Parc Regional de la Martinique to hire a guide or receive more information.

Montserrat

CHANCE'S PEAK: at about 3,000 feet, Montserrat's highest point in the Soufrière Hills.

Chance's Peak is traditionally scaled by a group on August Monday (the first Monday of the month) each year. Other times, a youngster will be glad to show you the way to the top. It's a good half-day climb, and most people start around dawn. The village of Trials is one takeoff point.

An excellent map of Montserrat may be purchased at many shops in Plymouth or from the chief surveyor's office on Parliament Street. This detailed map charts landforms, bays, ruins, donkey trails, other trails, and even houses; it's a must! Montserrat's long-dormant Soufrière Hills volcano is now active, erupting explosively in 1996. Check for current status.

St. Lucia

THE PITONS: nearly 3,000-foot craggy twin volcanic peaks on the southwestern shore are particularly popular with rock climbers.

RAIN FOREST WALK: about a three-hour loop through the Central Forest Reserve, which protects 1,600 acres. This is considered a real hike, not a stroll. Guides are essential and are provided with all tours that are arranged in conjunction with the forestry service. The hike usually includes bus transportation to and from the forest and some type of lunch. This lush rain forest with its orchids and lianas is the only habitat of the highly endangered St. Lucia parrot; only about a hundred birds are left.

For more information, contact the Forestry Office or the St. Lucia National Trust.

Camping

Camping is generally not encouraged in the Caribbean; it is against the law in the Bahamas and on Bonaire. On many other islands, camping on the beach is illegal. This isn't personal; it's purely economics. These are poor places, overall, and anything that subtracts from the incoming tourist dollar tends to have a negative reception. Understandably, the idea of visitors rich enough to travel *choosing* to rough it is seen as suspect by people happy to have any kind of roof overhead. So in order to have a successful and safe camping experience, it's best to stick to proven ground or make careful advance plans through local people and the tourist board.

With the exception of Puerto Rico and the U.S. Virgin Islands, where camping is fairly commonplace, it's best to carry your gear as inconspicuously as possible. You might want to tuck your packs into a suitcase or a conventional-looking piece of soft luggage. Customs officials are not shy about refusing entry, especially on islands with camping restrictions or where it is unsanctioned (that is, "officially not recommended"). The customs officials of many islands tend to react suspiciously to anyone who reflects the counterculture clichés in appearance or demeanor.

The entry forms for most countries require visitors to provide the name and address of their destination; only formal campgrounds are acceptable in this case. It's best to spend your first night or two in a guest house to become familiar with the area. In many cases, a charter boat can provide the ideal "camp" base. Camping out in the Caribbean is often untenable. Bugs, heat, dampness, the common night rains, and lack of security make coastal boating or hiking by day from a protected lodging better options. The following list provides some guidelines.

Bahamas

Absolutely *no* camping allowed.

Bonaire

Absolutely *no* camping allowed.

British Virgin Islands

Brewers Bay Campground, Box 185, Roadtown, Tortola, BVI; (809) 494-3463. Tula's N & N Campground, Little Harbor, Jost Van Dyke; write to Box 8364, St. Thomas, U.S. Virgin Islands 00801; (809) 774-0774.

Dominican Republic

Camping is generally informal and without facilities. Bring *everything* you need. If you'd like to have a few comforts, try a simple guest house in a rural town as a base. For instance, El Portillo, La Terrenas, Samaná, has eight bungalows right on the shore.

Extended treks into the Cordillera Central require guides, mules, and jeeps to get to a takeoff point. One approach is to go to the nearest village in advance, arrange the entire trip, including the route, and then return by jeep on the appointed date with all the food, camping gear, and personal items necessary for the excursion. The terrain is often rough and everything is very primitive. Pack for altitudinal cold in mountain areas and remember your Spanish phrase book.

Guadeloupe

PARC NATUREL ON BASSE-TERRE: prearranged campsites within 74,100-acre forest, with lakes, rivers, hiking trails, and semiactive volcano.

LES SABLES D'OR: on Grand Anse Beach near Deshaies. Offers all facilities and tent rental; telephone: (011) 596-81.39.10. Campers (camping cars) fully equipped to sleep four or five people rented by DLC (Découvertes et Loisirs Créoles) in Abymes; telephone: (011) 596-20.55.65.

Jamaica

HOLLYWELL FOREST CABINS: at 4,000 feet. Two studio cabins, one two-bedroom cabin; each has a bathroom, kitchen with stove, and fireplace. Can be reached by road. Part of the Hollywell National Recreation Park: picnic areas, trails, parking.

CLYDESDALE: at 3,700 feet. Bunk beds in thirty-person, two-section dormitory; flush toilets, showers, and fire pit for cooking. Can be reached by car except in rainy weather.

PORTLAND GAP: forest hut at 5,200 feet. Hikers can sleep on the floor of hut; tent space available. Outhouse, running water.

BLUE MOUNTAIN PEAK: rough hut at 7,400 feet. Sleeping bag space for thirty people; room for camping, as well. Firewood is generally provided, but water may be scarce. Prepare for altitudinal cold.

The above are all Forestry Department camps in the Blue Mountains (none provides blankets, linens, or cooking utensils): Advance registration and, for some, paid permits are required; permits must be picked up in person. For more information, contact Department of Forestry, 173 Constant Spring Road, Kingston, Jamaica; telephone: (809) 924-2667.

MAYA HIKING CENTRE, JACK'S HILL: at 2,000 feet in the Blue Mountains. Tents for rent, guides for hire, indoor cooking facilities, maps for sale. Can be reached by car or bus from Kingston. The center will also help visitors rent rooms in nearby Jamaican homes or plan their own Blue Mountain trip (for a fee). For more information, contact MAYA Hiking Centre, P.O. Box 216, Kingston 7, Jamaica; telephone: (809) 927-8282.

STRAWBERRY FIELDS: thirty-six miles east of Ochos Rios. No phone in Jamaica; call New York (212) 265-6088 or (800) 621-0048. Platform tents and cottages; weekly rates include bed linens. Beach hiking, music nightly, and informal restaurant on the grounds.

Martinique

Visitors can camp almost anywhere—mountains, forests, and many beaches. Do check with the local mayor's office and/or the property owner before setting up camp. Camps with cold showers and toilet facilities are on the southeast coast at Macabou; on the south coast at St. Luce, Le Marin, and St. Anne; and at Anse à l'Ane near Trois Ilets. Tents and camping cars can be rented.

Montserrat

While camping is not illegal, it is also "not advised." Customs officials are very discriminating here.

Puerto Rico

Camping carries no stigma on Puerto Rico, where there are a number of private and public campgrounds, both on the beach and in the mountains. A complete list may be obtained from the Puerto Rico Department of Tourism. In this book, check the national parks list and the section on Puerto Rico for more details.

CARIBBEAN NATIONAL FOREST: on El Yunque. The required camping permits are free at the visitors' center. For more information, write the Caribbean National Trust, Box B, Palmer, Puerto Rico 00721; telephone: (809) 887-2875.

Puerto Rico's two offshore islands, Vieques and Culebra, also have places to camp. On Culebra, Flamenco Beach is popular (overly so on three-day weekends). It's a public beach outside of the little town. You'll need transportation or stamina; there are no facilities, not even fresh water.

On Vieques, obtain prior permission to camp from the Recreation and Sports Department, which manages Sun Bay Beach.

St. Lucia

The official position on camping here is do it at your own risk, with prior permission of the landowner; "not advised" according to the tourist board.

Turks and Caicos

Camping is allowed, but visitors must obtain prior permission from the landowner. There are no prearranged sites or facilities. Probably it's best to start out in a small beachside guest house and go from there. Bugs are a problem in some places.

U.S. Virgin Islands
St. John

CINNAMON BAY CAMPGROUNDS: (30 Rockefeller Plaza, Room 5400, New York, NY 10112; telephone: 800-223-7637, in New York City 212-586-4459). Bare sites, tents, and one-room beach units available. Cottages and tents all have picnic tables, a charcoal grill, a two-burner propane stove, an ice chest, a water container, and eating utensils. Restaurant, commissary, water sports center; all accommodations within a five-minute walk of the beach. In the winter season, daily rates for bare sites are about $10, for tents $40, for cottages $50.

MAHO BAY CAMPGROUNDS: (17-A East 73rd Street, New York, NY 10021; telephone: 800-392-9004). Fully furnished tent-cottages concealed in hillside vegetation. Winding walkways lead down to private beach. Environmentally oriented, with evening lectures, music, and folk dancing. Commissary and restaurant on grounds. About $50 a day for a double during the winter season, less in the summer.

St. Thomas

LARRY'S HIDEAWAY & CAMPSITES: (10-1 Hull Bay, St. Thomas, U.S. Virgin Islands 00801; telephone: 809-774-8955). Thirty units for camping out on Hull Bay; water sports, commissary, bar and grill.

National Parks, Forests, and Protected Areas

The idea of a preserved natural area is somewhat new to the Caribbean, and many exquisite areas are as yet undesignated. Often, the more undeveloped islands where natural habitats are still relatively unscathed have had other priorities. So you're likely to find more parks listed for the more developed islands where the remaining forests are increasingly precious. Some of the older parks, such as the U.S. National Park on St. John, U.S. Virgin Islands, and the extensive Parc Naturel on Guadeloupe, have well-organized trail systems, guides, and information centers. Others, such as Morne Trois Pitons on Dominica, are still in the organizational phase; a large variety of natural wonders are protected but little explored. Whatever the habitat and state of development, these areas all have their own remarkable assets. Consider this list a sampler that will grow in the future. (See Underwater Parks for protected marine areas.)

Anguilla
FOUNTAIN NATIONAL PARK: nearly five acres of important archaeological sites.

Antigua
INDIAN TOWN NATIONAL PARK: in the northeastern part of the island; blowholes and rock sculpture on Atlantic coast.

NELSON'S DOCKYARD NATIONAL PARK: at English Harbour; includes historic restorations as well as surrounding natural areas, both land and sea.

Aruba
ARIKOK NATIONAL PARK: well-preserved Indian drawings; southwest of Oranjestad, near San Fuego.

Bonaire

WASHINGTON/SLAGBAAI NATIONAL PARK: 135 bird species, including flamingos; salinas; and salt lakes bordered by coral beaches and
an underwater park. Trails and dirt roads; no camping, no concessions.

British Virgin Islands

SAGE MOUNTAIN: 1,716-foot peak and ninety-two surrounding acres
on Tortola; remnants of rain forest with marked trails and spectacular
view.

CRAWL NATIONAL PARK: part of the Baths Protected Area on Virgin
Gorda; dramatic natural boulder formations and enclosures; the most
popular tourist site in the BVI; trails; area includes ruins of historic copper mine.

GORDA PEAK NATIONAL PARK: contains Gorda Peak, the highest
 point on Virgin Gorda; marked trail to summit winds through wild orchids (major flowering season is December).
    The British Virgin Islands has been developing a comprehensive park
system since 1978; about ten national parks and protected areas currently
exist. Plans are under way to establish the limestone island of Anegada,
with its unique limestone geology and endemic species, such as the rock
iguana, as a park, as well.

Cuba

GUAMA AND ZAPATA NATIONAL PARK: swamp canals; tour by
launch; crocodile breeding farm and the spectacular beach at Girón Bay
(Bay of Pigs).

Curaçao

CHRISTOFFEL NATIONAL PARK: extensive natural area established in
1978 to help protect typical flora and fauna; white-tailed deer and three
types of orchids.

Dominica

CABRITTS NATIONAL PARK: established in 1986 to protect both historic and natural features in the northwestern part of the island.

MORNE TROIS PITONS NATIONAL PARK: lavish foliage, giant ferns, lianas, bromeliads. Three lakes: Boeri, Fresh Water, and the Boiling Lake. Variety of hiking and walking possibilities on unmarked trails; guides a must for venturing out in this untouched central forest.

Dominican Republic

CABRON POINT (CABÓ CABRON) NATIONAL PARK: mangroves and exotic vegetation; near Samaná.

HAITISES NATIONAL PARK: exotic vegetation.

LAGO ENRIQUILLO AND ISLA CABRITOS NATIONAL PARK: in the mountains near the Haitian border; a lake full of crocodiles at 144 feet below sea level.

PARQUE NACIONAL DEL ESTE: southeast of Romana; various coastal habitats and mangroves; includes offshore Isla Saona with white-crowned doves and clear waters.

Grenada

GRAND ÉTANG NATIONAL PARK: in the central part of the island; includes heart-of-the-island vegetation near cacao and spice plantations; visitor center near Grand Étang Lake.

LEVERA POND NATIONAL PARK: unique habitat; in planning.

Guadeloupe

PARC NATUREL ON BASSE-TERRE: 74,000 acres of forest with waterfalls, lakes, rivers, picnic areas, smoking fumaroles of the semiactive soufrière. A full-blown park with marked trails (hiking guide gives length and difficulty); interpretive centers, camping.

ENGRAVED ROCKS ARCHAEOLOGICAL PARK TROIS-RIVIÈRES: petroglyphs dating from 300 or 400 A.D. Marked trail (thirty- to forty-minute easy walk) with displays and plantings.

Jamaica

NEW SEVILLE NATIONAL PARK: contains the sites of three Arawak settlements, the ruins of the first Spanish settlement on Jamaica, and Anglo-Jamaican plantation ruins.

BLUE MOUNTAIN FORESTS: guided hikes through this lush coffee-growing country can be arranged, including up the 7,902-foot Blue Mountain Peak. Jamaica's Forest Department manages retreats there. (See the individual island listings for more details.) Informal camping okay.

Martinique

PARC NATUREL REGIONAL DE LA MARTINIQUE, MOUNT PELÉE: semiactive volcano, ruins, trails, and interpretive material.

PARC NATUREL AND NATURE PRESERVE, PRESQU'ÎLE DE LA CARAVELLE: on the rugged Atlantic side of the island; tropical mountains and highlands; trails, campsites, and the ruins of Dubuc castle.

Puerto Rico

CARIBBEAN NATIONAL FOREST: 28,000 acres of tropical forest surrounding El Yunque Mountain (3,493 feet). Some 250 species of tropical trees and rain-forest plants. Marked trails, visitor center, restaurant, waterfall, and swimming hole. Listen for the singing tree frog—coqui (pronounced koo-KEE)—that repeats its name. About an hour's drive from San Juan and worth even a half-day visit.

AGUIRRE FOREST: on the southern coast near Salinas, next to Jobos Bay.

JOBOS BAY NATIONAL ESTUARINE SANCTUARY: area of protected mangroves.

GUÁNICA FOREST: diverse vegetation and a large bird population. Bordered by lovely beaches; west of Ponce.

PIÑONES FOREST: protected lagoons and mangrove swamps; east of San Juan.

GUAJATACA FOREST: twenty-five miles of marked trails through karst (limestone) reserves. Sinkholes, cliffs, caves, and forest-tufted haystack hills are outstanding features. Trail maps are available at the ranger station; between Arecibo and Aguadilla.

RÍO ABAJO FOREST: timber-management program for stands of pine, mahogany, and teak. Sawmill operates Monday through Friday from 7:30 A.M. to 3:30 P.M.; south of Arecibo.

CAMBALACHE FOREST: dirt roads for leisurely walking; east of Arecibo.

MARICAO FOREST: dry vegetation with lots of birds, especially hawks. Stone observation tower provides dramatic views of the coast and Mona Island. Fish hatchery for stocking freshwater ponds; near Mayaqüez. Open daily from 7:30 A.M. until noon and 1 to 4 P.M.

MONTE GUILARTE FOREST: heart of the coffee country. Short, slick trail leads to the peak; west of Adjuntas.

TORO NEGRO FOREST: bamboo-fringed Guineo Reservoir, the island's highest lake, and Ferro Punta, the tallest peak, at 4,390 feet. Streams and dense forest with sierra palms and tree ferns. Inabón Falls with its rocky cascades attracts experienced mountain climbers; east of Adjuntas.

CARITE (OR GUAVATE) FOREST: dense cool forests and bluish hued lake; east of Cayey, about an hour from San Juan.

All of these Puerto Rican forests are open daily from 8 A.M. to 5 P.M., unless otherwise noted; a $.50 admission fee helps maintain them. Since many sites and trails are unmarked, be sure to stop first at the ranger station for maps and orientation.

Campers need prior permission, which may be obtained directly from individual ranger stations, or through the Department of Natural Resources by calling (809) 724-3724 or 724-3623.

St. Kitts and Nevis

BRIMSTONE HILL NATIONAL PARK: massive fortress, visitor center, restaurant, and panoramic view of six nearby islands.

St. Lucia

CENTRAL FOREST RESERVE: varied true rain forest, protected habitat of parrots; arrangements for popular walks can be made through all tour representatives and hotels; guides are provided. No unaccompanied visitors.

MARIA ISLANDS NATURE RESERVE: off St. Lucia's southeastern coast; world's only home of a rare ground lizard and a harmless snake. Many seabirds, such as terns and boobies, may be seen here; no visitors during nesting season. Make arrangements to visit (by boat) at the reserve's interpretive center on the nearby mainland.

PIGEON ISLAND NATIONAL PARK: mainly a historical site, accessible by car. Small admission charge.

Turks and Caicos

FORT GEORGE CAY NATIONAL PARK: lots of iguanas, turk's-head cactus, prickly pear, casuarina pines; the fort's five cannons now provide a dive attraction.

CAICOS CAYS NATIONAL UNDERWATER PARK REEF: at the Meridian Club, Pine Cay.

U.S. Virgin Islands

BUCK ISLAND REEF NATIONAL MONUMENT, OFF ST. CROIX: protected site since 1961, includes 850 acres of steep, grassy slopes and a 2,000-yard-long fringing reef with a self-directing underwater trail. Land trails as well, but most visitors come to see the reef. A day trip from Christiansted, St. Croix; the short boat ride involved is easily arranged.

SALT RIVER NATIONAL PARK, ST. CROIX: protects a complex natural habitat at the site of Columbus's landing in 1493. Walking tours available through the St. Croix Environment Association. Includes endangered species and archaeological sites.

VIRGIN ISLANDS NATIONAL PARK, ST. JOHN: a short ferry ride from Red Hook, St. Thomas, to Cruz Bay; walk or take a cab from there. This is a full-blown park, U.S. style, crisscrossed with trails through varied terrain. A full program of guided walks, snorkel tours, and historical and cultural programs. Spectacular coral beaches, petroglyphs, plantation ruins, and numerous dive sites (a third of the park is underwater). The self-guided underwater trail at Trunk Bay reef is almost as famous as the powdery beach, rated among the world's top ten beaches. Camping in campgrounds only. Reserve well in advance (see Camping for addresses).

SANDY POINT, ST. CROIX NATIONAL WILDLIFE REFUGE: beach and surrounding waters have been declared critical habitat for leatherback turtles; near Frederiksted (see Exploring for information on turtle patrols).

National Parks: Addresses

The following addresses may be helpful if you would like more information about these parks and protected areas. You may want to join the national trust or a nature interest group on your favorite island; membership is often as low as U.S. $20 a year. Be sure to use airmail postage (and mark envelope as such) on all correspondence.

ANGUILLA

Permanent Secretary
Ministry of Tourism,
Agriculture, and Fisheries
The Valley, Anguilla

Chairman, Fountain Committee
Anguilla Archaeological and
Historical Society
P.O. Box 252
The Valley, Anguilla

ANTIGUA AND BARBUDA

Parks Commissioner
Antigua and Barbuda
National Parks Authority
P.O. Box 1283
St. John's, Antigua

Fisheries Department
Ministry of Agriculture,
Lands, and Fisheries
St. John's, Antigua

BARBADOS

National Conservation Commission
Codrington House
St. Michael, Barbados

Barbados National Trust
48 Blue Waters
Bridgetown, Barbados

BRITISH VIRGIN ISLANDS

Director
National Parks Trust

c/o Ministry of Natural Resources
Government Headquarters
Road Town, Tortola
British Virgin Islands

DOMINICA
Parks Superintendent
Forestry Division
Botanical Gardens
Roseau, Dominica

GRENADA
National Parks and Protected
Areas Programme
Forestry Division
Ministry of Agriculture
St. George's, Grenada

GUADELOUPE
Mission pour la creation du
Parc National de la Guadeloupe
Office National de Forets
Jardin Botanique
97,009 Basse-Terre
Guadeloupe, French Antilles

MARTINIQUE
Parc Naturel Regional de la Martinique
Tivoli
97,200 Fort-de-France
Martinique, French Antilles

MONTSERRAT
Montserrat National Trust
P.O. Box 332
Plymouth, Montserrat

SABA AND CURAÇAO
STINAPA
P.O. Box 2090
Curaçao, Netherlands Antilles

Tom van't Hof
Box 18
The Bottom
Saba, Netherlands Antilles

ST. KITTS AND NEVIS

Physical Planning Officer
Planning Unit
P.O. Box 186
Basseterre, St. Kitts

Brimstone Hill Society
P.O. Box 229
Basseterre, St. Kitts

ST. LUCIA

Chief Forest Officer
Ministry of Agriculture
Castries, St. Lucia

Director
St. Lucia National Trust
P.O. Box 525
Castries, St. Lucia

ST. VINCENT AND THE GRENADINES

Ministry of Agriculture
Kingston
St. Vincent

U.S. VIRGIN ISLANDS

Superintendent
Virgin Islands National Park
P.O. Box 7789
St. Thomas, U.S.V.I. 00801

Superintendent
Christiansted N.H.S. and
Buck Island Reef National Monument
P.O. Box 160
Christiansted
St. Croix, U.S.V.I. 00820

Animal Watching

Luck and perseverance may be required to get a good look at some of the Caribbean's special animals. In most cases you need to get out in the countryside or at least away from crowds to see an agouti or an iguana. If you don't care to walk, an early-morning or twilight drive may yield a glimpse of a frigate bird, a deer, or a mongoose. Animals sometimes turn up in the most unlikely places; you might see an iguana in a parking lot on St. Thomas. Stay alert and keep watching. You may want to check with a local naturalist; national trusts and national parks are good places to start asking. Be sensitive in inquiring, though, or someone may turn up with a dead version of the animal you'd like to see. Read up on the animal: What does it eat? What habitat best suits its needs? Also, pay attention to the names on maps; Turtle Cove may be precisely that.

For a more guaranteed encounter, an organized trip may suit your needs. Some opportunities follow.

Birds

General as well as serious bird-watching tours are organized by Bird Bonanzas, Inc., P.O. Box 611563, North Miami, FL 33161; telephone: (305) 895-0607. They arrange spring and winter tours to major bird habitats on the Dominican Republic, Puerto Rico, Jamaica, Grand Cayman, and the Lesser Antilles. Surface costs, including accommodations, are reasonable.

Flamingos

Flamingos can be seen on Bonaire and Great Inagua, Bahamas. There is also a small flock on North Caicos, Turks and Caicos. Access is limited—absolutely no visitors during nesting season. See the individual island listings for more details.

Dolphins

Dolphins are a familiar sight to boaters. A guaranteed encounter is offered by the Underwater Explorers Society (UNEXSO) at its dive center in Port Lucaya. The program begins with a dolphin seminar where you can join the dolphins in the water in a special dockside pen. Anyone eager to spend more time with the friendly mammals may become an assistant trainer and spend the entire day with the dolphins. For more information, contact Underwater Explorers Society, P.O. Box F-2433, Freeport, Grand Bahama Island, Bahamas; telephone: (800) 992-DIVE. Prices vary.

Whales

Humpback whales migrate south each year to breed. During their peak migration period (February through March), they are often seen swimming through Drake's Passage (between St. John and Tortola) as well as in nearby waters. Although the whales are often visible from the shores of many Caribbean islands, local excursions often provide a closer look (check with charter boats). More extensive viewing is offered by an organized, seven-day whale-watching tour, land-based on Tortola. For more information, contact Oceanic Society Expeditions, Fort Mason Center, Building E, San Francisco, CA 94123; telephone: (415) 441-1106.

Sea Turtles

It is always thrilling to see an animal, particularly an ancient and endangered one, in its own environment. Most visitors to Provo, on the Turks and Caicos, have had this experience. If you haven't, you may want to sign up for a turtle patrol. Nesting season is usually from April through August. In an effort to aid the survival of the species, many places have turtle patrols that walk nesting beaches each night to record scientific data and inhibit poachers. While some turtle patrols are formed by informal citizens' groups, others result from highly organized scientific studies. Earthwatch pairs interested volunteers with scientists in a number of programs, such as the Leatherback Turtle Recovery Program on Sandy Point, St. Croix. Volunteers who would like to help must pay for the opportunity, usually at rates lower than an ordinary vacation. Spending nights on the beach with 1,000-pound relics of the dinosaur age seems a privilege worth paying for. For more information, contact Earthwatch, P.O. Box 403N, Watertown, MA 02272; telephone: (617) 926-8200. Earthwatch also teams volunteers with researchers working on a variety of projects throughout the Caribbean. On the island of St. Lucia, the Naturalists Society and the Fisheries Management Unit let tourists join a turtle watch for a fee (see the individual island listings for more information).

Beachcombing

A Puerto Rican proverb with philosophical implications is often used to describe the finite space of an island and also, perhaps, the freedom of thought to be found in walking. It goes something like: Walk as far as you can in any direction, turn around, and you'll meet yourself going the other way.

Revelatory walking—the hypnotic pace of mile upon mile of white sand in sun—encourages thought to wander one way and feet, another. Beachcombing provides the perfect landscape for transcending time and space, especially if you're wandering rather than purposefully exploring.

The Caribbean's many types of shore (see Part 1, Islands and Sea, for more details) offer ample opportunity for dual exploration—daydreams and sea drift. Every beachcomber knows that some beaches are more generous than others. One may be heaped with driftwood, corals, and dried sea fans while another offers only honed fragments of shell—perhaps the perfect curve of a triton's lip or the inside spiral of a conch—the small bit that may lead to a line of verse, another place.

Beachcombing is irresistible, for it is not only what lives on the beach but everything that may come to rest there that captures the imagination. Although flotsam may be full of surprises, what ends up on any particular beach results from much more than wish and chance. Wind, tide, current, the type of coast, and the type of bottom directly offshore all play a part. And each stray bit of driftage that comes to rest among the drying seaweeds along the high-tide line carries its own message. Mollusk shells or egg cases hint of animals that have lived their hidden lives in the sand close by; fish buoys, plastic bottles, and driftwood bring evidence of human activity—of fishing and shipping offshore. One might receive messages from the open ocean—the soft bodies of jellyfish or the purple shell of a janthina snail that has lived its whole pelagic life suspended from its own bubble float.

Early curiosity about the way things ended up on a particular beach led to the discovery of the "rivers in the sea," which we now chart as the great global currents. One such current is the often-romanticized Gulf Stream, which moderates the marine climate between the eastern coast of the United States and the Bahamas. As its warm waters flow northward, they often carry tropical sea life, like the Portuguese man-of-war, far beyond its normal range. These colorful jellyfish—blue air bladders floating above the water, potent stinging tentacles dangling below—occasionally ride the current as far as Great Britain.

Season as well as current can affect the quantities and species of organisms that wash onto the beach. Hurricanes have changed complete shorelines in the Caribbean, as well as tossing boats and corals well above sea level. Storms can wash out sand animals that generally remain unseen except for sand trails, burrow holes, protruding antennae, and breathing siphons. The safest existence for beach animals is to breathe, eat, and reproduce under cover of sand, below the reach of the surf. But even animals as specialized to this burrowing life as clams, worms, cockles, moon snails, and whelks have little resistance against the surge of storm waves.

Wherever beach animals are thrown ashore, they reflect their native habitats. The coloring and thickness of their shells may reflect the local food supply. Milk conchs from different islands range from gray to peach, a variation within the species that is attributed to geographic diversity. The shells that end up on a particular beach may have grown up in the sands or grass beds offshore.

Beachcombing in different areas will give shell collectors an opportunity to find a great variety of species. Beaches protected by bordering headlands or sandbars and reefs offshore are potentially best for shell collecting. Perfect and, often, naturally cleaned shells can be found on many beaches. This is the only way to collect shells. Taking live specimens can totally destroy the fragile, intricately balanced shore microcosms.

The wave-torn beaches of the open shore (generally facing east in the Caribbean), which are usually too rough to harbor perfect shells, offer other treasures—tokens of shipwrecks, glass buoys, corks, and bottles with messages. The beaches are often piled with seaweeds—dried Sargasso and tendrils of mermaid's hair. It is among this wrack that one may find the remains of pelagic animals.

Frequently, the parts and pieces that finally reach shore give little information about the animals they once were, and their presence offers clues only to the currents that brought them. A dramatic example is the spirula, or ram's-horn shell, which washes up on beaches throughout the world without a trace of the animal that built it. At first glance, the spirula, less than an inch in size, appears to be some type of snail. But its loose, translucent coil is really a series of pearly chambers. This fragile coil is the internal shell of a small squidlike animal that schools in deep tropical waters. Apparently when the animal dies, the gases of decomposition carry the buoyant shell to the surface, where it then floats with the currents like a bottle without a message.

Not everything that travels the ocean currents carries a squid-to-chambered-shell story, but many things carry marks of their voyages. The size of the barnacles and the amount of sea growth on an object are usually proportional to the time each has spent at sea. Driftwood may become silky smooth or be riddled by teredo shipworms. Not really worms but mollusks, they are able to tunnel through wood with their calcareous shells. Like the gooseneck and acorn barnacles, teredos spend a larval period drifting freely with the currents. At a certain point in their development, they must attach themselves to wood, or die. Barnacles, on the other hand, can make do with any miscellaneous flotsam, from bamboo to Styrofoam.

Whatever the length of the journey, the driftage that ends up on any beach is an intricate composition with a story to tell—if you aren't distracted by one of your own.

Apparel and Accoutrement

Beachwear, sunscreen, a hat, sunglasses, cover-up; flipflops for the beach, tennis shoes for the rocky shore. Be comfortable. Carry as little as possible. A plastic bag tucked under the leg of your bathing suit will provide for take-homes; it will also be handy if you swim in to the beach from a boat. Avoid the hottest midday sun; early mornings and late afternoons are the best. You may need insect repellent and want binoculars and a camera, or perhaps a pencil or pen and a scrap of paper instead.

Exploring by Water

Snorkeling

Clear waters and balmy temperatures make year-round snorkeling one of the delights of the Caribbean. Almost all beach hotels rent or loan snorkeling gear—mask, snorkel (the breathing tube), and fins—and give instruction. Anyone with moderate swimming skills can snorkel successfully. If you have never tried it, take a quick class; it won't be long before you'll be enjoying the fascinations of the underwater world. If your hotel does not offer instruction with gear rental, try a local dive shop. Islands with underwater trails or parks (see the list that follows) often feature on-the-spot snorkeling instruction. In areas where boat charters are required to reach an underwater park, as with Buck Island Reef National Monument off St. Croix, U.S.V.I., use of snorkeling gear and instruction are usually part of the deal. It's best to bring your own gear if you're an avid snorkeler or are heading off the beaten path.

Seeing a living coral reef for the first time is an experience to treasure. If you are unsure of your skills, wear a personal flotation device and spend some time in shallow water. Put your mask and snorkel on and bend over at the waist; walk along the bottom with your face under water until you feel comfortable. The next step is to put on your fins and try it prone in water where you can still stand up. Practice for a while before you head for deeper waters.

Scuba Diving

The Caribbean with reefs, wrecks, and drop-offs has become a major destination for scuba enthusiasts. Warm shallow waters, which range from the mid-seventies in winter to the low to mid-eighties in summer (the depths are 65°F or so), don't even demand full wet suits. If you've always wanted to try scuba diving, the Caribbean is a good place to take some instruction; in addition, a number of intensive certification courses are offered.

Many well-run dive operations are scattered throughout the islands. Dive tours, both land- and boat-based, are popular; on Bonaire, where the entire marine area is a park, dive centers abound. The U.S. Virgin Islands and Puerto Rico are also popular islands for diving; the added advantage here is the safety backup provided by U.S. licensing requirements, the availability of decompression facilities, and the Coast Guard in case of emergency.

Islands with certified dive masters and instructors include:

Bahamas

Freeport/Lucaya—Underwater Explorers Society; Nassau—Bahama Divers, Ltd., Underwater Tours; Andros—Small Hope Bay Lodge; boat charters provide a good option.

Bonaire

More than forty dive sites within swimming distance of the shore; Don Stewart's Habitat is a complete dive resort; Dive Bonaire is at the Flamingo Beach Hotel; Hotel Bonaire Beach and the Carib Inn also have scuba centers. Year-round dive packages are available.

British Virgin Islands

A number of places to rent equipment and book tours. Try Aquatic Centers, Road Town, Tortola, or Dive BVI on Virgin Gorda.

Cayman Islands

More than a hundred charted dive sites and qualified shops and dive masters to go with them. A number of hotels offer scuba packages that include, rooms, boat trips, T-shirts, welcome drinks, and airfare from Miami. Ask the tourist board for current brochures.

Guadeloupe

Pigeon Island is on Jacques Cousteau's list of the world's ten best diving spots. It has reefs, wrecks, walls, caves, slopes, and drop-offs.
    Dive packages are available from some hotels.

Jamaica

Offers variety, from sponges to shipwrecks. Major resorts in Montego Bay, Negril, and Ocho Rios all have dive centers; Sea and Dive Jamaica offers trips, rental, and instruction.

Saba

The Saba Marine Park, which encompasses the entire island, has sparked an active dive community. This small island now supports three pro-dive shops and all hotels offer dive packages. Dive sites are rich with corals, fish, and unusual geological formations.

Trinidad and Tobago

Tobago offers some of the Caribbean's best diving, off its coast near Speyside. Some dive sites for novice divers and many for the experienced. A number of dive operators offer services.

Turks and Caicos

Clear waters and spectacular corals as well as the renowne(
drop-off at Turks Island Passage. Many dive operations, ofte
to resorts.

U.S. Virgin Islands

Underwater parks and more than twenty well-equipped dive shops with
facilities comparable to those on the mainland. A good place to learn
or enjoy.

For the experienced diver willing to bring equipment and a diving buddy,
the options are unlimited. Many islands such as the Dominican Republic,
the Caymans, the British Virgins, and the Turks and Caicos have shipwrecks on reefs offshore. Others such as Port Royal, Jamaica (see History
for an archaeological dive opportunity), and Oranjestad, St. Eustatius
(Statia), have entire sunken cities to explore. Be sure to check with your
airline about extra charges and regulations concerning transport of scuba
tanks. Check with the tourist board of the islands you are interested in
visiting for the latest information on diving.

For information on becoming a certified scuba diver, and for a list of
certified instructors, contact the National Association of Underwater Instructors (NAUI) or Professional Association of Diving Instructors
(PADI) through your local dive shop.

Safety for Swimmers and Divers

Common sense will serve you as well in the Caribbean as it does on Nan-
tucket or Catalina. The classic rule around water remains: Don't go alone.
Diving with someone of equal ability makes it more fun.

Watch your sun exposure; you can burn through water. And the exposed back of a snorkeler seems to burn twice as fast as that of a sun-bather, perhaps because the sun doesn't feel as hot when you're in the water. Use waterproof sunscreen; a tight-fitting cotton T-shirt (preferably with long sleeves) is also a good idea. Some people like to wear light cotton pants with a drawstring waist. Pants give protection from the sun as well as coral cuts, which inexperienced snorkelers may get from flailing their newly finned legs too vigorously.

There are two categories of weather to be concerned with here—internal (if you don't feel well, don't go; if you get "the creeps," get out) and external. Both tend to be ignored by travelers squeezing a lot of fun into a little time.

Light rain is usually nothing to worry about. Wind, however, is. Winds build heavy seas and can make boat dive trips uncomfortable and even dangerous. They also ruin visibility for divers by churning up bottom sediments. It's probably best to wait a day or two until seas settle down. The runoff resulting from heavy rains can also ruin visibility in inshore areas.

Currents are not often a factor in much of the Caribbean because tidal flow is minimal. There are always a few localized areas where currents are of concern; check charts and those with local knowledge when in doubt. Many islands have rough windward coasts with wily currents; these areas are best avoided. If locals advise you not to swim somewhere, take them seriously.

In the Bahamas, however, swimmers and divers must be constantly aware of the strong tidal flow; currents may run up to four or five knots. In many places it is possible to swim and dive only at slack tide. Obtain local knowledge and proceed with caution; you may want to float downstream and return in a dinghy, use a drag line, or swim in a more protected area.

Night dives are best made under controlled conditions with proper equipment and local experts.

The Divers Alert Network (DAN) operates a twenty-four-hour emergency hotline that provides advice on treatment of diving-related injuries. They also keep information on the status and location of decompression chamber facilities. The decompression chamber at Roosevelt Roads Naval Station on Puerto Rico is probably the best bet for most of the Caribbean. Membership to DAN is $10 per year and includes a manual on first-aid and symptoms of major diving-related injuries. For information, call (919) 684-2948 (Monday through Friday 9 A.M. to 5 P.M. EST); emergencies only (919) 684-8111. Or write Divers Alert Network, Box 3823, Duke University Medical Center, Durham, NC 27710.

Best Avoided: Hazardous Marine Life

While swimmers and divers new to the colorful bustle of tropical reefs may worry about sharks or barracudas, most potential hazards are far less showy. If you have an unpleasant encounter, check the following list for suggested treatments. Better yet, read it now and avoid the listed organisms.

Note: In any of the following cases, if more serious symptoms occur, such as difficult breathing, profuse sweating, vomiting, or fainting, seek emergency medical care immediately.

Bristle Worms

These fat worms range from four to ten inches in length and may be orange-red or green. They are covered with a fancy topping of white bristles that form a type of armament; brittle, glasslike bristles detach easily when the animal is touched, operating a bit like a porcupine's quills. Touching the bristles can cause severe pain that can last up to several hours, depending on the extent of your contact with the worm. It is best to resist their enticing colors.

Corals

Any coral will cut or scrape you if you bang into it. Coral scrapes have a tendency to become infected; they should be scrubbed with soap and water and treated with antiseptic and antibiotic ointment. Remember that if you get hurt on coral, you have also injured the coral's own delicate protoplasm.

Fire or stinging corals may be leafy, square, or encrusting, but all tend to be a tannish yellow in color. Although they are distant relatives of the more elaborate stony corals, their polyps do not form visible cups. The encrusting type of stinging coral may take on the shape of anything it covers. They are most easily recognized by their surface smoothness. They inflict a painful burn when touched or brushed against. Apply vinegar or alcohol to help remove any stinging cells clinging to your skin. Follow with antibiotic salve.

Fire Sponge

These sponges are bright red in color, but their shape varies. Contact will cause pain, itching, and swelling; apply vinegar.

Jellyfish

Moon jellies, sea nettles, and the Portuguese man-of-war, among others, are not fish at all but relatives of the corals. Jellyfish of all types have stinging cells, or nematocysts, that discharge when touched, injecting venom into the skin of the victim. Stings from the potent Portuguese man-of-war can cause intense pain and may even cause shock or respiratory paralysis. Avoid all jellyfish, whether they are floating or on the beach; even dried jellyfish may contain active stinging cells.

Treatment of all jellyfish stings should be directed toward inactivating any nematocysts that may remain undischarged on the skin. Pour vinegar over the sting and let it remain a few minutes. Then, using a towel or other protection for your hands, carefully remove any remaining tentacle fragments and wash the area with soap and water. Alcohol and papain may be used instead of vinegar. If none of these treatments is available, sprinkle the sting with fine dry sand. It's best to avoid rubbing, as it may activate more stingers.

Sculpin (Scorpion Fish)

This quiet, bottom-dwelling fish has venom in its dorsal and pectoral spines. If touched or stepped on, the poisonous spines can inflict a painful wound that may involve the entire extremity.

Wash the injury with soap and water. Then immerse the entire extremity in water as hot as the injured person can stand without scalding the skin for thirty to ninety minutes. The heat will help inactivate the venom and decrease the pain. Then seek medical care.

Sea Urchins

These spiny black pincushionlike animals are common throughout the Caribbean in all types of marine environments. They won't bother you if you don't touch or step on them. If you do, the urchins' brittle spines break off easily and can become embedded under the skin. Pain and localized swelling vary. Remove as many spine fragments as possible, clean well, and apply antiseptic. Any remaining fragments will probably be absorbed by the body in a few days. Warm candle wax dropped on the embedded spines may help cushion the injury. Keep checking for infection and clean with peroxide; in severe cases, consult a doctor.

Stingrays

Swimming rays are easily seen in the clear waters of the Caribbean. Napping rays are another matter. When walking in shallow waters, shuffle your feet so any napping rays will have a chance to flee. If you do step on a ray, treat the wound as you would a sculpin injury.

Underwater Parks

Antigua and Barbuda

SALT FISH TAIL REEF MARINE PARK, ANTIGUA, AND PALASTER REEF MARINE PARK, BARBUDA: both established in 1973. Numerous corals and fishes in clear waters.

Aruba

ARASHI UNDERWATER PARK: northeastern tip of the island.

Bahamas

EXUMA CAYS LAND AND SEA PARK, GREAT EXUMA ISLAND: underwater preserve with coral and limestone reefs, blue hole, drop-offs, caves, night dives. Make arrangements through dive centers on Georgetown and Staniel Cay for equipment rental, air fills.

Barbados

FOLKSTONE UNDERWATER PARK, ST. JAMES: on west coast, conservation area; all marine life is protected. Sunken freighter for dive site. Snorkeling and glass-bottom boat; equipment rental nearby.

Bonaire

BONAIRE MARINE PARK: entire coastline of Bonaire and Klein Bonaire from the high-tide line down to 200 feet. No fishing or collecting of shells or corals, dead or alive. Some of the most varied and beautiful coral formations in the Caribbean. Quarter-mile-long underwater trail for snorkelers.

British Virgin Islands

WRECK OF THE RHONE MARINE PARK: near Salt Island (about five sea miles from Road Town). The *Rhone* went down in the hurricane of 1867 in about thirty feet of water; its coral-encrusted remains and colorful fish population make it one of the Caribbean's most popular dive sites.

Curaçao

CURAÇAO UNDERWATER PARK: at Jan Thiel Bay on the eastern end of the island. Nearby Seaquarium has glass tanks for high-and-dry coral viewing, as well.

Guadeloupe

RESERVE COSTEAU DE PIGEON (UNDERWATER COSTEAU PARK): Pigeon Island off Guadeloupe's west coast. Snorkeling and scuba-diving areas. Variety of tropical fish and coral in clear waters.

Saba

SABA MARINE PARK: Clear waters surround the entire island. Various corals, fish, and unique geological formations such as lava flows and tunnels.

Turks and Caicos

CAICOS NATIONAL UNDERWATER PARK REEF: off the Meridian Club, Pine Cay. Rich reefs in clear waters. No spearfishing or live collecting.

FORT GEORGE NATIONAL PARK: near Pine Cay, not far from Provo. The underwater section of the park has five cannons from the fort that were blown into the water by a storm. Snorkeling and scuba diving. Equipment rented on Pine Cay or Provo; dive trips available.

U.S. Virgin Islands

BUCK ISLAND REEF NATIONAL MONUMENT, OFF ST. CROIX: a striking 2,000-yard-long example of a fringing coral reef. A marked underwater trail indicates types of fish and coral. Day-trip boat charters are easily arranged in Christiansted.

UNDERWATER TRAIL AT TRUNK BAY: U.S. National Park, St. John. A self-directed underwater trail, with labeled corals, off a powdery white beach. Good for even beginning snorkelers; the park service holds regular classes. Check the Visitors' Information Center in Cruz Bay for details.

Boating

The sea surrounds, separates, and connects this lovely string of islands. There is something particularly special about seeing islands from the sea, which after all is the way they were discovered. It is only from this vantage point that one gets the sense of the coast, the height of the mountains, the density of the colors in relation to the stunning blues of the water.

Arrange for a boat trip even if only for a few hours—for perspective, if not pleasure. There are lots of options, from dinghies to day or term charters to cruise ships. Most islands offer everything from glass-bottom boat tours to deep-sea fishing and Hobie Cat rentals. (See the individual island listings for more information.)

Make sure you select the sea outing that will be most meaningful for you, based on whether you want to fish, swim, picnic, bird-watch, sightsee, dive, beachcomb, sail, or party. In many places large floating rafts chug around the harbor while guests dance and drink rum. If you aren't fond of crowds, avoid the large boats that will have people lined up on the rail from stem to stern. People who feel more comfortable on the proverbial "even keel" will probably be happier on a powerboat than on a sailboat heeling at thirty degrees. Francis J. Waters, captain of *Diva,* who has long run successful day charters to Buck Island, St. Croix, says the most important thing to consider is whether you like being there or getting there. On a powerboat you'll spend more time being there; a sailboat will give you time to savor the trip itself.

Term charters (boat rentals for a week or more) can be arranged through a number of reputable companies. Boat charters contain a wealth of options, from bare bones to the luxury of private yachts and gourmet meals. Charters are of two types—bare boat and crewed. A bare-boat charter is without a paid crew, which means you need to know something about handling a boat. Each rental agency has its own requirements regarding qualifications and experience. One week is usually the minimum charter. Rates vary.

Crewed charters differ considerably from boat to boat. Many boat owners take charter parties out as their livelihood. Other boats are run by hired crews. When choosing a crewed charter, consider the size of the boat, the size of the party, and the facilities; if you like luxury and privacy, the shared bathrooms and hammocks of a Windjammer cruise are not for you. Many families and novice sailors like to charter a bare boat and hire only the captain; they do their own cooking but have the security of local experience on board.

Note: Outside of the U.S. Virgin Islands and Puerto Rico, visitors do not have the advantage of the safety measures required and licensed by the U.S. Coast Guard. Do inquire about life rafts, preservers, and other safety factors in advance.

Boat Charters

The following companies are well-known boat charters with various options—such as crews, bare boats, sail and dive packages—on different types of vessels.

The Moorings
Suite 402
Clearwater, FL 34624
telephone: (813) 535-1446 or (800) 535-7289
This is one of the biggest and most experienced chartering agencies. It now has seven Caribbean and Bahamian branches. Orientation and support services are well organized. It's a good place to start for either crewed or bare-boat charters from multiple locations.

Windjammer Barefoot Cruises Ltd.
P.O. Box 120
Miami Beach, FL 33119
telephone: (305) 534-7447 or (800) 327-2601
Windjammer offers sailing vacations of six or thirteen days on classic tall ships. Itineraries vary by ship. Reasonable.

Nicholson Yacht Charters
432 Columbia Street, Suite 21A

Cambridge, MA 02141-1043
telephone: (617) 225-0555 or (800) 662-6066
Nicholson's has a fine reputation for matching vacationers with charter yachts of all types and sizes throughout the Caribbean. It rents both motor and sailing yachts up to nearly 300 feet in length. Prices vary according to season, size, and the number of your party.

PART FIVE

The Islands

"Donkey say God make the world with hill and hallow, so when you climb the high hill, yo cud res' in the hallow."

Caribbean proverb

Anguilla

AREA: 35 square miles.

POPULATION: About 9,600.

CAPITAL CITY: The Valley.

LANGUAGE: English.

RELIGION: Anglican, Baptist, Methodist, Roman Catholic, Seventh-Day Adventist, Evangelical.

GOVERNMENT: Self-governing dependency of U.K.

LOCATION: The most northerly of the Leeward Islands, about 5 miles north of St. Martin; 160 miles east of Puerto Rico.

GETTING THERE: The nearest jet airports with flights to Anguilla are St. Maarten, Antigua, St. Kitts, St. Thomas, and Puerto Rico. The easiest and most frequent connections are from St. Maarten on Windward Island Airways (three scheduled flights daily) or by ferryboat from the Port of Marigot, French St. Martin (ferries leave at regular intervals between 9 A.M. and 5 P.M. daily). LIAT flies from Antigua (two scheduled flights a week) and St. Kitts to Anguilla.

CUSTOMS: Entering visitors need a valid passport or proof of citizenship and either a return or an ongoing ticket. Visitors may bring personal items in duty free, including either 200 cigarettes or 50 cigars, one bottle (40 oz.) of liquor, and some perfume. The importation of firearms including air guns is prohibited. Entering with prohibited drugs is a crime.

HEALTH: No special precautions. Anguilla is a dry island. It now has a new hospital, but travel with any medications you require.

CLOTHING: Informal, with an emphasis on swimwear, but you will need a cover-up for moving about the island, especially in shopping areas. An air of friendly small-town conservatism reminds visitors that swimwear is not appropriate in town and topless or nude bathing is illegal. You'll want a hat and canvas shoes for exploring and maybe a light wrap for breezy evenings.

ELECTRICITY: Most places have 110 volts/60 cycles AC, as in the U.S.

TIME ZONE: Atlantic standard time year-round, which is the same as eastern daylight saving time; in winter, Anguilla is an hour later than eastern standard time.

MONEY: Eastern Caribbean dollar (or E.C.) is the official currency, although some places will accept U.S. and Canadian dollars. Money is easily exchanged (E.C. $2.65 to $2.70 equals U.S. $1); the official exchange rate fluctuates. Both Bank of America and Barclay's International have branches in The Valley, open 8 A.M. until noon Monday to Friday plus 3 to 5 P.M. Friday; closed weekends and holidays. Don't count on using credit cards; ask in advance.

TAX AND TIPS: Airport departure tax is U.S. $10 per person. Generally there is an 8 percent government tax and a 10 percent service charge on hotel bills. Tipping is discretionary at 10 to 15 percent for waiters and cabdrivers.

Overview

Anguilla with its twisting coast seems to sit off by itself in a special sea of tranquility, although it's only 5 miles from busy St. Martin to the south and about 160 miles east of Puerto Rico. Billed as the best-kept secret in the Caribbean, Anguilla—all 16 by 4 miles of it—is home to about 9,600 people. It's quiet, dry, beach bound, and flat; Crocus Hill at 213 feet marks its highest point. Anguilla just may have some of the most spectacular coral sand beaches in the Caribbean. Each cove offers its own ambience, from the shell-sprinkled crescent of Rendezvous Bay to palm-linked nooks and crannies.

Relatively new to the tourist trade, Anguilla offers a vacation centered around the sea. Some accommodations have tennis courts and pools, but this is really an island for beach-lovers, bird-watchers, divers, and dreamers.

History

Anguilla was called Malliouhana by the Carib Indians. In 1493, Columbus sailed close enough to note Anguilla's wriggling length and to christen the island for the eel it resembled, but by all accounts he didn't tarry.

The first settlers were the British, who arrived to claim the island in

Anegada Passage

LEEWARD ISLANDS

⌇ SOMBRERO

 ANGUILLA

Marigot ● ST MARTIN
▲ Philipsburg

ATLANTIC OCEAN

ST BARTHÉLEMY

◌ SABA

◌ ST EUSTATIUS

 ST CHRISTOPHER (ST KITTS)

Basseterre

BARBUDA

Charlestown ◌ NEVIS

St John's ◌

ANTIGUA

◌ MONTSERRAT
Plymouth

Guadeloupe Passage

CARIBBEAN SEA

GRAND
TERRE

𝒩

GUADELOUPE

BASSE
TERRE

Pointe-à-Pitre

Basse Terre ●

MARIE GALANTE

ÎLES DES SAINTES

Dominica Passage

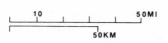
10   50MI
50KM

Portsmouth ●

DOMINICA

Roseau ●

Martinque Passage

about 1650. Early Anguillans sent to St. Croix by Governor John Richardson in 1680 helped settle the Virgin Islands. Anguillans repelled two French invasions during the colonial period of international musical chairs—one at Crocus Bay in 1745, another at Rendezvous Bay in 1796. Anguilla remained British.

In 1825, the royal government made Anguilla part of a St. Kitts-Nevis combination colony under a St. Kitts seated legislature. Anguilla was ruled as such for several centuries. By the 1950s, Anguillans began to feel discontent with the distant rule of St. Kitts, some sixty miles south. In May 1967, they revolted. The quiet island made international news as "the eel that squealed." Anguilla demanded self-government, and two years later declared complete independence. Britain responded dramatically in March 1969 by dropping a force of peacekeeping paratroopers.

When the dust—and the revolt—settled (no lives were lost), the point was well made that Anguilla should be an individual entity, as the people wished, and as such the island was taken back into the colonial fold. In early 1976, the island's new and separate constitution was implemented. It provides for an island-run government of ministers and elected representatives. It is this government that is carefully—controlled tourism is the byword—leading Anguilla into the tourist arena.

Things to See and Do
Please ask before photographing local people.

Historic Sites

Governor Richardson's (1679–1742) tomb at Sandy Hill; ruins of Dutch fort on Sandy Hill—scene of 1796 battle; Wall Blake House—restored seventeenth-century plantation house, at Wall Blake. More information about these historic sites is available from Anguilla's active Archaeological and Historical Society, P.O. Box 252, The Valley, Anguilla, West Indies.

Lobster Fishing Village
At Island Harbour.

The Fountain
Underground cave at Shoal Bay, with skylight opening and continuous supply of fresh water.

TENNIS: Available at various hotels.

FISHING: Trips can be arranged through your hotel; local skippers usually go out for about U.S. $20 per person.

BOATING: Some local craft are available for informal charter (ask around and agree on terms beforehand). Jet skiing is banned.

DIVING: Tamarian Watersports has PADI scuba certification courses, equipment rental, and dive trips—both scuba and snorkel. Some hotels also rent snorkel gear.

BEACHES: Anguilla has more than thirty superb coves and beaches, all with snowy coral sand and interesting offshore waters. It's best to rent a car and explore. A few beaches to get you started: Rendezvous Bay, a long, sandy crescent on the south shore, is a popular choice. Shoal Bay is somewhat L-shaped, with shade trees, good snorkeling, and a nearby ledge for tank dives. Maundays Bay and Cove Bay (one of the few with palms) are also wonderful spots on the south shore. Gentle Sandy Ground sits barricaded between a salt pond and the sea—a great place for rough, windy days and timid children. Don't forget to see the unusual rock formations on the Atlantic coast side.

Note: Nude bathing is illegal.

Nearby islets also have wonderful beaches and make nice day trips for picnics. Sandy Island, with its white sands ringed with coconut palms, is about fifteen minutes by water from Sandy Ground Harbour. Scrub, Dog, and Prickly Pear Islands are all easily reached by powerboat as well. Sombrero Island, about thirty-eight miles northwest of Anguilla, is not quite as accessible, but many find its remote, manned lighthouse appealing. Visit by charter boat. Boat excursions to the closer cays can be arranged through your hotel, the local Tourist Board, Anguilla Travel Services in Sandy Ground, or Malliouhana Travel and Tours.

NIGHTLIFE: May be even quieter than day life. Most visitors find that nightlife consists mainly of watching for the green flash at sunset, dining out, and talking. Live music—from jazz to steel band—can be found most nights at various restaurants and hotels.

SHOPPING: Somewhat limited but it does include handcrafted items such as carved schooners, handwoven baskets, and crocheted items. Anguilla's colorful tropical stamps are collector's items; at the post office in

The Valley, British-made goods are cheaper here than in the U.S. Hallmark on Airport Road handles some well-known porcelains and linens. Avid shoppers will want a day on nearby St. Martin, with its profusion of duty-free shops. The ferry trip from Blowing Point, Anguilla, to Marigot, French St. Martin, takes about twenty minutes; boats run every 30 minutes starting about 8 A.M. Check locally for the exact times.

FESTIVALS AND HOLIDAYS

Anguilla Day, 30 May.

Queen's Birthday, June.

Summer Carnival, first full week in August. Biggest island celebration, with boat races and planned events. Reservations a must at carnival time.

August Monday, first Monday in August.

Separation Day, 19 December.

Christmas Fair, December.

Boxing Day, 26 December.

Local businesses are closed on holidays; nonreligious holidays often have boat races or "jump-up" dances. Events vary from year to year and often include tennis tournaments and other sporting events.

FOOD: Anguilla's bountiful seas and its variety of restaurants make for delicious fare. Most restaurants specialize in seafood—fresh lobster, fish, conch, whelks—prepared with a French flair. From simple beach bars to the expensive and oft-touted Malliouhana. Less expensive restaurants highly recommended for local specialties are Lucy's Harbour View, Aquarium Bar and Restaurant, Johnno's, and the Ferryboat Restaurant; The Pepper Pot serves Trinidadian *roti* as well as local dishes.

Because this is a small island, reservations, especially for dinner, are always a good idea.

HOTELS: For such a small island, Anguilla offers diverse accommodations, many right on the beach. Choices range in price from upward of U.S. $500 per day for two at Malliouhana to U.S. $35 to $50 per day for a double at a guest house off the beach. Rental villas and apartments start at about U.S. $300 a week.

Information on the island and hotels, apartments, villas, and guest houses can be obtained from the Anguilla Tourist Office.

HOTELS

Cinnamon Reef Beach Club, Box 141, Anguilla, W.I.; telephone: (809) 497-2727. On Little Harbour. Use of snorkeling equipment, sailboats, and tennis courts included. Expensive. Fourteen units, pool, and beach.

Rendezvous Bay Hotel, Box 31, Anguilla, W.I.; telephone: (809) 497-6549. Boating, fishing, and tennis; bar and dining room. Moderately priced. Twenty units, pool, and beach.

Malliouhana Hotel, on remote Mead's Bay; telephone: (809) 497-6111 or (800) 835-0796; fax: (809) 497-6011. Sleek, complete resort with fifty-three units scattered around its twenty-five acres. Expensive. Three pools, boutique, water sports, bar and restaurant, fully equipped exercise hall and supervised children's playground.

Rainbow Reef Villas, Box 130, Anguilla, W.I.; telephone: (809) 497-2817. Six well-furnished villas. Weekly rate includes housekeeping service. Moderately priced. On Sea Feather's Bay with a reef-fringed beach.

Write for a complete listing of other accommodations. Color brochures and rates will help you choose. Since most facilities are small, make reservations well in advance for popular in-season getaways. Don't forget Anguilla's inexpensive guest houses; on an island four miles wide, you're never far from the beach. They include Casa Nadine, Florencia's, Lloyd's, Maybern, Norman B, Farrington Manor, and Pond Dipper; details are available from the Tourist Board.

For More Information

ANGUILLA

Department of Tourism
The Valley
Anguilla, W.I.
telephone: (809) 497-2451 or 2759
Telex: 9313 ANGGOVT LA

U.S.

Anguilla Tourist Office
775 Park Avenue, Suite 105
Huntington, NY 11743
telephone: (800) 553-4939

Once you arrive on the island, you may want to stop by the tourist office in The Valley, for a copy of the latest brochures; *What We Do in Anguilla* is a good guide. Detailed maps are available at the Department of Lands and Survey.

Antigua and Barbuda

AREA: Antigua, 108 square miles; Barbuda, 62 square miles; Redonda, 1 square mile.

POPULATION: About 67,000.

CAPITAL CITY: St. John's, Antigua.

LANGUAGE: English.

RELIGION: Varied Christian sects with a majority of Anglicans.

GOVERNMENT: Parliamentary democracy with a seventeen-member House of Representatives and an elected prime minister.

LOCATION: Often called the "Heart of the Caribbean," Antigua is one of the Leeward Islands and sits about midway down the chain if you start from Puerto Rico. That's about 17° latitude, in the neighborhood of Nevis and Montserrat and north of Guadeloupe. Barbuda is twenty-five miles north of Antigua; Redonda, an uninhabited rock twenty miles southwest of Antigua, is really much closer to Montserrat.

GETTING THERE: Antigua's V.C. Bird (formerly Coolidge) International Airport is a true Caribbean crossroads that makes the island easily accessible from a number of places, with nonstops from New York, Toronto, Miami, San Juan, and other major cities. Windjammer cruises and several major cruise-ship lines also put in here.

CUSTOMS: British, Australian, and Japanese visitors need passports; Canadian and U.S. visitors need only proof of citizenship (driver's license, voter registration card, or birth certificate); all other nationalities must have visas. Everyone needs either a return or an ongoing ticket.

HEALTH: A dry, well-developed island; no special precautions. Water is generally safe to drink, and bottled water is readily available.

CLOTHING: Standard tropical wear, on the conservative side with variations for fun and formality. Dress standards on Antigua reflect its British heritage. Swimwear and shorts belong seaside. You'll need summery street wear for sight-seeing and shopping in St. John's. Most resorts insist on cover-ups once you leave the beach, and many, especially in season, require jackets (and comparable garb for women) for dinner.

ELECTRICITY: Most hotels have 110 volts/60 cycles AC, as in the U.S. and Canada; others have 220 volts, and several variations in outlet styles are included in this mix. Most places keep transformers and adapters on hand, sometimes for a fee; as always, check details in advance.

TIME ZONE: Atlantic standard time, the same as daylight saving time; in winter, Antigua is one hour ahead of eastern standard time.

PHONE: Dial direct, using area code 809-46 plus five local digits.

MONEY: Eastern Caribbean dollars, usually called E.C. (or sometimes the old beewee), are the official tender. Official exchange rates usually work out to about E.C. $2.65 = U.S. $1. U.S. and Canadian money is cheerfully accepted most places, where on-the-spot conversions take place. Credit cards not widely accepted, although some resorts and stores take American Express and sometimes Barclay's; you're much better off with traveler's checks. Banks are open from 8 A.M. to 1 P.M. Monday through Thursday and 8 A.M. to 1 P.M. and 3 to 4 P.M. Friday; closed weekends and holidays.

TAX AND TIPS: Hotels and restaurants add 10 percent service charge to all bills; no other tipping is necessary,. A government tax of 7 percent may also be added to your hotel bill. In restaurants without an added service charge, 10 to 15 percent is standard. Airport porters get U.S. $.50 to $1 per bag, depending on the number of bags and the distance they must be carried.

GETTING AROUND: Taxis are easy to come by and a good way to get around. The Antigua Taxi Association has a well-run stand at the airport. Fares are set by the government; cabs don't have meters. It costs about U.S. $10 from the airport into St. John's and about U.S. $25 to Nelson's Dockyard. Rates to hotels differ; check with the Tourist Information Desk inside the airport for exact fares. All-island tours that include Nelson's Dockyard and shopping and sights in St. John's start at U.S. $55 and take most of the day. Shorter variations can be negotiated. Taxi drivers are usually tipped about 10 percent of the fare for good service.

Car Rental: Probably your best choice for long stays and leisurely exploration. Rentals cost about U.S. $45 to $60 a day, unlimited mileage, you buy the gas—about U.S. $2 per gallon. Roads are left-hand drive, but they're in good condition, and there are no precipitous mountain curves. You will need a local driver's license available in the airport or police station for U.S. $12 and a peek at your U.S. driver's license.

There are a number of car rental agencies on Antigua, all locally owned, although they may be affiliates of major chains. You'll need to make reservations during Christmas week, Easter week, carnival, and sailing week. Your travel agent or hotel should be able to help, or you can call the following firms directly: Antigua Car Rental (Avis), telephone: (809) 462-1815; Budget, telephone: (809) 462-2544; Carib Car Rental, telephone: (809) 462-2062; Hertz, telephone: (809) 462-3397; and National, telephone: (809) 462-2113. A complete listing of car rental firms is available through the tourist office.

Overview

Antigua (pronounced An-TEE-ga) is a pleasant cross between frenetically touristed isles and those so rural you can't buy toothpaste. It's just big enough to offer lots of vacation options and it's friendly. The people here are as ambling and relaxed as the easy roll of the hills. Beaches are Antigua's claim to fame; there are supposed to be at least 365 of them. Story has it that Queen Elizabeth herself found one so irresistible that she actually entered the water—the only time she is said to have done so. It all took place in complete seclusion, the story emphasizes.

The island is relatively dry, with only forty inches of rain a year, so the landscape undergoes definite changes of face in wet and dry seasons. There are times when it looks like a golden African savanna and others when it's spring green.

In recent years, pineapples and sea island cotton have replaced sugarcane as the major crops, and tourism has become the leading industry. Antiguans enjoy a better standard of living than that on some nearby islands, and most of the people can read and write.

Along with its marvelous beaches and variety of water sports, Antigua has a first-rate restoration of an eighteenth-century sea base—Nelson's Dockyard in English Harbour. There are a number of other historical buildings, ruins, and museums as well as Amerindian sites. Tourist facilities are very complete, with full services and entertainment varying from casinos to calypso.

History

Columbus sighted this island in 1493 and named it Santa Maria de Antigua after a church in Spain. Both Spanish and French attempts to settle Antigua were foiled by the fierce resident Carib Indians. It wasn't until 1632 that the British successfully settled and called the island by a shortened and uniquely pronounced version of its original name.

The island remained a quiet colonial outpost for three centuries. African slaves were imported to work on the sugarcane plantations that formed the island's main industry. Slavery was abolished in 1834.

Under British dominion from 1871 to 1962, Antigua belonged first to the Federation of the Leeward Islands and then, as a separate colony, to the British Federation of the West Indies. The government of Antigua received complete control over internal affairs in 1967.

Amid a million-dollar celebration, Antigua became officially independent from Britain on 1 November 1981. A long-popular leader, Vere Cornwell Bird, then seventy-one years old, became the first prime minister. Throughout the eastern Caribbean, Antigua is admired for its political stability and its preparation for and subsequent graceful transition to independence.

Things to See and Do

St. John's, Antigua

Antigua and Barbuda's picturesque waterfront capital has an open-air market, historical buildings, and new shopping areas in restored warehouses. Wander and shop, then choose a spot for lunch; this is a friendly, just-busy-enough town. Most visitors like to see St. John's Cathedral, an Anglican church originally built in 1683, then replaced by a stone structure in 1745. The stone church was destroyed by an earthquake; the present building, on the same site, dates from 1845. There's a small botanical garden on the east side of the city. The ruins of eighteenth-century Fort James still guard the north on St. John's Point.

English Harbour and Nelson's Dockyard National Park, Antigua

Lord Horatio Nelson's Dockyard is probably the best restoration in the eastern Caribbean. This complete facility, which still includes a sail loft, the paymaster's office, and some workshops, was used by the British from 1707 to 1899, when most ships had become too large to execute the winding harbor entrance. Then-Captain Nelson was in charge from 1784 to 1787. Other buildings around the yard also help capture the feeling of eighteenth-century nautical life. The restored Admiral's Inn, constructed of ballast bricks, is now a hotel and restaurant. It's a visitors' tradition to tarry there for a rum punch. The Admiral's House is now a museum with lots of Nelson memorabilia. The former Capstan House and Copper and Lumber Store are now called Prince William Careenage and are part of a time-share apartment development. Across the harbor from the Dockyard is Clarence House, once the home of the Duke of Clarence, who later became King William IV of England. Now open to the public when the governor or visiting royalty are not in residence, it's worth a visit. The entire English Harbour area is still a major boating center, and many enjoy looking at classic yachts at anchor or marveling at their diverse crews costumed in everything from blue blazers to cutoffs and bikinis.

The town of English Harbour sits north of Nelson's Dockyard below the historical area known as Shirley Heights. The Antigua Historical Society has a map to the ruins that identifies the fortifications that were built here by General William Henry Shirley in 1787. Barracks and powder magazines run along the well-fortified ridge that protected the crucial dockyard (which, by the way, was never attacked). Fort Berkeley sits at the west end.

For a multimedia presentation of Antigua's history, visit the Interpretation Centre at Dow's Hill on the way to Shirley Heights. The center also offers a striking 360-degree view of the park.

National park guides at the entrance to the Dockyard can be consulted about historical details. Boat tours of English Harbour are also available.

Indian Town National Park, Antigua

Out on the northeastern corner of the island where the Atlantic rollers have sculpted the rocky coast into blowholes and the span called Devil's Bridge.

Arawak Museum and Archaeological Site, Antigua

Near English Harbour; Amerindian relics.

TENNIS: There are courts with resident pros at Half Moon Bay, Curtain Bluff, and Anchorage. Courts are also available to guests (no charge) at Jolly Beach, Antigua Beach, Halcyon Cove, Halcyon Reef, Galley Bay, Blue Waters, and Hawksbill. Antigua's annual pro tournament is held in January.

GOLF: Cedar Valley has an eighteen-hole course, par 70; clubs and carts for rent, greens fees about U.S. $16. Half Moon Bay has a nine-hole course, par 34; guests there have priority.

HORSEBACK RIDING: The St. James Club and Galley Bay have horses. Take note: The government is trying to phase out beach riding.

SPORTFISHING: About U.S. $150 to $200 for two for a day includes boat, bait, rods, and, often, sodas. Most hotels will make arrangements for you, or you can try Dive Antigua, the Catamaran Hotel, or See by Sea at Basil Hill Tours; to reserve in advance, call (809) 462-4882.

WATERSKIING: Offered by many hotels at about U.S. $15 per half hour per person.

WINDSURFING: Equipment available at many hotels, or try Village Watersports for rental or lessons.

BOATING: Blessed with good natural harbors, Antigua has long been a yachting center. You may want to go day sailing, or take a lunch, cocktail, or dinner cruise. There's also a glass-bottom boat in Halcyon Cove. Many hotels have sunfish, Hobie Cats, sailfish, or catamarans available for their guests, often free of charge. For day excursions on larger boats, both motor and sail, check with your hotel desk. Be sure to ask about beaches and snorkeling equipment; all day trips are a little different.

The *Jolly Roger,* a converted wooden sailing ship built in 1944 for the Swedish navy, is another popular day boat that now sails under the skull and crossbones pirate flag and has been outfitted with red sails and cannons. Trip includes lunch, swimming, and pirate festivities. Book at your hotel desk or call 462-2064.

WALKING AND HIKING: Besides strolling the streets of St. John's or exploring the English Harbour area, visitors often beachcomb or simply wander Antigua's varied coast. Long stretches of sand are broken by quiet coves and mangroves or, on the Atlantic side, dramatic rock formations. However, since public transportation is not dependable, and these natural variations are often a considerable distance from each other, it's best to rent a car to get you to walking areas. Otherwise, explore only half as far as you can comfortably walk so the return trip won't be a trial. There are no marked trails on Antigua, but the trek up Monk's Hill (inland from the Catamaran Hotel) has become a popular one. It'll take a good chunk of the day (be sure to carry drinks and a snack), but the ruins of Great

George Fort and the view make it particularly rewarding. It's also possible to explore parts of the rain forest remnant on Boggy Peak, at 1,300 feet, the highest point on the island. Remember, you'll be walking in the tropical sun, so wear a hat, start early, and always carry something to drink when venturing off the beaten path.

SWIMMING AND DIVING: There's lots of interesting inshore reef snorkeling; most hotels offer equipment free or for a small charge. The St. James Club, Blue Waters Beach, Halcyon Cove, Jolly Beach, Curtain Bluff, Hawksbill, Half Moon Bay, and Long Bay (as well as Dive Antigua, telephone: 462-0256) rent scuba gear to certified divers. Dive Antigua also holds classes and makes regular day and night dive trips; trips include reef and wreck dives off the west, south, and northeast coasts. There's also good diving—both scuba and snorkel—off the shores of Barbuda. For dive trips in the English Harbour area, check with Dockyard Divers in Nelson's Dockyard or call 460-1178 or channel 68 on VHF radio.

BEACHES: For sunning, dreaming, swimming, and walking, Antigua's reported 365 beaches are unparalleled. Most of them are public and well-protected by reefs, so the surf is as soft as the powdery sands. Almost all of the major hotels are right on the beach or will get you there fast; even small guest houses are never far from the sea.

NIGHTLIFE: Casinos, hotel floor shows, nightclubs, and discos. Check your hotel desk for complete listings. Remember to pack appropriate clothing.

SHOPPING: The main shopping area in downtown St. John's extends from Newgate Street on the north to Redcliffe Street on the south, heading away from the water. Temple Street is about the end of the most interesting section. Walk the waterfront south to find the public market that bustles early mornings and especially Saturdays. It's a great place to savor local color as well as produce. Locally made flour-sack shirts and skirts as well as handmade dolls and baskets are available in many places. Batik cloth and clothing—some local, some imported (ask, if you care)—are also popular. Liquor prices are low here; local rum—Cavalier—is inexpensive. Antigua's colorful stamps are collector's items. Some visitors like to return with wooden *wari* boards, a popular game on Antigua. The Artist's Guild has grown in recent years, and more shops and galleries carry watercolors and oils by local painters. The nicely restored Redcliffe Quay and Nelson's Dockyard shops are also interesting.

FESTIVALS AND HOLIDAYS: Along with all the traditional English holidays, Antigua has several annual week-long festivals. Sailing Week, in late
April, has races, rum, and dancing, alternating seaborne exertion with
shoreside exuberance. Daytime sailboat races are recounted at nighttime
parties that hop from hotel to hotel for seven days. The final day of the
festival is called Dockyard Day, with tugs-of-war and greased pole racing
contests between sailboat crews. Lord Nelson's Ball that night ends the
festivities amid awards, dancing, and more rum.

The next serious all-island partying comes at carnival time, usually the
last week in July, the first week in August on Antigua. This colorful ten-
day-long festival celebrates the abolition of slavery on 1 August 1834. Just
as the former slaves once took to the streets to exult their freedom with
song and dance, the entire island now turns out to "jump-up" and dance
to the music of calypsonians and steel bands. Parades, calypso competitions, food, and a carnival queen are all part of the festivities.

Business holidays include New Year's Day, Good Friday, Easter, Whitmonday, Queen's Birthday, Independence Day (1 November), Christmas,
and Boxing Day (26 December).

FOOD: A spicy blend of curries, sauces, and local fruits of the land and
sea marks Antiguan cuisine. Try pumpkin soup, conch chowder, coconut-
breaded seafood, or lobster in its infinite variations. Every price range is
available, from twenty-dollar-a-plate elegance to the several-dollar walking lunches at local chicken stands and delis. Shirley Heights Lookout,
expensive, is furnished with antiques and overlooks English Harbour;
serves seafood and is open for lunch and dinner. Calypso Cafe and Lemon
Tree specialize in local fare. Redcliffe Quay has a deli and a pizza bar (two
separate places). The Red Snapper at Nelson's Dockyard serves local fish
at moderate prices. Most of the hotel dining rooms can provide continental and American dishes such as U.S. prime steaks and lettuce salads.
There are any number of interesting places to eat in St. John's; use some
care in venturing out, but, by and large, health standards are quite good
on Antigua.

HOTELS: Hotels on Antigua are almost as plentiful as beaches. Prices
range from the luxury of all-inclusive resorts to simple guest houses. Helpful women with telephones and rate guides meet every flight into Antigua
to steer the spur-of-the-moment and aimless traveler toward suitable
lodgings. If you wish to reserve in advance, write for the complete list or
see your travel agent. Remember, off-season rates—from 16 April to 15
December—are as much as 30 to 40 percent lower. Be sure to reserve well
in advance for festival weeks. Jolly Beach Resort (U.S.: 800-321-1055),
with 400 rooms and expansive grounds, is Antigua's largest hotel and one

of the most popular. Rates include all water sports (complete with topless beach), tennis, and evening entertainment. Galley Bay Surf Club is more expensive; twenty-eight double rooms five miles from St. John's; horse-back riding, beach, and water sports. Admiral's Inn at English Harbour in Nelson's Dockyard is not on the beach, but its 200-year-old ambience makes up for it.

This gives you some idea of choices; there really is something for everyone. The official listings include twenty-two small guest houses with rooms for less than U.S. $20 and many other small hotels for U.S. $30 to $40 a day.

For More Information

ANTIGUA
Antigua and Barbuda Department of Tourism
P.O. Box 363
St. John's, Antigua, W.I.
telephone: (809) 462-0480
fax: (809) 462-2483

U.S.
Antigua and Barbuda Department of Tourism and Trade
610 Fifth Avenue, Suite 311
New York, NY 10020
telephone: (212) 541-4117
fax: (212) 757-1607

CANADA
Antigua and Barbuda Department of Tourism
60 St. Clair Avenue East, Suite 304
Toronto, Ontario M4T IN5
Canada
telephone: (416) 961-3085
fax: (416) 961-7218

ENGLAND
Antigua House
15 Thayer Street
London W1M 5LD, England
telephone: 0171-486-7073
fax: 0171-485-9970

Barbuda

This small island just twenty-five miles north of Antigua is described as "genuine wilderness." About 1,200 people live on its sixty-eight square miles, most of them in the village of Codrington. There are only a few tourist accommodations—one lodge and several guest houses. The tourist office in St. John's, Antigua, can provide the details. Most of Barbuda's visitors come for a day trip to bird-watch, horseback ride, dive, swim, or wander its isolated beaches.

Barbuda is a low coral island, almost all beach; it clears the sea by only 143 feet at its highest point. Snorkeling, scuba diving (there are wrecks offshore), parasailing, and waterskiing can be arranged. The only two ways to see Barbuda's Caves at the Highlands with their Amerindian drawings are by Honda scooter or a horse (wear long pants).

You may also want to spend some time at the bird sanctuary, where giant frigate birds with five-foot wingspans perform their mating dances and then nest. Martello Tower, an undated stone ruin, perhaps an old Spanish lighthouse, is another point of interest. So is old Codrington Village, founded in 1685, now in ruins but once a family stronghold. You'll want to find the modern Codrington for Barbuda's traditional lobster lunch. Don't ignore the beaches, where shells and solitude wind in every direction.

Aruba

AREA: 70.9 square miles; 19.6 miles long, 6 miles across at widest point.

POPULATION: 81,507.

CAPITAL CITY: Oranjestad.

LANGUAGE: Officially Dutch, but Spanish, English, and Portuguese are also spoken as well as the local tongue, Papiamento, a blend of these languages with a sprinkling of Amerindian and African.

Needless to say, Arubans are good with languages and almost everyone speaks English.

RELIGION: Catholic, Jewish, and many types of Protestant services are held (Aruba has forty different nationalities).

GOVERNMENT: No longer part of the Netherlands Antilles, Aruba is now a separate entity within the Kingdom of the Netherlands. A crown-appointed governor and an elected parliament and a council of ministers regulate local affairs.

LOCATION: 15 miles off the north coast of Venezuela, 42 miles west of Curaçao; the most westerly of the ABC (Aruba, Bonaire, Curaçao) Islands.

GETTING THERE: Airline service to Aruba includes daily flights from New York and Miami on American Airlines, ALM (Dutch Antillean Airlines), or VIASA; three flights a week from Puerto Rico on ALM; daily from Caracas on ALM. Many cruise ships make regular stops on Aruba.

CUSTOMS: U.S. and Canadian citizens need proof of citizenship—passport, birth certificate, or U.S. voter registration card; all other nationalities need a valid passport. Everyone must have either a return or an ongoing ticket. Visitors are allowed to bring articles for personal use, including a fifth of liquor and 200 cigarettes (for those over twenty-one years of age).

HEALTH: Aruba's dry climate and steady trade winds help make it a very healthy place; there are no tropical diseases and insects are scarce. All drinking water is distilled seawater from the island's large desalinization plant, so tap water is perfectly safe to drink. It is said that this processed water is so pure that it must be run through limestone to give it a "water" taste.

CLOTHING: Mostly informal tropical wear; both men and women may wear shorts in town even though locals don't. Swim wear should be kept to the beach and hotel pool areas. Casinos, nightclubs, and some restaurants require evening wear—cocktail dresses for women, jackets for men. Hairdo-conscious women will want some type of scarf or headgear to help combat the trade winds.

ELECTRICITY: 110 volts/60 cycles AC, as in the U.S.

TIME ZONE: Atlantic standard time, the same as eastern daylight time, all year.

MONEY: The official currency is the Aruban florin (written AFL) and also referred to as a guilder. The exchange rate fluctuates but is about U.S. $1 to AFL 1.78. U.S. dollars and major credit cards are accepted everywhere, and few find the need to change money.

TAX AND TIPS: Airport departure tax is U.S. $12.50 per person. Government room tax is 5 percent. Hotels add 10 to 15 percent service charge to cover tips; many restaurants do this as well; check your bill before tipping additionally. Porters at the airport expect about U.S. $.50 per bag; generally no tips for the taxi driver.

GETTING AROUND: *Taxis:* Plentiful and unmetered, best to establish the rate in advance. The Dispatch Office may be called at 22116 or 21604. The ride from the airport to most resort hotels costs about U.S. $8 to $12. Sight-seeing taxi tours cost about U.S. $30 per hour, maximum of four passengers.

Tours: Sight-seeing by bus costs about U.S. $15 per person for a three-and-a-half-hour tour. De Palm Tours (telephone: 24400) has several sight-seeing options, including daily snorkeling tours, beach barbecues, deep sea fishing, and excursions; call for details or check with your hotel.

Car Rental: Aruba has right-hand-drive cars. Among the car rental agencies are Hertz, Avis, National, Budget, and several local agencies, including Jansen's and Marco's. To rent a car, you must hold a valid foreign driver's license and be over twenty-one years of age. Cars rent for U.S. $28 to $65 a day, depending on the make. Motorcycles and scooters are available for about U.S. $27 to $29 a day—unlimited mileage, you buy the gas. Aruban roads are well marked and maintained, so car rental is a good option. Ask your hotel desk or the Tourist Board to help with arrangements if you haven't reserved before arrival.

Bicycling: Another good way to see the island. Many hotels have bikes for rent, or try Aru Rentals (telephone: 22498); they charge about U.S. $9 a day.

Overview

Aruba is one of the islands where natural beauty has not been sacrificed for casinos and comforts. It's a good destination for those who want to get away but not from it *all*. (Kentucky Fried Chicken and Burger King have beaten you here. There's also a bowling alley.) Even with its huge oil refinery and its strip of high-rise hotels on Palm Beach, most of Aruba is wide-open space.

It's a low, arid island with exotic cacti, aloes (a cash crop), and wind-

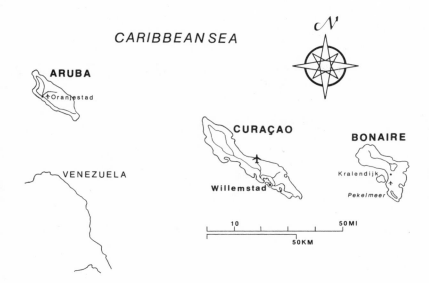

CARIBBEAN SEA

ARUBA
+Oranjestad

VENEZUELA

CURAÇAO

Willemstad

BONAIRE

Kralendijk

Pekelmeer

10   50 MI

50 KM

sculpted divi-divi trees that always stream toward the southwest away
from the cooling trade winds. Aruba has areas with high, powdery sand
dunes, massive diorite boulders, caves with Amerindian drawings, and a
dramatic natural bridge on its Atlantic coast.

The Arubans are polite and friendly and take pride in traditional Dutch
tidiness. This island enjoys one of the highest standards of living in the
West Indies and sees happy tourists as one way of keeping it so. Restaurants offer a wide range of cuisines. You may have to share the beach here,
but you won't have to live on peas and rice unless you want to!

History

History doesn't specify Aruba's exact discovery. However, we do know
it was claimed for Spain by Alonso de Ojeda in 1499.

Aruba's name is also subject to certain mystery. Some scholars think
it came from the Amerindian word *oruba,* meaning "well placed and
handy to the mainland." Others prefer the label that the Spanish conquistadores may have given the island—Oro Uba, "there was gold."

The island was inhabited by a peaceful Arawak tribe, the Caiquetios,
when the Spaniards arrived. Fortunately, the Spanish found Aruba "value-
less" and spared the Indians from colonial "policy," that is, extermination.

In fact, Charles V actually forbade foreign settlers, and Aruba became the one island where the Indian population survived to interbreed with the Spanish and Dutch. Some Arawak features can still be seen on Aruban faces.

In 1825, gold was discovered on Aruba. Although the mine produced more than 3 million pounds of gold, by 1916 it became uneconomical to operate it. Ruins of the gold mills and smelters can still be seen at Balashi and Bushiribana.

It was black gold that brought continuing prosperity to Aruba. In 1924, Lago Oil and Transport Company, now a subsidiary of Exxon, built a large oil refinery on the southern end of the island near San Nicolas. In recent years, tourism, along with the refinery, has helped maintain Aruba's high standard of living.

On January 1, 1986, Aruba became a separate entity within the Kingdom of the Netherlands.

Things to See and Do

Oranjestad

Aruba's picturesque capital city with its quaint pastel houses and busy port. You'll probably want nearly a full day to shop, wander, and lunch here. Walking is the way to see this spotless city. Fresh produce and fish are sold directly from island traders (boats) tied at the wharf.

You may want to stroll through Wilhelmina Park with its tropical plantings and marble statues of Queen Mother Wilhelmina by Italian Arnoldo Lualdi. Fort Zoutman is also right downtown. It was built in 1796 to help protect Aruba from the buccaneers. DeMan's Shell Collection, located at Morgenser 8, is an extraordinary private shell collection; phone ahead for appointment (telephone: 22460).

Arashi: Underwater park off northwest coast.

Bubali Bird Sanctuary: North of Oranjestad.

California Dunes and Lighthouse: On Aruba's northernmost tip.

Bushiribana and Boedoei: Abandoned gold mines and smelter mines.

Rock Formations: At Ayo and Casibari; natural bridge carved by ocean waves is on the coast south of Boedoei.

Indian Drawings: Fontein cave, on the coast south of Boca Prins; Arikok National Park.

Boca Prins: High and powdery dunes, traditional spot for dune sliding (best to wear long pants and tennis shoes).

BEACHES: Aruba is blessed with stretches of white coral sand. The western and southwestern coasts offer the best in terms of sunning and swimming. Eagle Beach just north of town is a free public beach with thatch-covered picnic facilities. Palm Beach, just north of Eagle, has a very gentle slope—ideal for children and floaters. Most of the hotels lining Palm Beach let nonguests use their facilities for a small fee.

Most of Aruba's surf-swept northern and eastern shore beaches are posted "No Swimming" or "At Your Own Risk." Some surfing is done at Dos Playa and Aneiconfi. These coasts are noted for treacherous currents and wave action; caution is in order.

DIVING: Aruba's waters are warm and clear, often with 100-foot visibility. Tropical fish and corals can be seen at a number of locations. Snorkeling equipment rents for about $4 an hour to $8 a day at most hotels. One-hour boat trips with equipment and a guide are also available. See your hotel activities desk, or call De Palm Watersports (telephone: 24400 or 24545).

Scuba diving lessons and dive trips may also be arranged through your hotel or directly through De Palm or Red Sails Sports (telephone: 35721). One of Aruba's most popular dives is down to a German freighter scuttled in World War II. Most dive trips include equipment rental and cost about $40 per person. Be sure to count on an additional 10 percent service charge.

WATERSKIING: Possible at most hotels.

WINDSURFING: Divi Winds Center (telephone: 23300, extension 623) rents equipment.

BOATING: Sunfish are available for rent or loan at most hotels. Pedal boats rent for $7 for 30 minutes at most resorts. Sea jeeps (small motorboats designed for two or four people) are also available at most hotels. Larger boats are often available for charter directly from boat owners. Check the Aruba Nautical Club in Spanish Lagoon or the Bucinti Yacht Club.

SPORTFISHING: Charters arranged through De Palm Watersports (telephone: 24400). Count on spending about $250 per half day for a boat for six. Price includes bait, tackle, soft drinks, and beer.

TENNIS: Free to hotel guests during the day; a small charge for lights at night. Most hotels have courts. The trade winds often seem like another player; the Holiday Inn is said to have the best wind shields.

GOLF: Aruba's world-class golf course, Tierra del Sol, opened in 1995. Designed by the Robert Trent Jones II Group, the eighteen-hole course on the northwest coast near the California Lighthouse brings a full-featured golf community to the island. Greens fees are about U.S. $10 for eighteen holes. Carts and clubs can be rented on site.

The nine-hole Aruba Golf Club near San Nicolas claims to make golf a new experience, complete with oiled sand greens (telephone: 42006).

NIGHTLIFE: Casinos, discos, and nightclubs abound. Aruba's casinos are all in large hotels—the American Aruba Beach Resort, the Aruba Concorde, the Aruba Caribbean, the Aruba Palm Beach, the Aruba Holiday Inn, the Hyatt Regency Aruba, Aruba Hilton and Casino, and the Royal Cabana Casino. These hotels also offer nightclub shows, dining, drinks, and dancing. Check the Tourist Board's monthly calendar for regularly scheduled folkloric shows and cultural events.

SHOPPING: With its 3.3 percent duty, Aruba is not technically a free port, but there are lots of imported bargains. Nassaustraat in Oranjestad is the main shopping district with stores that offer Delft ware, silver, pewter, perfume, china, crystal, cameras, and many other luxuries. Holland cheeses, such as Edam and Gouda, and chocolates are tasty good buys.

Lovely commemorative stamps are available at the post office. As always, compare with stateside prices before assuming everything is a great deal.

Local crafts include wood carving, leather goods, and a typical red and white pottery.

FESTIVALS AND HOLIDAYS

New Year's Day, 1 January. Midnight fireworks, strolling musicians.

Pre-Lent Carnival, February or March. Street dancing, food, costume parades, and general all-island festivities.

Queen's Day, 30 April. Parades, sports.

Labor Day Holiday, 1 May.

Annual Aruba Marathon, third weekend in June.

St. John's Day, 24 June. Folkloric celebration.

Watapana Festival, Tuesday nights in summer. Local crafts, foods, dancing shows.

San Nicolas Day, 5 December.

Kingdom Day, 15 December.

Christmas Day, 25 December.

Boxing Day, 26 December.

FOOD: Aruba offers many choices when it comes to eating. Restaurants specializing in Indonesian, Chinese, American, French, Spanish, and Italian food come in most price ranges. All the big hotels have terrace coffee shops as well as formal dining rooms. There are many small "refresquerias," where light meals and snacks are served. Late nights and early mornings you might want to try some local snacks from the white mobile restaurant trucks that park on L. G. Smith Boulevard, near Wilhelmina Park. Some Aruban specialties include *cala* (bean fritters), *ayacas* (meat roll wrapped in leaves), and *pastechi* (meat turnovers). Another oft-served dish is *keshi yena,* a whole Edam cheese stuffed with a savory filling and then baked. Check the brochures for a complete listing.

HOTELS: Unfortunately, there aren't any moderately priced hotels on Aruba. They're mainly full-service resorts and start at about $80 for a double (without meals) in winter and go upward from there. The Tourist Board says it will provide information on guest houses and apartments upon request.

Here's a short list of some of the big hotels with all amenities (on the beach, pools, restaurants, tennis, et cetera).

To direct-dial Aruba, dial 011 (international access code), then 297 (Aruba's country code), and then 8 (area code) before the local number. Americana Aruba Hotel and Casino, 405 rooms; telephone: 24500 (Aruba); (800) 447-7462.

Aruba Caribbean Hotel and Casino, 220 rooms; telephone: 22250 (Aruba); (800) 223-1588.

Aruba Concorde Hotel and Casino, 490 rooms; telephone: 24466 (Aruba); New York State (800) 442-8436; all other states (800) 223-7944.

Aruba Holiday Inn and King International Casino, 390 rooms; telephone: 23600 (Aruba); (800) 238-8000.

Aruba Palm Beach Resort and Casino, 163 rooms; telephone: 23900 (Aruba); (800) 345-2782.

Best Western Manchebo Beach Resort, 72 rooms; telephone: 23444 (Aruba); (800) 223-1108.

Best Western Talk of the Town Resort, 62 rooms; telephone: 23380 (Aruba); (800) 223-1108.

Divi Aruba Beach Resort, 203 rooms; telephone: 23300 (Aruba); (800) 22-DORAL; food and lodging discounts for children aged 3 to 12.

Hyatt Regency Aruba, 340 rooms; telephone: 31234 (Aruba); (800) 233-1234; supervised activities for children and teens.

Sonesta Hotel, Beach Club and Casino, 275 rooms; telephone: 36000 (Aruba); (800) SONESTA.

For More Information

ARUBA Aruba Tourism Authority
L. G. Smith Boulevard 172
Oranjestad, Aruba
telephone: 23777

U.S.
Aruba Tourism Authority
199 14th Street N.E., Suite 1506
Atlanta, GA 30309
telephone: (404) 892-7822

Aruba Tourism Authority
2344 Salzedo Street
Miami, FL 33144
telephone: (305) 567-2720

Aruba Tourism Authority
1000 Harbor Boulevard
Weehawken, NJ 07087
telephone: (201) 330-0800fax: (201) 330-8757

CANADA
Aruba Tourism Authority
86 Bloor Street West, suite 204
Toronto, Ontario M5S 1M5
Canada
telephone: (416) 975-1950

Bahamas

AREA: 5,380 square miles, more than 700 islands covering a sea area of 90,000 square miles.

POPULATION: About 255,000.

CAPITAL CITY: Nassau, New Providence Island.

LANGUAGE: English.

RELIGION: Anglican, Roman Catholic, and many other sects.

GOVERNMENT: An independent member of the Commonwealth, with a two-house parliament and cabinet headed by the prime minister.

LOCATION: Islands scattered from off the coast of Florida nearly to Haiti.

GETTING THERE: By air or sea from Miami and other eastern cities.

CUSTOMS: Citizens of U.S., Canada, U.K., or colonies need only valid proof of citizenship for stays of less than three weeks. Other nationalities may need visas.

HEALTH: No special considerations; however, Out Islands may lack or have limited medical care.

CLOTHING: Informal tropical wear; no bathing suits in downtown areas, churches, restaurants, or casinos. In Nassau and Freeport, visitors may need evening wear at some night spots and casinos.

ELECTRICITY: 120 volts/60 cycles AC, as in the U.S.

TIME ZONE: Eastern standard time in winter; daylight saving time in summer.

MONEY: The Bahamian dollar (B$) is on a par with the U.S. dollar. Traveler's checks and major credit cards are honored widely, but check in advance on the Out Islands. Change is not readily available in many places, and you will need to cash travelers' checks at local banks.

TAX AND TIPS: Same as North America; some resorts add a service charge. When in doubt, ask.

GETTING AROUND: Motor scooters (you *must* wear a helmet), bicycles, and cars are available for rent in Nassau, Freeport, and on some of the larger islands. Roads are good and uncrowded on Grand Bahama. Remember, roads are left-hand-drive here. Taxis are plentiful in these cities. Most Out Islands have informal taxi services and boat rentals; some accommodations have bicycles available. Bahamahost guides offer tours in Nassau and Freeport. Touring Nassau in a horse-drawn surrey is a favorite with visitors to the island of New Providence.

Overview

The Bahamas are low, sandy sea islands scattered over some 90,000 square miles of the southwestern part of the Atlantic Ocean. The name came from the Spanish *baja mar*, or low sea, and indeed the extensive shallow waters of the Bahama Banks remain a remarkable feature of this island group. More than 700 islands, cays, islets, and sand spits make up the Commonwealth of the Bahamas. Many of these islands are uninhabited; others are small outposts where settlements are limited by the availability of fresh water. Still others such as Freeport and Nassau are bustling centers of international trade.

The sparse scrub vegetation and low profile of the Bahamas may disappoint the visitor expecting tropical forests; the highest point is only a few hundred feet above sea level. While these islands lack the lush vegetation and dramatic mass of the mountained Antilles, they more than make up for it in beaches and crystalline waters. So clear is the water that one can easily see ten to fifteen feet below the surface by moonlight.

The clarity of the water, as well as the moderate marine climate, is due mainly to the influence of the Gulf Stream, one of the great global currents that runs strongly north between the Bahamas and the coast of Florida. All of the normal sedimentation that would cloud the offshore waters is swept away by the stream, leaving the Bahamas with some of the world's clearest waters. Extensive coral reef formations—Andros has the world's second-largest barrier reef—wrecks, tropical fish, and moderate temperatures combine to make these islands notable dive attractions.

Some of the world's most extensive stretches of white sand are found here. In the shimmering warmth of a deserted Bahamian beach, the whole world seems to be an unending expanse of blue and white and blue again. The blurred distinction between land and sea becomes dizzying. The elu-

BAHAMA and
TURKS and CAICOS ISLANDS

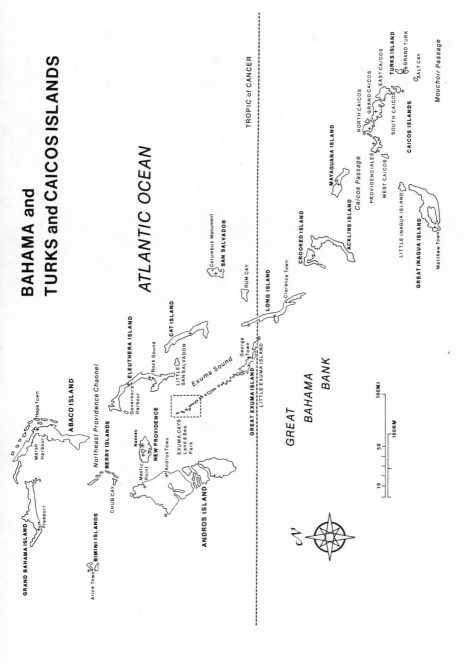

ATLANTIC OCEAN

TROPIC of CANCER

GRAND BAHAMA ISLAND

Freeport

Alice Town BIMINI ISLANDS

ABACO ISLAND

Marsh Harbour

Hope Town

Northeast Providence Channel

BERRY ISLANDS

CHUB CAY

Nassau

Mastic Point

NEW PROVIDENCE

Andros Town

ANDROS ISLAND

ELEUTHERA ISLAND

Governors Harbour

Rock Sound

CAT ISLAND

LITTLE SAN SALVADOR

EXUMA CAYS Land & Sea Park

Exuma Sound

George Town

GREAT EXUMA ISLAND

LITTLE EXUMA ISLAND

RUM CAY

Columbus Monument

SAN SALVADOR

LONG ISLAND

Clarence Town

GREAT BAHAMA BANK

CROOKED ISLAND

ACKLINS ISLAND

MAYAGUANA ISLAND

Caicos Passage

PROVIDENCIALES

WEST CAICOS

NORTH CAICOS

GRAND CAICOS

EAST CAICOS

SOUTH CAICOS

CAICOS ISLANDS

TURKS ISLAND

GRAND TURK

SALT CAY

Mouchoir Passage

LITTLE INAGUA ISLAND

GREAT INAGUA ISLAND

Matthew Town

N

10   50   100 MI

100 KM

Conch meat has provided protein for islanders since pre-Columbian times. A fisherman in Nassau Harbour, Bahamas, displays his catch. (Photo by Ellen Milan.)

sive concept of "islandness" seems to run on, forever lost in subtleties of color and the vague dampness that divides land and sea.

There are places here where anyone would love to sun, dream, bird-watch, or beachcomb. The shops, restaurants, and casinos of Nassau and Freeport offer contrasting diversions.

History

The Bahamas were originally settled by Lucayan Indians, who came north from the Caribbean sometime around the ninth century. These were the people who later met Columbus on the shores of what many believe is today's San Salvador.

The conquistadores, eager for easy gold, followed Columbus. It was during this time that the Lucayans were wiped out by enslavement, disease, and other hardships.

The next phase in Bahamian history involves the early English settlers, who came to the Bahamas seeking religious freedom. They settled on the island of Eleuthera, which they named for the Greek word for freedom. A prosperous agricultural economy developed as other English settlers joined them. The Bahamas became a Crown Colony in 1717.

At about the same time the convenient geography of the Bahamas attracted many well-known marauders. Ann Bonny, Captain Avery, and Captain Teach, more notoriously known as Blackbeard, were all familiar in the Bahamas at that time.

Woodes Rogers, the first royal governor of the Bahamas, an ex-privateer himself, was appointed to rid the islands of pirates. The motto of the islands, still part of the Great Seal of the Bahamas, became the Latin version of "Pirates Expelled, Commerce Restored." After a long English colonial period, the Bahamas became completely self-governing in 1967.

Things to See and Do

Nassau, New Providence

The capital of this island nation offers a great variety of things to do. This bustling metropolis has picturesque street markets and chic casinos. You can charter a boat or an airplane, play golf or tennis, or dive in clear waters. You may have to do it with lots of other people, but you can try almost anything here. Check the Tourist Board or your hotel for details. When strolling historic Nassau, you may want to include Parliament Square, Fort Charlotte, the Botanical Gardens, and, of course, the colorful Straw Market.

The popular People-to-People Programme matches visitors with Bahamian hosts for "a truly Bahamian experience." Contact the coordinator (326-5371), your hotel, or the Tourist Board to participate.

Freeport, Grand Bahama

This cosmopolitan city, with its casinos, resorts, restaurants, and international shopping, was built primarily as a tourist attraction. And, indeed, its close proximity to Florida has made it easy to visit. Grand Bahama Island offers great swimming, diving, and the relaxed resorts of West End. There are many beautiful natural areas once you get out of town. Try a nature walk at Rand Memorial Nature Centre or visit the Grand Bahama Museum to learn more about the early Lucayans. The Underwater Explorers Society (UNEXSO), across from the Lucayan Beach hotel, offers multiple marine attractions such as dive classes and excursions, a museum, movies, dolphin interactions, and a tank where divers can be photographed holding fiberglass sharks.

The Out Islands

Geographically the Out Islands include all the isles and cays (pronounced keys) out and away from the big-city bustle of Nassau and Freeport. Most of them are wonderful and unspoiled, more notable for beaches and sea than settlements. Many of the larger Out Islands have a well-rounded balance of facilities; others are delightfully primitive. If you decide to head out, get current information from the Tourist Board. Many of these islands are accessible by limited flights or only by boat; accommodations are often limited, and camping is illegal everywhere in the Bahamas. Advance planning is a good idea. The Out Islands Promotion Board may be reached at 800-OUT ISLANDS (800-688-4752). A few Out Islands:

The Abacos

A sailing center with a world-class reputation. Marsh Harbour, Hope Town, Green Turtle Cay, and Walker's Cay all have complete marinas with charter boats, guides, and dive centers. Pelican Cay National Park, an underwater preserve, even affords the opportunity for night dives. Shipbuilders on Man-o-War Cay still practice the adz-and-hatchet style of boat building that their ancestors used some 200 years ago. Great beaches, swimming, diving, and snorkeling; many shore facilities.

Andros

Bonefishing and scuba diving top the list of water sports on the largest island in the Bahamas. There is lots of fresh water on Andros, and it supports dense pine forests, mangroves, and great untouched tracts of natural growth. The forests of Andros are said to shelter mythical red-eyed elves called "chick charnies." Legend has it that these mischief makers hang from the trees by their tails. The second-largest barrier reef in the world runs some 100 miles along the east coast of Andros; shipwrecks add allure to natural undersea wonders.

Berry Islands

Thirty small islands ninety-two miles from Andros, mainly known for fishing and diving. Great Harbour Cay has a nine-hole golf course.

Bimini

Big game fishing, Hemingway, and Bimini are nearly synonymous in the Bahamas. Bimini, only sixty miles from Florida, is often a first stop for yachters and a weekend destination for Floridians. There are lots of attractions for Hemingway buffs: Blue Marlin Cottage was his home from 1931 to 1937; Angler Hotel Bay and Museum displays some of his work; other memorabilia is spread throughout Alice Town (don't overlook the bars). A small straw market, a "Fountain of Youth," where fresh water bubbles up in a mangrove lagoon, beaches, and diving complete the picture.

Eleuthera

This long, skinny island offers pink sand beaches, cliffs, coves, and perhaps the sweetest homegrown pineapples in the world. Swimming, diving, and sunning top the list here; hotels are scattered the length of the island, so there's no sense sharing with a crowd.

Exuma

Some 365 cays and islands make up the group called the Exumas. George Town, Great Exuma, is the capital; it's very relaxed although most of the island's activity takes place here. This is a big boating center for visitors and islanders alike. The annual Out Island Regatta held in mid-April is a weeklong festival of boat racing, local foods, and fun. Exuma National Land and Sea Park is a major dive attraction. Boat charters are available. The Tropic of Cancer runs through Little Exuma.

Inagua

This island supports one of the world's largest flamingo colonies. Up to 40,000 birds live on Lake Windsor, which is a wildlife preserve. You may arrange a tour by writing to The Bahamas National Trust, P.O. Box 4105, Nassau, New Providence, Bahamas, or call (809) 323-1317. Access is strictly monitored; advance arrangements are a must. Two simple guest houses service Inagua; both are in Matthew Town.

Long Island

Miles of white powdery beaches are the big attraction on this scenic island divided by the Tropic of Cancer. The Long Island Regatta is held at Salt Pond each May. Dive trips to more than thirty wrecks at nearby Conception Island leave from Stella Maris, a fairly complete resort with fifty rooms.

San Salvador

One of the main contenders for the first Columbus landing site, the island itself offers visitors tranquility and fantastic snorkeling and diving. The marina at Riding Rock Inn has twenty-four rooms and a dive shop; telephone: (809) 332-2694 or (800) 272-1492. There is also a 550-room Club Med overlooking Bonefish Bay. All Club Med activities are included in the weekly rate. Call (800) CLUB MED for details. Discovery Day on 12 October is the island's biggest celebration.

SHOPPING: Outside of Nassau and Freeport, shopping is limited largely to local basketry and T-shirts. Nassau and Freeport have a large selection of imported luxury goods such as Irish linens, British woolens, and perfumes. Be sure to do some gentle bargaining in the Straw Market and at Saturday markets on the Out Islands; buying more than one item is a good way to get a lower price.

FESTIVALS AND HOLIDAYS: Vary somewhat from island to island; annual regattas are listed under Out Islands. The Tourist Board, which is quick to respond, prints a complete calendar of events each year.

The 26 December Boxing Day Junkanoo Parade in Nassau is a high point, as is the New Year's Day Junkanoo in both Freeport and Nassau. (Junkanoo is a Christmas carnival with costume parades and partying.)

FOOD: Seafood specialties and Continental dishes in Nassau and Freeport. You might try conch fritters, conch salad, grouper fingers, and, of course, peas 'n' rice, the national dish. (Use some caution in ordering fish; see Health in Part 3 for more information on ciguatera fish poisoning.)

HOTELS: On New Providence, the main island, all standard chains are well represented, along with Club Med, a yoga retreat, and any number of guest houses. Other islands have a limited number of resorts. The Tourist Board will happily supply a complete list.

For More Information

Contact the nearest Bahamas Tourist Office.

U.S.

2957 Clairmont Road, Suite 150
Atlanta, GA 30329
telephone: (404) 633-1793
fax: (404) 633-1575

8600 West Bryn Mawr Avenue, Suite 820
Chicago, IL 60631

telephone: (312) 693-1500
fax: (312) 693-1114

World Trade Center, Suite 116
2050 Stemmons Freeway
P.O. Box 581408
Dallas, TX 75258-1408
telephone: (214) 742-1886
fax: (214) 741-4118

3450 Wilshire Boulevard, Suite 208
Los Angeles, CA 90010
telephone: (213) 385-0033
fax: (213) 383-3966

One Turnberry Place
19495 Biscayne Boulevard, Suite 809
Aventura, FL 33180
telephone: (305) 932-0051 or (305) 937-0585
fax: (305) 682-8758

150 East 52nd Street
28th Floor North
New York, NY 10022
telephone: (212) 758-2777
fax: (212) 758-6531

CANADA

121 Bloor Street East, Suite 1101
Toronto, Ontario M4W 3M5
Canada
telephone: (416) 968-2999 or (800) 667-3777
fax (Canada only): (416) 968-6711

Barbados

AREA: 166 square miles; 21 miles long, 14 miles wide.

POPULATION: Approximately 260,000.

CAPITAL CITY: Bridgetown.

LANGUAGE: English.

RELIGION: Anglican.

GOVERNMENT: Parliamentary democracy.

LOCATION: Most easterly island of the Caribbean, Barbados sits off by itself, nearly 100 miles east of St. Vincent.

GETTING THERE: A number of scheduled airlines fly into Barbados.

CUSTOMS: U.S. and Canadian citizens need only proof of citizenship and either return or ongoing tickets for stays of less than six months; all other nationalities need passports. Visitors may be asked to show evidence of having sufficient funds for their stay.

HEALTH: No special considerations.

CLOTHING: Casual tropical wear; some hotels offer formal dining; remember to restrict beachwear to pool and shore; street clothes (this means at least knee-length shorts) are necessary in town.

ELECTRICITY: 100 volts/50 cycles AC.

TIME ZONE: Atlantic standard time, one hour ahead of eastern standard time.

MONEY: Barbados dollar; U.S. dollars and credit cards are widely accepted.

TAX AND TIPS: 5 percent government hotel tax and airport tax; 10 percent service charge at most establishments.

GETTING AROUND: Taxicabs are plentiful and have set fares. There is also a good bus system. Several local touring companies offer lots of different excursions; some include both land and sea views of Barbados. Visitors may rent bikes, motor scooters, or cars from a number of agencies. Barbados has more than 800 miles of roads, all of which are left-hand-drive; a temporary license (you need a valid U.S. driver's license) is easily obtained from your car rental company or a police station for BD $10.

Overview

Barbados is the most densely populated island in the West Indies. It is also the most civilized, in the opinion of many. Relatively flat—central Mt. Hillaby is the highest point at 1,104 feet—Barbados is green with fields of sugarcane. Indeed, its prosperity remains based on sugar and, of course, tourism.

Rather early in its history, Barbados earned the nickname of "Little England," and the popularity of afternoon tea and cricket bear witness to strong British traditions. No other Caribbean island can offer a capital city (Bridgetown) with Trafalgar Square, a fountain, and a statue of Lord Nelson. Bridgetown also offers the Caribbean's cleanest commercial harbor and safest downtown shopping district.

In addition to maintaining the delights of civilization, Barbados enjoys the benefits and beauty of natural areas. The protected west coast is lined with classic pink and white sand beaches. The rugged Atlantic shore is steadily pounded by rollers that have come the distance. Ecological awareness is strong on Barbados, and the National Trust monitors the use of protected areas like Welchman Hall Gully. The island has several botanical gardens with exotic species, as well as many parks and gardens.

Barbados is a diverse island nation full of citizens satisfied with themselves and their country and willing to share graciously with visitors. This island is one of the best choices for first-time visitors to the Caribbean or for those uncomfortable with the on's and off's of developing nations. Barbados is stable and safe as well as beautiful.

History

Amerindians inhabited the island when a Portuguese navigator first charted it in 1536. Unlike most of the other Caribbean islands, Barbados eluded Columbus because of its eastern position. Although the Portuguese named the island, they were intent upon Brazil and never even bothered to claim Los Barbados, the Bearded Ones. Presumably the name was sparked by the island's abundant ficus trees, which have hairy aerial roots that look like beards.

Apparently, the Amerindians had abandoned Barbados by the early 1600s. When the first English settlers arrived in February 1627, the island was uninhabited. They called their settlement Jamestown (now Holetown). This began the uninterrupted British tradition in Barbados. The island's parliament, established in 1639, is one of the oldest in the Americas. In addition to having only one colonizer, Barbados is the only island in the Caribbean that has always had an elected assembly.

This is not to say that the island avoided the pitfalls of slavery and the plantocracy that were so essential to the prosperity of the sugar era. Although the slaves were freed in 1834, the plantation owners retained political control of Barbados. White political dominance was not broken until universal suffrage was achieved in 1951.

Barbados became completely independent from Britain on 30 November 1966. Its long parliamentary history paved the way for today's stable democratic government; modern Barbados is often pointed out as a role model for other emerging island nations.

Things to See and Do

Barbados is organized; a great deal is available in a small space. The island is divided into eleven parishes, and attractions and diversions are listed accordingly. Pick up the Tourist Board's informative pamphlets for more specifics. You'll probably want to spend a day in historic Bridgetown, the capital, which was founded in 1628. There are many historic public buildings, a bustling harbor, duty-free shopping, and Trafalgar Square.

Barbados Museum

About 1¼ miles from Bridgetown, the museum, housed in a former British military prison, contains glassware, furniture, books, and more that chronicle the history of the island.

Chalky Mount Potteries

In the Scotland District of St. Andrews Parish, families of potters still make their wares much as their ancestors have for some 300 years. Items are for sale and include bowls, jugs, pots, and unique water pitchers called "monkeys." The view from the village is spectacular.

Flower Forest

At Richmond plantation, St. Joseph; open daily from 9 A.M. Ruins of a sugar plantation among gardens. This is a good place to see exotic fruit trees (fruit and drinks are sold, as well). Spectacular views of surrounding countryside; wild monkeys; local handicrafts.

Farley Hill National Park

Off Highway 1 in St. Peter, the park was once the property of a famous British planter who often entertained royalty in this 1880s Georgian mansion. The grounds and house, before it was destroyed by fire in 1965, were used in the movie *Island in the Sun*. The gardens offer views and delightful picnic areas.

Gun Hill

Small signal fort built by an early regiment; on a cliff overlooking the valley of St. George. Restored by the National Trust, the station houses a collection of military memorabilia.

Harrison's Cave

Near Welchman Hall Gully in St. Thomas Parish. Visitors ride a special tram on a mile-long excursion that showcases indirectly lit stalactites and stalagmites and underground pools. Open every day. Book in advance.

Welchman's Hall Gully

Maintained by the National Trust, this lush ravine with a profusion of spice trees, palms, and ferns is a good place to cool off in tropical splendor or to watch for wild monkeys.

SHOPPING: Broad Street in Bridgetown is the center of the shopping district, where imports such as crystal, cameras, perfume, and china are readily available. Local products include Mount Gay rum, pottery, baskets, custom-made clothing, jewelry, and artwork. Try Pelican Village near the Deep Water Harbour for local crafts; this newly developed and landscaped area along Princess Alice Highway houses the small shops of many island artisans.

FESTIVALS AND HOLIDAYS

New Year's Day, 1 January.

Holetown Festival, February. Three-day-long street festival, with parades, song, dance, markets, and sports, commemorating the landing of the first permanent settlers in 1627.

Good Friday, Easter Monday (dates vary).

Whit Monday, May.

Crop-Over Festival, last two weeks in July. Cultural festival that origi-
nated as a celebration at the end of the sugarcane festival.

Kadooment Day, first Monday in August. Giant costume parade.

National Festival of Creative Arts, October and November.

Independence Day, 30 November.

Christmas Day, 25 December.

Boxing Day, 26 December.

FOOD: Specialties include fried flying fish, sea eggs (sea urchins generally
steamed and then fried with onion and lime juice), pepper pot, breadfruit,
yam pie, *roti,* and pudding and souse. Be adventurous. You may want to
buy some local confections or preserves to take home. Specialties include
coconut sugar cake, tamarind balls, shaddock rind, and guava cheese. Try
the supermarkets and Women's Self Help, opposite Nelson's statue in
Bridgetown. Street vendors also offer a variety of wares.

HOTELS: Hotels, guest houses, apartments, and cottages are plentiful on
Barbados. Prices start at less than U.S. $50 a day for a double room in a
simple guest house and run to well over U.S. $350 a day for a double in
a resort hotel. If you're after a quiet vacation, consider a more remote site
on the east coast where Atlantic rollers are more prominent than people.

For More Information

Contact the very helpful Barbados Board of Tourism office nearest you.

BARBADOS

Box 242, Harbour Road
Bridgetown, Barbados, W.I.
telephone: (809) 427-2623 or (800) 744-6244
fax: (809) 426-4080

U.S.

800 Second Avenue
New York, NY 10017
telephone: (212) 986-6516/6518 or (800) 221-9831
fax: (212) 573-9850

3440 Wilshire Boulevard, Suite 1215
Los Angeles, CA 90010
telephone: (213) 380-2198/2199
fax: (213) 384-2763

CANADA
Barbados Tourism Authority
2160 Yonge Street, Suite 1800
North York, Ontario M2N 6L9
Canada
telephone: (416) 512-6569/6570/6571 or (800) 268-9122
fax: (416) 512-6581

ENGLAND
263 Tottenham Court Road
London W1P 9AA, England
telephone: (44) 71-636-9448/9449
fax: (44) 71-637-1496
telex: 051-262081

GERMANY
Staatliches Fremdenverkehrsamt Barbados
Neue Mainzer Strasse 22
D-60311 Frankfurt/Main, Germany
telephone: (49) 69-23-23-66
fax: (49) 69-23-00-77

Bonaire

AREA: 122 square miles; 24 miles long, 3 to 7 miles wide.

POPULATION: Approximately 12,000.

CAPITAL CITY: Kralendijk.

LANGUAGE: Papiamento and Dutch; English and Spanish widely
spoken.

RELIGION: Varied, mainly Christian.

GOVERNMENT: Member of the Netherlands Antilles, a coequal part
of the Kingdom of the Netherlands; an elected council governs local affairs.

LOCATION: 50 miles north of Venezuela, 30 miles east of Curaçao, 86 miles east of Aruba.

GETTING THERE: Daily flights on American Airlines through several U.S. gateways via Curaçao or Aruba. ALM through Miami and Atlanta, nonstop twice weekly. ALM Antillean Airlines may be called toll free from the U.S. at (800) 327-7230 (twenty-four hours). Air Aruba may be reached at (800) 827-8221. Weekly boat from Curaçao (*Isidel III*). Dive packages with air charters are often available in winter season.

CUSTOMS: Transit visitors from U.S. and Canada need only proof of citizenship; passports are a good idea for longer visits. Either ongoing tickets or return tickets and confirmed hotel reservations required. Non-U.S. citizens need passports.

HEALTH: No special considerations. All water is desalinated and pure.

CLOTHING: Informal tropical wear (bathing suits, cover-ups, shorts) for day; casual evening wear for casinos and dining out (jackets optional for men).

ELECTRICITY: 127/220 volts/50 cycles AC.

TIME ZONE: Atlantic standard time year-round.

MONEY: Netherlands Antilles florin or guilder, written NAF. U.S. $1 is about NAF. $1.77. Credit cards may be subject to limitations; check with your hotel in advance. U.S. dollars and traveler's checks accepted in most places.

TAX AND TIPS: Airport tax NAF. $10, interisland tax NAF. $5. Bank hours: 8:30 A.M. until noon and 2:00 P.M. to 4:00 P.M. Monday through Friday. Service charges—10 to 15 percent added to hotel and restaurant bills; no extra tips necessary except for special service. Airport porters expect NAF. $1 per bag (about U.S. $.55).

GETTING AROUND: *Taxis* are unmetered with fixed government rates; fare from airport to hotels is about U.S. $10 (10 percent tip is standard). Rates increase at sundown, after 8 P.M., and again after midnight. Taxis often do sight-seeing tours.

Car Rentals: Bonaire has well-maintained roads with right-hand-drive. U.S. and Canadian driver's licenses are valid on the island. Cars rent for about U.S. $29 to $60 a day. Car rental can be arranged directly or through your hotel when you make reservations. Bon Car, Avis, Dollar Rent a Car, and Budget all have offices on Bonaire.

Bus Tours: Bonaire Sightseeing (telephone: 8300, ext. 212), Flamingo Tours (telephone: 8310), or Archie Tours (telephone: 8630).

These guided tours usually take two hours, and cost U.S. $13 per person; your choice of the northern route (not including the national park) or a southern one. Longer tours are also available.

Jeep Tours: Bonaire Safari Tours at Habitat (telephone: 8290) has air-conditioned, four-wheel-drive vehicles that go to otherwise inaccessible sites—caves, grottoes, and remote areas of the national park.

Boat Trips: Flamingo Beach and Bonaire Beach have sunset cruises. Glass-bottom boat rides offered by Bonaire Scuba Center. Water taxis to islet Klein Bonaire (Habitat, Dive Bonaire, and Bonaire Scuba Center). Other trips and boat excursions, including picnics, may be arranged through Bonaire Scuba Center and Vistamar Bonaire.

Overview

Bonaire is small, unspoiled, and blessed with natural diversity. Bonaire's flatlands have dunes, mangroves, salinas, and the salt pans that an international salt company happily shares with flamingos. Other parts of the island have giant cacti, divi-divi trees, and ancient Indian caves. Bonaire is ringed with beautiful beaches, crystal waters, and unique reef formations, which make it a diver's paradise. Excellent support facilities, including a decompression chamber, add to its allure. Bonaire is listed as one of the world's top three dive destinations.

Bonaire's natural world is dominated by a great variety of birds. Along with one of the world's largest flocks of flamingos, Bonaire shelters some 130 species; the Tourist Board will send you a checklist on request. Many species can be seen in the 15,000-acre Washington/Slagbaai National Park. Within the park, Bonaire's highest peak, Mount Brandaris at 746 feet, is the dominant feature. At the foot of the mountain, colorful parroquets and pigeons congregate around a watering spot. Careful observers may glimpse an iguana, as well.

History

When Amerigo Vespucci sighted the island in 1499, he named it after the Arawak word *bo-nah* or "low country." The peaceful Arawaks had inhabited Bonaire for centuries.

The first attempts at colonization were made by Spain between 1527 and 1633. The Dutch claimed Bonaire in 1634, however, and established a military stronghold. The Dutch West India Company developed salt production; livestock breeding and corn planting started in 1639. African slaves were imported to work the salt pans when the salt industry became the economic mainstay. Bonaire's next 160 years were spent under the management of the Dutch West India Company.

The early 1800s were tumultuous throughout the Caribbean. Bonaire was briefly occupied by the British and suffered raids from both French and British pirates. In 1816, the Dutch regained control and set up government plantations where slaves tended commercial crops like Brazil wood, aloes, and cochenille. When slavery was abolished in 1863, the plantations became unprofitable and the island was divided up and sold.

Many people left Bonaire to find work during the next ninety years or so of recession. It wasn't until well into the 1950s that tourists discovered Bonaire and its economy began to recover. Since then, Bonaire has made important environmental strides by establishing an extensive marine park and a 15,000-acre national park.

Things to See and Do

Sports

Naturally water sports top the list with scuba diving, snorkeling, and windsurfing as the top three. The island hosts several week-long underwater photo and video festivals. Visitors also have the opportunity to enjoy mountain biking, eco-hiking, sailing, parasailing, sea kayaking, deep sea fishing, horseback riding, and tennis.

Kralendijk

Bonaire's capital (the name translates "coral reef" or "dike") is a picturesque waterfront town worth exploring. Bright colors splash the Dutch colonial facades of quaint shops. The fish market is designed like a mini Greek temple, and the old fort echoes the past.

Natural Areas

Bonaire's natural assets are its big attraction. The island has three distinct land zones. The north is greener and hillier than the rest of the island. The middle section resembles parts of the U.S. southwest. The flat southland is mainly mangroves, dunes, and salt works.

Goto Meer

In the northwest, right outside the entrance to the national park, is an inland lake that was once connected to the sea. It is now a flamingo sanctuary. Bonaire is home to some 10,000 flamingos that have learned to share the salt pans, one of their habitats, with the Antilles Salt Company.

Washington/Slagbaai National Park

The park takes up the entire northwestern section of Bonaire. Open to visitors from 8 A.M. to 5 P.M. every day except major holidays; admission is U.S. $3 per person at the gate. Absolutely no camping, hunting, or fishing allowed. Bring your own food and drink; there are no concessions. Most people like to include swimming or snorkeling in a day's tour; some of the island's best beaches are within the park. These 15,000 protected acres showcase Bonaire's natural wonders—unique arid terrain, salinas, caverns, and secluded beaches. Along with the showy flamingo, some 135 other species of birds make use of this area. Early mornings and late afternoons are best for bird-watching. Poosdi Mangel and Bronswinkel Wekk, at the foot of Mount Brandaris, are two popular watering holes good for bird-watching. Salina Bartol and Salina Slagbaai are also good places to watch birds.

Bonaire's seven lizard species, including iguanas, can also be seen in the park. Fortunately, the ruggedness of the park roads superimposes a pace suitable to seeing flora and fauna. Visitors have a choice of two routes—a fifteen-mile "short" route (follow the green arrows) and a twenty-two-mile "long" route (marked by yellow arrows). Maps and guidebooks are sold at the entrance gates.

There are a number of beaches for picnicking and cooling off. There's good snorkeling at Playa Funchi. The Onima Indian Caves are decorated with red pre-Columbian symbols. The source of this red dye may have been the Brozia tree, with its twisted trunk, which still grows in the area.

Bonaire Marine Park

This park includes the entire coastline of Bonaire and the neighboring islet of Klein Bonaire from the high-water mark down to 200 feet (60 meters). All marine life is completely protected here; no collecting of fish, shells, or corals, dead or alive.

Bonaire is the peak of a submerged mountain formed by volcanic eruptions that occurred beneath the sea some 70 million years ago; hence, there are deep, sloping reefs very close to shore, with many dive sites right off the beach. The narrow reef terrace slopes seaward, dropping off around thirty-three feet. After this, the slope varies from 30 degrees to 90 degrees down to about 100 to 200 feet. Extensive fringing reefs of elkhorn and staghorn corals are found in the shallow water.

Water temperatures around Bonaire remain near 80°F year-round, to the delight of both snorkelers and scuba divers. Every visitor will have favorite coves and dive sites (more than forty are mapped), so take some time to find yours. Pink Beach is generally considered one of the finest bits of sand on Bonaire.

Dive Centers

Many of Bonaire's dive centers either offer accommodations or are associated with hotels. They include:

BONAIRE SCUBA CENTER

P.O. Box 200
Bonaire, N.A.
telephone: (011) 599-7-5736
fax: (011) 599-7-8846
Located at the Black Durgon Inn

DIVE INN

Kaya C.E.B. Hellmund 27
Bonaire N.A.
telephone: (011) 599-7-8781
fax: (011) 599-7-8513
Locations at Sunset Inn, Sunset Beach Hotel, and Sunset Oceanfront Apartments

GREAT ADVENTURES

P.O. Box 312
Kralendijk, Bonaire, N.A.
telephone: (011) 599-7-7500
fax: (011) 599-7-7507

HABITAT DIVE CENTERS

P.O. Box 88
Bonaire, N.A.
telephone: (011) 599-7-8290
fax: (011) 599-7-8240
Located at Captain Don's Habitat

NIGHTLIFE: Planned nightlife on Bonaire centers around hotel evenings with local bands, folk dancers, or slide shows. The Bonaire Beach Hotel has a casino and the Flamingo Beach Hotel has a game room billed as "the world's first barefoot casino."

SHOPPING: Shops offer a variety of goods, from luxury imports to handicrafts. Open 8 A.M. to noon and 2 to 6 P.M. Monday through Saturday.

Fundashon Arte i Industria Bonairiano in Kralendijk runs a nonprofit organization to train young people in local crafts.

FESTIVALS AND HOLIDAYS

Masquerade, January. Street dancing.

Carnival festivities, February.

Carnival parade, Queen Juliana's Birthday and Ricon's Day, April.

Good Friday, Easter (dates vary).

Labor Day, May.

Ascension Day, May.

St. John's, St. Peter's, and St. Paul's Day, and International Regatta, October.

St. Nicholas parade, Aquinaldo Song Festivities, December.

Kingdom Day, 15 December.

FOOD: Naturally, seafood heads the list; pickled conch is a specialty. International cuisine is available. You might want to try Bistro Des Amis for smoked eel mousse or sweet red pepper soup (entrées range from U.S. $10 to $22) and the Zeezicht Bar Restaurant on the waterfront for seafood specialties (complete dinners U.S $10 to $22). Den Laman Aquarium Bar and Restaurant houses a 9,000-gallon saltwater aquarium and offers a variety of dishes (ask to see if they have removed turtle from the menu); entrées U.S. $10 to $21. Several hotels have dining rooms, and there are a number of small bars and restaurants. Reservations are recommended almost everywhere.

HOTELS: Most of Bonaire's major accommodations are connected with the dive centers listed under Things to See and Do. Remember, camping is not allowed on this island.

For more information, contact:

Bonaire Tourist Office
10 Rockefeller Plaza, Suite 900
New York, NY 10022
telephone: (212) 956-5911 or (800) 826-6247

British Virgin Islands

AREA: 59 square miles (36 islands and islets).

POPULATION: Approximately 17,000.

CAPITAL CITY: Road Town, Tortola (population: 2,260).

LANGUAGE: English.

RELIGION: Anglican.

GOVERNMENT: British dependency; appointed governor with local officials.

GETTING THERE: Several airlines fly into Tortola from Caribbean gateway cities; visitors also may fly on short shuttles or take ferryboats from the U.S.V.I. (St. Thomas and St. John are close by.)

CUSTOMS: U.S and Canadian visitors need proof of citizenship; valid passports for all other nationalities. All visitors must have either return or ongoing tickets. Backpacking is actively discouraged.

HEALTH: No special considerations. Facilities are scarce—a small hospital on Tortola, a clinic on Virgin Gorda, and nurses only on the other major islands.

CLOTHING: Informal tropical wear. No bare chests or midriffs in commercial or residential areas. Nudity is an offense punishable by law.

ELECTRICITY: 110 volts/60 cycles AC, as in the U.S.

TIME ZONE: One hour ahead of eastern standard time.

MONEY: U.S. currency; check in advance about credit cards.

TAX AND TIPS: Departure tax U.S. $5 per person by air, $4 per person by sea; 7 percent hotel tax.

GETTING AROUND: Taxis provide the only public transport. Cars, mopeds, and bicycles are available for rent; walking is safe and pleasant. Interisland ferries and small planes (Air BVI) run between Tortola, Virgin Gorda, and Anegada. A number of boats run day charters to nearby isles, including Norman Island and Jost Van Dyke.

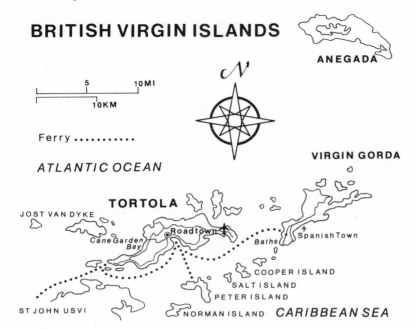

BRITISH VIRGIN ISLANDS

ANEGADA

5   10MI
10KM

Ferry ....

ATLANTIC OCEAN

VIRGIN GORDA

TORTOLA

JOST VAN DYKE

Cane Garden Bay
Roadtown

Baths   Spanish Town

COOPER ISLAND
SALT ISLAND
PETER ISLAND

ST JOHN USVI   NORMAN ISLAND   CARIBBEAN SEA

Overview

This group of islands is as distinctive as their names—Tortola, Anegada, Virgin Gorda, Jost Van Dyke, Norman Island, Fallen Jerusalem, Necker Island, and Great Dog, to name a few. More than fifty isles and islets, many uninhabited, make up the British Virgin Islands. All are surrounded by notably clear waters and most have striking white sand beaches. The British Virgins are the old stomping grounds of privateers and buccaneers, as is testified to by names like Sir Francis Drake Channel. Sometimes at twilight you can almost visualize deep bays and anchorages sheltering old square-riggers, and secluded coves with cooking fires flickering on the shore. Many of these islands haven't changed much; sun and sea remain their trademarks.

History

When Columbus supposedly anchored off Virgin Gorda in 1493, he likened the many nearby islands and cays to the legendary St. Ursula and her 11,000 virgins.

Long a favorite haunt of seafarers, from Sir Francis Drake to Blackbeard, the islands were first settled by the Dutch in the seventeenth century. They were later raided by the Spanish and the British.

In 1872, the British Virgin Islands became a separate colony of Britain under the Leeward Islands Administration. Today, these politically stable islands remain a British colony with their own elected chief minister and government.

Things to See and Do

Natural attractions—secluded beaches and clear waters—highlight the islands of the BVI. All thirty-six islands and scattered islets have extraordinary stretches of white coral sand, perfect for sunbathing and shell collecting. The protected offshore waters offer delightful swimming, snorkeling, and diving. The configuration of this group of scattered isles, the steady trade winds, and the safe anchorages have made the BVI a major boating center; many charter boat companies are located here. A relaxed atmosphere and friendly people add to the islands' charms.

Tortola

This is the main island in the group, and the capital of Road Town offers the little shopping available. Most visitors with an urge to shop take the boat to St. Thomas for a day. The J. R. O'Neal Botanic Gardens, right in Road Town, is a cool, peaceful getaway. This four-acre garden includes an interesting collection of plants, both indigenous and exotic. Sage Mountain National Park has well-marked trails that lead to the peak at 1,716 feet. Sage Mountain, with its remnants of primeval rain forest, orchids, ferns, and cool quiet, also has a great view. Beaches are plentiful on Tortola; try Cane Garden Bay for snorkeling, and Beef Island beach near the airport for shell collecting.

Norman Island

It's only a short sail from Tortola to this rustic cay with good snorkeling. You can swim or dinghy into well-known sea caves. Some say this is the island that inspired Stevenson's *Treasure Island* (treasure really was found here!). Bring a picnic; there are no facilities onshore.

Salt Island

Two evaporating salt ponds are still worked here. Most visitors come to dive the Wreck of the Rhone Marine Park off the southwestern coast. The *Rhone*, a royal mail steamer that sank in the hurricane of 1867 with 125 people aboard, has become a major dive site in the area. Part of the wreck is in only about thirty feet of clear water, so even surface snorkelers can get a glimpse. The wreck, which was featured in the film *The Deep,* and the surrounding area, is a BVI National Park.

Virgin Gorda

The mountainous northern section of this peaceful isle, topped by Gorda Peak at 1,370 feet, part of Gorda Peak National Park, is marked by trails and abundant orchids. The major blooming season coincides with December rains. The southern section of Virgin Gorda is flat, low, and strewn with giant boulders; it is part of the Baths protected area. The Baths, with its natural granite sculpture, grottos, pools, and coral beaches, is the most heavily visited tourist area in the BVI, but it is still worth a visit. This area is crisscrossed by a network of interesting trails. Buy a copy of the informative *North Sound, A Guide for Yachtsmen and Explorers* for detailed trail maps and interpretive material. Proceeds help the British Virgin Islands National Trust maintain protected areas.

Anegada

This is the only coral island in the BVI. Its low, reef-ringed profile has been (and still is) the demise of many vessels. The island is all beach and water—a great getaway for divers, beachcombers, and sunbathers.

SHOPPING: A few local handicrafts—some lovely traditional baskets are still woven here—and a few imports. Visitors don't come to the BVI to shop; most come because they don't want to shop.

FESTIVALS AND HOLIDAYS
New Year's Day, 1 January.
Commonwealth Day, March.
Easter Festival on Virgin Gorda (date varies).
Easter Monday (date varies).
Whit Monday, May.
Sovereign's Birthday, June.
Territory Day, July.
BVI Festival on Tortola, August.
St. Ursula's Day, October.
Birthday of heir to the throne, November.
Christmas Day, 25 December.
Boxing Day, 26 December.

FOOD: Seafood and Caribbean specialties. Try Road Town's Saturday morning market for local fruits and vegetables.

Hotels

These islands offer a good variety of accommodations, from the deluxe Little Dix on Virgin Gorda to Tula's Campground on Jost Van Dyke. The British Virgin Islands Tourist Board publishes a complete list and is quick to respond to inquiries. The pamphlet "Intimate Inns and Villas" lists the BVI's small hotels. Call (800) 835-8530 for the latest information from the Tourist Board.

For More Information

Contact the nearest British Virgin Islands Tourist Board office.

BVI

P.O. Box 134
Road Town, Tortola
British Virgin Islands
telephone: (809) 494-3134
fax: (809) 494-3866

U.S.

BVI Press Office (North America)
767 Fifth Avenue
New York, NY 10153
telephone: (212) 705-1264
fax: (212) 705-1345

370 Lexington Avenue
New York, NY 10017
telephone: (212) 696-0400 or (800) 835-8530
fax: (212) 949-8254

1686 Union Street
San Francisco, CA 94123
telephone: (415) 775-0344 or (800) 835-8530
fax: (415) 775-2554

ENGLAND

FCB Travel/Marketing
110 St. Martin's Lane

London WC2N 4DY, England
telephone: 44-71-240-4259
fax: 44-71-240-4270

GERMANY
Sophienstrasse 4, D-65189
Wiesbaden, Germany
telephone: 49-611-300262
fax: 49-611-300766

Cayman Islands

AREA: 100 square miles (three islands).

POPULATION: About 31,200.

CAPITAL CITY: George Town, Grand Cayman.

LANGUAGE: English.

RELIGION: Varied.

GOVERNMENT: Crown Colony of Great Britain.

LOCATION: 150 miles northwest of Jamaica, 500 miles south of Miami.

GETTING THERE: Cayman Airways flies nonstop from both Miami and Houston.

CUSTOMS: U.S. citizens need only proof of citizenship and either a return or an ongoing ticket.

HEALTH: No special considerations; fully staffed hospital on Grand Cayman.

CLOTHING: Casual tropical wear; sports jackets for men optional for dinner; women will want dressy cottons for hotel dining.

ELECTRICITY: 110 volts/60 cycles AC, as in the U.S.

TIME ZONE: Eastern standard time year-round.

MONEY: Cayman Islands dollar (CD) = U.S. $1.25; Canadian and U.S. currencies both readily accepted throughout the Caymans. Check in advance about credit cards.

TAX AND TIPS: 6 percent room tax; most places add 15 percent service charge; departure tax $8 CD.

GETTING AROUND: Taxis, cars, and bicycles can be rented. Temporary driver's license available at police station for a small fee; you'll need to show your valid U.S. driver's license. Most car rental agencies require advance reservations—between six and thirty-six hours before pickup. Check Bob Soto's and Red Sail Sports for boat trips.

Overview

Three sandy islands—Grand Cayman, Cayman Brac, and Little Cayman—make up this grouping. Grand Cayman, the main island, is about twenty-two miles long and eight miles wide; its highest point is only sixty feet above sea level. Most of the population resides here. Little Cayman lies about eighty miles east-northeast of Grand Cayman and has only a few permanent residents. Cayman Brac (from the Scottish word for bluff, as in cliff) rises nearly one hundred forty feet above sea level and is home to about 2,000 residents.

The islands are notable for spectacular white sands, crystal waters, offshore banking, and quiet. Tourism is the major industry, and some 20,000 scuba divers visit the islands each year.

History

The islands were sighted by accident by Columbus on his fourth voyage in 1503; they were not settled until the following century. Columbus called them Las Tortugas—the turtles—because so many were in the vicinity. The name didn't stick, however, and today's islands bear another animal's name—the crocodiles.

Grand Cayman was first settled in 1655 when a group of British army deserters from Jamaica made rapid career changes. In the Treaty of Madrid in 1670, Spain ceded the Caymans to Britain. The islands continued to be colonized by British from Jamaica. Since the land was unsuitable for the large plantations that marked life on other islands for the next few centuries, slavery was nearly nonexistent. Piracy, however, did have its heyday.

The Caymans were a dependency of Jamaica until 1959. In 1962 they became a separate British Crown Colony.

Things to See and Do

The pleasures of the Caymans center around shore and sea. Diving, snorkeling, and sportfishing are the main draws.

Bat Caves

For intrepid (nonsqueamish) bat and cave fans. On Grand Cayman; get local directions. A visit requires climbing down a ten-foot cliff and crawling in on hands and knees. You may rather take a twilight stroll and watch for the little mammalian crescents to wing by.

Queen Elizabeth II Botanic Park

A mile-long nature trail takes visitors by more than two hundred labeled plants, including orchids and mahogany and ironwood trees. You may catch a glimpse of banahaquits, parrots, tree frogs, and the endangered Grand Cayman blue iguana.

Pirate Caves

At Bodden Town, the island's first capital, these are said to be the haunts of Sir Henry Morgan and Blackbeard; small admission charge.

Turtle Farm

This is touted as a tourist attraction—the world's only commercial turtle nursery. Some people feel that rearing for slaughter a highly endangered species is a somewhat misdirected use of resources. If you've never seen these magnificent creatures close up, do make a visit, but don't buy any turtle souvenirs or tortoise shell products; they will be confiscated when you pass through U.S. customs. The U.S. Endangered Species Act makes it illegal to import or possess any product derived from an endangered species.

DIVING AND SNORKELING: There are 300 wrecks in nearby waters, which are clear and full of colorful fish and corals. Many dive sites are right offshore. The wreck of the *Balboa* is only twenty yards off George Town dock. All hotels rent masks and snorkels (U.S. $4 to $7 a day); if you're an avid diver, you'll want to bring your own. Dive packages, which include accommodations, equipment rental, et cetera, are the best deal for serious divers; they cost about U.S. $100 per day per person, depending on the season. A single two-tank dive costs about U.S. $35. See Part 4, Exploring, for a list of Caymans' dive operators.

SHOPPING: Duty-free shops in George Town are stocked with British woolens, linens, Scottish plaids, Irish crystal, French perfumes, silver, and other luxury imports. Try the Cayman Craft Market for locally made leather and straw goods. In Bodden Town, try Eastern Queen for handicrafts. Stamps are a collector's item; the main post office is on Edward Street, George Town. Remember that turtle products cannot be taken into the U.S.

FESTIVALS AND HOLIDAYS: Standard U.S. and British holidays, plus the annual Pirate's Week in late October, when the entire island dresses up and celebrates its history. The Annual Agricultural Show is held on Ash Wednesday.

FOOD: Seafood such as lobster and conch; the local specialty breadfruit puffs complements American and Continental cuisine.

HOTELS: World-famous Seven Mile Beach on Grand Cayman is dotted with mostly expensive hotels, condominiums, and villas. Off-season double occupancy of a one-bedroom villa or condominium costs about U.S. $100 a day. Moderately priced accommodations include Royal Palms, Le Club Cayman, Seagull, and Victoria House. Across the road from the beach, Cayman Islander provides an inexpensive option.

Several scuba centers around the island also offer moderately priced lodgings (a package is your best bet); these include the simple Cayman Diving Lodge on the East End, South Cove Resort of George Town, and Spanish Cove Resort on the remote North Shore (where meals are included).

Little Cayman has Little Le Club, a moderately priced, twelve-room fish camp; Pirates Point, a tiny dive center with eight gazebo rooms at a moderate price; and Southwestern Cross Club, an expensive fishing and diving center that can house twenty-four guests.

Cayman Brac has two well-run, moderately priced choices: Buccaneer's Inn, with thirty-nine rooms and a pool (rates include meals); and Divi Tiara Beach Hotel, (packages, tennis, and pool, on the beach).

For More Information

Contact the nearest Cayman Islands Department of Tourism.

U.S.
Two Memorial City Plaza
820 Gessner, Suite 170
Houston, TX 77024
telephone: (713) 461-1317

3440 Wilshire Boulevard, Suite 1202
Los Angeles, CA 90010
telephone: (213) 738-1968

420 Lexington Avenue, Suite 2733
New York, NY 10170
telephone: (212) 682-5582
fax: (212) 986-5123

6100 Blue Lagoon Drive, Suite 150
Miami, FL 33126
telephone: (305) 226-2300
fax: (305) 267-2930

ENGLAND
Trevor House
100 Brompton Road
Knightsbridge, London SW3 1EX
England
telephone: (071) 581-9960

Cuba

AREA: 44,218 square miles; 760 miles long, between 22 and 124 miles wide.

POPULATION: About 10 million.

CAPITAL CITY: Havana.

LANGUAGE: Spanish.

RELIGION: Remains predominantly Roman Catholic in spite of communism.

GOVERNMENT: Communist dictatorship under Fidel Castro.

LOCATION: 90 miles off Key West, Florida, about 100 miles from Jamaica.

ELECTRICITY: 110 volts/60 cycles AC, same as in the U.S.

TIME ZONE: Eastern standard time most of the year, changes to daylight saving time slightly different from that on the East Coast, so
that there will be an hour's difference for a few weeks each spring
and fall.

MONEY: Cuban peso; exchange rate varies. Use of credit cards by
U.S. citizens is forbidden, but traveler's checks are okay. Currency
is tightly controlled; visitors must list purchases, including meals,
on vouchers. Money can be exchanged at the airport and at major hotels.

Overview

Cuba, the Caribbean's largest island, is only 90 miles off the coast of Florida and was once an accessible weekend getaway. The very thought of Havana was likely to evoke images of unending sunny days and casino nights,
Hemingway, and the high life all laced with glitz, glamour, and rum. Today, Cuba is no longer accessible, and its image resides in the striking features of Fidel Castro and his government.

While travel to Cuba is still restricted for most U.S. citizens, there are
intermittent signs of change. Recently, Cuban-Americans, researchers,
artists, clergy, students, journalists, and humanitarian groups have been
allowed to travel to Cuba with U.S. permission. For current information,
call the Treasury Department's Cuba hotline (800) 306-CUBA.

Citizens of Canada, Denmark, France, Sweden, Switzerland, and Italy,
do not need visas.

Since Cuba will be out of the realm of most Caribbean vacationers, it
is dealt with only briefly here.

Things to See and Do

Old Havana; Hemingway's house, La Finca Vigía; and the world-famous
Varadero Beach probably top the list. Cuba also has an interesting selection of national parks and protected areas. This is a large, diverse island
with tremendous natural features. Try to arrange a tour that includes
some of them.

SHOPPING: Very limited. Tourist hotels have political posters and T-
shirts; a few straw items and various crafts are also available. Oddly
enough, U.S. citizens are allowed to return with up to 100 Cuban cigars
and one liter of rum (Carta Blanca is the common choice) if they are purchased in Cuba.

For More Information

The U.S. Treasury Department's Cuba hotline: (800) 306-CUBA

The Center for Cuban Studies
124 West 23rd Street
New York, NY 10011
telephone: (212) 242-0559
(has arranged tours for special interest groups when tours are permitted)

Marazul Tours, Inc.
4100 Park Avenue
Weehawken, NJ 07087
telephone: (201) 319-9670 or (800) 223-5334

Curaçao

AREA: 180 square miles; 38 miles long, from 2 to $7^{1}/_{2}$ miles wide.

POPULATION: 170,000.

CAPITAL CITY: Willemstad.

LANGUAGE: Dutch, Spanish, local papiamento; English widely spoken.

RELIGION: Mainly Christian; services in many denominations.

GOVERNMENT: Member of the Netherlands Antilles, a coequal part of the Kingdom of the Netherlands; an elected council governs local affairs.

LOCATION: 35 miles north of Venezuela.

GETTING THERE: Through New York on American Airlines; through Miami or San Juan on ALM.

CUSTOMS: U.S. visitors need proof of citizenship; Canadians need passports or birth certificates. All visitors need either return or on-going tickets.

HEALTH: No special considerations. All water is desalinated and pure.

CLOTHING: Informal tropical wear; shorts are okay in Willemstad. Cocktail dresses and ties and jackets may be needed at night.

ELECTRICITY: 110 to 130 volts/50 cycles AC, 220 volts/50 cycles AC.

TIME ZONE: Atlantic standard time year-round.

MONEY: Netherlands Antilles florin or guilder NAF. U.S. $1 is about NAF $1.77. U.S. dollars and traveler's checks widely accepted.

TAX: U.S. $10 airport tax; 7 percent government room tax.

GETTING AROUND: Taxis are marked; confirm fares before departure. All major car rental agencies operate here; right-hand drive and international road signs make this an easy option. U.S. driver's license acceptable. Public buses; many hotels provide scheduled transportation to Willemstad.

Overview

Just 35 miles north of Venezuela, Curaçao has some lovely open countryside and a large capital city, Willemstad, with some 150,000 people. Relatively flat and arid, the island is punctuated with cactus and divi-divi trees. It is ringed with delightful beaches and clear waters. The National Underwater Park is hoping to attract some of nearby Bonaire's divers. The 4,000-acre St. Cristoffel nature reserve protects many of the island's indigenous species.

History

Curaçao was put on the map in 1499 by Alonso de Ojeda and was initially settled by the Spaniards in the early 1500s. The Dutch captured it in 1634 and founded a settlement. The English and the French alternately squabbled with the Dutch over the island from 1666 until the early nineteenth century. Curaçao was briefly British from 1800 to 1802, was regained by the Dutch, and then was recaptured by the British in 1807. The Treaty of Paris in 1815 gave the Dutch the upper hand, and Curaçao remains so Dutch in character today that it is sometimes called "Holland in the Caribbean."

Things to See and Do

Willemstad

Curaçao's picturesque capital has some of the best shopping and most historic buildings in the Caribbean. Pick up the walking tour at your hotel or the Tourist Board. You may want to include Fort Amsterdam, the Queen Emma Pontoon Bridge, the floating market (you might try some local fruit), and Mikve Israel-Emanuel Synagogue, the oldest in the Western Hemisphere (with a courtyard museum).

Cunucu (Countryside)

Bays, beaches, and plantation houses are scattered throughout Curaçao outside of Willemstad. The Botanical Garden and Zoo, Amstel Brewery, Curaçao Liquor Distillery, Ascencion Plantation, and Octagon House are among the offerings.

Hato Caves

These limestone caverns formed of fossilized coral are open Tuesday through Sunday from 10 A.M. to 5 P.M.; there are guided tours on the hour. The caves contain "rooms" of limestone formation, an underground lake, and ancient petroglyphs. Entrance fee is $4.25 for adults.

Beaches

Curaçao is ringed with lovely beaches; those on the wild north coast are more for views than swimming. Boca Tabla, with its sea-carved grottoes and thundering waves, is probably the best known. Boca Sun Pedro is great for beachcombing. Santa Barbara is popular for swimming and sunbathing; entrance fee is NAF $6 per car; all facilities; snacks and refreshments available. Blauw Bay, near the old fishing village of St. Michael, also has changing facilities and a snack bar.

Curaçao Underwater Park

Especially for snorkelers. A marked trail runs 975 feet through corals and leads to the eighty-year-old wreck of the SS *Oranje Nassau* that is now home to colorful fish.

Cristoffel National Park

Some 4,500 acres in the north (about a forty-five-minute drive from Willemstad) protecting a variety of plants and animals. Visitors may see rare sabal palms, orchids, divi-divi trees, and cactus. Animals that live in the park include rabbits, iguanas, birds, feral donkeys, and shy little Curaçao deer.

The park has a 35-mile network of roads; driving the circuit takes about three-and-a-half hours. Park hours are from 8 A.M. to 4 P.M. Monday through Saturday (no one is admitted after 2 P.M.), Sunday from 6 A.M. to 3 P.M. Entrance fee is $5 for adults, $3 for children. All the roads are well marked and easy to follow whether you walk or drive.

The footpath that winds the 1,239 feet up Mount Cristoffel, Curaçao's highest peak, is marked with white stripes and takes about one-and-a-half hours. Get an early start to avoid the heat. The panorama from the top makes it worth the effort. Remember to bring your own food and drinks; there are none in the park.

SHOPPING: Some of the best in the Caribbean, including imported luxury goods and locally made Curaçao liquor and Dutch cheese (U.S. citizens can return with $25 worth for personal use). Curaçao's free guide includes detailed shopping tour directions. If you drive out of town, you may want to stop in Santa Marta Landhuis at the crafts workshop for the handicapped.

FESTIVALS AND HOLIDAYS

New Year's Day, 1 January.

Chinese New Year, January.

Carnival, weekend preceding Lent.

Harvest Festival, March.

Passover, April.

Good Friday, Easter (dates vary).

Queen Juliana's Birthday, April.

Labor Day, 1 May.

Ascension Day (date varies).

Curaçao Day, July.

St. Nicholas Day, 5 December.

Kingdom Day, Antillian Flag Day, 15 December.

Christmas Day, 25 December.

Boxing Day, 26 December.

FOOD: Food has an international flavor. Specialities include *erwtensoep*, a pea soup, and *keshi yena*, a whole Edam cheese stuffed with meat or fish and baked. For seafood, try Pisces restaurant off fisherman's wharf; it serves only the catch of the day and is a favorite with locals. The less adventurous have Pizza Hut and Kentucky Fried Chicken to fall back on.

HOTELS: Large hotels on the island with casinos include: Curaçao Caribbean Hotel and Casino, Curaçao Plaza Hotel and Casino, Las Palmas Hotel and Vacation Village, Otrobanda Hotel and Casino, Princess Beach Hotel and Casino, and Sonesta Beach Hotel and Casino. Some other hotels on the island are: Avila Beach Hotel, Coral Cliff Resort and Beach Club, Club Seru Coral, Hotel Holland, Kadushi Cliffs, Lions Dive Hotel, Porto Paseo Hotel, and Trupial Inn.

FOR MORE INFORMATION

Curaçao Tourist Board
330 Biscayne Boulevard, Suite 806
Miami, FL 33132
telephone: (305) 374-5811

Curaçao Tourist Board
475 Park Avenue South, Suite 2000
New York, NY 10016
telephone: (212) 683-7660 or (800) 332-8266

Dominica

AREA: 290 square miles; 20 miles long, 16 miles wide.

POPULATION: Approximately 73,000.

CAPITAL CITY: Roseau.

LANGUAGE: English and French patois.

RELIGION: Mainly Roman Catholic and Anglican.

GOVERNMENT: Parliamentary republic; independent member of Commonwealth headed by an elected prime minister.

LOCATION: Between Guadeloupe and Martinique.

GETTING THERE: On LIAT via Puerto Rico, Barbados, Antigua, or Guadeloupe; Air Guadeloupe also flies into Dominica.

CUSTOMS: U.S. visitors need proof of citizenship and either a return or an ongoing ticket.

HEALTH: Dominica is remote and has limited medical facilities. Bring insect repellent, and plan to be self-sufficient on hikes. (See Health in Part 3 for more details.)

CLOTHING: Informal tropical clothing; absolutely no swim wear on the streets, please. You'll need a wrap or jacket for cool mountain evenings. Men do not need ties.

ELECTRICITY: 220 to 240 volts/50 cycles AC.

TIME ZONE: One hour ahead of eastern standard time.

MONEY: Eastern Caribbean dollar. Canadian and U.S. dollars often accepted. Limited credit cards; check in advance.

TAX AND TIPS: U.S. $8 departure tax, 5 percent government room tax, 3 percent tax on alcoholic drinks and food.

GETTING AROUND: Taxis, cars, and jeeps may be rented. Apply for temporary permit at the police station or airport; about U.S. $8 and a valid U.S. driver's license needed. Several companies offer day tours. Hiking is a popular mode of transport, too.

Overview

Dominica is a naturalist's paradise. It's often said that this is the only Caribbean island that Columbus would still recognize. Belief in this statement occurs as suddenly as Dominica's airstrip, which appears like a last-minute mirage in the thick forest. Conviction grows as the centuries spin away on the two-hour ride into the capital of Roseau over rough, twisting roads. There are avenues of great bamboos as thick as men's arms. Tree ferns, guavas, and giant gommier trees reach for the sky. Bromeliads and lianas layer the trees with their junglelike twists and tangles. Dominica has its own definition of green, with nuances given by sunlight and mist. Water drifts from passing clouds and rushes down hillsides. Roadside rivers are often filled with bathers and people beating their laundry on water-smoothed rocks.

Dominica isn't for everyone. If you want luxury or beaches, this is not the island for you. However, if you want to sense the pureness of untouched rain forest and the smoldering power of volcanism, there's no better place. History—geologic, natural, and human—is alive and well on Dominica.

Note: Please ask before picking fruit; fruit trees have owners. Also, many islanders prefer not be photographed; please ask first.

History

Dominica was sighted by Columbus on a Sunday (for which it is named) in 1493. The first settlers were French, who arrived in 1632. The French and the British traded the island back and forth in battle for the next two centuries. Britain took the island in 1759; France recaptured it in 1778. The British held control from 1805. This mixed French-English tradition still is evident today in many aspects of Dominican life, from cooking to language. Although English is the official language, most of Dominica's 73,000 people still speak a French patois.

Dominica became independent from Britain on 3 November 1978. Agriculture—mainly bananas, coconuts, citrus fruits, and cocoa—remains the major industry.

Things to See and Do
Roseau

Dominica's picturesque capital is worth exploring. Most people include a visit to the Botanical Gardens on the edge of town; they will help acquaint you with some of the exotic species you'll see around the island. The garden's hall of giant bamboo is as popular as the delicate orchids and the red claws of the heliconia. Trail maps, brochures, and booklets published by the forestry division are on sale at the division's office in the garden. These illustrated publications contain a wealth of information and range in price from 25 cents to $11.

Scotts Head—Soufrière Marine Reserve

The reserve offers some outstanding diving for both scuba divers and snorkelers. It includes an underwater peak, offshore reefs, and an underwater hot spring. Experienced divers often descend "The Wall" to admire the black coral. Boat tours and sport fishing are also available.

Trafalgar Falls

Somewhat inland from Roseau. A visit requires about a fifteen-minute walk; the slope to the base of the falls is too steep for most vehicles. Breadfruit trees, tree ferns, and orchids surround a rocky pool where three falls splash in.

Sulfur Springs

Northeast of Roseau, near Trafalgar Falls. An accessible miniview of volcanic fumes and brimstone. A sulfurous look and smell for those who don't want to trek to the Boiling Lake.

Portsmouth

In the north, a colorful little town built around a bay that is the best anchorage on the island. Several notable natural areas are nearby.

Syndicate Nature Trail

In the foothills of Morne Diablotin at about 1,800 feet, the forestery division has developed a short, easy nature walk. At only 0.8 mile, walkers can enjoy a trail through the mature rain forest of the much larger parrot preserve.

Cabrits National Park

Peninsula north of Portsmouth where Dominica's only dry woodland is now a protected area. The park also contains eighteenth-century Fort Shirley.

Indian River Mangroves

Just south of Portsmouth. Canoe rides take visitors up this mangrove-lined river.

Morne Trois Pitons National Park

Dominica's natural wonders are showcased in this untouched central rain forest preserve. If you aren't up for a vigorous hike, at least drive in this forested area. The easy, five-minute walk to the Emerald Pool is recommended to all; a stroll through this plant-lined grotto will give you a glimpse of the lushness, sights, and smells of the rain forest. Many swim in the pool (please, no soap). This is a well-marked trail; no guide needed. Both the shy agouti (a large relative of the guinea pig) and the manicou (a small opossum) live in the area, but you are more likely to see and hear some of the many birds.

Freshwater Lake

Also within Morne Trois Pitons National Park, two miles northeast of the village of Laudat. Several hiking trails start from the picnic area at the edge of this crater lake. A walk of less than an hour to the north will take you to Boeri Lake. A walk of an hour-and-a-half or so will take you back to Laudat; it's nearly two hours to get to the village of Rosalie on foot. Freshwater Lake itself is Dominica's largest lake. The purple flowers floating in it are water hyacinths, and the emergent vegetation around its shores is unique among crater lakes. The short walk around the lake provides a good look at different types of forest: montane forest, elfin woodland, and cloud forest. As always, please stay on the trails. Everything in this park is protected by law.

Middleham Trails

Walking trails that traverse a 950-acre tract of rain forest on the northeast boundary of Morne Trois Pitons National Park. Access to the trails, which are marked, is from Sylvania or Cochrane via the Laudat road. Each trail is about a two-hour walk. There is a rain shelter on the Cochrane/Providence trail right before the viewpoint overlooking Middleham Falls, one of Dominica's tallest. Whether you start from Cochrane or Sylvania, you will walk through several cultivated or culturally abandoned areas before you enter true rain forest with its intertwining layers of plant life. Both trails pass Tousanti (Stinking Hole), a collapsed laval tube that still emits hot air.

Boiling Lake / Valley of Desolation

Hire an experienced guide for this hike and take a hearty lunch. It's a rugged 6 miles from Laudat to the Boiling Lake; the Valley of Desolation is thrown in free along the way. This is in the heart of Morne Trois Pitons National Park, and anyone who completes this venture will have seen a good bit of the park and have a fair idea of what it must smell like inside a volcano (or, at least, a region of active fumaroles). Titou Gorge, at the beginning of the trail, is another geographic reminder of volcanism. The varied vegetation on Morne Nicholls shows altitudinal striations; remember as you climb to watch as the montane forest gives way to elfin woodland. It is especially important to stay on the trail at all times, especially in the Valley of Desolation, where only a thin crust covers the hot lava. This hike is not for everyone. Be sure of your own physical condition and stamina before you attempt it. (See Part 4, Exploring, for more information on hiking and mountain climbing.)

Carib Indian Reserve

In the northeast, Salybia is the largest village. Rent a jeep or take a tour, but go. This will give you a chance to see Dominica's rugged windward shore, where Caribs still launch dugout canoes, as well as the reserve itself. These Indians are part of the Caribbean's living history (see Part 2, People and Culture—Social History, for more background), the last enclave of a proud people still governed by a tribal chief. Superb baskets, woven as they have been for centuries of various natural-colored local reeds and grasses, are for sale along the roadside. You'll have to look hard to find basket-making of this caliber elsewhere in the Caribbean.

SHOPPING: Baskets and local straw work, verti-vert grass mats (try the convent workshop downtown), and various bamboo and coconut shell crafts are available throughout the island. The Carib Reserve is the best place for baskets. There is an interesting bookstore in Roseau that handles books on local history and hard-to-find editions by Jean Rhys, who was born nearby.

FESTIVALS AND HOLIDAYS: Pre-Lenten carnival is the island's biggest festival; it begins the Sunday afternoon before Ash Wednesday and ends Tuesday night; lots of music, a parade of floats, and street dancing. All regular U.S. and British holidays as well as August Monday and Independence Day (3 November) are celebrated.

FOOD: Mountain chicken, the muscular legs of a large frog (or crapaud), is a local specialty. There is a closed season (March through August) to help protect the dwindling stocks. Be conscientious about not encouraging poaching. Local rum, freshwater crayfish, and tropical fruits are also favorites.

Food is reasonably priced; a good hotel dinner for two will cost about U.S. $20 to $30. Castaways is a local favorite just north of Roseau. Papillote Rain Forest Restaurant serves inexpensive American food (open 10 A.M. to 6 P.M.). It's often better to adventure out for lunch rather than at night, since many hotels on Dominica expect their guests to dine with them in the evening (meals are often included in the room rate).

HOTELS: Accommodations include the Anchorage Hotel and Dive Center, Castaways Beach Hotel, the Emerald, Fort Young Hotel, the Garraway Hotel, Lauro Club Hotel, Layou Valley Inn, Papillote Wilderness Retreat, Picard Beach Cottage Resort, Roxy's Mountain Lodge, and various guest houses, apartments, and cottages. Ask the Dominica Tourist Board for details.

For More Information

DOMINICA
Division of Tourism
National Development Corporation
P.O. Box 293

Roseau, Dominica
telephone (809) 448-2045
fax: (809) 448-5840

U.S.
Caribbean Tourism Association
20 East 46th Street
New York, NY 10017
telephone: (212) 682-0435
fax: (212) 697-4258

┌─────── Dominican Republic

AREA: 18,816 square miles (about twice the size of the state of New Hampshire).

POPULATION: 6,502,600 (about 345 people per square mile).

CAPITAL CITY: Santo Domingo.

LANGUAGE: Spanish (take a dictionary or phrase book).

RELIGION: Roman Catholic (about 97 percent of the population).

GOVERNMENT: Republic.

LOCATION: The Dominican Republic shares the large island of Hispaniola with Haiti on the west; the wily currents of the Mona Passage separate it from the island of Puerto Rico on the east.

GETTING THERE: Several airlines fly regularly from New York (3½ hours by air); Miami (2 hours by air); San Juan, Puerto Rico; and Port-au-Prince, Haiti. Cruise ships—Royal Caribbean Line, Cunard, Norwegian Caribbean, Sun Line, and others—dock in Santo Domingo and Puerta Plata. Private yachts may also enter at major ports.

CUSTOMS: Citizens of the United States, Canada, Mexico, Venezuela, and Jamaica need proper identification—passport, voter registration card, birth certificate—and a tourist card, which may be purchased for U.S. $10 upon arrival, or avoid the lines and purchase it as you check in for your flight to the Dominican Republic. The card—a postcard with a fill-in information sheet attached—is good for 60 days. Citizens of Austria, Germany, Belgium, Holland, France, Finland, Spain, Denmark, Italy, Great Britain, Switzerland, Japan, Luxembourg, Panama, Israel, Sweden, and Norway need only a valid passport, no card purchase. Possession or use of marijuana and other controlled substances is prohibited and punishable by fine and/or prison terms from 6 months to 10 years.

HEALTH: Bottled water is recommended; no other special considerations.

CLOTHING: Take the usual items with an awareness toward Latin formality and fashion. The Dominicans, influenced by their native son designer Oscar de la Renta, tend to be fashion conscious, and you will see, especially in Santo Domingo, a very citified flamboyance (earrings and high heels even accompany bathing suits).

Shorts in the Dominican Republic are only for poolside and within resort compounds. However, slacks, jeans, and pantsuits are all fine for city excursions. Dining out requires summer dresses for women, summer-weight jackets and ties for men. For night spots, you may want to add cocktail dresses and a light wrap; for men, a suit or sport coat and tie.

ELECTRICITY: 110 volts/60 cycles AC, as in the U.S.

TIME ZONE: Atlantic standard time, one hour ahead of eastern standard time.

MONEY: The Dominican peso, which was once on a par with the U.S. dollar, fluctuates.

Cambio (change): After you purchase your tourist card—which must be done with U.S. dollars before your baggage is inspected—you'll be able to change money. Be sure to do so; the porters and taxis clamoring for your business in the confusion outside expect and will take only pesos.

Banks: Official government exchange banks (easily distinguished from the unofficial by the presence of young, uniformed, machine gun–toting guards) are open from 8 A.M. to 2:30 P.M., closed Saturdays. Special tourist offices are open on Sundays.

There is said to be a thriving black market exchange that gives one a slightly better rate; it's probably best avoided. Hotels will not change money or take traveler's checks when their cashier's office is closed (and it seems to be closed often).

Remember to save your receipts—if you have leftover pesos

when you leave, you will need your receipts in order to convert the pesos back into U.S. dollars.

Credit Cards: Most major cards are accepted by hotels, larger restaurants, and shops. However, there is often a service charge on top—up to 20 percent—so shoppers are enticed to spend American dollars cash instead. This is true in several stores in the Old Town.

TAX AND TIPS: Resorts, hotels, and restaurants add 10 percent service charge to the total bill. In restaurants it is customary to reward good service with an additional 5 to 10 percent tip. Government tax of 5 percent is also added to hotel bills as well as an 8 percent food and beverage tax. (Remember to figure this 23 percent tax when budgeting for your hotel.) There is an airport departure tax of U.S. $10. Once you pay this tax, which applies even to ticketless infants and children, and get your exit stamp on your passport at customs, you are in an area of duty-free shops that take only U.S. dollars.

Tipping seems standard—about U.S. $.50 per bag. Tourist publications advise tipping porters, bellhops, and taxi drivers according to your usual custom.

GETTING AROUND: *Taxis* from the airport into Santo Domingo cost from U.S. $15 to $25, depending on the exchange rate. It's a pleasant 30- to 40-minute ride along the coast. Short rides and half-day tour rates tend to be high as well.

Buses: Lots of visitors recommend the overall view and price offered by tour buses—about U.S. $5 around the city. There are several big companies, including Prieto, Vimecca, and Amber, with air-conditioned buses. Arrange tours through your hotel desk. If you speak Spanish or crave adventure (or both), you might try riding the local buses; stops are marked by curbside yellow obelisks. Or you can ride the jitney, usually a van that makes regular stops and is also inexpensive. If your Spanish is marginal, be sure to carry your destination written clearly on a piece of paper, and, needless to say, your hotel and address for the return trip.

Car Rental: Dominicans drive on the right. All one needs is a valid driver's license from another country or, of course, an international driver's license (both good for 90 days in the D.R.).

Rental agencies abound, but the cars are often poorly maintained. In addition, the roads are poorly marked, and you may not get much help in the event of a breakdown. Check everything (seat belts, spare tire, jack, gas, water) yourself before you leave the agency (some people do so before signing) and again before setting

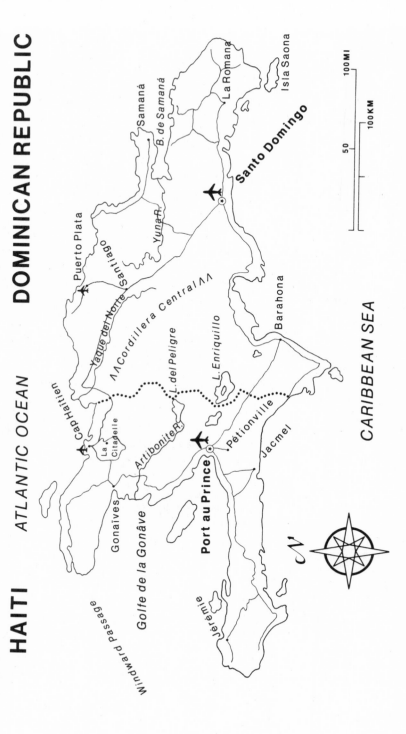

out on a long excursion. And as always in unfamiliar, poorly mapped terrain, avoid driving at night. Be sure to pick up a new road map at the Tourist Information Center if the agency does not provide it.

Major companies—Avis, National, Hertz—with rates at U.S. standards are located in the airport; some smaller local rentals may be found outside. Don't hesitate to bargain, especially with smaller operators (taking a peek at the vehicle in question). The paperwork is somewhat time-consuming, and speaking Spanish is most helpful.

Fly / drive travel packages or hotel and car packages are often available. All arrangements are made in advance by your travel agent, and you are spared the tedious details—and know the price in advance.

If you want to go to La Romana, Samaná, or Puerto Plata, there are inexpensive air-conditioned bus trips available. Again, see your hotel activities desk for details. There is also somewhat regular domestic air service. As always in the islands, schedules are casual, so it is a misconception to believe that flying will save you time; it's best to allow an entire day to change locales whether driving or flying, regardless of distance.

Local Walking Guides: Often young students learning English are only too eager to walk around with you, point out the sights, and help in bargaining for trinkets. Some students even carry cards as government-certified guides. They provide a good way to gain insight for a few pesos' tip. Just be sure you find out if yours is congenial before setting out; it can make or break the day. The same goes for cab guides.

Overview

Occupying the eastern two-thirds of the large island of Hispaniola, the Dominican Republic (D.R.) is blessed with a variety of natural assets. Steep peaks fall away to fertile valleys that lead off into rolling hills and fields lush with sugarcane, the main crop and industry. The Cordillera Central mountain range is topped by Pico Duarte, at well over 10,000 feet, the highest peak in the West Indies; the country has three other mountain ranges and four major rivers. There are a number of small lakes; the large Lago Enriquillo, with its crowd of crocodiles, at 144 feet below sea level is unique in the Caribbean. Almost a third of the coast is lined with beaches; much of the rest drops away dramatically in rocky headlands.

Only the hairclips place the century in this photo of a smiling cook by the late Wilfredo Garcia of the Dominican Republic.

Similar in many ways to nearby Puerto Rico, just seventy-five miles east across the Mona Passage, the D.R. does not enjoy the same standard of living. Their common Spanish heritage is readily evidenced in language, religion, history, music, food, and the architectural similarities of their colonial cities. In fact, the D.R. is a favorite vacation spot for the more affluent Puerto Ricans. While a middle class is slowly emerging on the D.R., most of the people are farm workers; a third of the population cannot read or write.

A visitor probably would not sense this from the many resort hotels of Santo Domingo, a huge, modern city. But wander off to quiet residential streets in the shadow of high rises. You'll see brightly painted stucco facades, potted flowers, and open sewers. The struggle is more obvious here.

As in all places in transition, there is an undercurrent of unrest; the machine gun–toting guards in the banks and exchange houses are disconcerting. It seems unnatural for boys barely growing mustaches to spend their days indoors caressing the slick barrels of their guns.

All of this does little to spoil the pleasures of the countryside. About

200,000 American visitors a year enjoy the Dominican Republic's friendly people, beaches, mountainsides, and the unending tropical nights filled with merengue music or Spanish guitar.

Whereas Santo Domingo is an interesting and diverse city, many find the noise and complexities of modern life more easily bypassed in smaller towns such as Puerta Plata on the north coast, where there is a budding resort area in the old crescent-shaped port, or in the still-rural fishing village of Samaná.

History

When Columbus anchored off the island on 5 December 1492, it was the home of the Taino Indians (see History/Time Frames in Part 2 for details). Columbus called the island La Española, which evolved into Hispaniola, and said never had human eyes seen a fairer land, or something to that effect.

Santo Domingo was founded in 1496, becoming the first permanent European settlement in the New World. Its military buildings, the fort, and the safe port became a center of Spanish strength, not only for the expeditions of the conquistadores, but also a religious and educational headquarters. Sir Francis Drake sacked the city in 1586, and it was some time before it recovered its previous grandeur. As well as leaving it considerably poorer, Drake left a good portion of the city in cinders.

The Treaty of Ryswick in 1697 forced Spain to leave the western end of Hispaniola—Haiti—to France. France took over the rest of the island in 1795 and ruled until about 1809, when the Dominicans revolted against the French rule. In 1814, the Treaty of Paris returned the country to the Spanish. To add to this confusion, Haiti took over the country in 1822 and ruled until 1844, when Juan Pablo Duarte organized a revolution, beat the Haitians, and proclaimed a republic on 27 February 1844.

Oddly enough, in 1870, the Dominicans proposed a treaty that would have annexed their country to the U.S., but the U.S. Senate did not ratify it. Even so, to prevent debt collection by foreign powers, the U.S. ended up taking control of Dominican customs in 1905, and in 1916 it actually occupied the country and set up a military government that ruled until 1924.

The U.S. retained control of Dominican customs until 1941, overlapping the beginning of the Trujillo era. General Rafael Leonidas Trujillo Molina came to power in 1930, and the iron-willed dictator ruled the country (Santo Domingo was then Ciudad Trujillo) until his assassination in 1961.

The conservative Joaquín Balaquer, a Trujillo appointee, continued to rule. The first free elections in forty years were held in 1962, putting leftist Juan Bosch in power—for about seven months. Then a military coup left a junta in control. Balaquer ruled until 1996.

This may all seem confusing and irrelevant to your suntan or amber necklace, but even a once-over of this political roller coaster will add depth to your visit and a flicker of insight into the tenuous hope for stability and prosperity placed in young boys and their guns.

Colonial Santo Domingo

The Old City is still being restored as a monumental (so to speak) government project. Millions of dollars have been spent tearing down modern walls to reveal the "colonial core" of old arches and doorways and reconstructing new-old buildings around those solid enough to remain.

Old Santo Domingo was founded near the end of the fifteenth century on the eastern bank of the Ozama River. After the original town was destroyed by a hurricane, it was rebuilt on the opposite bank of the river in the sixteenth century, but many of the original foundations are still in evidence.

The second founding of Santo Domingo was on 5 August 1502. It was the fifth Spanish settlement on the island (the others barely remain). This second town was laid out by Friar Nicolás de Ovando, the governor. The harbor became a strategic launching point for Spanish explorations, and the town itself, a center of culture, religion, and education.

Since the traffic, heat, and apparent confusion in the maze of the Old City's crowded streets can be overwhelming, perhaps the best approach is a city bus tour; it will give you the overall picture and, hopefully, your bearings. After that, you can take time to wander, shop, dine, and see the sights. A rundown of the high spots follows. For more detailed information, look for a paperback guide with a picture of the statue of Columbus pointing on it—*Santo Domingo* by Carmenchu Brusiloff and Juan Alfredo Biaggi. One of the few guides available, it can be found in most hotel gift shops. It is filled with details and good architectural photos, and it has a map.

Note: Historic sites are often closed on Mondays and for siesta from noon to 3 P.M.

The Cathedral

A grand weather-beaten vault of a building full of arches and crosses and crypts in an age-old shadowiness that evokes the meek shiver of appreciation that even the most uninformed feel in the presence of history.

The Chapel of Saint Ann or the Bastidas Chapel (the first to be entered after passing through the side gates) is where Sir Francis Drake slept on his troublemaking twenty-four-day stay in Santo Domingo in 1586. When Drake left, he took his sword to the Bishop's statue lying in repose on his tomb; Drake's swordplay left the statue minus a hand and nose. This chapel has its original ceramic tiles, which were crafted in Seville.

A labyrinth of tombs, chapels, arches, pillars in varying styles, altars, crypts (the fifth-generation grandfather of Simon Bolívar, also named Simon Bolívar, is one of note), and baptismal fonts crowd the cathedral interior along with oil paintings, carved mahogany altarpieces, and a coat of arms. The cathedral's main entrance is a great hingeless door that ingeniously swings open and closed on its own pivot. Outside, the facade is decorated with a frieze that includes the whimsy of griffins, centaurs, and lobsters.

The Monumento al Gran Almirante Cristóbal Colón (Monument to the Great Admiral Christopher Columbus) dominates one end of the cathedral and is what most visitors come to see. Despite some controversy, this is where Dominicans believe the explorer's bones rest. Every Columbus Day (12 October), the coffer holding his remains is opened with great ceremony in honor of the anniversary of his arrival in the New World.

Museo de las Casas Reales (Royal Houses Museum)

This museum covers more than three centuries—the period of first Spanish occupation to the country's independence from Spain in 1821. It is in these contiguous buildings, the Palace of Governors and the Royal Court of Appeals, that one can see the only existing coat of arms of the eccentric Spanish Queen Juana La Loca, who ordered the establishment of the Royal Court in 1511. It also contains Taino Indian artifacts, ancient navigational instruments, an eighteenth-century sugarcane grinder, and antique maps and documents.

Alcazar (Castle) or the Casa de Colón

The Alcazar is near the post office and telecommunications facility, if you want to make a double venture. Built from about 1509 to 1512 by Don Diego Colón (Columbus's son), it was constructed so solidly that Colón was accused of building a fortress; it does appear to be a house-fortress with a Renaissance air.

The restoration of the Alcazar, finished in 1968, converted the building to a living center and furnished it with objects of rich daily life, including a fifteenth-century tapestry and musical instruments. A unique sixteenth-century Flemish wood carving of the death of the Virgin is also considered a treasure of the Alcazar.

Museo Virreinal (Viceroyal Museum)

Paintings, sculpture, art objects from the fourteenth to the sixteenth century.

Casa del Cordón (House of the Cord)

Generally considered the first stone house in Santo Domingo. Built at the beginning of the sixteenth century, it now houses the Banco Popular Dominicano, which restored the building. This is the house where Drake weighed the jewels the Dominican women brought to pay the ransom he demanded of the city.

Casa de Bastidas

The former house of Santo Domingo mayor Rodrigo de Bastidas, it opened in 1977 as a museum for treasures recovered from sunken ships.

La Atarazana

The first arsenal in the New World constructed as a storage area for military equipment and as a training base. It's been completely reconstructed to reflect the sixteenth century, using the old walls and arches where possible. Once the area where conquistadores brought their ships for repairs and supplies, it is now an arcade of small shops and restaurants.

La Forteleza (The Fort)

Obviously a fort from any perspective, La Forteleza commands the Caribbean–Ozama River corner of the colonial city. Built in the early sixteenth century, the fortress was the first military building in the colony. In the center of the complex stands the impressive Torre del Homenaje (Tower of Homage), named because homage was given to entering ships from its great height. Its old stones and spiral staircases reach a height of well over fifty feet. Restored in the 1970s, the tower and fortress have as many stories told about them as they have building stones. One tale claims that the spirits of executed prisoners take on different shapes and wander the walls on moonless nights to frighten any who might intrude upon their peace.

There's a marvelous view of the Ozama River from the tower. The very obvious industrial complex is Molinos Dominicanos (Dominican Flour Mills). You may notice three huge boulders at the river mouth. They're called the Three Sisters: The largest is the base for a bridge; the other two are trapped by the fortress. The Ozama River, at the end of its meandering journey through the country, opens into the busy port of Santo Domingo. In the seventeenth century, the harbor was chained closed with logs reinforced with iron to help protect the city from intruding ships.

Modern Santo Domingo

Plaza de la Cultura (Plaza of Culture)

On Pedro Henriquez Urena Avenue, a group of museums and galleries built on the grounds of the mansion that was Trujillo's last residence. The National Library, Museum of Natural History, Modern Art Gallery, and Teatro Nacional are all here among fountains and gardens.

Museo del Hombre Dominicano
(Museum of the Dominican Man)

Contains valuable Taino Indian artifacts, including vomit spatulas used in religious rituals, and dioramas of pre-Columbian life.

Jardín Botánico Nacional Dr. Rafael M. Moscoso
(Botanical Gardens)

Inexpensive boat, train, or carriage tours take visitors through the grounds that contain 200 varieties of palm trees, an orchid garden, many other tropical plants, the world's largest flower clock, and a research center. Small admission charge.

Parque Zoológico Nacional (Zoo)

A modern zoo of 250,000 acres, opened in 1975, with irregular topography, man-made waterfalls, and an open-air cage for 4,000 birds.

Parque de Atracciones Infantiles
(Children's Amusement Park)

The old zoo and gardens, downtown, have caves, animals, a Ferris wheel, and pony rides.

Near Santo Domingo

Los Tres Ojos de Aqua (The Three Eyes of Water)

A few kilometers from the center of Santo Domingo on the road to the airport, these subterranean caverns with their underground lakes—the eyes—and ferns and cool quiet offer a certain escape from the fervor of the city. The only intrusions are insistent guides and the carping of souvenir vendors in the landscaped park around the entrance to the caves. They are quick to say that the carved objects of stalactites and stalagmites that they sell are from other caves; cheap amber and trinkets are also available. Be prepared for lots of steep stair climbing and breathtaking drops. Until 1972, when the stairs were installed, visitors had to use the old Indian entrance, which entailed sliding down the slick trunk of the centerpiece tree that arches out through an opening in the cave. The opening bathes the caves with a dappled sunlight that allows plants to grow in this unique setting, called by an appreciative child, "a little bit spooky, but not too much."

Museo Panteón y Yacimiento Arquelógico de la Caleta (Pantheon Museum and Archaeological Site at Caleta Point)

The site, on the road to the airport, east of Santo Domingo, was once a small fishing village until a Taino Indian cemetery was discovered beneath the town. The museum contains thirty-three Indian skeletons, which have been left exactly as they were buried there centuries before.

This is the village that began the folk art tradition of carving travertine stone from caves into fake Indian relics, which were once sold for the real thing. Now the imitation is openly admitted, and the stone carvings have become a national handicraft.

Ingenio de Engombe (Engombe Sugar Mill)

Described as the least known but most romantic of ruins, this two-story palace, a small chapel, and another building that may have sheltered slaves or been a warehouse remain from the early sixteenth century. About 9 miles west of Santo Domingo on the left bank of the Haina River.

Other Places of Interest Around the Island

Altos de Chavón (The Heights of Chavón)

A re-creation of a sixteen-century Spanish village built by Gulf-Western Corporation (also the creators of Casa de Campo) high on the banks of the Chavón River, just east of the town of La Romana. It's about a two-hour drive from Santo Domingo, fifteen minutes by shuttle bus from Casa de Campo. Art galleries, boutiques, cafes, and restaurants are scattered around cobbled courtyards; there's also a regional museum of Taino Indian history and artifacts.

Isla Saona (Saona Island)

An animal and forest preserve off the coast to the southeast. A large number of white-crowned doves nest in the national park here. Clear waters for diving.

Samaná and Samaná Peninsula

About a four-hour drive from Santo Domingo over rugged terrain, this small fishing town on the northeast coast has many descendants of settlers from the British West Indies who still speak English. A rural area with spectacular natural assets. Cabron Point (Cabó Cabron) and the Haitises are natural parks protecting an intriguing zone of mangrove swamps and exotic vegetation.

Balaquer, during his last term as president, planned to make Samaná a tourist center; he razed the old town with its small wooden houses and built two-story buildings for free-port shops. Although Norwegian Caribbean Line cruise ships land on occasion, the town is still decidedly rural. Samaná is a good place for fishing, diving, and exploring, but be sure to bring all of your own equipment.

Puerta Plata

The major port on the north coast, about 145 miles from Santo Domingo, about a one-hour flight with a stop in Santiago. It's a regular stop for a number of cruise ships, and private yachts may clear customs here as well. Story has it that when Columbus approached this harbor on his first voyage, the high mountain looked snowcapped from out at sea, glistening like silver in the sun; so the port was called Silver Port, or Puerta Plata. A cable car goes to the top of Isabel de Torres Mountain, offering a spectacular view; the car usually runs on cruise ship days (if it's not broken).

Once a haven for pirates and smugglers, Puerta Plata with its wooden Victorian houses still seems to be a lovely colonial town. The old stone fort—Fuerte de San Felipe (Fort of Saint Phillip)—guarded the north shore in Spanish days. Amber is mined in the hills nearby. It's easy to see why sailors sometimes called this lovely port on a rugged coast "The Sweetheart of the Atlantic."

Natural Areas

The Dominican Republic is richly endowed with natural wonders—caves; rivers; spectacular mountains, indeed the highest peak in the West Indies, Pico Duarte (more than 10,000 feet); rocky headlands; white sand beaches; mangroves; and quiet lakes. Lago Enriquillo (Enriquillo Lake), in the southeast near the Haitian border, at 144 feet below sea level is unique in the Caribbean. The largest group of crocodiles (*Crocodylus acutus*) in the world is said to sun on the shores of this vast lake within the national park.

Camping in natural areas is generally informal and without facilities; bring everything you need. If you want to explore but prefer to have a few comforts nearby—showers, groceries, restaurants—Samaná or a similar rural town will make a good base. Be sure to take a Spanish phrase book or dictionary. It's often a good idea to enlist a guide, especially if you strike out for the hinterlands. Write directly to the Tourist Board for more specific information once you've selected a destination.

NIGHTLIFE: The Dominican Republic has the Latin flair for life after dark. Most casinos, discos, floor shows, and nightclubs are connected with (and are often in) large hotels. Check with the hotel activities desk for details. They should also have the schedule for opera, theater, and visiting artists at the Teatro Dominicana in the Cultural Plaza. You can also check with the Dominican Information Center in the colonial city near the cathedral for help in getting tickets. Events are often sold out, so make arrangements as soon as you arrive. Dress appropriately.

BEACHES: Unfortunately the lovely waters right around Santo Domingo are obviously polluted, and in places the distinct odor of raw sewage is overwhelming. Beaches not too far out of town include Boca Chica, Caribe or Embassy Beach, Guayacanes, and Juan Dolio on the road between Caleta Point and San Pedro. Punta Cana in the town of Higuey has a tourist complex with clean water and a beautiful beach. Another place near Higuey, Macao, is listed as one of the top 100 beaches in the world. The luxurious Gulf-Western resort Casa de Campo at La Romana makes a good day trip out of Santo Domingo. It's about a two-hour drive each way and tours are available from major hotels. The town of La Romana is the center of the sugarcane industry on the island; cane fields and a huge refinery share the verdant countryside with the resort. There are plenty of good spots for lunch in La Romana, as well as at Casa de Campo, which has complete facilities.

SPORTS: Casa de Campo is the center for organized sports in the Dominican Republic. From tennis to polo to golf and fishing, you won't find more offered anywhere on the island. The resort is the site of the Pete Dye Golf Course, and the hotel stables fifty quarter horses near its polo field and rodeo ring. A small sportfishing fleet (mostly Bertram 35s) is docked nearby.

Here's a quick roundup of sports offerings:

Tennis: Plaza Dominicana, Sheraton, Hotel Santo Domingo, Playa Dorada, and a complete tennis village at Casa de Campo (seventeen courts and special tennis holiday deals).

Golf: Casa de Campo Pete Dye Course is country-club style and can be expensive and busy; reserve in advance in season. Santo Domingo Country Club's eighteen-hole course is available to guests reserving twenty-four hours in advance (see hotel desk). Robert Trent Jones Course (eighteen holes) is at the Jack Tar Resort, Playa Dorada, Puerta Plata; package plans available.

Polo: Matches to watch on Saturdays and Sundays from January through April at Sierra Prieta in Santo Domingo; matches to play or watch from September through May at Casa de Campo.

FISHING: Informally, almost everywhere. If you want deep-sea trips, try Casa de Campo with its Bertram 35's. Island-style fishing trips on traditional boats are easily arranged out of Samaná. The Boca de Yuma Fishing International Tournament (white and blue marlin, sailfish, and tuna for points) is usually held in May (check with the Tourist Board for the dates).

DIVING: Bring your own equipment and know-how. There are pool-side classes for scuba certification at larger hotels, but you would do better to learn where diving is more of a specialty; for the most part, diving in the D.R. is for experienced divers only. Casa de Campo offers scuba excursions, and Catalina Island just offshore has good snorkeling areas. Several diving firms take people to La Caleta Reef and Playa Palenque with its submerged cannons. The waters here are lovely and clear, and much can be seen just by snorkeling. As always, ask for local knowledge beforehand; most fishermen know the reefs and currents in their areas.

SHOPPING: As well as amber crafted into countless types of jewelry, you'll find handmade furniture, baskets, leather work (even handmade sandals), macramé, embroidery, and the opaque sea-blue stone called *larimar,* a sort of Dominican turquoise. It comes in different grades, from primitive to finely crafted, and at different prices that don't necessarily reflect quality.

Shop carefully. Take your time. Look things over well, especially items offered by street vendors. And bargain. Get an idea of prices before you confront the street vendors; the hotel shops are a good place to start. Most items offered on the street are initially priced at about twice what they will be sold for. Lots of galleries and shops sell Haitian as well as Dominican art and handicrafts. Be sure to ask about origin if this is important to you.

Shipping parcels home from the D.R. is slow and risky. Most of the furniture sold in tourist areas—mahogany rocking chairs are popular— can be disassembled into an easily transported parcel. The vendors will be delighted to package it for you so you'll be able to check it as luggage on the flight home.

There are streets lined with shops in the colonial city; Duarte Street is one of the big ones, as is Calle El Conde. La Atarazana also has a number of shops and galleries. El Mercado Modelo (The Model Market) in Santo Domingo was once solely a local market. At the behest of the Tourist Board, souvenirs are now offered alongside spices, market baskets, and saucepans. An interesting mix, but shop carefully and bargain for everything.

Amber is undoubtedly one of the best buys in the country. A petrified resin from ancient conifer trees—it can be as much as 60 million years old—amber often contains bits of plant or animal remains; a dramatic-looking insect or a delicate fern always increases the price. Amber varies in color from nearly clear to cool lemon yellow to a rich brown. There's a great deal of it available here, from cheap children's rings to intricately tooled necklaces; one Dominican artist even sculpts large blocks of amber. To be sure you're buying real amber and not plastic, hold a match under it; if it begins to smudge or melt, it's plastic.

Mendez Artesania (José Reyes and Arzobispo Nouel) is a reliable source for amber jewelry. Miguel Mendez is the jeweler who popularized the unique bluestone larimar (named for his daughter Larissa and the sea). A shop called María Ambar (Calle Duarte 9) is also reliable, matching high quality with price.

Shops are generally open from about 8:30 or 9 A.M. until noon, and from 2:30 to about 6 or 6:30 P.M.

Note: A number of tortoiseshell items are sold in the Dominican Republic; most of them are fabricated from the shells of endangered sea turtles. Since these animals are on the endangered species list, it is illegal to bring items made from them into the U.S.; customs will confiscate tortoiseshell.

FESTIVALS AND HOLIDAYS

New Year's Day, 1 January.

Three Kings Day (Epiphany or Little Christmas), 6 January.

Feast of Our Lady of Altagracia (High Grace), pilgrimages to the Basilica in Higuey, 21 January.

Duarte Day, 26 January.

Independence Day, 27 February.

Labor Day, 1 May.

Corpus Christi Day, 25 May.

Boca de Yuma International Fishing Tournament, May or June (date varies).

Merengue Festival, July.

Restoration Day, 16 August. (The children dress up as little devils in some places.)

Feast of Our Lady of Mercy, pilgrimages to Santo Cerro (Holy Hill), 24 September.

Columbus Day, 12 October.

Christmas Day, 25 December.

FOOD: Dominicans like to eat, and any place without a cafe, you're likely to find a food stand or a vendor with a pushcart. For the most part, the street food here is safe. Just make sure you're buying from a vendor or stand that looks viable and busy. Follow the local customers and use common sense. The oranges (or *chinas*), mangoes, and pineapples sold from street carts are usually fresh and sweet (the mangoes should be peeled). Eat in the hotel coffee shops if you want an American-style sandwich or have an aversion to fried and spicy foods.

Dominican beverages couldn't be more pleasant. Strong, rich local coffee and El Presidente beer are tops. The local rum is also good—try Bermudez, Sibonney, or Brugal; it's also a lot cheaper than imported alcohol, which carries a high duty. There is lots of good seafood as well as Dominican beef. You may want to try some of the local specialties such as *modongo* (tripe), *chicarones* (crispy fried pork rind—a sort of bacony potato chip), *bollito de yucca* (deep-fried ground yucca root and cheese), *sanchocho* (mixed vegetables and meat), or some variety of *pastelitos* or empanadas. Pastelitos are little fried pastries, a sort of turnover filled with beef, chicken, pork, or fish in a usually spicy sauce; empanadas are simply larger pies along the same lines. Wonderful Spanish omelets are served for breakfast, along with a variety of tropical fruits. You may also want to try some of the plantain variations—fried when ripe and sweet (sometimes called *amarillos*), fried when they're green (*tostones*), or simply boiled and served like a tropical potato.

Hotels

The Dominican Republic Tourist Office has a ten-page list of hotels and guest houses by city. The list includes amenities (beach, pool, water sports, tennis, golf, kitchen, casino, restaurant, disco) and classifies each establishment as inexpensive, moderate, first-class, or all-inclusive.

There are also many money-saving packages available if you ask. And remember that a 23 percent tax goes on top of your hotel bill.

SAMANÁ

Cayacoa Beach Resort. 60 rooms, air-conditioning, dining room, disco (operates at busy times); above the beach. Moderate.

El Portillo, Las Terrenas. 8 bungalows with plumbing and kitchens, right along the shore, rustic—pack as you would for camping.

PUERTA PLATA

Hotels vary considerably, from housekeeping condominiums out of town to simple downtown inns.

Dorada Naco Hotel, Playa Dorada; telephone: (800) 322-2388. 150 condominium apartments. Complete resort, including supermarket, beach, free riding, and golf. Expensive.

Jack Tar Village, Playa Dorada; telephone: (800) 999-9182. 208 rooms on the beach, restaurant, nightclub, pool, shops, golf course. Package plan with sports included is recommended.

Hotel Montemar, Avenida Circunvalación del Norte; telephone: (800) 545-8089. 44 rooms, 6 bungalows, pool, asphalt tennis courts, restaurant, bar. Five-minute walk to beach. Dominican-style informality; reasonable.

Playa Dorada, Playa Dorada; telephone: (800) 545-8089. 254 rooms with all amenities.

SANTO DOMINGO

Santo Domingo has all types of hotels; if you decide to stay at a small, old, and picturesque one, it's not out of line to inquire about bathroom facilities, showers, and how regularly the water runs. Information on Dominican hotels is easily obtained from travel agents and the Tourist Office, so the following brief list contains only hotels with toll-free U.S. phone numbers. Remember, off-season rates are considerably less (even at Casa de Campo) and package deals abound.

Santo Domingo. (800) 877-3643. 220 rooms, air-conditioning, pool, tennis, restaurant, nightclub.

Hispaniola Hotel and Casino. (800) 877-3643. 164 rooms, air-conditioning, pool, restaurant, nightclub. Moderate.

Sheraton. (800) 334-8484. 260 rooms, air-conditioning, pool, tennis, restaurant, nightclub, disco.

El Embajador. (800) 463-6902. 316 rooms, air-conditioning, pool, tennis, restaurant, nightclub, disco.

LA ROMANA

Casa de Campo. (800) 877-3643. 176 rooms, air-conditioning, pool, tennis, golf, restaurant, nightclub, disco.

PUENTA CANA

Club Mediterranne at Puenta Cana. (800) 528-3100. 334 rooms, air-conditioning, pool, tennis, restaurant, nightclub, disco.

All the hotels listed for Santo Domingo, La Romano, and Puenta Cana provide help arranging sightseeing, car rental, et cetera; they also have gift shops.

For more information, contact the nearest Dominican Republic Tourist Office or call the toll free information hotline (800) 752-1151.

D.R.
Secretaría de Estado de Turismo
P.O. Box 498
Santo Domingo, Dominican Republic
telephone: (809) 535-3276

U.S.
100 North Biscayne Boulevard
Miami, FL 33132
telephone: (305) 371-2813

1501 Broadway, Suite 410
New York, NY 10036

1300 Ashford Avenue
Santurce, Puerto Rico 00902
telephone: (809) 725-4774

GERMANY
Grosse Brockenheimer
Strasse 6D-6000
Frankfurt, Germany
telephone: (069) 287551

ITALY
Via Serbelloni 7
Milano, Italia
telephone: (059) 323073

SPAIN
Nuñez de Balboa 37
4to. izquierda
Madrid, España
telephone: 431-5354

SWITZERLAND
Zolliderstrasse 141
8034 Zurich, Switzerland
telephone: 01 550242

VENEZUELA
Final Avenida Casanova
Centro Comercial 777
Local 18, Primer Piso
Chacaíto-Caracas, Venezuela
telephone: 71320-713239

Information is also available from Dominican Airlines, 1200 NW 78th
Avenue, Miami, FL 33126; telephone: (305) 592-3588.

Once you arrive in the D.R., the Tourist Information Center in the colonial city, right across from the cathedral, is a good source of information; telephone: 685-3282. Look for English tourist publications in your

hotel. *Bohío* (mostly ads but interesting), the *Santo Domingo News,* and the blue handout called "dominican fiesta!" all have items of interest; "fiesta" is probably the most helpful. Check the gift shops for the inexpensive "Official Guide to the D.R."

Grenada

AREA: 133 square miles (3 islands); Grenada itself is 21 miles long, 7 miles wide.

POPULATION: About 96,000

CAPITAL CITY: St. George's.

LANGUAGE: English.

RELIGION: Mainly Roman Catholic and Anglican.

GOVERNMENT: Parliamentary democracy (independent member of the British Commonwealth).

LOCATION: Most southerly of the Windward Islands, about 100 miles north of Venezuela.

GETTING THERE: By air direct from Miami or New York or through San Juan. Connections via Trinidad and Barbados.

CUSTOMS: U.S. and Canadian citizens need only proof of citizenship and either return or ongoing tickets.

HEALTH: No special considerations.

CLOTHING: Tropical sportswear; visitors are asked to "cover up in town." Most people dress for dinner in season (cocktail or long dresses, jackets and ties).

ELECTRICITY: 220-240 volts/50 cycles AC.

TIME ZONE: Atlantic standard time, one hour ahead of eastern standard time.

MONEY: Eastern Caribbean dollar; the value fluctuates, usually about E.C. $2.70/2.90 to U.S. $1.

GETTING AROUND: Taxis, tour buses; mini-mokes and cars are
rented (present your valid U.S. driver's license to Police Traffic Department).

Overview

Mountainous and volcanic, yet blessed with unlikely white coral beaches,
Grenada has every Caribbean attribute of scenic beauty. One of the
world's smallest nations, Grenada depends on spice plantations and tourism to maintain its economy; it is a main world supplier of nutmeg. The
most southerly of the Windward Islands, Grenada includes a few of the
small Grenadines to the north; Carriacou, Petit Martinique, and small
islets and sand spits like Île de Ronde, Green Bird, and Kick-em-Jenny are
all administered as dependencies.

History

Grenada was sighted by Columbus, who named it Concepción. But early
on, the island with its green hills reminded passing sailors of Granada in
Spain. The French, who began to settle the island in the 1600s, altered
the name to "Grenade." The British took possession in 1763 and the island became known as "Grenada" (pronounced Gre-NAY-da). It became
a Crown Colony in 1877 and independent in 1974.

Most visitors are likely to be familiar with the more recent upheaval
that resulted in the 1983 U.S. invasion. Things have settled down into
new expansion, business investments, and the revival of tourism. The new
airport, begun by Cuba and once much in the news, has been finished with
U.S. money.

Things to See and Do

St. George's

A walk through and up and around this picturesque harbor town will give
you the sights at a leisurely pace. The Tourist Board office on the Carenage, St. George's inner harbor, actually the crater of an ancient volcano,
will provide maps and information; it also makes a good starting point.
You may want to include the Grenada National Museum, Fort George
(originally built by the French in 1705), Fort Frederik, and the Botanical
Gardens and Zoo (here's your chance for a glimpse of many rarely seen
Caribbean animals).

Bay Gardens

Another showcase for tropical flora, including spice trees; three acres northeast of town.

Annandale Falls

This is a favorite picnic spot in the mountains about a fifteen-minute drive from St. George's, where falls cascade some 50 feet into a pool below. Bring your lunch and swimwear to enjoy this area of lush vegetation and hiking trails.

Grand Étang National Park and Forest Reserve

This park sits in the center of the island and includes rain and elfin forests and the blue-blue waters of Grand Étang Lake, which fills the crater of an extinct volcano. Crisscrossed by hiking trails of all levels, the park gives visitors a close look at the variety of Grenada's plants and animals. Trails lead to the 2,309-foot summit of Mount Sinai, through the mists to the top of 2,373-foot Mount Qua Qua, as well as a thirty-minute jaunt along the edge of Grand Étang Lake.

You can drive to the Grand Étang Forest Center, the park's interpretive hub, for more information. You'll need a four-wheel-drive vehicle to negotiate the mountain roads. Hiking guides are available but must be arranged for in advance through your hotel or the Grenada Board of Tourism office on the Carenage.

Grand Anse Beach

This is probably one of the most famous stretches of sand in the Caribbean. On the dry southern shore; most of Grenada's hotels are nearby. Facilities on hotel beaches are available to nonguests for a small fee.

Other Beaches

On the southern part of the island, try Musquetta or Horseshoe Bay. Levera Beach, on the northwestern tip of the island where the Atlantic and the Caribbean meet (but few people do), is palm-lined and lovely. Bring your lunch. Nearby Carriacou and Sandy Island also have nice sandy stretches.

Carriacou

Most visitors can't resist a short trip to the nearby island of Carriacou, twenty-three miles northeast of Grenada. A small airline makes the short flight regularly; boats also make the trip several days a week. This rural, 13-square-mile island has an interesting combination of African and Scottish heritage. With good anchorages and lovely beaches, it is the perfect getaway for beachcombers and dreamers. Expect to pay for this relaxed atmosphere; doubles often cost $100-plus a day without meals.

SHOPPING: Every visitor will want to take in St. George's bustling Saturday morning market in Market Square. It's a good place to buy local fruit or little baskets of fresh spices to take home. The nearby Straw Mart offers shoppers the best of island handicrafts, including straw work and coconut shell jewelry. (Remember, it is illegal to bring turtle products into the U.S.)

Yellow Poui has two art galleries in St. George's where Caribbean artwork and historical prints are sold.

Tikal, an arts and crafts shop next to the National Museum in St. George's, features fine handicrafts from Grenada as well as Latin America. Dolls, straw work, jewelry, batiks, and sculpture can be found here.

FESTIVALS AND HOLIDAYS: Carnival in mid-August is the big bash here; all traditional festivals, music, and "jump-up," where revelers jump up and dance. The August Regatta on Carriacou is also one big party. Businesses are closed on traditional British and American holidays.

FOOD: Seafood, including conch (or *lambi*), specialties are popular. Be sure to try local fruits and vegetables and local rum punch laced with Grenadian spices. Almost everyone who visits the island has at least one meal in the old plantation house at Morne Fendue, where local specialties are charmingly served; call for reservations (442-9330). Ross Point Inn is a favorite dining spot with locals.

HOTELS: Grenada's hotels are low-key and comfortable. At most of them, you can expect to pay about U.S. $150 and up for a room for two in season. Many hotels include the use of sports equipment such as tennis courts and boats.

Accommodations (and prices) vary from the lush suites of the Calabash Hotel (around $400 a day, double, in season, with breakfast, tea, and dinner) to simple guest houses throughout the island in the $50-a-day range. The moderately priced La Sagesse Nature Center offers beach cottages or rooms in its old manor house for less than $100 a day.

For complete hotel listings, request "The Greeting," a booklet from the Grenada Board of Tourism.

For More Information

U.S.

Grenada Board of Tourism
820 Second Avenue, Suite 900D
New York, NY 10017
telephone: (212) 687-9554

CANADA

Grenada Board of Tourism
439 University Avenue, Suite 820
Toronto, Ontario M5G 1Y8
Canada
telephone: (416) 595-1339

Guadeloupe

AREA: 687 square miles.

POPULATION: Approximately 387,000.

CAPITAL CITY: Basse-Terre.

LANGUAGE: French and Creole; English in most hotels.

RELIGION: Roman Catholic.

GOVERNMENT: Overseas region of France.

LOCATION: Leeward Islands, north of Dominica (310 miles from San Juan).

GETTING THERE: All major airlines fly into Guadeloupe's international airport.

CUSTOMS: U.S. and Canadian citizens need either a valid passport or proof of citizenship (an expired passport less than five years old works); other nationalities need a valid passport and, in some cases, a visa.

HEALTH: No special considerations; modern facilities. Tap water is okay.

CLOTHING: Informal tropical wear; men may need sport coats and women long skirts for dining in some places. Pack a sweater if you plan to hike in the Parc Naturel.

ELECTRICITY: 220 volts/50 cycles AC.

TIME ZONE: Atlantic standard time, one hour ahead of eastern standard time.

MONEY: French franc; U.S. and Canadian currency accepted.

GETTING AROUND: Rental cars, taxis, cars with guides, tours, and public buses. Drivers need more than a year's experience and a valid driver's license for car rental. Flat, modern Grand-Terre has good roads and easy driving, but it may be safer to let someone else negotiate the steep, mountainous twists of Basse-Terre. All sight-seeing companies have tours that include Parc Naturel.

Overview

Guadeloupe is relatively undiscovered by American visitors, maybe because they are lured to other French islands with more romantic images or are put off by the industrialized metropolis of Pointe-à-Pitre, Guadeloupe's principal city. Guadeloupe is two islands, shaped like open butterfly wings; the eastern wing of land is called Grand-Terre, the western, Basse-Terre. La Rivière Sallée is the strait that separates them.

Grand-Terre and Basse-Terre differ right down to their geology. Grand-Terre is flat and calcareous, ringed with white coral sand beaches, and consequently has most of the resorts. Basse-Terre is volcanic, with craggy mountains and lush forests. The smoldering La Soufrière at 4,813 feet is its most famous landmark. La Soufrière is only one of the natural wonders that are protected within the extensive Parc Naturel on Basse-Terre. With its fumaroles, thick forests, spectacular waterfalls, and well-marked trails in diverse habitats, this park is one of the best hiking areas in the Caribbean.

French flair and food round out the offerings of this lovely country. Don't overlook Guadeloupe's small dependencies offshore; Le Desirade, Marie-Galante, and Îles des Saintes also offer visitors quiet seaside scenery.

History

When Guadeloupe was sighted by Columbus in 1493, it had long been the home of the Amerindians. Their extensive rock carvings and petroglyphs at scenic Trois Rivières are thought to be over a thousand years old. The Caribs that met Columbus called the island Karukera, "Island of Beautiful Waters." Columbus rechristened it for Santa Maria de Guadalupe de Estremadura. The fierce Caribs were able to repel early Spaniards who tried to settle the island.

The first European settlement was made by the French in 1635, when they claimed Guadeloupe. The French fought the Caribs and managed to drive them to neighboring islands. They then set about sugar production with imported African slaves. The king of France officially annexed the island in 1674.

The prosperous island then became the stage for the British-French battles that have marked Caribbean history. The British occupied Guadeloupe from 1759 to 1763, when it was exchanged for all French rights in Canada. It was not until the Treaty of Paris in 1815 that the international tug-of-war officially ended.

The island became an overseas department of France in 1946, giving islanders the same social welfare benefits as French citizens on the Continent. The island's economy remains based on tourism and agriculture; the main crops are sugarcane, bananas, and pineapples.

The explosion of La Soufrière volcano on 30 August 1976 resulted in the wide-scale evacuation of southern Basse-Terre. This semiactive volcano, which is closely monitored, is one of the main attractions within Guadeloupe's extraordinary Parc Naturel.

Things to See and Do

Hiking and exploring top the list, although there are also lovely beaches with all water sports, and some city diversions, as well.

Pointe-à-Pitre

This bustling harbor town is Guadeloupe's principal city. Visitors usually enjoy a stroll through the covered marketplace and along the Darse (dock) market, where the vendors in madras are as colorful as their wares. The nearby Place de la Victoire is lined with grand sablier trees and colonial houses. The modern edifices of the post office, city hall, and other government buildings are in the northern part of town.

The Musée St. John Perse, named for the 1960 Nobel Prize-winning poet who was born on Guadeloupe, exhibits mementos, documents, and photos in a charming nineteenth-century house. Not too far away, the Centre St. John Perse, on the waterfront, is a new architectural complex that includes duty-free shops, restaurants, a hotel, and a bank. Many years in the planning, this complex has tastefully transformed old warehouses and buildings to renew the area.

Basse-Terre

Guadeloupe's quiet capital is tucked away between the smoldering Soufrière and the ocean. A seventeenth-century cathedral and stalwart Fort St. Charles, built in 1643, are high points.

Trois Rivières and the Engraved Rocks Archaeological Park

On the southern coast of Grand-Terre, this little settlement has a number of pre-Columbian relics. The archaeological park has interpretive material on local plants, as well as ancient petroglyphs. An easy thirty- to forty-minute walk is mapped with wooden markers. Another path leads down to the stream mouth, where more drawings can be seen. This primitive site remains a beautiful area.

Nearby, the ferry to Îles des Saintes leaves from the dock in town.

Parc Naturel

This 74,100-acre preserve in the heart of lush Basse-Terre is one of the Caribbean's exemplary parks. Exhibition huts give information on various subjects, including the volcano, coffee, the forest, and the sea. The park has more than 200 miles of marked foot trails, which are color-coded and rated by difficulty. Approximate hiking times, mileage, and descriptions of the terrain and flora and fauna are included in the booklet called "Walks and Hikes/Promenades and Randonnées." Visitors can then decide if they'd like to explore for half a day or half a month. The park's diverse assets include rivers, hot springs, waterfalls, a rain forest, lava flows, and, of course, the Soufrière itself. The park has no gates, no opening or closing hours, and no admission fee.

If you want company on your explorations, try a guided hiking tour through the Organisation des Guides de Montagne de la Caraïbe (O.G.M.C.); telephone: 81.45.79. Scaling La Soufrière with their guides takes about four hours one way and costs about 300 francs. Shorter and less arduous treks have different fees. Contact the park's visitor center or the Tourist Office for more information. Guides are recommended, particularly to La Soufrière.

Within the park, briefly:

Grand Étang (Great Pond): The surface area of the pond (now some 50 acres) shrinks each year as aquatic weeds encroach. A one-hour circuit (classed as an "easy walk") lets visitors enjoy lush vegetation as well as the pond itself. (You can drive to the edge of the pond.)

Galleon Fall: The Galleon River falls 131 feet just a mile from its source. A two-hour walk with some steep places.

Carbet Falls: Three falls of the Carbet River, which originates on the face of the Soufrière, where the waters are boiling and sulfurous. The waters cool and become clear after these dramatic falls. The first and second can be seen from the shore; the third fall, although only 66 feet high, is more impressive for the volume of its flow. The second and third falls may be reached easily on foot (about thirty minutes to the third falls, only twenty minutes or so to the second). The hike to the first fall is somewhat more demanding. It takes an hour and a half to get there and is described as "somewhat difficult hiking." Better take lunch on this one.

La Soufrière: This towering peak at 4,813 feet is often locally called the "Old Lady." Probably best categorized as a semiactive volcano, Soufrière still bubbles and rumbles, emitting sulfurous fumes from its craggy fumaroles. The trek directly to the summit (red trail) can be made by the sturdy in about four hours; a guide is a good idea. More leisurely trails lead to other craters, fumaroles, and Sulfur Lake. The Citerne, one of Soufrière's neighboring volcanoes, with a completely round crater, is more accessible, although part of the trail requires climbing ladders straight up the wall of Sulfur Lake.

Offshore Islands

Marie-Galante: daily ferry from La Darse, Pointe-à-Pitre; two-hour crossing, about 160 francs round-trip.

Îles des Saintes: ferries leave Trois Rivières twice daily; thirty-minute crossing, about 85 francs each way.

Le Desirade: Monday through Friday departures from Marina de St. François; forty-five-minute crossing, about 100 francs roundtrip.

Note: These crossings may be rough. If you tend toward seasickness, you may be happier flying. Local tour operators often have excursion packages.

BEACHES: For white stretches of coral sand, head for Grand-Terre. Public beaches are usually free but may charge for parking; don't count on facilities. Motel beaches offer changing rooms, chairs, and towels to nonguests for a fee. Topless is common at hotel beaches. There are several official nudist beaches; Pointe Tarare is the most popular. For a change of scene, you may want to swim and sun on one of the black beaches of western Basse-Terre.

SHOPPING: French imports, wines, cheeses, and local rum are all readily available. Locally made straw work and Creole dolls are popular. Certain stores offer discounts when you pay with traveler's checks. Remember, in French fashion, stores close at noon for a long lunch, then reopen later.

FESTIVALS AND HOLIDAYS: All Catholic holidays are celebrated, including pre-Lenten Carnival, which begins on Epiphany (6 January) and runs through Ash Wednesday, with different events each Sunday. Partying ends with King Vaval's pyre on Ash Wednesday night.

Bastille Day, 14 July.

Schoelcher Day, 21 July.

Fête des Cuisinières (Cooks' Festival), early August. Mass feasting, parades, Creole costumes.

Festival of the Sea (Îles des Saintes), mid-August.

All Saints' Day, 1 November. Cemeteries are candle lit.

St. Cecilia's Day, 22 November. Musical fetes.

FOOD: Food is a pleasing mix of French and Creole dishes. An interesting lunch spot is Hotel-Relais de la Grand Soufrière in Saint-Claude, in the mountains near Soufrière. This hotel training school serves distinctive meals for about 65 francs, fixed price, service included. The Moulin Blanc in Basse-Terre serves moderately priced meals. You might want to try *calalou* soup or local crayfish in broth. Have a take-out lunch of French bread, cheese, wine, and fruit at least once. Guadeloupe is full of beautiful places to enjoy it.

HOTELS: Guadeloupe is a large diverse island with accommodations to suit all tastes and pocketbooks. The four-star Auberge de la Ville Tour on the beach in Grosier is Guadeloupe's oldest inn; all facilities, including a good restaurant, in a restful, tropical setting with balconied rooms. Off-season packages are available for considerably less (telephone: 84.23.23). There are a number of small, privately owned hotels as well as a Club Med on Guadeloupe.

Camping is also an option on Guadeloupe. Sites are basic except at Les Sables d'Or, near Deshaies on Grand Anse Beach. Sites have good facilities and tents can be rented (call 28.44.60). Camping cars, fully equipped to sleep four or five, can be rented from Alligator Vacances (telephone: 23.17.52), Locap' Soleil (telephone: 84.56.51), and Vert' Bleu (telephone: 28.51.25).

To direct-dial Guadeloupe from the U.S., use international access code 011, prefix 590, and then dial local numbers as listed.

For More Information

Office Départemental du Tourisme
5 Square de la Banque
B.P. 422
97163 Pointe-à-Pitre, Guadeloupe
telephone: (011) 590-82-09-30/590-89-46-89
fax: (011) 590-83-89-22

U.S.

French Government Tourist Office
676 North Michigan Avenue, Suite 3360
Chicago, IL 60611
telephone: (312) 751-7800

French Government Tourist Office
9454 Wilshire Boulevard, Suite 715
Los Angeles, CA 90212
telephone: (310) 271-7800

French Government Tourist Office
610 Fifth Avenue
New York, NY 10020
telephone: (900) 990-0040
fax: (212) 247-6468

CANADA

French Government Tourist Office
1981 Avenue McGill College
Montreal, Quebec H3A 2W9
Canada
telephone: (514) 288-4264

French Government Tourist Office
30 St. Patrick Street, Suite 700
Toronto, Ontario M5T 3A3
Canada
telephone: (416) 593-6427

Haiti

NOTE: Due to the civil unrest and the dire economic situation that constantly interrupt the flow of goods and services, U.S. visitors should be aware of the potential for random violence and crime, particularly in urban areas. All U.S. travelers to Haiti are encouraged to register with the U.S. Embassy, on Harry Truman Boulevard in Port-au-Prince, immediately upon arrival. To register, telephone (509) 22-0200, 22-0368, or 22-0612. Travelers are urged to use extreme caution, avoid public gatherings, and maintain contact with the embassy while in Haiti.

AREA: 10,714 square miles (about the size of the state of Maryland).

POPULATION: Nearly 6,500,000 (about 690 people per square mile).

CAPITAL CITY: Port-au-Prince.

LANGUAGE: French (official) and Creole patois; a great deal of English is spoken in the tourist areas.

RELIGION: Predominately Roman Catholic.

LOCATION: Haiti sits on the western third of the large island of Hispaniola—the second-largest island in the Caribbean—which it shares with the Dominican Republic. Cuba is its nearest island neighbor, 22 miles to the northwest.

GETTING THERE: Several airlines fly into Port-au-Prince.

CUSTOMS: U.S. citizens need proof of citizenship—a valid passport, voter registration card, or birth certificate—and either a return or an ongoing ticket. Tourists may bring one carton of cigarettes and one quart of liquor into Haiti; drug laws are strictly enforced. Tourist cards are issued on arrival. The whole process is generally a formality, quite pleasant enough.

HEALTH: Haiti has the tropical health problems that go with poverty, poor hygiene, poor nutrition, and overpopulation. Although strides in general health have been made in recent years, tuberculosis, hepatitis, and malaria remain common. So go only when your general health is good. Malaria prophylaxis (chloroquine) is advised. Wear insect repellent, especially in the evening and early morning hours; eating only in major hotels and restaurants where the water is bottled and the milk boiled will reduce your risk considerably.

Drink only bottled water. If you're on a tight budget or traveling with children, it's a good idea to take some boxed drinks and snacks along with you; it can get expensive to sit down to sodas every time someone gets thirsty. Food from street vendors is a definite no-no. You may also want to bring long-life boxed milk, which needs no refrigeration.

If you are on a private yacht and need fresh fruits and vegetables, the best advice is to choose easily peeled bananas, avocados, oranges, and such. If you must have lettuce, soak it at least twenty minutes in water with a little chlorine bleach or iodine solution to be extra careful, and then rinse. You might consider it worth the trip up to the Baptist Mission Store on Mt. Kenscoff, where fresh produce is grown and sold under controlled health conditions. The mission also runs a marvelous bakery and a small restaurant with good sandwiches.

One last health note: Don't overlook the value of lots of soap and water hand washing. Also, carry premoistened towelettes for freshening up en route. You may want to bring a small plastic bottle of bleach; you never know when you may want a few drops to wash your hands, purify bathwater, or clean your shoes after a day of adventurous walking through streets with open sewers.

This all sounds discouraging, I'm sure, and recent publicity including Haitians in the high-risk group for AIDS makes the health outlook there even bleaker.

CLOTHING: Informal tropical wear is fine, but dress conservatively outside of hotels and resorts; you'll be obvious enough without wearing shorts in downtown Port-au-Prince. Evening dress (jackets, dresses) may be needed in some hotels and restaurants; light sweaters for evenings and the mountains. Bring a hat, bathing suits, sunglasses, cover-ups, as usual. It's a good idea to bring jeans or sturdy pants if you plan to ride a mule back up to the Citadelle or hike in the bush.

ELECTRICITY: Generally 110 volts/60 cycles AC. Some beach hotels use DC; ask ahead if it matters to you.

MONEY: The basic unit of Haitian currency is called the gourde: 5 gourdes to U.S. $1. U.S. dollars are accepted (indeed preferred) everywhere, and there's no need to change money if you bring enough with you. (There is no charge for changing money.) American Express traveler's checks seem to work equally well, and are accepted even in the Iron Market. Hotels accept most major credit cards, but several of the larger shops take only American Express cards.

TAX AND TIPS: Airport departure tax, about U.S. $10 per person. Porters expect about U.S. $1 per bag. Tipping seems expected and is often (especially in your hotel) directly related to service; it seems to even out at about U.S. $1 for nearly everything—all a little baffling since the hotel adds U.S. $2.50 per day for the maids, who expect you to add to that (and are likely to hold out on your towels if you don't). The hotels also add a 10 percent service charge to your total bill, supposedly for all those other people who also expect tips. Count on another few dollars per day energy surcharge. All tallied, this increases the bill considerably, so find out exactly what will be added when you make your reservations or check in, so you won't be stunned when you leave. (There aren't many tourists in Haiti, and in this country, where the average yearly income is less than U.S. $300, we all appear very rich. Count on hidden costs.)

GETTING AROUND: Don't go far, especially in Port-au-Prince, without a Haitian to lead the way. Walking guides can be acquired outside most hotels most of the time. They are usually happy to show you around for a few dollars a day; it's traditional to throw in a soda or lunch, depending on the length of the tour and the time of day. Agree on the fee in advance, and if you want to be shown a particular art gallery or restaurant, be adamant or you'll probably be charmed into a similar place the guide just happens to know.

Tap-taps, large trucks lined with seat boards for passengers and room on top for livestock and produce, are the quintessential traveling cultural exhibition. Every inch of every tap-tap is painted with folk art, proverbs, religious messages, and often its own name and the name of the driver. Like everything else, tap-taps are more than crowded. Rides on Haiti's unique mass transit system are best left to the young and hardy. If you do want this experience, go with a guide.

Taxi rates are set by the government.

Cab guides will go almost anywhere, and wait while you shop, or personally see you through the Iron Market for a daily fee, depending on the distance you want to travel. Hold out for a driver with a good car; vans are preferable—the extra height gets you up above the road dust and makes for a much nicer outing. As always, establish price and route in advance.

Car rentals. Nobody recommends driving within Port-au-Prince; to say the roads are crowded is laughable. It *is* possible to drive from

Port-au-Prince to Cap-Haïtien without being a former New York City cabdriver as long as one takes reasonable precautions. Be sure to leave with a full tank of fuel (all gas stations are closed at night) and check for a spare tire and jack; don't assume anything. It's probably best to leave Port-au-Prince as early in the day as possible (absolutely no later than 2 P.M.) since heavy afternoon showers are common in the mountains. Remember that many animals also use the roads.

Tour operators. Don't overlook the convenience of prearranged tours; nothing in Haiti is "canned." It's more than likely that even the most organized sight-seeing will contain charming elements of the unexpected. Most hotels will help with the arrangements or you may contact tour agencies directly.

Overview

Haiti is exactly as the tourist brochures promise, a place "like nowhere else." Perhaps because Haiti is so hard to categorize, most first-time visitors don't know what to expect and fall quickly into love-it or hate-it camps; few are neutral. Whatever the reaction, the word "color," which in the tropics seems an even flatter label for something of great dimension, is always used in describing this island.

The colors vibrate, blend, and swirl in such a way that a street scene or marketplace seems to become a work of art, balanced by the even distribution of ebony skin, its sheen reflecting the rainbow.

Life is hard here; the average life span is only fifty years, the average income less than U.S. $300 per year. And yet there is no lack of joie de vivre, and poets, painters, wood-carvers, embroiderers, and papier-mâché makers abound. It is as though the whole nation has found small ways to fabricate their visions of a colorful, controllable universe. And to sell them.

Haiti can be overwhelming; nothing quite prepares you for its richness, poverty, density, diversity. With an average of 690 people per square mile, Haiti is one of the most densely populated countries in the Western Hemisphere. On the road to Port-au-Prince from the airport are cars, trucks, donkeys, vans, taxis, and tap-taps (Haiti's hand-painted answer to mass transit). Dirt byways are lined with goats and people, some carrying produce on their heads. New car dealerships pop up in the roadside mélange that belongs to another century, instantly reminding one of certain inequities. There is a small group of the very affluent, a small emerging middle class, and a great multitude of poor who seem to subsist on a diet of ingenuity.

Political violence is a tradition. After the end of the Duvalier regime in 1986, Haiti was in a state of violent political upheaval. Since the U.S. military returned Haitian President-elect Jean-Bertrand Aristide, the dust has shown signs of settling. The presidency was peacefully transferred to Rene Preval in 1996. However, with 46 percent inflation and little work, the Haitian people continue to be challenged. If you go, check with the U.S. State Department for Travelers Advisories before your visit.

History

The original Caribbean tourist, Christopher Columbus, claimed Haiti for Spain on his first voyage, when he landed near Cap-Haïtien on 5 December, 1492. He called the island "La Isla Española." It remains in its Latinized form, Hispaniola.

The Spaniards quickly conquered the million or so indigenous Arawak Indians and proceeded to kill all of them within a relatively short time. Then they started to import Africans for slaves, beginning the exploitive plantation culture that lasted for the next 300 years.

In 1697, the Treaty of Ryswick formalized the bargain in which Spain officially ceded the western end of Hispaniola to France. The French changed its name to Saint Domingue and continued to import large numbers of Africans for slaves. Saint Domingue flourished and, under this harsh system of exploitation, became one of the richest colonies in the New World.

The ideals of liberty and equality proclaimed by the French Revolution, which began in 1789, were not unheard-of in Saint Domingue, where they fueled slave rebellions. Plantations were burned and many of the white slave lords fled or were killed.

French troops were sent in 1792 to crush the revolt, but they were defeated by the local armies of Toussaint L'Ouverture, the self-educated slave grandson of an African king. Toussaint agreed to rule for France, abolished slavery, and organized a constitutional convention.

Napoleon saw this as an act of secession and sent seventy warships and 25,000 men to restore French authority. Toussaint was captured by one of those petty schemes of treachery so common to war and was put on board a warship for France as a criminal. He died soon thereafter from the duress of prison in the French Alps, but the revolution was carried on by his generals—Henry Christophe, Alexander Pétion, and Jean-Jacques Dessalines. The French troops, decimated by yellow fever as well as war, withdrew in 1803; 50,000 had died trying to restore slavery.

On 1 January 1804, Haiti became the second country in the New World to declare its independence and the world's first black republic.

Dessalines's secretary read the declaration of independence on the very spot where Toussaint had been captured.

But the story does not ride this victory to peaceful prosperity. Politics divided the country. Christophe became emperor of the north (indeed, the autocratic prototype for Eugene O'Neill's *Emperor Jones*) and Pétion controlled the south.

Christophe called himself King Henry I and involved himself and his subjects (conscripting 20,000 of them back into slavery) in monumental building projects. Many died hauling rocks and cannons 3,000 feet up the mountain to fabricate Christophe's fortress, the massive Citadelle Laferrière, built to withstand invasion by Napoleon, who, of course, never came.

After Christophe's suicide with a silver bullet in 1820, Haiti was united under the leadership of Jean Pierre Boyer, who governed for the next twenty-five years.

Haiti was ruled by twenty-two dictators from 1843 to 1915, when the United States seized control. U.S. troops occupied the island until 1934, and the U.S. maintained economic control until 1947.

After being elected president in 1957, François "Papa Doc" Duvalier became dictator. Unable to deal with great social and economic problems along with political unrest, his regime became repressive. Haiti, under Duvalier's strong arm, featured the terrors of his secret police—the *tontons macoute*. Graham Greene's *The Comedians*, a novel vividly portraying this era, is still "unavailable" in Haiti. As well as amassing a private fortune, Papa Doc saw the completion of the new jetport and some attractive administrative buildings.

When Duvalier died in April 1971, he was succeeded by his nineteen-year-old son Jean Claude, "Baby Doc," who was president until 1986, when he fled Haiti. Young Duvalier's deposé left Haiti in violent political turmoil.

Ongoing political unrest coupled with severe economic hardships marked Haiti's next years. Attempts to hold elections ended in violence and a series of military coups. In 1990, the popular Reverend Jean-Bertrand Aristide defeated a former Duvalier supporter for the presidency, but when General Raoul Cedras seized power in October 1991, Aristide was forced to flee.

In an effort to curb the political violence in Haiti and to restore democracy, the Organization of American States established severe trade sanctions against Haiti. Then, in October 1994, the U.S. military returned Aristide to power. A peaceful election in 1996 placed Rene Preval as president. Needless to say, however, Haiti has still not recovered—tremendous inflation and the lack of employment impede its progress toward stability.

Things to See and Do

Port-au-Prince

Museums, statues, parks, galleries, shops, the Iron Market, gingerbread houses (Defly Mansion is restored and open to the public). Wandering recommended.

Champ de Mars: The Square of Heroes of Independence, a city park complete with pigeon houses; surrounded by statues. Le Maron Inconnu (the Unknown Slave) blowing the conch for revolt is probably the most famous.

The National Palace: An imposing white building looking out on the square. Visitors' hall has some busts and tombs of famous people; most impressive from the outside.

Musée du Panthéon National Haïtien: Modern underground museum on the square; its striking architecture makes it unmistakable. Exhibits change. Admission charge.

Cathédrale de la Sainte Trinité: An Episcopal church with biblical murals painted in 1951 by the Haitian masters Obin, Bottex, and Bigaud. These paintings gave great impetus to the Haitian art movement, portraying all biblical figures with black faces except Judas, whose is white.

Le Musée d'Art Haïtien du College St. Pierre: Houses the works of Haiti's leading artists collected by Bishop Voegli for the Episcopal Church and by Dewitt Peters of Le Centre d'Art.

The National Museum: Historical relics—the anchor from Columbus's flagship the *Santa Maria*, the small silver pistol with which Christophe shot himself, and more.

Kenscoff and Vicinity

Fort Jacques Artisanat: One mile above Port-au-Prince; a primitive forge—handmade wrought-iron furniture and figures for sale at moderate prices.

Jane Barbancourt Distillery: About twenty minutes by car out of Port-au-Prince on the road to Kenscoff. Free tastes of exotic liqueurs—hibiscus, mango, coconut—served with an ambience that recaptures the style of an eighteenth-century distillery.

Baptist Mission Craft Shop: If you have only one place to shop, this is a good choice (it's officially in Fermathe, in the heart of Haiti's vegetable garden community). A variety of handicrafts—furniture, baby clothes, wood carvings, papier-mâché, even hand-painted rocks and little kerosene lanterns made from old cans. Fixed prices and they take American Express cards. A hand-embroidered woman's dress sells for U.S. $10–$12. Save time for lunch at the Mountain Maid Tea Terrace run by the mission. You can enjoy a wonderful sandwich, hot dog, hamburger, and a fruit soda or complimentary herb tea while looking out over the terraced vegetable gardens and the mountains. Stop in the small bakery next door for some great cookies or bread. The elevation at the mission is 4,350 feet; there are pine trees and cool breezes. A wonderful stop after a morning in the heat and bustle of Port-au-Prince. Visitors are encouraged to take self-guided tours of the extensive grounds, which include a school, a hospital, greenhouses, chicken coops, and a pet monkey.

Fort Jacques: A nineteenth-century fort complete with cannons in the Fermathe mountains. A nice walking trail (about an hour long) and great views of both Port-au-Prince harbor and Lake Azuei on the Haiti–Dominican Republic border.

Furcy: Near the top of Kenscoff Mountain; a small village set in pines and mountain foliage. Good for hiking, picnicking (most hotels will pack a lunch), and horseback riding (horses can be rented there).

Mirebelais

Saut d'Eau: Beautiful waterfall about three hours' drive out of Port-au-Prince; a driver-guide and jeep are required. The site of a mid-July pilgrimage.

Cap-Haïtien

Historic port city on Haiti's north coast, the site of Columbus's first landing. Mountains and colonial charm.

The Citadelle: Henry Christophe's monumental fort, 3,000 feet above sea level with walls twelve feet thick, took ten years to build. Cannons everywhere, a room that holds 45,000 cannon balls, and in the center Christophe's tomb. The fort was designed to shelter 10,000 people; the royal family was allotted only forty rooms. Most visitors arrange to ride a mule up the rocky mountain.

Sans Souci Palace: In the town of Milot, gateway to the Citadelle. Also built in Christophe's reign, designed to rival Versailles in France. Left in ruins by an earthquake, its grandeur is now mainly in the imagination.

Cathedral: Well-preserved nineteenth-century architecture; built at the time of Sans Souci.

Jacmel

Quiet colonial town overlooking black sand beaches.

Coffee-sorting Plant: Locally grown beans are graded and sorted.

Bassin Bleu: A day trip requiring a horse (rentals available) to a natural pool fed by waterfalls. Take a lunch; the trip will take most of the day, about one-and-a-half hours by horseback each way. Legend has it that nymphs live in three mountain grottos. The goddess of the waters herself sits on a rock next to Palm Lake and combs her hair by moonlight. Of course she disappears at the approach of any mere mortal, but the story says anyone lucky enough to find her golden comb will become as rich as a king.

SPORTS: Soccer is the national sport and is played at the Sylvio Cator Stadium in Port-au-Prince. Many larger hotels have tennis courts; almost all have pools. Fishing can sometimes be arranged but is not highly developed. There is one nine-hole golf course, described as not overly rewarding for the serious golfer. Some interesting hikes and horseback rides are suggested under specific locations earlier in this section.

SNORKELING, SCUBA DIVING: There are no customs restrictions on private scuba gear. Several beach resorts rent equipment. The biggest dive operation in Haiti is run by an American, Alan Baskin, at Baskin in the Sun at Kaliko Beach Club, about an hour's drive out of Port-au-Prince. If you're serious about diving in Haiti, check with him.

Note: The first place always mentioned for snorkeling is Sandy Cay right in Port-au-Prince harbor; it is polluted and best avoided for health reasons. There is some good snorkeling in Haiti, but, as always, stay away from population centers.

BEACHES: *Archie Beach* area, thirty to sixty minutes north of Port-au-Prince. Ibo Beach, Kyona, Kaloa Beach, Ouanga Bay, Mai-Kai, and Amani-Y are all beach resorts with a large, open lodge, accommodations with private baths, showers, and dressing rooms. Clear water, golden sand. Scuba and snorkeling equipment rentals. Food served right on the beach.

Southwest Beach area, less than sixty minutes from Port-au-Prince. Taino Beach and Sun Beach in Grand Goave are two of the secluded beach resorts in this area.

North Coast Beaches, near Cap-Haïtien: Cormier Plage, an informal beach resort just minutes from Cap-Haïtien. La Badie, also nearby, has old colonial ruins and good snorkeling. Bring your own equipment or rent it in Cap-Haïtien.

Jacmel area: Raymond les Bains, white sand beach on the gentle south coast.

Cyvadier Cove, uncrowded small white sand beach. Recommended for picnicking; excellent snorkeling.

NIGHTLIFE: In season, each Port-au-Prince hotel has a special night to present some sort of entertainment, from folk dancing to cabaret acts along with a buffet or barbecue. Events vary; check with your hotel. Special voodoo ceremonies open to visitors show ancient rituals with symbols, music, and dance. The arrangements may be made through your hotel. Nightclubs, casinos (all under government supervision), and discotheques are located around the island.

SHOPPING: Shopping in Haiti is nearly synonymous with the word *bargain*—bargain as in good deal and bargain as in barter. The Haitians seem to make just about everything (often out of nothing) and much of it very well. Baskets, wood carvings—lots of dark mahogany and an interesting pale gray wood—embroidery work, papier-mâché (from taps-taps to tigers), voodoo-inspired copper jewelry, handmade chairs with cane seats, toys, and oil paintings are all available in great variety.

Do bargain; it is considered, well, stupid, not to. Most sellers give an initial price about two or even three times higher than what they'll settle for. Take your time; bargaining is as much a social act, a traditional verbal give and take, as it is a way to buy. The Haitians are patient and, indeed, help out in the Iron Market with a little remedial bargaining. ("No, no, you don't say 'no.' I give you price. You give me price. Soon we both be happy.")

However, once you begin to bargain in earnest for something, it is considered extremely bad form to walk away without buying. Either say no outright or think about it (there is no rush; try to fall into that tropical time zone).

One last bit of advice: Go to a big store like Carlos, which has fixed prices, before you are overwhelmed by the Iron Market. You're far less likely to pay too much for something if you have a relative idea of what the going rate is beforehand. Also, the Iron Market is best earlier in the day before the heat settles. Driving up Kenscoff Mountain makes a perfect afternoon after the excitement (and heat) of the Iron Market.

FOOD: Haitian food is most often described as Creole, a mix of Afro-French with a few local specialties thrown in. It's best for health reasons not to eat anything from street vendors or hole-in-the-wall "restaurants." (See Health in Part 3.)

Haiti may have the best *pommes frites* (French fries) west of Paris, but they aren't considered specialties like *pois ac duriz coles* (rice and beans), *grillot cochon avec banane pesse* (pork chop with bananas), *tassot avec sauce pimentee* (salted dried beef in spice sauce), *duriz ac djondjon* (rice with black mushrooms), or *chou palmiste* (palmetto shoot salad).

HOTELS: Most of Haiti's hotels have U.S. representatives that can be contacted through a travel agent. The Holiday Inn in Port-au-Prince is popular with business travelers. Haiti's Club Med, forty-five minutes north of Port-au-Prince, near Montrouis, presents a safe travel option, as do other "complete environment" resorts out of town.

For More Information

Office National du Tourisme
Avenue Marie Jeanne
Port-au-Prince, Haiti

Jamaica

AREA: 4,244 square miles; 142 miles long, 52 miles wide.

POPULATION: 2,506,000.

CAPITAL CITY: Kingston.

LANGUAGE: English, Jamaican patois.

RELIGION: Mainly Anglican, Baptist, and Roman Catholic.

GOVERNMENT: Parliamentary democracy; independent member of the British Commonwealth.

LOCATION: About 90 miles south of Cuba, 590 air miles from Miami.

GETTING THERE: Air Jamaica from many U.S. cities; American, Air Canada, as well as several other carriers also fly into Jamaica. Many cruise ships stop at Jamaican ports.

CUSTOMS: U.S. and Canadian citizens vacationing in Jamaica need proof of citizenship (with photo) and either a return or an ongoing ticket. All other visitors must apply for a visa or work permit.

HEALTH: No special considerations.

CLOTHING: Standard tropical wear; you'll need a sweater or jacket in the mountains. Many hotel dining rooms require jackets and ties for men; women will want to dress accordingly. No beachwear or shorts on city streets.

ELECTRICITY: 110 volts (some 220)/50 cycles (single and three phase).

TIME ZONE: Eastern standard time year-round.

MONEY: Jamaican dollar (J$) with fluctuating exchange rate. You must use Jamaican money; airport exchange bureaus service incoming flights. Since it is illegal to take Jamaican dollars out of the country, allow time to reverse the process when you depart. Traveler's checks and credit cards are widely accepted.

TAX AND TIPS: Hotel room tax U.S. $2 to $6 a day, depending on season; airport departure tax U.S. $15. Tip the same as you would in North America when a service charge is not added to your bill.

GETTING AROUND: Internal air service linking major cities; railroad service between Kingston and several areas; also sight-seeing buses, local buses, taxis, and rental cars.

Overview

With 2.5 million people and an area about the size of Connecticut, Jamaica is an island with everything. The lush heights of the Blue Mountains that rise to 7,402 feet dominate the central landscape. A generous coastal plain ends in sparkling white beaches. Rivers wind through the countryside and splash dramatically down climbable falls. There are limestone caves and bamboo forests. Historic plantation houses, pirate hideouts, and ancient Indian sites dot the landscape. The capital of Kingston is full of cultural attractions and diversions.

Jamaica has long wooed the tourist dollar and offers virtually every sport and leisure activity. Want to go hot air ballooning, river rafting, or parasailing? This is the place. Water sports, golf, tennis, and horseback riding are all options. If you aren't interested in getting overstimulated while you're having fun, try one of the less-resorty towns like Port Antonio, or choose a small beach establishment.

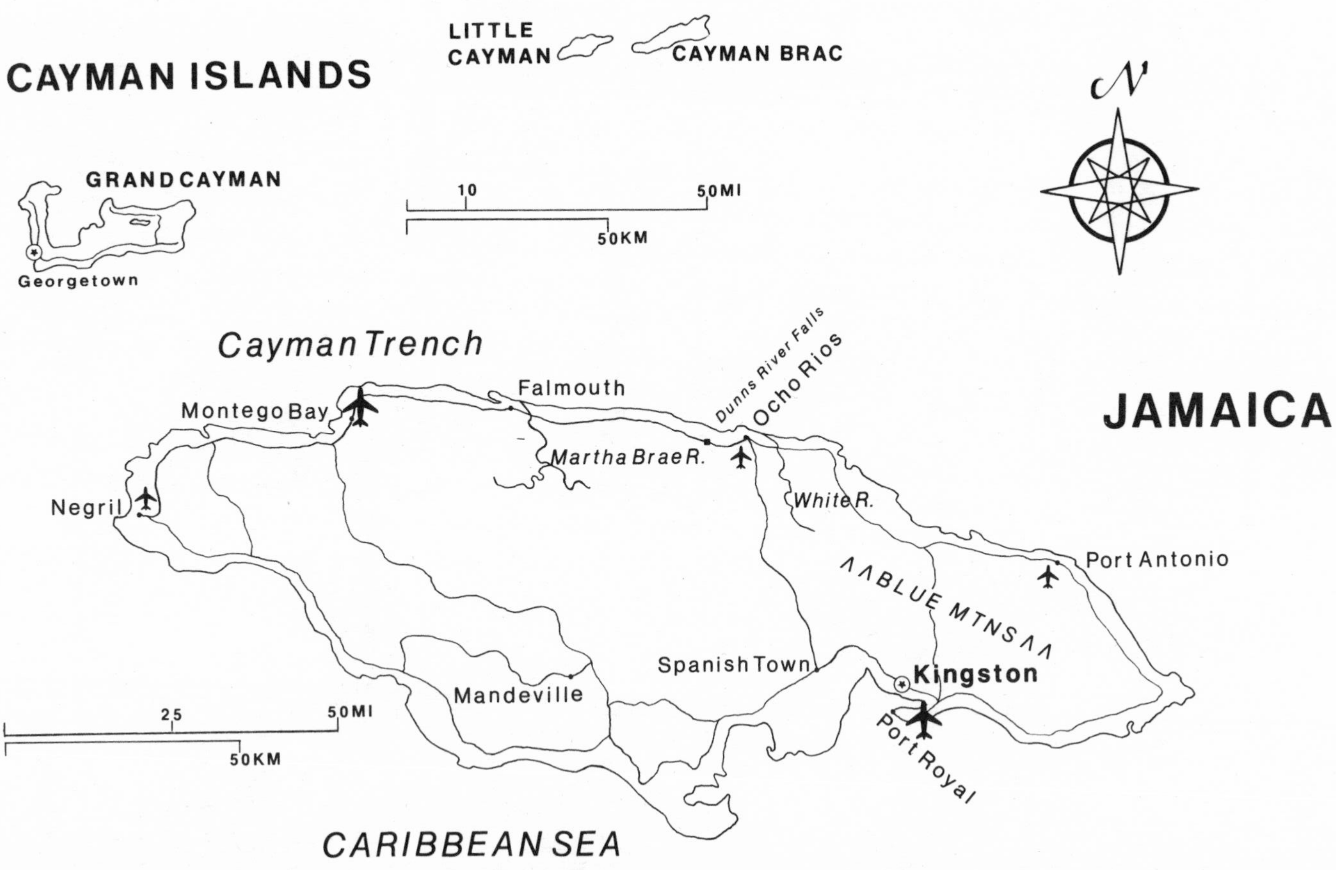

CAYMAN ISLANDS

GRAND CAYMAN

* Georgetown

LITTLE
CAYMAN

CAYMAN BRAC

10   50 MI

50 KM

N

JAMAICA

Port Antonio

Port Royal

Kingston

BLUE MTNS

White R.

Ocho Rios

Dunns River Falls

Spanish Town

Martha Brae R.

Falmouth

Cayman Trench

Mandeville

Montego Bay

Negril

CARIBBEAN SEA

2 5   50 MI

50 KM

History

When Columbus sighted Jamaica in 1494, it was inhabited by the docile Arawak Indians. They were soon exterminated by early Spaniards who tried to enslave them to work their sugarcane fields. African slaves were then imported as laborers.

England captured the island in 1655, in a side battle of a war with Spain. The Spaniards left after freeing their slaves, who took to the hills and became known as "Maroons." They so harassed the settlers that they were granted certain lands and freedom in 1739.

This overlapped somewhat the period during which Jamaica became a pirate stronghold; particularly notorious was Port Royal. The plunder from Spanish galleons enriched the local economy. The sugar era followed the pirates' heyday, and the English imported large numbers of African slaves to work their extensive plantations.

Slavery was abolished in 1838. Jamaica became a Crown Colony in 1866 and fully independent on 6 August 1962.

In recent times, agricultural products, long Jamaica's economic backbone, dropped to less than a fifth of the island's exports. This shift in economic importance brought many rural families to the cities and caused serious unemployment. After a bitter election struggle in the early 1980s, Jamaica's present government is trying to restore the economy by revitalizing tourism and free enterprise. The mixing of bauxite (aluminum ore)—Jamaica is the world's second-largest producer—sugar, and tourism continue to be the cornerstones of the island's economy.

Things to See and Do

Jamaica is a large, diverse island. Even the most intrepid visitor will only be able to scratch the surface in a week's time. There are more than 200 miles of white sand beaches, spectacular waterfalls, rivers for rafting, the famous Blue Mountains, caves, tropical forests, and formal gardens. This wealth of natural assets is matched by cultural ones.

Plan to get off the beach for at least a day or two and see some of the countryside. Choose selectively; the following suggestions may help you decide where to base yourself. This is a big country; select accommodations near most things of interest to you. Look at a map to get some idea how far it is from Montego Bay to Kingston, for example (a four-and-a-half-hour train ride—a good way to see a bit of the countryside). As you'll notice, Jamaica's major resorts are spread out from one end of the island to the other. For hiking trips into the Blue Mountains, it's best to start in Kingston.

Kingston

Jamaica's cosmopolitan capital is overlooked or avoided by many visitors, but you really haven't seen Jamaica unless you've been to Kingston. Several museums showcase Jamaican culture and West Indian history. The Institute of Jamaica, founded in 1879 to stimulate interest in the island's arts and sciences, houses an outstanding collection of West Indian material. It's at 12 East Street and is open from 8:30 A.M. to 5 P.M. Monday through Thursday (no admission charge). The National Gallery of Art (near the waterfront) houses historical prints and engravings as well as the colorful paintings and sculptures of modern Jamaicans.

Although Hope Botanical Garden is famous for its orchid house, the 200 acres of ornamentals—both trees and flowers—are equally pleasing. (See Shopping, below, for several more Kingston stops.)

Devon House is a nineteenth-century mansion built by George Stiebel, one of the Caribbean's first black millionaires. Now administered by the Jamaica National Trust, the house features period furnishings and a restaurant with good Jamaican food and a patio bar. Blue Mountain coffee is served on the "coffee terrace." Some of the best island crafts are for sale in the garden house shop. There's a small admission charge.

The late Bob Marley's home is now the Bob Marley Museum and will delight reggae fans. There is an admission charge. Check for open hours in advance.

Port Royal

Once called the world's "richest and wickedest" city, Port Royal is across the harbor from Kingston on a thin peninsula called the Palisadoes. This was the stomping ground of the notorious pirate Henry Morgan and the Brethren of the Coast. Most of Port Royal is now in Kingston Harbor as a result of an earthquake in 1692. Nevertheless, the site attracts lots of visitors. Many artifacts recovered by divers are in the Archaeological Museum; open daily from 9 A.M. to 5 P.M.; small admission fee. (See History/Time Frames in Part 2 for more information on Port Royal and archaeological projects on Jamaica.)

White Marl Arawak Museum

Outside of Kingston, on the way to Spanish Town, this museum contains an interesting display of Arawak Indian artifacts; open daily from 10 A.M. to 5 P.M., admission fee.

Spanish Town

Jamaica's first capital has some of the world's finest Georgian architecture. Take a guided walking tour. The city's museums are open from 9 A.M. to 5 P.M.

Montego Bay Area

Rocklands Feeding Station: In nearby Anchovy, this bird sanctuary has more than 100 species, both exotic and otherwise. It opens daily at 3:30 P.M. for feeding time at 4 P.M. Admission fee (children under four not permitted).

Doctor's Cave Beach: Probably the most popular and crowded beach on Jamaica; thought to be fed by healthful mineral springs.

Rose Hall Great House: Legend has it that this restored great house is still haunted by the cruel Annie Palmer, the "White Witch," who met a violent death.

Martha Brae Rafting: Daily one-and-a-quarter-hour river excursions; raftsmen pole downriver from Rafter's Village.

Montego Bay Marine Park

This is a 6,000-acre preserve of enticing waters for divers, snorkelers, sailors, and windsurfers. Underwater attractions include the Canyon and Chimney, a 70-foot fish-feeding station.

Negril, Mandeville, and South Coast

Rick's Cafe: You can snorkel in and around the caves at this popular beach; the bar on shore is just as popular.

Marshall's Pen: A 300-acre wildlife sanctuary at an eighteenth-century great house.

Bamboo Avenue: On the way to Kingston, the road is sheltered by great canopies of giant bamboo.

Ocho Rios

Columbus Park: The site and museum commemorate Columbus's landing; at Discovery Bay.

Runaway Caves-Green Grotto: Subterranean caverns 120 feet below the earth's surface, said to be an old pirate hangout; boat tours.

Plantation Tours: These are working plantations that have grown crops such as sugarcane, bananas, coconut, and breadfruit for more than two centuries. Ride back in history in an open jitney. Choose from Brimmer Hall, Prospect Plantation, or Friendship Plantation, all nearby.

Dunn's River Falls: You can climb 600 feet to the top. Most people wear bathing suits; it can be moist going and the cold water is exhilarating when you arrive.

Firefly, Noel Coward's House: In Port Maria, the playwright's house is maintained as it was when he lived there.

Jamaica Night on the White River: On Sunday evenings, take a canoe ride by torchlight and African drums. A folklore show and feast onshore are part of the deal.

Port Antonio

This small harbor town about 67 miles from Ocho Rios is one of Errol Flynn's old haunts; he is said to have initiated river rafting for tourists. As well as rafting down the Rio Grande, visitors may want to enjoy Reach or Somerset Falls, the seemingly bottomless Blue Lagoon, or the Caves of Nonsuch, with the fossilized testimony to life in ancient seas. You can even visit Errol Flynn's ranch east of Port Antonio for a horseback ride or a tour, held when cruise ships are in port. The lushly forested Blue Mountains, home of the world-famous coffee, are worth at least a day's excursion from Kingston. (For extended hikes, see Part 4, Exploring.)

SHOPPING: Local crafts include wood-carvings, straw work, baskets, and gemstone jewelry (stones are mined on Jamaica); the best outlet for quality items is Things Jamaican Ltd. (shops in Devon House, Kingston; both airports; and Sam Sharpe Square in Montego Bay). Contemporary artwork is also popular, as is locally made rustic furniture. Check government crafts markets, Made in Jamaica Gift Shops, and market stalls.

Handmade fashions are very popular and are well done on Jamaica. Island designs are stylish, and custom-made clothing is a great buy.

FESTIVALS AND HOLIDAYS: Standard British holidays plus Junkanoo, a Christmas carnival with costume parades and partying. Jamaican Independence Day, the first Monday in August, is also a festive occasion and includes an arts festival.

The Jamaica Tourist Board publishes a yearly schedule of events. The calendar includes reggae celebrations, jazz festivals, yacht races, cricket tournaments, craft fairs, flower shows, parades, sports fishing tournaments, and many other interesting events. Be sure to request a copy.

FOOD: Salt fish and *ackee* is Jamaica's national dish. Peas and rice, pumpkin, pepper pot, jerked pork, and Creole specialties and curries are served throughout the country. Fritters of all kinds and patties with various fillings are popular with visitors. Be sure to try Blue Mountain coffee, the local Red Stripe beer, and Jamaican rum. Look for native fruits at Saturday morning markets.

HOTELS: Packages abound; you can frequently get airfare and hotel deals for the price of the flight alone. Ask your travel agent or the tour desk at the airline reservation number.

Jamaica has every option in accommodations, from all-inclusive couples-only resorts to luxurious plantation inns to chain hotels, campgrounds, and guest houses. Ask the Tourist Board for a complete listing with prices. The tourist business is highly competitive here; most hotels have their own enticing color brochures.

For more information on camping, see Part 4, Exploring. For more information on the island in general, contact the nearest Jamaica Tourist Board (in London it's called the Jamaica High Commission). You may want to ask about the popular "Meet the People" program designed to give visitors a chance to spend time with Jamaicans who may share their interests.

For More Information

U.S.

500 North Michigan Avenue, Suite 1030
Chicago, IL 60611
telephone: (800) 233-4582
fax: (312) 527-1472

1320 South Dixie Highway, Suite 1100
Coral Gables, FL 33146
telephone: (800) 233-4582
fax: (305) 666-7239

3440 Wilshire Boulevard, Suite 1207
Los Angeles, CA 90010   *requested 5/24/95*
telephone: (800) 233-4582
fax: (213) 384-1780

801 Second Avenue, 20th Floor
New York, NY 10017
telephone: (800) 233-4582
fax: (212) 856-9730

CANADA
1 Eglinton Avenue East, Suite 616
Toronto, Ontario M4P 3A1
Canada
telephone: (416) 482-7850

ENGLAND
Jamaica House
1-2 Prince Consort Road
London SW7 2BZ, England
telephone: (071) 224-0505
fax: (071) 224-0551

GERMANY
Pan Consult
Falkstrasse 72-74
60487 Frankfurt, Germany
telephone: (069) 70-74-065
fax: (069) 70-1007

Martinique

AREA: 425 square miles; 50 miles long, 22 miles wide.

POPULATION: 360,000.

CAPITAL CITY: Fort-de-France.

LANGUAGE: French and Creole; English in tourist areas.

RELIGION: Roman Catholic.

GOVERNMENT: Overseas region of France.

LOCATION: Between Dominica and St. Lucia.

GETTING THERE: Many major airlines fly direct or via Guadeloupe; LIAT flies from other Caribbean islands.

CUSTOMS: U.S. and Canadian citizens need passports or proof of citizenship (an expired passport less than five years old will do); other nationalities need valid passports and, in some cases, visas. A return or ongoing ticket is also required of all visitors.

HEALTH: No special considerations. Modern facilities available; tap water is safe.

CLOTHING: Informal tropical wear; men may need jackets for dining, and women may want long skirts.

ELECTRICITY: 220 volts/50 cycles AC.

TIME ZONE: Atlantic standard time, one hour ahead of eastern standard time.

MONEY: French franc; U.S. and Canadian currency accepted.

TAX AND TIPS: Most hotels and restaurants add a 10 percent service charge to the bill. Porters and bellhops expect about one franc per bag. Cabdrivers are not usually tipped.

GETTING AROUND: Taxis, rental cars, cars with guides, public buses. Drivers must have a valid driver's license and more than one year's driving experience.

Overview

The Caribs, Martinique's fierce original inhabitants, called the island Madinina, "Island of Flowers." Although the Indians disappeared long ago, the flowers and the gallicized version of the name remain.

When Columbus sighted Martinique in 1502, he described it as "the best, richest, sweetest country in the whole world." The island's physical beauty—deeply forested mountains, waterfalls, gorges, and fertile lowlands—still delights visitors. Martinique has all the appealing attributes of a Caribbean island as well as the very French atmosphere and accoutrements of civilization. Visitors may divide their days between relaxing on beaches of either black or white sands and exploring the ruins of St. Pierre in the shadow of tempestuous Mount Pelée at 4,428 feet, then spend their evenings dining, dancing, or gaming in four-star restaurants and hotels. Martinique is an especially good destination for people who like their outdoor activities tempered by fine food and cultural options. Take your French phrase book and get ready to wake up to croissants.

History

Although Columbus visited the island in 1502, Pierre D'Esnambuc officially claimed it for France in 1635, when the island's first European settlers arrived. The native Carib Indians were rousted from their homeland

WINDWARD ISLANDS

Martinque Passage

Sainte Marie

Caravelle Park

Montagne Pelée

Fort de France

MARTINIQUE

Pointe d' Enfer

St Lucia Passage

ATLANTIC OCEAN

Castries

ST LUCIA

Soufrière

Vieux Fort

Grenada Trough

CARIBBEAN SEA

St Vincent Passage

Barbados Ridge

ST VINCENT

Speightstown

Holetown

Kingstown

Bridgetown

BARBADOS

BEQUIA

THE

GRENADINES

MUSTIQUE

CANOUAN

Tobago Trough

MAYREAU

UNION

CARRIACOU

GRENADA

St George's

Point Salines

10   50MI

50KM

over the next few centuries in a series of fierce battles. As well as skirmish-
ing with the Caribs, the French, Dutch, and British fought among themselves. The British occupied the island from 1762 to 1763 and from 1794
to 1815. Martinique has been an overseas department of France since
1946, as visitors will quickly notice when using traditional French francs
and postage stamps.

The sudden eruption of Mount Pelée in 1902 changed the face of Martinique forever; in three terrifying minutes it wiped out the entire population (save one) of the island's first capital city of St. Pierre. Most visitors
make the trip to the north to reflect on the powers of nature so evident
in the lava-encrusted ruins of this once-monumental city.

Today, Martinique's thriving tourist industry contributes considerably
to its economic well-being. Agriculture as well continues to be a mainstay;
bananas, pineapple, sugar, and rum are the main products.

Things to See and Do
Fort-de-France

Martinique's capital surrounds the harbor, and green mountains provide
the backdrop. Most visitors like to spend a day here getting the feel of the
island, shopping, lunching, et cetera. You may want to include La Savane
(the central park with gardens and fountains), historic Fort Saint-Louis,
the Musée Départemental, and the Saint-Louis Cathedral. Don't miss the
rococo La Bibliothèque Schoelcher, originally built for the Paris Exposi-
tion of 1889 and imported right down to the doorknobs.

Mount Pelée and St. Pierre

Many tours make this trip, about an hour's drive north from Fort-de-
France, which includes the tropical beauty of cloud-shrouded Mount Pelée and the curiosities of St. Pierre. Once called the Paris of the West Indies,
the cultural center of St. Pierre—Martinique's first capital—became the
New World's Pompeii after the devastating 1902 eruption of Mount Pelée
killed all but one of its 30,000 inhabitants. Auguste Siparis, a prisoner in
the dungeon, survived to become a circus curiosity. Today, a visit to the
site's Musée Volcanologique will add another dimension to the tragedy.
Common objects such as petrified spaghetti, fused glassware, melted
clocks, and twisted musical instruments are shocking testimony to the
sudden eruption. Open daily from 9 A.M. until noon, and from 3 to 5
P.M.; small admission fee. Wandering among the ruins helps complete
the picture.

La Pagerie, Martinique, the birthplace of Empress Josephine, Napoleon's first wife. (Photo courtesy of French West Indies Tourist Board.)

Centre d'Art Musée Paul Gauguin

A visit to this memorial to Gauguin, at Turin Cove between Carbet and St. Pierre, is easy to combine with a visit to the ruined city of St. Pierre. Gauguin spent four months in 1887 painting on Martinique. This small museum houses reproductions of the work he did while on the island, as well as other information and memorabilia. Open daily from 9:30 A.M. to 5:30 P.M.; admission fee.

Parc Naturel Regional de la Martinique

This extensive park area covers a great deal of the island and is divided into various preserves and recreation areas. Park personnel organize inexpensive guided excursions year-round. Special arrangements for small groups may be made by contacting the Parc Naturel Regional de la Martinique, Caserne Bouille, Fort-de-France; telephone: 73.19.30.

Serious hikers who wish to climb Mount Pelée or explore Gorges de la Falaise or the thick coastal rain forest between Grand Rivière and Precheur should also contact the park staff. These hikes are organized with guides only at certain times of the year.

Presqu'île de la Caravelle Nature Preserve

This unique peninsula is also part of the park. It contains the safest beaches on the Atlantic side of the island, as well as mangroves and well-marked trails. One of Martinique's most popular hikes winds through tropical wetlands to the ruins of Chateau Dubuc (guides not needed).

Musée de la Pagerie

The birthplace of Napoleon's Empress Josephine is near the village of Trois Îlets, a twenty-minute ferry ride across the bay from Fort-de-France. In a luxurious tropical setting, this old stone building, once La Pagerie's kitchen, now houses memorabilia of Josephine's early life. Visitors are free to wander about the lovely grounds of the former sugar plantation, where Josephine was born in 1763. One of Napoleon's indiscreet love letters will color the faces of most readers. Open daily except Mondays from 9 A.M. to 5:30 P.M.; admission fee.

Musée d'Art en Coquillage

This tiny museum, devoted to seashell art, is in Anse à l'Ane near Trois Îlets. Seashell tableaux depict various scenes. Open daily except Tuesdays from 10 A.M. until noon and from 3:30 to 5 P.M.; admission fee.

BEACHES: The beaches south of Fort-de-France are of white sand, those in the north have typical gray or black volcanic sands. Plage des Salines, in the south near St. Anne, with its palms, white sand, and Diamond Rock offshore, is a favorite. There are no nudist beaches per se, but most large hotels permit topless bathing. The rough Atlantic coast is not recommended for swimming (experts only!) except at Cap Chevalier and Presqu'Île de la Caravelle Nature Preserve.

CAMPING: Martinique is one island where visitors can camp almost anywhere—mountains, forests, and many beaches. During the season, visitors are required to camp where facilities are available; a nominal fee is charged. Between June and September, camping is allowed in areas that have no facilities. For details check with the Office National des Forêts, 3.5 Km, Route de Moutte, Fort-de-France; telephone (596) 71.34.50. Camping cars can be rented. Ask the Tourist Office for its current list of camps.

NIGHTLIFE: Dancing, entertainment, and casinos; centered around resort hotels.

SHOPPING: French imports—fashions, perfumes, wines—top the list. The greatest variety is available in Fort-de-France, where discounts are often given on luxury items paid for by traveler's checks (at certain stores). Local rum, Creole dolls, and appliquéd cloth wall hangings of island scenes are also popular purchases. Remember, most shops close at noon for a long lunch, then reopen later in the afternoon.

FESTIVALS AND HOLIDAYS: All Catholic holidays are celebrated, including Pre-Lenten Carnival, which begins weekends in January and goes through Ash Wednesday. King Carnival's funeral procession and pyre at dusk on Ash Wednesday end the festivities, which are held in La Savane, Fort-de-France.

Labor Day, 1 May.

Bastille Day, 14 July.

All Saints' Day, 1 November. Cemeteries all over the island are candlelit.

Armistice Day, 11 November.

FOOD: Specialties include French cuisine and spicy Creole dishes (take it easy with these if you aren't used to highly seasoned foods). *Petit punch blanc* (little white punch) or *petit punch vieux* (little old punch), made with light or dark rum, respectively, are traditional meal starters. You may want to try *blaff,* a tasty local fish stew, sometime during your stay. You can make a simple lunch of real French baguettes, cheese, fruit, and wine and carry it to a scenic spot. The Matador comes highly recommended for evening dining.

HOTELS: Accommodations run the price and luxury gamut on Martinique. Ask the Tourist Office for a current listing and rates.

For More Information

U.S.

French Government Tourist Office
676 North Michigan Avenue, Suite 3360
Chicago, IL 60611
telephone: (312) 751-7800

French Government Tourist Office
9454 Wilshire Boulevard, Suite 715
Los Angeles, CA 90212
telephone: (310) 271-6665

French West Indies Tourist Board
444 Madison Avenue

New York, NY 10020
telephone: (800) 391-4909
fax: (212) 838-7855

CANADA
French Government Tourist Office
1981 Avenue McGill College, Suite 480
Montreal, Quebec H3A 2W9
Canada
telephone: (514) 844-8566

French Government Tourist Office
30 St. Patrick Street, Suite 700
Toronto, Ontario M5T 3A3
Canada
telephone: (416) 593-6427

Montserrat

AREA: 38 square miles; 12 miles long, 7 miles wide.

POPULATION: About 11,000.

CAPITAL CITY: Plymouth.

LANGUAGE: English.

RELIGION: Anglican, Roman Catholic, Baptist, Methodist, and Seventh Day Adventist.

GOVERNMENT: British dependency, local government with a crown governor.

LOCATION: 27 miles southwest of Antigua, which is about midway down the Lesser Antilles.

GETTING THERE: Via Antigua, connect with LIAT's Montserrat Air. This fifteen-minute flight connects with most international flights, of which there are several per day. Be sure to reserve in advance.

CUSTOMS: Visitors from the U.K., the U.S., and Canada may use a passport, driver's license, birth certificate, or voter registration card as ID. People from other countries must have valid passports. All visitors are required to have either a return or an ongoing ticket and may be asked for evidence of sufficient funds while visiting the island. Visitors may also bring in their personal effects; wines and spirits not exceeding 40 ounces; 6 ounces of perfume; and either 200 cigarettes or 60 cigars. Gift articles worth up to E. C. $250 may also be brought in duty free provided that the visitor has not been on the island for the last six months.

HEALTH: No major considerations. Tap water is generally safe, but, as always, in rural areas it is best to boil milk and water. Medical facilities are basic—a small hospital and a few resident doctors. Be sure to travel with any prescriptions you might need.

CLOTHING: Standard lightweight tropical wear. Dress on Montserrat tends to be rather conservative. The Tourist Board actually prints a dress code pamphlet that's available in airports and hotels, reminding visitors that beachwear, short shorts, and crop tops are unwelcome in town. Men as well as women are expected to wear shirts. Topless and nude bathing are unacceptable.

ELECTRICITY: 220-230 volts/60 cycles; U.S. and Canadian appliances require transformers.

TIME ZONE: Atlantic standard time, one hour ahead of eastern standard time.

MONEY: The Eastern Caribbean dollar, or E.C., is the official currency. Traveler's checks from the U.S. and Canada may be changed into E.C. at local banks, and some shops accept them; check ahead about credit cards.

Bank hours are from 8 A.M. until noon Monday through Thursday, 8 A.M. until noon and 3 to 5 P.M. on Friday. All banks are closed on weekends.

TAX AND TIPS: Airport departure tax per person is U.S. $8. There's also a 7 percent government tax on all hotel bills plus 10 percent service charge. Tipping is discretionary.

GETTING AROUND: *Taxis* are plentiful, and often the drivers will also act as guides. The fares are fixed and the listings are available in the airport, Tourist Board office, and most hotels. Count on about U.S. $11 one way from the airport into Plymouth, slightly more to outlying hotels.

Car rentals are also available. Driving is on the left-hand side of

the road. A valid driver's license is required to obtain a temporary
Montserrat license, available at the airport and at the Traffic Office
in the police station in Plymouth between 9 A.M. and 1 P.M. on
Monday, Tuesday, Thursday, and Friday. Rental cars cost from U.S.
$25 to $50 a day depending on the make and the time of year. Prearranged day tours are another option. Runaway Travel offers various
packages that include transportation and sometimes lunch.

Overview

This verdant island is off by itself, although it's only some 27 miles west
of Antigua. It rises to 3,000 feet at Chance's Peak, then drops through
the fertile planted valleys to a narrow coastal plain edged by black sand
beaches. The semiactive volcano, Galway's Soufrière, on the eastern end
of the island erupted in 1996, sending a cloud of ash skyward and thrusting a lava spine upward within the crater. This recent volcanic activity
forced the evacuation of some 5,000 people living in Montserrat's southern areas. Volcanists expect more activity to follow.

Montserrat is dotted with the ruins of sugar mills and plantations as
well as colorful wooden houses ringed with porches and laced with gingerbread. The capital city of Plymouth is picturesque and civil, offering
necessary commodities, some informal lunch spots, and a few souvenirs.

This quiet island is a delightful getaway for those willing to provide
their own nightlife and to spend days of ease with a walk or a horseback
ride for excitement. One of the top spots for unspoiled natural wonders,
it's ideal for naturalists and hikers (it's quite safe to wander here). Bird
life is varied, and this is one place where even a short stay might yield a
glimpse of an iguana.

Check on the current status of volcanic activity before you plan a visit.

History

Columbus named Montserrat on his second voyage, but by all accounts
he never stepped ashore. From the sea, the rugged mountains of the island
reminded him of the land near a Spanish monastery called Santa Maria
de Montserrati. The island remained Montserrat even though the Spanish
never settled here. Montserrat was first colonized in 1632 by Irish Catholics from St. Kitts, who came to the island to escape religious persecution.
Other settlers from Ireland, Barbados, and Virginia followed suit, and by
1648 there were some 1,000 Irish families on the island.

The seventeenth century was one of turmoil, with the English and
French involved in some bloody skirmishes over the island. The French

captured Montserrat in 1644; the island was won back by the English in 1688. After a peaceful interlude Montserrat was recaptured by the French in 1782 and finally ceded to Britain in 1783. There are fortification ruins and cannons from this era in several places—historic Wapping, out near Carr's Bay, and in the old infirmary in Trials, where French soldiers once lived.

Montserrat remained quietly British throughout the sugar era and still has an agriculturally based economy, with sea island cotton as one of its main crops. The island became a self-governing dependency of Britain in 1960, and most local people would like to keep it that way. While tourism and the building and development that go with it have increased within the last ten years, Montserrat remains unspoiled and relatively undiscovered.

Things to See and Do

Get out and see the island and countryside—wander, bike, horseback ride, drive. Montserrat is beautiful—truly the other Emerald Isle. Although organized sports and entertainment may seem lacking, Montserrat more than compensates in peacefulness and natural wonders.

Montserrat Museum

A historic panorama housed in a restored sugar mill in Richmond Hill. Don't miss this. Sundays and Wednesdays from 2:30 to 5:30 P.M.; free admission.

Government House

The shamrock on this lovely old Victorian structure pays homage to Montserrat's early Irish heritage. Wednesdays only from 10:30 A.M. until noon; however, the gardens are open to visitors from 10:30 A.M. until noon on Mondays, Tuesdays, Thursdays, and Fridays.

Ruins

Numerous ruins dot Montserrat, but so far only a few have been labeled. Bransby Point Fortification (easy to combine this with Fox's Bay Bird Sanctuary or the Montserrat Museum) has a great view and cannons; the old fort at St. George's Hill also provides breathtaking views. The ruins of the sugar plantation at Galway's Estate (currently closed due to nearby volcanic activity) are being excavated in a project directed by the Montserrat National Trust. Volunteers may join the dig in the summer months (see Sites, Ruins, and Museums for more details).

Galway's Soufrière

A cab ride out of town and a short, very steep climb down into the still-steaming cauldron of the volcano. Some days the smell of sulfur is overwhelming. Boiling gray water tumbling over the crystallized rocks down a deep ravine to the sea presents a dramatic scene. You don't really need a guide for this one; it's just down the slope and off to the left. Plan on a twenty- to thirty-minute hike each way. Recently, due to volcanic activity, this area has been closed to hikers. Check locally for current status.

Great Alps Waterfall

A fifteen-minute ride south of town; you can usually pick up a guide by the roadside at the turn in St. Patricks. Somewhat more than an hour's moderate walk each way. Depending on the recent weather, there are places on the rocky trail that require a bit of scrambling, and sometimes the path is overgrown. There won't be much water flow in the falls during long dry spells. You might want to tackle this hike on a cool morning; wear a bathing suit under your clothes and take a picnic. This is a good place to observe iguanas and enjoy tropical foliage.

Chance's Peak

At 3,200 feet, this is the highest mountain on Montserrat. A guide is a must for this strenuous, all-day venture. Island tradition is such that a large group of people (mostly young) climb Chance's Peak blowing conch horns each year on August Monday (the first Monday in August).

Fox's Bay Bird Sanctuary

A pleasant walk on a well-marked trail with signs pointing out tamarind trees and red mangroves. It's relatively flat and can be muddy in the rainy season. Best to avoid the early morning and evening bug hours (wear insect repellent). If you would like to watch the egrets return to their roosts (it's quite dramatic), walk left down the beach from the sanctuary and watch from there. Leave time for a swim at Fox's Bay after your walk.

Other Walks

You may want to circle Broderick's Estate (which is government property) on the path; about a mile or so round-trip. It has a great view. The hike into Gage's Soufrière, some two miles or so, is also to be considered; take a guide for this one. There are many other old roads and paths, as well. Consult the large-scale map and ask for local recommendations.

DIVING AND SNORKELING: Minimal on this rough coast. There is some snorkeling around the rocks at Little Bay and on isolated coral heads there and in Rendezvous Bay. A car wreck and tire reef has been started off Fox's Bay and ought to have plenty of fish in a few years. For now, it's very relaxing to skim over the black sand off Fox's Bay or Little Bay looking for sand dollars and watching the batfish. There are, however, several interesting scuba sites for experienced divers. Aquatic Discoveries, the island's dive center next to Vue Pointe Hotel, offers dive trips, equipment rentals, boat charters, and scuba classes.

WALKING AND HIKING: This is one of the best islands for exploring on foot. It's pretty safe to just wander on Montserrat, but respect private land and get a local guide if you plan any major off-the-path exploring. Check with the Tourist Bureau in downtown Plymouth for recommendations.

You will also need the detailed tourist map of Montserrat for sale on the island. This large-scale, full-color map even charts vegetation, donkey tracks, *ghauts* (ravines), and ruins and is a must for serious travelers.

For seniors and the faint of foot or heart, recommended walks are on the beaches, in town, on flat country roads (many country roads are hilly), and on the relatively flat path that winds through Fox's Bay Bird Sanctuary. The treks to the waterfall and down into the volcano at Galway's Soufrière are *not* moderate walks, no matter what the taxi drivers say. However, the ride up to the Soufrière is lovely; it's worth the trip just to feel the magnitude of the mountains, smell the sulfur, and perhaps look over the edge. You may want to stop at the ruins of Galway's Plantation on the way, if this area is not closed due to volcanic activity.

MOUNTAIN BIKING: Island Bikes, on Harney Street in Plymouth, offers guided trail rides, bike rentals, and other related services. Owners Susan Goldin and Butch Miller also offer accommodations at Island Bikes' guest house. Call (or write) for details: (809) 491-4696; fax: (809) 491-3599.

SPORTS: Tennis at Montserrat Springs and Vue Pointe Hotel. Golf at the Montserrat Golf Club in Belham Valley; telephone: 5220.

BEACHES: Not Montserrat's strong point but they are pleasant—all of powdery black sand with the exception of Rendezvous Bay, and many are tree lined. Fox's Bay Beach (right out of town) and Little Bay in the north are favorites. Plan to spend the day if you venture out to Little Bay. Take a picnic and plenty of sunscreen; shade is scarce. Rendezvous Bay, Montserrat's only gold sand beach, can be reached only by boat (make arrangements in Carr's Bay) or by a stiff hike over the mountain. Woodlands also has a pleasant beach with a covered picnic area and changing facility. This is one of the wetter sections of the island and provides a lovely drive through lush tropical growth.

NIGHTLIFE: Largely self-generated. On Wednesday nights the Vue Pointe Hotel has a barbecue with a steel band; reservations required. Wade Inn and Montserrat Springs often have live entertainment on Friday nights.

SHOPPING: Shopping on Montserrat is limited, but you might be surprised by what you find. Many have been enchanted by the quality of a mahogany carving or coconut jewelry. Or you might find a hand-crocheted Rasta hat, calabash bowls, a watercolor by a local artist, or a hand-painted T-shirt. Wander and browse; it's a good way to see downtown Plymouth as well. You can start in historic Wapping (just south of Plymouth over the walking bridge) with Montserrat tapestries and the Philatelic Center. Montserrat's elaborate stamps are prized by collectors. Wander over the bridge past HM's Prison and into Plymouth. Don't miss Tradewinds and the downtown art galleries. There are also several T-shirt shops, where visitors can pick up a unique shirt or beach dress.

Local specialties you may want to shop for include woven sea island cotton products (in the store on the waterfront across from the cannons), bay rum (after-shave, not liquor), the local sorrel drink, hot sauce, and guava or pineapple jam. Perks Punch, a rum drink, is also considered a specialty.

Remember, most stores close for lunch from noon to 1:00 P.M. every day, and *everything* closes for the day at noon on Wednesdays and Saturdays.

FESTIVALS AND HOLIDAYS

New Year's Day, 1 January.

Good Friday, Easter, and Easter Monday (dates vary).

St. Patrick's Day, 17 March. Often with some type of festivities or a fair.

Whitmonday (date varies).

Queen's Birthday, June.

August Monday, first Monday in August. It's traditional to hike up Chance's Peak, although this is not carried out by a large number of the population.

Carnival time, 16 December. Festivities continue through New Year's Day and include parades, street dances, masquerades, and lots of singing, steel bands, and calypso music.

FOOD: The national food is goat water, which most say is a local version of traditional Irish stew. Mountain chicken, the legs of local frogs found only on the islands of Montserrat and Dominica, is also served. This frog is a threatened species and is said to taste like watery chicken, so follow your conscience here.

There's lots of local fish, along with fritters and traditional peas and rice. Restaurants vary from informal takeouts such as the Evergreen (ice cream, pizza, fried chicken, and perhaps the best french fries in the world) to the expensive, everything-cooked-to-order Belham Valley Restaurant (reservations are a must). Vue Pointe Hotel in Montserrat Springs also offers multicourse dinners (expensive, and the service can be spotty).

In the moderate price range, try the Wade Inn at Plymouth or the Blue Dolphin in Parsons on the hill overlooking town.

HOTELS: The hotels on Montserrat vary from what the Tourist Board describes as "modern" (that is, expensive) to "quaint and rustic." Vue Pointe Hotel is the most expensive; there are a few guest houses on the island that fall in the quaint-to-rustic category, with prices ranging from U.S. $20 to $34 for a double year-round. The summer rates for Vue Pointe, Montserrat Springs, and the other hotels are considerably lower than the winter rates.

HOTELS

Vue Pointe
P.O. Box 65
Montserrat, W.I.
telephone: (809) 491-5210 or (800) 235-0709
fax: (809) 491-4813

Montserrat Springs
P.O. Box 259
Montserrat, W.I.
telephone: (809) 491-2481 or (800) 253-2134
fax: (805) 491-4070

Flora Fountain
P.O. Box 373
Plymouth
Montserrat, W.I.
telephone: (809) 491-6092
fax: (809) 491-2568

GUEST HOUSES

Providence Estate House
St. Peter's
Montserrat, W.I.
telephone: (809) 491-6476
fax: (809) 491-8476

Marie's Guest House
P.O. Box 28
Plymouth
Montserrat, W.I.
telephone: (809) 491-2745

The phones work well on this island, and calling directly is the easiest way to establish a reservation.

Villas, apartments, and houses are also available for rent; prices vary. Check with the Tourist Bureau or the following establishments for listings:

Runaway Travel
P.O. Box 54
Plymouth
Montserrat, W.I.
telephone: (809) 491-2800
fax: (809) 491-6207

Shamrock Villas
P.O. Box 221
Plymouth
Montserrat, W.I.
telephone: (809) 491-2431
fax: (809) 491-4660

Lime Court Apartments
P.O. Box 250
Plymouth
Montserrat, W.I.
telephone: (809) 491-6985
fax: (809) 491-2513

For More Information

W.I.

Montserrat Tourist Bureau
P.O. Box 7
Plymouth
Montserrat, W.I.
telephone: (809) 491-2230
fax: (809) 491-7430

U.S.

Medhurst & Associates Inc.
The Huntington Atrium
775 Park Avenue
Huntington, NY 11743
telephone: (516) 425-0900
fax: (516) 425-0903

CANADA

New Concepts-Canada
2455 Cawthra Road, Suite 70
Mississauga, Ontario L54 3P1
Canada
telephone: (905) 803-0131
fax: (905) 803-0132

ENGLAND

RBPR
3 Epirus Road
London SW6 7UJ, England
telephone: (011) 071-730-7144
fax: (011) 071-938-4793

GERMANY

Montserrat Tourist Committee
The West India Committee
Lomer Strasse 28
22047 Hamburg, Germany
telephone: (011) 49-40-695-88-46
fax: (011) 49-40-380-00-51

Puerto Rico, Culebra, and Vieques

AREA: 3,515 square miles; one principal land mass, 110 miles long, 35 miles wide, and offshore cays.

POPULATION: Approximately 3,500,000.

CAPITAL CITY: San Juan.

LANGUAGE: Spanish and English.

RELIGION: Predominantly Roman Catholic.

GOVERNMENT: U.S. commonwealth with its own constitution; an elected governor is head of state.

LOCATION: 1,000 miles southeast of Miami, 80 miles east of the Dominican Republic.

GETTING THERE: Most major airlines fly into San Juan International; some connect through Miami or Houston.

CUSTOMS: U.S. Customs; no formalities for U.S. citizens coming from the U.S.

HEALTH: Health facilities are the best in the Caribbean; many English-speaking doctors.

CLOTHING: Light tropical wear; it's best to avoid shorts in downtown areas. Proper evening dress and jackets and ties are required at nightclubs, casinos, and resorts. You'll need a sweater for nights in the mountains. Essentially, commonsense packing; a camper will need different attire than a night owl intent on resort life.

ELECTRICITY: Mainly 100 volts/60 cycles AC.

TIME ZONE: One hour ahead of eastern standard time, the same during daylight saving time.

MONEY: U.S. currency, traveler's checks, and credit cards are accepted everywhere in San Juan. Check in advance if you're heading out into the countryside.

TIPS: Same as in North America.

GETTING AROUND: There are many choices here. City buses operate regularly in San Juan, as do metered taxis (agree on price in advance). Intraisland buses (*guaguas*) run between San Juan, Mayagüez, and Ponce. Public cars or *públicos* (look for "P" or "PD" on the license plate) make frequent runs between all towns on the island; they operate in daylight hours from various town plazas to *público* centers in San Juan, such as Rio Piedras plaza and the international airport. Routes and rates (very reasonable) are fixed by law. All major car rental agencies operate on Puerto Rico (best to reserve in advance). Right-hand drive makes driving easy; a valid U.S. driver's license is required.

Overview

Puerto Rico is probably the most underrated tourist destination in the Caribbean. It is truly an island with everything. From the beautifully restored colonial city of Old San Juan to the beaches of the east coast and the rain forest of El Yunque, Puerto Rico is large and diverse. A Spanish heritage, U.S. currency, and a tropical landscape blend to form a unique multifaceted island. If you want casinos and shopping malls with the latest Spanish and Venezuelan fashions one day and crab *asopao* in the mountains the next, Puerto Rico is the place for you. In order to appreciate both the culture and the landscape, you must take time to get out on the island; the Condado might as well be Miami Beach; Fajardo, Ponce, Luquillo, and Humacao are distinctly their own places.

Puerto Rico is large as islands go; people actually fly between its larger cities. With size come a number of options and a cultural sophistication that are not found on smaller islands. Puerto Rico has a complete system of forests with trails, campsites, and accommodations. It also has caves, mangroves, lakes, striking deserts, and long stretches of coral sand fringed with palms. As well as natural assets, if offers the annual Casals Music Festival, the Ballet Folklorico, galleries, historical and archaeological sites, theater, and the wonderful art museum in Ponce, which contains a remarkable collection of Pre-Raphaelite paintings.

On top of all this, Puerto Rico is very easy to get to, especially from the eastern seaboard of the U.S.; and there are no customs formalities for entering citizens coming from the U.S., no money to change, and English (or some variation) is virtually a second language. Resorts, hotels, and guest houses in all price ranges are plentiful, and Puerto Rican food is outstanding. This island has something for everyone; do a little research

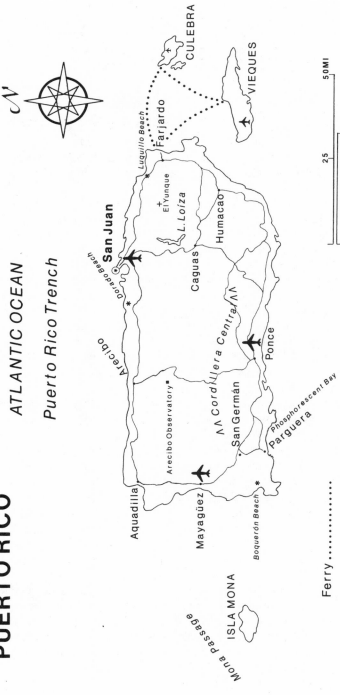

PUERTO RICO

ATLANTIC OCEAN

Puerto Rico Trench

CARIBBEAN SEA

Mona passage

ISLA MONA

Aquadilla

Mayagüez

Boquerón Beach

Arecibo Observatory

Arecibo

San Germán

ΛΛ Cordillera Central ΛΛ

Parguera

Phosphorescent Bay

Ponce

Caguas

Humacao

L. Loíza

El Yunque

Dorado Beach

San Juan

Luquillo Beach

Farjardo

CULEBRA

VIEQUES

Ferry..............

50MI

25   50KM

N

and make sure you find the "habitat" right for you. Puerto Rico is one of the best choices for an economical family vacation, when there may be differences of opinion on the "entertainment program."

History

Before Columbus's second voyage to the New World, Puerto Rico was inhabited by the Taino Indians, who called it Borinquen. On 19 November 1493, Columbus claimed Puerto Rico for Spain and named it San Juan Bautista. This began the island's long tradition of Spanish heritage, which is still evident today.

Ponce de León became the governor of the first settlement, which was established in 1508. Peaceful interaction with the Tainos was short-lived (not to mention the Indians themselves). Early Spaniards came in search of gold, but its limited supply soon forced them to move or to settle down to agricultural pursuits.

During the next three centuries, the settlers defended Puerto Rico. Early islanders fought the enemies of the Spanish Empire from their New World bastion—the Dutch in 1625 and the English in 1595, 1598, and again in 1797. The massive fortresses of Old San Juan remain eloquent testimony to these early grudges.

Along with fighting colonial skirmishes, the Puerto Rican settlers struggled to develop an island-based economy concentrated on cattle, coffee, sugarcane, and tobacco.

In 1897, Spain granted Puerto Rico an autonomous government headed by Luis Muños Rivera. Soon after, the hostilities of the Spanish-American War led to an invasion by U.S. troops. Spain ceded Puerto Rico to the U.S. in 1898 as a part of the war settlement.

Puerto Ricans became American citizens in 1917. The island became a commonwealth with its own constitution in 1952. Industrialization, which began after World War II, has become a major part of the economy. Puerto Rico, with its growing middle class, is now a major exporter of manufactured goods, which range from electronics to pharmaceuticals.

Things to See and Do

Pick up or send for your complimentary copy of *Qué Pasa*, the official visitors' guide to Puerto Rico. This nearly 100-page booklet, with its maps, photographs, and information, is essential. There is so much to see and do on Puerto Rico that it may take some time to make your choices. Towns and cities such as Boquerón, Mayagüez, Aibonito, Barranquitas, and Coamo all have their special offerings. Rent a car and head out.

Old San Juan

Originally founded in 1521 and now a restored area, the seven-square-block old city was once enclosed by fortress walls. It is a National Historic Site with restored homes, churches, shops, and restaurants as well as public buildings.

El Morro Castle, the imposing fort that the Spanish began in 1539, still dominates the headland at the entrance to San Juan Harbor. Its massive walls, ramparts, and cannons remain an impressive historical testimony. The fort is magnificently restored, and the view alone from its 140-foot height above the sea is worth a visit. This is a must stop for anyone with children. (The park outside is a good place for picnics and kite flying.) The fort itself is administered by the U.S. National Park Service. Open daily from 8 A.M. to 6:15 P.M. Tours available.

The massive city walls of Old San Juan, their shadows unchanged by the centuries, and the narrow cobblestone streets make exploring on foot the best way to get a sense of this historic neighborhood. You'll also get a chance to pop into a shop or two to admire local handicrafts or stop in a cozy restaurant that serves traditional Spanish dishes. You may want to visit the San Juan Cemetery, the Museum of Art and History, the Pablo Casals Museum, San José Church, Casa Blanca, La Fortaleza, the Fine Arts Museum, Casa del Libro, Cristo Chapel, La Princesa Jail, El Arsenal, Plaza de Colón, or San Cristóbal Fort, among other places. Plan at least half a day, including lunch; a full day will allow for a more "historic" pace.

Naturally, this barely starts on the metropolitan San Juan area. Don't forget nearby Río Piedras with the University of Puerto Rico and its botanical garden. Check tourist brochures for details.

El Yunque

Probably your best chance to see a rain forest if you have only a short time is El Yunque in the Caribbean National Forest, on Route 191, about an hour's drive from San Juan. A half day will give you time for the drive from San Juan, which passes through some lovely countryside and by the famous Luquillo Beach, as well as time for a short walk in the forest or a dip in a waterfall, and lunch. You may want to stop to eat en route— the food stands at Luquillo Beach offer a sampler of local foods and the popular drink of chilled coconut water called *cocos fríos*—or eat at the mountaintop restaurant in the forest. There are many picnic areas, as well.

The Caribbean National Forest is a 28,000-acre preserve that was originally set aside by the Spanish crown in 1876. One of the oldest preserves in the Western Hemisphere, the forest is now administered by the U.S.D.A. Forest Service. This is the only tropical U.S. national forest; it is also the rainiest, with up to 240 inches of rain per year. This heavy rainfall and the warm climate nurture a dense evergreen forest that contains 240 native tree species and a luxuriant tangle of vines, epiphytes, and giant ferns. This is true rain forest, generally called *tabonuco,* which is found on slopes less than 2,000 feet in elevation. The forest shelters more than fifty species of birds, including the rare Puerto Rican parrot. (A complete bird checklist is available from the forest service.) A number of lizards, crabs, and frogs, including the tiny singing *coqui,* also live throughout the forest. There are no poisonous snakes here or anywhere on the island; observant visitors may see the shy Puerto Rican boa in the forest.

Walking or hiking is the best way to get the feel of this special area. Get out of your vehicle and sit on a bench if you are frail; the smells, the mist, the hush combine to evoke the essence of the rain forest. Don't travel this far to miss it. Trails crisscross the entire forest; many start in El Yunque Recreation Area, which is in the central portion of the forest. Other trailheads are located off nearby highways. There are some rugged trails that are for experienced, well-conditioned hikers only; others have gentle slopes and frequent rest stops. The staff at El Yunque Interpretive Center will be happy to provide advice about trail difficulty and condition. They also stock detailed topographical maps, which are available for one dollar each.

The popular El Yunque Trail loops through three of the four forest types on the way to the 3,496-foot El Yunque Peak; it is well maintained and not difficult. The lower trail begins at the central picnic area near the interpretive center and wends its way through palo colorado forest. This forest type has stouter trees than the *tabonuco* forest (the only category not in evidence on this trail) but contains similar varieties of tree ferns, bamboos, mosses, and vines. As the trail winds up the slope, it passes through an extensive and magical palm forest, where the trees are layered with bromeliads and patterned by filtered sunlight. At the top of the trail is elfin woodland, a terrain that suits its name. Here among the clouds, dwarfed and contorted trees live under an encrusting layer of mosses, liverworts, and bromeliads. The epiphytes that cling to the trunks of these gnarled trees hold so much moisture that they actually support pond and stream animals. Take one of the short side trails to the towers for spectacular views of both forest and coast. The openness there also provides a good vantage point for birders (the hawks like it for the same reason).

El Toro Trail, which leads to the highest peak in the forest, at 3,532 feet, is for more serious hikers. It is 12 miles round-trip and takes in four forest types (*tabonuco,* palo colorado, palm, and dwarf) on the way to El Toro Peak. This weathered trail straddles the wooded ridge for much of its length and is often slick. El Toro Trail takes in some of Puerto Rico's remotest areas. Hiking boots and a picnic are recommended.

Camping is permitted in most areas of the Caribbean National Forest. Camping permits and visitors' guide pamphlets are free at El Yunque Interpretive Center.

For More Information

Forest Supervisor
P.O. Box AQ
Río Piedras, Puerto Rico 00928
telephone: (809) 763-3939; 753-4335/4336

Resident Forester
Catalina Field Office
Bo. Barcelona Km 4.4
Palmer, Puerto Rico 00721

Forest Reserves

Along with the national forest, Puerto Rico has a number of forest reserves (see Part 4, Exploring, for a complete list). Some are truly wild areas, others are delightful parks; some protect mangroves and lagoons, others, sinkholes and caves.

Toro Negro Forest (east of Adjuntas), with Puerto Rico's highest peak, Ferro Punta, at 4,390 feet, often attracts serious mountain climbers. There are stunning drop-away views of both the Atlantic and Caribbean. Sierra palms and tree ferns contribute to the dense forest, where streams and the multiple cascades of Inabon Falls complete the paradisaical landscape.

All of these parks are open daily from 8 A.M. to 5 P.M.; your $.50 admission fee helps maintain them. Weekends you may find quite a crowd in some of the parks, but during the week you can have them almost to yourself.

Always check in at the ranger station (*casa del guardabosque*) for orientation; most trails are unmarked.

For camping, obtain prior permission and information from the Department of Natural Resources at (809) 724-3724 or 724-3623, ext. 225.

Fajardo

This delightful seaport is the place to go for boating and water sports. Day charters to nearby cays are available from Villa Marina or Isleta Ma-

rina. If you prefer to journey forth on a native sloop, inquire at Las Croa-
bas Beach, slightly north of Fajardo. Day trips and destinations vary;
some include snorkeling, picnicking, or both. Fajardo is also the takeoff
point for the regular ferries to Culebra and Vieques. *Públicos* run regularly between the wharf and the central plaza downtown. It's a quiet,
pleasant town worth wandering. If you don't have time to go downtown,
you may want to have a sandwich at the Fajardo-Vieques-Culebra Restaurant or the bar of the Hotel Delicioso on the waterfront. Hotel Delicioso
has clean, moderately priced rooms if you need to overnight in Fajardo.
For longer stays, Isleta Marina, on a cay just offshore, often has condos
available by the week.

Culebra Island

A quiet, dry island of some 2,000 inhabitants, Culebra is all relaxed
charm. Flamenco Beach, with its nightly turtle patrol, is an unsurpassed
crescent of coral sand. The island also has extensive mangrove labyrinths,
rocky shores, coral reefs, and rolling hills of gray-foliaged thorn forest.
The Culebra National Wildlife Refuge protects Flamenco Peninsula,
Mount Resaca, the Ensenada Honda mangrove area, and the nearby cays
of Culebrita and Luis Peña, as well as twenty-three other islets and rocks.
Accommodations are limited, so reserve in advance. Obtain the current
listing from the Tourist Board.

Vieques Island

Vieques is only 6 miles from Fajardo, and many people make day visits
to beach or snorkel there. Sombé (Sun Bay) Public Beach near Esperanza
has picnic and camping areas. Vieques is low key, with marvelous swimming and diving. Most accommodations are in guest houses.

Mona Island

This rugged, uninhabited island off the west coast of Puerto Rico is now
a nature refuge. Once home to Taino Indians, pirates, treasure-seekers,
and guano miners, it has been set aside for the vast colonies of seabirds,
iguanas, and marine life. Overnight camping is permitted but most visitors come by boat for the day only. Boats leave from Puerto Real in Cabo
Rojo. Contact the Department of Natural Resources by calling (809) 722-
1726 for information and to make camping reservations.

Ponce

This old city, with its airy plaza, distinctive buildings (the red and black
fancy one is the century-old firehouse), and seafaring traditions is well

worth a visit. Above the city, on El Vigía Hill, visitors may climb a 100-foot observation tower. Ponce's earlier inhabitants once used this summit to keep track of nearby ships. Observers hoisted flags that identified a vessel as friend or foe. Today, the view includes the mansion of the Serralles family, makers of Don Q rum; the city; and the sea and Caja de Muertos Island in the distance.

Caja de Muertos, with its 100-year-old lighthouse and sparkling beaches, is accessible only by ferry. Ferries leave La Guancha Pier in Ponce at 8:30 A.M. on Friday, Saturday, and Sunday.

The Ponce Museum of Art on Las Americas Avenue houses a collection of some 1,000 paintings and 400 pieces of sculpture. It contains one of the Western Hemisphere's best collections of Pre-Raphaelite paintings. Small admission fee. The museum is open from 10 A.M. to 4 P.M. most days; closed on Tuesdays and for lunch from noon to 1 P.M. each day.

You may want to explore nearby Playa de Ponce, where local artisans make spectacular papier-mâché masks for their carnival parades, or visit the Tibes Indian Ceremonial Center. This ancient site, with its 187 skeletons, is the oldest known cemetery in the Antilles. Calabash trees, with global gourdlike fruit, which has long been used for bowls in the Americas, shade the ceremonial ballparks there. The site also includes two dance grounds, with stone points that line up with the sun during equinoxes and solstices.

Arecibo Observatory

This observatory houses the largest radio and radar telescope in the world. A 20-acre dish, set in the sinkhole of a primeval karst forest, gathers radio waves from space. Operated by Cornell University under a contract with the National Science Foundation, the observatory is open for tours Tuesday through Friday at 10:30 A.M. and 2:30 P.M.; closed Monday, Saturday, and holidays. The grounds are open from 1 to 4 P.M. on Sundays; however, there are no tours. For more information, call (809) 878-2612.

Rio Camuy Cave Park

The 300-acre Rio Camuy Cave park, about two and a half hours west of San Juan, near Arecibo, is in Puerto Rico's primeval karst limestone region. The park includes caverns, canyons, and sinkholes carved out by the world's third-largest underground river. Two of the sinkholes, with their giant stalactites and stalagmites, have been adapted for visitors. Once the haunt of the Taino Indians, the caves now include a modern visitors' center with a cafeteria and theater. The park is open Wednesday through Sunday and holidays, 8 A.M. to 4 P.M.; admission is $6 for adults, $4 for children under 12, and $3 for seniors.

South of Arecibo

The 800-year-old Caguana Indian Ceremonial Park near Utuado includes 13 acres of landscaped grounds as well as the ancient ball courts, petroglyphs, and small museum. No admission charge. Open daily 9 A.M. to 5 P.M.

San Germán

This is the second urban center that settling Spaniards founded on Puerto Rico. The town remains noted for its colonial architecture and Old World charm. Two plazas and a restored church dating back to 1606 are highlights.

Lajas/La Paraguera

This fishing village cum resort has guest houses, seafood restaurants, and a shell museum. Phosphorescent Bay nearby is one of the main attractions. Here, especially on moonless nights, visitors are able to see the mysterious sparkle of "sealight"—the luminescence of millions of dinoflagellates that glow when the water is disturbed. Boats leave La Paraguera hourly between 7:30 P.M. and 12:30 A.M., depending on demand.

NIGHTLIFE: Nightlife is centered around the casinos and nightclubs of the Condado strip and the major resorts. Check with your hotel or *Qué Pasa* for details. Concerts and plays are presented regularly.

BEACHES: There are literally hundreds of beaches circling Puerto Rico, not to mention on nearby cays. Luquillo Public Beach, with its palm-lined sand and booths of cheerful food vendors, is a classic example. Public beaches (*balnearios*) are open Tuesday to Sunday from 9 A.M. to 5 P.M. Parking and showers are included in the small entrance fee. Many of the beaches also have provisions for tent camping or have cabins or trailers for rent. Public beaches include Añasco, Boquerón, Caña Gorda, Cerro Gordo, Escambrón, Isla Verde, Luquillo, Punta Guilarte, Punta Salinas, Punta Santiago, Sardinera, Seven Seas, and Sombé. Call the Department of Recreation and Sports at (809) 722-1551 or 721-2800 for information about overnight stays. Check a map for locations.

Many hotels and guest houses have their own beaches. Guests from other hotels may often use these private beaches for a small fee or after having dined there for lunch. Palmas del Mar in Humacao, for example, is on its own lovely beach. Explore.

SHOPPING: That Puerto Rico is an island with everything is underscored by its available goods. From luxury items to hand-carved wooden religious figures, called *santos*, it is simply a matter of finding the place that has what you want. Old San Juan is an easy place to get a feel for goods and prices. It offers a blend of imports and handcrafted items in a relatively compact area.

Recently, Puerto Rico's Institute of Culture has done a great deal to preserve and stimulate interest in local handicrafts. It maintains a list (with maps) of artisans throughout the island, many of whom welcome visitors into their studios. Masks of papier-mâché, musical instruments of local woods, handmade bobbin lace, *santos,* and handwoven baskets are handicrafts you might want to look for.

FESTIVALS AND HOLIDAYS
All U.S. holidays plus:
Three Kings' Day, January.
De Hostos's Birthday, 9 January.
Abolition of Slavery, 22 March.
Semana Santa (Holy Week); date varies.
De Diego's Birthday, 17 April.
Luis Muñoz Rivera's Birthday, 17 July.
Commonwealth Day, 25 July.
Barbosa's Birthday, 24 July.
Lares Uprising Anniversary, 23 September.
Discovery of Puerto Rico, 19 November.

FOOD: Food of all types is available in cosmopolitan San Juan. Out on the island, native specialties include thick soups called *asopaos* and little fried turnovers called *pastelillos*. The turnovers come with a variety of somewhat spicy fillings, from fish to chicken, and are good with local beer. *Cocos fríos,* cold green coconuts with the tops sliced off and straws popped in, are often sold as roadside drinks.

HOTELS: Lodgings of all sorts and prices, from tents to luxurious villas, are available in Puerto Rico. All of the major hotel chains are well represented. A complete list is available from the Tourist Board; most travel agents also have lots of suggestions.

For More Information

Contact the Puerto Rico Tourism Company in the following cities. Be sure to ask for *Qué Pasa*.

PUERTO RICO

Puerto Rico Tourism Company
La Princesa Building
Old San Juan, PR 00901
telephone: (809) 721-2400

U.S.

Puerto Rico Tourism Company
901 Ponce de Leon Boulevard, Suite 604
Coral Gables, FL 33134
telephone: (305) 445-9112

Puerto Rico Tourism Company
3575 West Cahuenga Boulevard, Suite 248
Los Angeles, CA 90068
telephone: (213) 874-5991

Puerto Rico Tourism Company
575 Fifth Avenue
New York, NY 10017
telephone: (212) 599-6262 or (800) 223-6350

CANADA

Puerto Rico Tourism Company
41-43 Colbourne Street, Suite 300
Toronto, Ontario M5E 1E3
Canada
telephone: (416) 368-2680/2689

Saba

AREA: 5 square miles.

POPULATION: 1,200.

CAPITAL CITY: The Bottom.

LANGUAGE: Officially Dutch, but English is most commonly spoken.

GOVERNMENT: Part of the Netherlands Antilles.

LOCATION: 28 miles south of St. Maarten.

GETTING THERE: Windwards Islands Airways STOL planes fly from Juliana Airport, St. Maarten, several times a day. There is also a ferry from St. Maarten three days a week.

CUSTOMS: U.S. and Canadian citizens need proof of citizenship.

HEALTH: No special considerations.

CLOTHING: Informal tropical wear, but no bathing suits on the streets. You will definitely need a sweater for cool evenings and rubber-soled shoes for walking.

ELECTRICITY: 110 volts/60 cycles AC, as in the U.S.

TIME ZONE: Atlantic standard time.

MONEY: Netherlands Antilles guilder (NAF) but U.S. dollars are widely accepted. Major credit cards accepted most places.

TAX AND TIPS: Hotel rooms have 5 percent government tax plus 10 percent service charge.

GETTING AROUND: Several taxis. A two-hour tour of the island runs about U.S. $40 per jeepful. There are five rental car operations, but unless you're eager for a thrill and are an expert at precipitous driving, this isn't a good choice. "Standing by the road" (hitchhiking) is a viable, safe, and acceptable way of getting around. Walking is also pleasant, although you'll need rubber-soled shoes and perseverance for the steep inclines.

Overview

Saba is a beachless green mountain going straight up to Mount Scenery's 2,854-foot peak with 1,064 steps. Three storybook villages with ginger-bread houses in Caribbean colors cling to the hillsides. Although the island lacks beaches, there are boat dive trips to nearby crystal waters full of coral and bright fish. Mountain trails, a bit of shopping, lots of scenery, and delightful people make Saba a great choice for visitors happy to do little or nothing.

History

Columbus sighted the island in 1493. Saba has lived under sixteen different flags; the island changed hands twelve times in the seventeenth and eighteenth centuries alone. Holland ended up with it in 1816 and it's been Dutch ever since. English, the spoken tongue, remains the legacy of early settlers from the Shetland Islands.

Saba is the smallest of the Dutch Windward Islands (St. Maarten and St. Eustatius are the other two), which are part of the Netherlands Antilles. About 25,000 people visit Saba each year, most on a day trip from St. Maarten or on three-to-seven-night dive-trip packages.

Things to See and Do

You can see all of Saba in a relatively short time. The best way to start is with a two-hour taxi tour. This will include a look at Hell's Gate, Upper Hell's Gate, the English Quarter, Windwardside, The Bottom, and Fort Bay.

Windwardside at 1,804 feet is Saba's second-largest settlement; it has tourist shops and a number of guest houses. The hand-hewn steps up to Mount Scenery (2,854 feet), which start a bit beyond town, will take you through a lovely rain forest filled with ferns and wild orchids (please, no picking). The climb takes about three hours one way; bring a picnic and enjoy. Interpretive material and identifying signs by the Saba Conservation Foundation line the trail. For more details about Saba's many nature trails and walking tours, pick up brochures at the Tourist Bureau. Visitors may become members of the Saba Conservation Foundation for a yearly donation of U.S. $25.

The Bottom, Saba's capital, in a valley at a mere 820 feet, is full of quaint buildings and Old World charm.

DIVING: The Saba Marine Park, established in 1987, protects the waters around the entire island. It includes a number of unique snorkeling and scuba sites. A small charge for each dive helps maintain the park. Above water boat tours are also available. Saba now has three pro-dive shops and all hotels offer dive packages. Saba's clear waters include lava tunnels, hot springs, unique boulder and coral formations, as well as a colorful array of fish life.

DIVE SHOPS
Saba Deep Diving Center
P.O. Box 22
Fort Bay, Saba
Netherlands Antilles
telephone: (011) 599-4-63347
fax: (011) 599-4-63397

Sea Saba Dive Center
P.O. Box 530
Windwardside, Saba
Netherlands Antilles
telephone: (011) 599-4-62246
fax: (011) 599-4-62362

Wilson's Dive Shop
P.O. Box 50
Saba
Netherlands Antilles
telephone: (011) 599-4-62541
fax: (011) 599-4-63334

SHOPPING: Saba offers interesting crafts in its small shops. Some of Saba's women make a patterned pulled-thread linen lace called Spanish Work; try Saba Tropical Arts. Silk-screened clothes are sold at the Saba Artisans Foundation. Around the Bend has T-shirts and papier-mâché. A morning or afternoon will give you time to browse through them all. Shop hours are 8 A.M. until noon and 2 to 6 P.M. Saban spice, a locally made blend of 151-proof rum, fennel, cinnamon, cloves, and nutmeg, is a popular souvenir: about U.S. $10 per quart.

FESTIVALS AND HOLIDAYS
Saba Summer Festival and Carnival, July.
Saba Days, early December.
Plus all standard holidays.

FOOD: Mainly restricted to guest houses and hotels (usually included in the room price). For a change of pace, try the several bars and eateries where you can enjoy pizza, hamburgers, sandwiches, or Chinese food.

HOTELS: Saba's hotels tend to be small and friendly. They can be booked directly or through the Tourist Bureau's toll-free number. To direct dial Saba (if your phone company offers the service), dial the international access code 011, then 599 (country code for Netherlands Antilles), and 4 (area code for Saba) plus the local number. Follow the same pattern for a fax. Hotels include:

Captain's Quarters
Windwardside
telephone: 62201
fax: 62377

Caribe Guesthouse
The Bottom
telephone: 63259
fax: 63259

The Cottage Club
Windwardside
telephone: 62486/62386
fax: 62434

Cranston Antique Inn
The Bottom
telephone: 63203

Gate House
Hell's Gate
telephone: 62416
fax: 62415

Juliana's
Windwardside
telephone: 62269
fax: 62389

Scouts Place
Windwardside
telephone: 62205
fax: 62388

Willards
Booby Hill
telephone: 62498
fax: 62482

There are also a number of cottages and apartments available. Obtain the complete list from the Tourist Bureau.

For More Information

Tourist Bureau
Windwardside
Saba, Netherlands Antilles

U.S.
Saba Tourist Office
P.O. Box 6322
Boca Raton, FL 33427-6322
telephone: (407) 394-8580 or (800) 722-2394
fax: (407) 394-8588

⌐ St. Barthélemy (St. Barts)

AREA: 8 square miles.

POPULATION: Approximately 5,000.

CAPITAL CITY: Gustavia.

LANGUAGE: French; quite a bit of English spoken in hotels.

RELIGION: Roman Catholic.

GOVERNMENT: Dependency of Guadeloupe, an overseas department of France.

LOCATION: 15 miles southwest of St. Maarten.

GETTING THERE: Connect through St. Maarten (principal gateway) or San Juan, St. Thomas, or Guadeloupe. There's also daily catamaran service from Philipsburg, St. Maarten, to Gustavia.

CUSTOMS: U.S. and Canadian citizens need either a valid passport or proof of citizenship (an expired passport not more than five years old will do) and either a return or an ongoing ticket; other nationalities need a passport and in some cases a visa.

HEALTH: No special considerations; one clinic on the island.

CLOTHING: Informal but fashionable tropical wear (bikinis, T-shirts, jeans). Men don't need jackets and ties for dining; women may want something casual but chic.

ELECTRICITY: 220 volts/50 cycles AC.

TIME ZONE: Atlantic standard time, one hour ahead of eastern standard time.

MONEY: French franc; exchange rate varies; U.S. dollars are widely accepted.

TAX AND TIPS: A 10 percent service charge is added to most bills. Taxi drivers are generally self-employed and do not expect tips. Airport departure tax is about 15 francs.

GETTING AROUND: Taxis; rental cars, mainly mini-mokes and VWs; agencies include Avis, Hertz, and Budget. Rental cars are available at the airport (best to reserve in season) and all are stick shifts. Minibus tours of the island are also available.

Overview

Steep green mountains and meadows divided by low stone fences run down to white sand beaches and the blue waters of coves and inlets. St. Barts is tiny, quiet, and picturesque. Quiet Gustavia, the capital, would not look out of place at Disneyland.

French ambience, not to mention food and wines, blends well with the balm of Caribbean sun and sand to make St. Barts an ideal getaway. If you aren't happy amusing yourself and relaxing, better look for another island.

History

Although St. Barts was sighted by Columbus in 1493 and named for his brother Bartoloméo, the island's first colonists were French. The first settlement, started around 1645, did not prosper; it was sold to the Knights of Malta and was later raided by Carib Indians and subsequently abandoned. St. Barts was resettled in 1674 by French people from Normandy and Brittany. The young colony succeeded this time partially because of French buccaneers who brought bounty plundered from Spanish galleons.

The British took the island briefly in 1758, but St. Barts remained essentially French until it was suddenly sold to Sweden in 1784. The Swedes renamed the harbor Gustavia after their king, declared it a free port, and prospered in trade. St. Barts' original population continued to farm quietly. France repurchased the isle in 1878, and it remains French today, with hints of Sweden's only Caribbean legacy.

Things to See and Do

Gustavia

The capital of St. Barts is a picturesque little harbor town best explored on foot. Many combine lunch and shopping with a look at Gustavia's historic architecture, a mix of Swedish colonial and French.

Corrossol

Northwest of Gustavia, where St. Barts echoes Brittany. Older women still wear French provincial dress, including the winged shoulder-length sunbonnets called *quichenottes;* their bare feet are the only concession to the tropics. They don't like to be photographed, but they do sell lovely straw work.

BEACHES: Tourist life on St. Barts is centered around the sea; beaches, swimming, snorkeling, and other water sports are all available. Many visitors like to sun at the airport beach, where the reverie of sunbathing is interrupted by the exciting comings and goings of planes on St. Barts' tiny airstrip. Nude sunbathing is prohibited, but going topless is common. On the south shore, Anse du Gouverneur is popular.

SHOPPING: Gustavia has some casual French designer clothes at freeport prices in its small boutiques. There is also a limited selection of other duty-free luxuries (avid shoppers may want to take a day on nearby St. Maarten). Local crafts include straw work and shell items such as jewelry and mobiles.

FESTIVALS AND HOLIDAYS: The Festival of St. Barthélemy is the big event here. It's celebrated in late August and turns Gustavian streets into a tropical country fair. Other festivities include Regatta Week in July and a small pre-Lenten Carnival with "black and white" parades and parties, for which revellers dress only in those colors. Bastille Day, 14 July, is also a day of local partying.

Many traditional cafés serve French and Creole specialties. You may want to try Hotel Hibiscus, L'Ananas, the Coté Jardin, or Le Brigantin. Almost every visitor makes it up to Castelets for dinner or a nightcap. Au Port in Gustavia often receives rave reviews from diners.

HOTELS: The largest hotel on this tiny island, the Guanahani, has only 76 rooms (there are perhaps some 800 rooms on the island altogether). Service in all tends to be relaxed and casual. The simple Tom Beach (12 rooms with kitchenettes) on St. Jean Beach is popular with sun worshippers who don't want a lot of frills. For a complete list, including apartments and villas, with current prices, contact the Tourist Office.

French Government Tourist Office
9454 Wilshire Boulevard, Suite 715
Beverly Hills, CA 90212
telephone: (310) 271-6665

French Government Tourist Office
676 North Michigan Avenue, Suite 3360
Chicago, IL 60611
telephone: (312) 751-7800

French Government Tourist Office
444 Madison Avenue
New York, NY 10022

St. Eustatius (Statia)

AREA: 8 square miles; 2 1/2 miles long, 5 miles wide.

POPULATION: Approximately 2,200.

CAPITAL CITY: Oranjestad.

LANGUAGE: Officially Dutch, but almost everyone speaks English.

RELIGION: Varied.

GOVERNMENT: Part of the Netherlands Antilles.

LOCATION: 38 miles south of St. Maarten, about 11 miles northwest of St. Kitts.

GETTING THERE: Windward Island Airways from St. Maarten.

CUSTOMS: U.S. and Canadian citizens need only proof of citizenship and either a return or an ongoing ticket.

HEALTH: No special considerations, except limited facilities.

CLOTHING: Casual tropical wear. This is one island where fashion means little; dressing for dinner (other than in clean casual clothes) would be suspect.

ELECTRICITY: 110 volts/60 cycles AC, as in the U.S.

TIME ZONE: Atlantic standard time.

MONEY: Netherlands Antilles guilder (NAF). U.S. currency is okay for all tourist purposes; Canadian money is best changed to guilders beforehand on St. Maarten. Don't count on being able to use credit cards.

TAX AND TIPS: A 7 percent government tax on hotel bills plus a 15 percent service charge added to restaurant and hotel bills; no need to add to that except for extraordinary service. Airport departure tax is U.S. $5 to the Dutch islands; U.S. $10 to other destinations.

GETTING AROUND: Taxis meet incoming flights and offer day tours. Prices are fixed (no meters) and should be confirmed in advance. There are also two car rental agencies.

Overview

St. Eustatius, almost always called Statia, is one of the Caribbean's smallest and quietest islands. Be sure of your own capacity for doing nothing and amusing yourself before you commit to more than a day here. This is the place to go if you really want to get away from it *all*. There is lovely territory for wandering, along the shore, among the ruins, and in Statia's forested crater.

History

Statia was once one of the most prosperous ports in the Caribbean. Its population was well over 7,000 in 1790, as compared with today's 2,200. In the 1600s and 1700s, rows of warehouses faced Oranjestad harbor, where merchant ships waited to unload. This all ended when the British sacked the island in 1780. Apparently, the British had declared war on the Dutch for a number of reasons. Certainly one of their grievances was the official cannon salute of recognition that the Dutch fired from Fort Oranje in answer to the U.S. *Andrew Doria* on 16 November 1776. The French and British fought over the island until 1816, when it became Dutch again, but Statia's prosperity was over.

The island remains a member of the Netherlands Antilles. Statia's government is one of the island's larger employers. The island also has some oil-related industry. About 30,000 tourists visit each year.

Things to See and Do

People don't come to Statia to do things. Walking, hiking, swimming, sunning, and limin' (which in the vernacular means not really doing anything) are all easy on Statia.

Oranjestad

Statia's capital is divided into an upper and lower town, separated by pink-gray cliffs. The restored Fort Oranje is in Upper Town, as are several fine examples of period architecture. One of the finest eighteenth-century houses in the Caribbean is now the St. Eustatius Historical Foundation Museum. The foundation's inexpensive "Walking Tour" booklet may be purchased at the museum. Pick up a copy and head out. Plan to picnic along the way (bring your own) or lunch at the popular Old Gin House.

The graveyard at the Dutch Reformed Church, just out of town, has lots of unique headstones if you are interested in stone rubbing.

The Quill

From the Dutch *kuil*, or pit, this is the crater of Statia's now-dormant volcano; it is the island's highest point. After the top of the mountain blew out, the inside of the crater eventually became forested. This is a half-day trek that requires more stamina than anything else. The quiet trails through the lush rain forest make it a nice break from the beaches. Allow two to three hours for the round trip so you have time to savor the flora, fauna, and view.

BEACHES: Most visitors prefer the quiet black sand beaches of the southwest shore. You can surf on the Atlantic side at Concordia Bay; take a friend, since there are no lifeguards.

DIVING: The sunken ruins of Oranjestad in Oranje Bay are the most popular destination. Snorkelers and divers can have a close look at masonry (the foundations of many old buildings are still intact) and cannons in the coralled depths. For equipment rental or dive trips, try Golden Rock Dive Center or Dive Statia. Dive sites include wrecks, cliffs, canyons, and reefs.

SHOPPING: "Not much" sums it up. You might find a few locally made items and imported Dutch wares. Mazinga Gift Shop and Old Gin House's boutique are your best bets. "Serious" shoppers should stop on St. Maarten either going or coming. The Hole in the Wall and Park Place also offer some unique wares.

FESTIVALS AND HOLIDAYS
Coronation Day, April. Fireworks, music, sports.
Statia-America Day, 15 November. Parades and parties.

FOOD: A blend of Creole, American, and Dutch foods is served in Statia's few eateries. La Maison sur la Plage, on the beach with a spectacular view, serves French-style dishes.

HOTELS: Hotels include the Old Gin House, an eighteenth-century tavern with 20 rooms; the hilltop La Maison sur la Plage; the Golden Era Hotel at the water's edge; the Talk of the Town Hotel; and Daniel's Guesthouse. Check Caribbean Connections (toll free) or the St. Eustatius/Statia Tourist Office for the latest listings.

For More Information

St. Eustatius Tourist Office
Fort Oranjestraat
Oranjestad, St. Eustatius
Netherlands Antilles
telephone: (011) 599-3-82433/02213/02209
fax: (011) 599-3-82433

U.S.
Caribbean Connections
P.O. Box 261
Trumbull, CT 06611
telephone: (800) 692-4106

Caribbean Tourism Organization
20 East 46th Street
New York, NY 10017
telephone: (212) 682-0435
fax: (212) 697-4258

CANADA
New Concepts Canada
2455 Cawthra Road, Suite 70
Mississauga, Ontario L5A 3P1
Canada
telephone: (905) 803-0131
fax: (905) 803-0132

St. Kitts and Nevis

AREA: St. Kitts, 65 square miles; Nevis, 36 square miles.

POPULATION: St. Kitts, 36,000; Nevis, 9,000.

CAPITAL CITY: Basseterre, St. Kitts; Charleston, Nevis.

LANGUAGE: English.

RELIGION: Mainly Anglican and Catholic.

GOVERNMENT: Independent member of the British Commonwealth.

LOCATION: Leeward Islands, between Montserrat and St. Maarten.

GETTING THERE: By air via San Juan.

CUSTOMS: U.S. and Canadian citizens need proof of citizenship and either a return or an ongoing ticket.

HEALTH: No special considerations; small hospital on each island.

CLOTHING: Tropical wear; sweaters and jackets for breezy evenings.

ELECTRICITY: 230 volts, single phase; 400 volts, three phase/60 cycles AC.

TIME ZONE: Atlantic standard time, one hour ahead of eastern standard time.

MONEY: Eastern Caribbean dollar.

TAX AND TIPS: Hotels add a 10 percent service charge and a 5 percent government room tax. Airport departure tax is U.S. $10 per person.

GETTING AROUND: Taxis, buses, bicycles, and rental cars (temporary license for U.S. $10); Four Island Airways and government ferries run between St. Kitts and Nevis (forty-five-minute ferry crossing). Taxi tours are popular; just be sure to work out details and prices in advance. Ask specifically if the price is E.C. or U.S. dollars.

Overview

One of the world's smallest nations is made up of St. Kitts (officially St. Christopher) and Nevis, volcanic islands with colorful histories and a friendly populace. About a third of the people make their living from agriculture, as they have for centuries. From the air, St. Kitts looks like one huge sugarcane field. Nevis grows more fruits and vegetables.

Both sister islands are happy to have tourist dollars. St. Kitts now welcomes cruise ships and has a full-fledged resort complex with a golf course and casinos. Nevis has a handful of plantation inns but remains, for most, a day stop. Both islands offer a stylish version of a Caribbean getaway— lush forests, green hillsides, beaches of all colors, and the vestiges of British colonial hospitality and elite country lodgings.

History

Both islands were named by Columbus on his second voyage in 1493. He named St. Kitts for his own patron saint, St. Christopher, which the British later shortened. He named the smaller island Las Nieves, Spanish for "The Snows." Apparently, from out at sea, the cloud covering on the island's central peak looked like snow. The British version of the name, Nevis, remains.

The first British colony in the Caribbean was established on St. Kitts by Sir Thomas Warner in 1623; French colonists arrived the following year. The British began to settle Nevis in 1629. Thus began the long struggle between Britain and France for possession of the islands. The remarkable fort Brimstone Hill remains a massive stone testimony to this dispute. Once called "The Gibraltar of the West Indies," Brimstone Hill was actually attacked only twice—by the French in 1782 and then by the recapturing British a year later.

The following centuries saw the sugar era and the plantocracy at its height. In 1967, St. Kitts, Nevis, and Anguilla were grouped as a self-governing associated state of Britain, but a newsworthy uprising on Anguilla quickly ended the association. St. Kitts and Nevis became an independent member of the Commonwealth on 19 September 1983. Sugar still accounts for two-thirds of the nation's exports; the main crop on Nevis is sea island cotton.

Things to See and Do

St. Kitts

Most visitors take the circular 23-mile tour around the island. It *can* be done in about two hours; it's also possible to make a day of it with the addition of bathing suits and a picnic. The Golden Lemon at Dieppe Bay is a popular lunch option (make advance reservations).

Basseterre: This quaint capital of St. Kitts is one of the loveliest cities in the Caribbean. Brightly painted buildings (often classed as perfect examples of West Indian architecture) are complemented by the blue waters of the harbor. The main square, called The Circus, has a clock tower and a fountain. A stroll through Basseterre with its government buildings and ancient townhouses can easily roll away the centuries. You may want to stop at St. George's Anglican Church, which dates from 1670, or the Philatelic Bureau, which sells the islands' beautiful stamps.

St. Kitts Sugar Factory: Tours explain the sugar-making process; cane is ground from February through July. On the edge of Basseterre.

Old Road Town: Once capital of the island, this settlement was the first permanent British enclave in the West Indies.

Wingfield Estate: Carib Indian petroglyphs; near Old Road Town.

Romney Manor: Home of Caribelle batiks; you can watch this traditional wax and dye process. A bit past Wingfield.

Brimstone Hill: One of the most dramatic and imposing forts in the Caribbean, this site is well worth a day's trip; it's also a perfect place for a picnic. From its 750-foot elevation, the fort has a panoramic view of six nearby islands. It took slaves more than 100 years to build the massive 7- to 12-foot-thick walls of Brimstone Hill. The fort's name refers to volcanic brimstone; faint whiffs of sulfur can still be noticed.

Brimstone Hill has been beautifully restored and now houses a visitors' center, souvenir shop, and restaurant. Don't miss this imposing legacy, where old cannons and thick stones dramatize history-book battles.

Mount Liamuiga: Once called Mount Misery, this 4,000-foot volcanic peak has been rechristened with the Caribs' original name for St. Kitts, which means "fertile land." Hikers can descend into this dormant volcanic crater by the roots and vines mud-slide method—after they've scaled the peak; this trip is for the sturdy only. A full day's adventure takes hikers through lush rain forest inhabited by numerous birds and vervet monkeys (descendants of those left by French colonists, who kept them as pets). Plan on at least eight hours, and take a lunch and a guide. Several companies offer guided hikes, walks, and rambles. Check with your hotel or the Tourist Office for recommendations.

Monkey Mountain: At 1,319 feet, this is a better choice than Mount Liamuiga for adventurers with doubts about their physical condition. Generally thought an easy climb, this walk can be started behind Fairview Inn, west of Basseterre. You'll see monkeys if you look closely. You don't need a guide here unless you want one.

Nevis

Spend at least a day on nearby Nevis. The ferry from Basseterre leaves from St. Kitts several times a day, except on Thursdays and Sundays; the forty-five-minute crossing costs about U.S. $6 per person, round-trip. Driving on Nevis can be a bit tricky; it's left-hand drive and goats have the right-of-way. Best hire a cab for a one-day visit.

Charleston: "Welcome to Nevis: Birthplace of Alexander Hamilton" proclaims the sign at Charleston's public pier. On Nevis, the word "welcome" is sincere, as will be evidenced by a stroll through picturesque Charleston. Most people stop at the Alexander Hamilton House and at the Trott's next door, where there is a small museum in the cellar. St. Paul's Church and St. Thomas Church both date from the seventeenth century. Turn north on the street between Williams Grocery and Bata Shoes to reach the Nevis Bakery—a side trip with its own rewards.

Bath House and Spring House: Soon after the 50-room Bath Hotel was completed in 1778, it became a fashionable retreat for the elite. The wealthy guests came to drink, gamble, and enjoy the mineral hot springs. The hot springs, with temperatures rising as high as 108 degrees, were said to have medicinal qualities. Although most of the original structure was destroyed by an earthquake in 1950, visitors may take a mineral bath (the simple bath house still functions) and tour the hotel.

Museum of Nevis History: The museum, which opened in 1992, is just beyond the Bath Hotel. It contains a large collection of Lord Horatio Nelson memorabilia, as well as Amerindian relics. There's a small admission charge.

Pinney's Beach: A picture-postcard beach with reef-protected water for snorkeling, palms for shade, and 3 miles of sand for sunning. Be sure to see the lagoon as well. If you're over for only a day, this is a good choice for an interlude and a picnic.

Nisbet Plantation: This restored great house, overlooking a superb beach, has operated as a hotel since the 1960s. Many consider it one of the finest plantation inns in the entire Caribbean. The scenery combined with good island lunches also make it a popular stop on one-day excursions.

Mount Nevis: Hiking to the cloud-covered 3,232-foot peak is not ovoerly strenuous, although in the rainy season it involves some steep scrambling and root-clinging. It's certainly an all-day adventure into thick rain forest. Ask your hotel to pack a lunch; they can also get you a guide.

SHOPPING: Shopping on both St. Kitts and Nevis is delightfully low key and offers Caribbean handicrafts such as banana and palm fiber mats, baskets, coconut shell objects (from bird feeders to jewelry), Caribelle batiks, and traditional unglazed pottery. Local preserves such as pineapple jam, mango jam, and hot-pepper sauce are popular take-home items. Try the new Pelican Mall in Basseterre for luxury imports.

FESTIVALS AND HOLIDAYS: All British holidays as well as the Arts Festival and Culturama on Nevis in July and August, Independence Day on both islands on 19 September, and Carnival on St. Kitts in December.

FOOD: West Indian specialties and Continental tradition blend to produce superb Caribbean cuisine. Seafood and local fruits and vegetables provide the focus for many dishes. On Nevis, most plantation inns have dining facilities; Golden Rock and Nisbet Plantation are favorites, although all are good.

HOTELS: Hotels on St. Kitts range from the elite Golden Lemon on Dieppe Bay, run by Arthur Leaman (formerly of *House & Garden* magazine), to simple guest houses. Sun 'n Sand Beach Resort on Frigate Bay (Atlantic side) offers cottages with weekly rates, as do several other establishments.

Small inns are the order of the day on the quiet isle of Nevis. Many of them were once sugar plantations; it's possible to sleep in a remodeled sugar mill. As elsewhere, summer rates are considerably lower than in-season rates. Call or write for a complete listing and current prices.

For More Information

ST. KITTS AND NEVIS
St. Kitts and Nevis Hotel and Tourist Association

P.O. Box 438
Liverpool Row, Basseterre
St. Kitts, W.I.
telephone: (809) 465-5304
fax: (809) 465-7746

Department of Tourism
P.O. Box 132
Basseterre
St. Kitts, W.I.
telephone: (809) 465-2620/4040
fax: (809) 465-8794

Nevis Tourism Bureau
Main Street, Charlestown
Nevis, W.I.
telephone: (809) 469-1042
fax: (809) 469-1066

U.S.

St. Kitts and Nevis Tourist Office
1464 Whippoorwill Way
Mountainside, NJ 07092
telephone: (908) 232-6701
fax: (908) 233-0485

St. Kitts and Nevis Tourist Office
414 East 75th Street
New York, NY 10021
telephone: (212) 535-1234 or (800) 582-6208

CANADA

St. Kitts and Nevis Tourist Office
11 Yorkville Avenue, Suite 508
Toronto, Ontario M4W IL3
telephone: (416) 921-7717
fax: (416) 921-7997

ENGLAND

St. Kitts and Nevis Tourist Office
10 Kensington Court
London W8 5DL, England
telephone: (011) 44-171-0881
fax: (011) 44-171-937-3611

St. Lucia

AREA: 238 square miles; 14 miles wide, 27 miles long.

POPULATION: 140,000.

CAPITAL CITY: Castries.

LANGUAGE: English, French patois.

RELIGION: 90 percent Roman Catholic.

GOVERNMENT: Independent member of the British Commonwealth.

LOCATION: One of the Windward Islands, between Martinique to the north and St. Vincent to the south.

GETTING THERE: By air via New York, Miami, or San Juan; LIAT from nearby islands.

CUSTOMS: U.S., Canadian, and U.K. citizens need passport or birth certificate and photo ID and either a return or an ongoing ticket; all others need a passport. Visitors' permits are issued on arrival.

HEALTH: No special considerations.

CLOTHING: Casual tropical wear. No minishorts or beachwear in town; visitors may want long skirts or jackets and ties for hotel dining in season. Bring a sweater for the mountains and breezy evenings.

ELECTRICITY: 220 volts/50 cycles AC.

TIME ZONE: Atlantic standard time.

MONEY: Eastern Caribbean dollar (E.C. $2.65 = U.S. $1).

TIPS: Restaurants and hotels add 10 percent service charge.

GETTING AROUND: Taxis, rental cars, bus tours, and several sea excursions.

Overview

Pure physical beauty is St. Lucia's biggest asset. From the dramatic heights of the Pitons to the inviting shores—some black, some white sands—this island is well endowed. Nearly 11 percent of St. Lucia is still rain forest where epiphytes and lianas festoon the thick foliage that supports a wealth of birds, insects, and small animals. The island has waterfalls, rivers, tranquil bays, and a smoldering soufrière as well. On St. Lucia, a visitor can hike rain forest trails, tan at a beachside resort, snorkel protected reefs, explore eighteenth-century ruins, or breakfast at a sidewalk café.

History

Beautiful, fertile St. Lucia was fought over for much of its history. Early Arawaks were driven out by invading Carib Indians. The Caribs repelled the early English settlers, who arrived in 1605 and in 1638. The fierce Caribs were finally subjugated by the French in 1660.

Over the next 150 years, the English and French battled for possession of the lovely island. St. Lucia, sometimes called "The Helen of the West," changed hands between the British and French a number of times. The last battle was in 1803, during the Napoleonic wars, when British troops stormed ashore and defeated the French who were holding Morne Fortune. The 1814 Treaty of Paris ceded St. Lucia to Britain for the last time.

A relatively quiet era followed. Slavery was abolished in 1834. St. Lucia became an independent member of the British Commonwealth on 22 February 1979.

Coconuts, bananas, and citrus fruits help provide agricultural income for the country; tourism, the other leading industry, provides a matching amount.

Things to See and Do

Castries

This old harbor town, once called La Carenage, has been rebuilt after natural catastrophes and fires, so many buildings are made of concrete. Derek Walcott Square, in the old center of town, is a lovely area with gardens and a fountain. It's named for the St. Lucian poet and recipient of the Nobel Prize for Literature and contains a 400-year-old samah tree. The harbor, in the crater of an extinct volcano, is one of the Caribbean's most popular. There are interesting restaurants, shops, and street markets throughout this colorful city. Many important historic sites are on Morne Fortune behind Castries.

Historic Sites

Pre-Columbian artifacts are displayed at the Archaeological and Historical Society's minimuseum on Morne Fortune overlooking Castries harbor. Also there is the nineteenth-century Apostles' Battery and a number of other old military buildings; the Prevost's Redoubt is one of the best preserved and provides a wonderful view. Pigeon Island National Park also has important military ruins, including Rodney's Fort.

Banana Plantations

Three large banana plantations are open to visitors—Cul-de-Sac (north of Marigot Bay), La Caye (in Dennery on the east coast), and Roseau Estate (south of Marigot Bay).

Marigot Bay

One of the Caribbean's most beautiful coves and a popular yacht anchorage, Marigot Bay is serene and palm-lined. Part of the movie *Dr. Doolittle* was filmed here. You may want to lunch at one of the bayside restaurants or head south to watch fishermen at Anse La Raye, where dugout canoes are still built Carib-fashion.

St. Lucia National Trust

The St. Lucia National Trust offers a number of interesting excursions. From land and sea adventures and estate tours to nature walks and cultural presentations, the National Trust tours give visitors an inside look at St. Lucia. Tours include the Marguis Estate, Errard Plantation, rain forest walk, Pigeon Island, Fregate Island, the Maria Islands, Cactus Valley, and the Soufrière, among others. Prices vary. For more information, contact The St. Lucia National Trust, P.O. Box 595, Castries, St. Lucia; telephone: (809) 452-5005 or 453-2504, fax: (809) 453-2791.

Soufrière

This is St. Lucia's second-largest city. Nearby Mount Soufrière is the world's only drive-in volcano. This sulfur-clouded moonscape provides a dramatic view and smell of volcanic activity. Visitors can wander among pits of bubbling mud and stinking steam, and even indulge in the sulfur mineral baths.

Central Forest Reserve

You may want to pick up a copy of the Tourist Board's pamphlet "Natural History Guide to Soufrière," or contact the very helpful Forest Service for more information before you explore. The circular Rain Forest Walk trail leads through the lush landscape of the reserve, the only habitat of the highly endangered St. Lucia parrot (*Amazona versicolor*). No unaccompanied visitors. Arrangements for the walk, which requires stamina, can be made through tour companies or directly with the Forest Service (telephone: 23231). The fee for the walk includes transportation to the forest, lunch, and a contribution to the forest preservation fund. This is true rain forest, layered with ferns, epiphytes, lianas, and orchids and full of bird song. Dress for mud and moisture.

Viewpoint and Mount La Combe, also within the reserve, are musts for people who would like a rain forest experience but not the extended hike. Viewpoint has a quarter-mile circular trail. Following the signposts another mile or so will take you to La Combe. Even this minitour will give you a greater appreciation of the complex and dwindling rain forest ecosystem. These short trails are open to all, without prior Forest Service arrangements; guides are unnecessary.

Pigeon Island National Park

Accessible by car—a causeway now connects this offshore island with St. Lucia at Pigeon Point, north of Castries. There's a small admission fee. The ruins of Rodney's Fort are within the park; he sailed from Pigeon Point to defeat de Grasse at the Battle of the Saints in 1782. Although mainly a historical site, Pigeon Island is also a natural area with lovely beaches. Many visitors like to bring a picnic and spend the day. The St. Lucia National Trust offers tours of Pigeon Island twice weekly.

Turtle-Watching

The St. Lucia Naturalists' Society and the Fisheries Management Unit monitor leatherback turtle nesting from April to August each year. A limited number of tourists can participate in these all-night watches for a fee that includes transportation and food. If interested, please make arrangements through the St. Lucia Tourist Board prior to departure.

The Pitons

St. Lucia's twin volcanic peaks, towering nearly 3,000 feet into the clouds, provide an unmistakable landmark that can be seen from far out at sea. These craggy pinnacles have long provided a challenge to experienced rock and mountain climbers. Experience, conditioning, and guides are musts here.

For those interested only in admiring the view, try an all-day sea excursion down the coast. It starts in Castries's yacht basin, stops at Soufrière's Sulfur Springs, and continues on to the Pitons, which are spectacular from the sea as the surf breaks on their bases. The trip includes lunch and often a steel band and snorkeling stop. Several boats make the trip; check your hotel for details.

SWIMMING AND DIVING: The best beaches include Vigie Beach, Choc Bay, Reduit Bay, La Toc Bay, and Pigeon Island. There's black sand at Soufrière's beach and good reef-protected beaches around Vieux Fort. Many hotels (most are on the beach) loan snorkeling equipment free to guests. There's good diving and snorkeling right off the beach at popular Anse Chastanet. For scuba equipment rental and instruction or dive trips, try Scuba St. Lucia at the Anse Chastanet Beach Hotel or Dive St. Lucia on Vigie Beach.

SHOPPING: Local handicrafts such as straw work, wood carvings, dolls, hand-screened fashions, and batiks top the list. Hand-carved mahogany plaques that detail island scenes bas-relief style are a real find. Local pottery is showcased at the Pottery Shop in Soufrière; try Noah's Arkade in Castries for West Indian crafts. Don't miss the Castries market for island sights and sounds, spices and straw work. Many visitors enjoy the duty-free shopping at Pointe Serephine, a Spanish-style mall near Castries.

FESTIVALS AND HOLIDAYS

Le Jour de l'An, 1 and 2 January. Old French celebration, dances, parties.

Carnival, February. Parades, queen, calypso.

St. Lucia Jazz Festival, May.

St. Lucia Day, 13 December.

Stores are closed for all traditional holidays.

FOOD: This is a good place to try Caribbean specialties such as callaloo, stuffed breadfruit, pumpkin soup, and fried flying fish. Fresh seafood and local fruits and vegetables prepared with historic French know-how produce tasty results. You'll be able to find plenty of choices, especially for expensive meals. For something simpler and cheaper, try Le Boucan in Castries, with its sidewalk cafe and St. Lucian specialties; or Doolittle's in Marigot Bay (take the ferry from Marigot jetty). Bring your swim gear and have a dip or go snorkeling before lunch. Windjammer Landing has four restaurants with a variety of choices.

HOTELS: St. Lucia has all types of hotels (with nearly 3,000 rooms); most line the beach around Castries. Several offer complete vacation packages, as do several charter boat companies, such as Moorings St. Lucia, telephone: (800) 535-7289; Cahoni; Endless Summer Destination St. Lucia;

Escape to Paradise; Motor Yacht Vigie; Stevens Yachts; Surf Queen; and Tradewind Yachts.

The Tourist Board will be happy to send you a complete list with prices of the island's hotels. These include the Anse Chastanet, Club St. Lucia, East Winds, Islander, Jalousie Plantation, Ladera Resort, Le Sport, Rendezvous, Royal St. Lucian, Sandals St. Lucia/Halcyon, Rex St. Lucian, Windjammer Landing Villas, Wyndham Morgan Bay, among others. On Morne Fortune, there are the Green Parrot Inn and Top O' the Morne.

For More Information

U.S.

St. Lucia Tourist Board
820 Second Avenue, Suite 900E
New York, NY 10017
telephone: (212) 867-2950 or (800) 456-3984
fax: (212) 867-2795

CANADA

St. Lucia Tourist Board
3 Robert Speck Pathway, Suite 900
Mississagua, Ontario L4Z 2G5
Canada
telephone: (905) 270-9892
fax: (905) 270-8086

ENGLAND

St. Lucia Tourist Board
10 Kensington Court
London W8 5DL, England
telephone: (071) 937-1969
fax: (071) 937-3611

GERMANY

St. Lucia Tourist Board
Postfach 2304
6380 Bad Homburg 1, Germany
telephone: (061) 72-30-44-31
fax: (061) 72-30-50-72

⌐ St. Martin/Sint Maarten

AREA: 37 square miles (16 Dutch; 21 French).

POPULATION: 28,000 on St. Martin; 32,000 on St. Maarten.

CAPITAL CITIES: Philipsburg (St. Maarten), Marigot (St. Martin).

LANGUAGE: French, Dutch, and much English.

RELIGION: Varied.

GOVERNMENT: French St. Martin is a dependency of Guadeloupe, an Overseas Region of France; Dutch St. Maarten is part of the Netherlands Antilles.

LOCATION: 144 miles east of Puerto Rico.

GETTING THERE: The international Dutch airport of Juliana is serviced by most major airlines. Small Caribbean lines offer interisland transport. There are direct flights from New York, Miami, and San Juan.

CUSTOMS: U.S. and Canadian citizens need proof of citizenship and either a return or an ongoing ticket. No formalities between sides of the island.

HEALTH: No special considerations.

CLOTHING: Casual tropical wear; no beachwear in town, please; a light wrap for evenings.

ELECTRICITY: 220 volts/60 cycles AC, as in the U.S.

TIME ZONE: Atlantic standard time, one hour ahead of eastern standard time.

MONEY: French franc, Netherlands Antilles guilder; U.S. money widely accepted, as are traveler's checks and credit cards.

TAX AND TIPS: Hotels rooms on the Dutch side have a 5 percent government room tax. Airport departure tax is $10 at Juliana airport; 15 francs at Esperance.

GETTING AROUND: Taxis, tours, buses, boat trips, car rentals (roads are good, for the most part). Major rental agencies at the airport

View of Marigot, capital of the French side of St. Martin, which is shared with the Dutch. (Photo by Ellen Milan.)

and in town. Most hotels will reserve a car for you if you ask in advance (the only way to get one in season).

Overview

Happily split between the French and Dutch, this island is one of the most popular tourist destinations in the Caribbean. It has rolling green hills that rise to 1,278 feet at Mount Paradis, free-port shopping, casinos, and irresistible white sand beaches. There are no spectacular natural assets or, for that matter, historical, architectural, or cultural ones. Yet, the island remains totally booked almost every winter. The secret is probably linked to ease; the island is accessible (Juliana is an international airport) and friendly. This is an easy place to relax without the pressures of sightseeing; visitors can swim or lie in the sun without feeling guilty about missing out.

History

Columbus named St. Martin in 1493. The French and Dutch both settled it in the 1630s; the Spanish became interested in the island in the 1640s. It was here that Peter Stuyvesant (later of New York) lost his leg in a struggle with the Spanish. The Spanish were ousted in 1648, when legend has it that the island was then divided between the French and the Dutch in a most civilized fashion. A Frenchman and a Dutchman, after fortifying themselves with a bit of drink, stood back-to-back and took off walking in opposite directions. Their meeting place on the other side of the island would be the border. The Frenchman was slightly quicker and the French still have 21 square miles, the Dutch 16. Thus began three centuries of happy coexistence. From 1651 to 1665 St. Martin became a possession of the Order of Malta and then was ceded to the French West Indies Company. During the Franco-British rivalries that bloodied most of the Caribbean in the seventeenth and eighteenth centuries, the island was twice occupied by the British. It became a free port in 1850. Today, tourism is the major industry.

Things to See and Do

Most visitors enjoy just puttering around this civilized, friendly island. It's the best way to see abandoned mills and quiet views. Wandering is also recommended in the two capital cities, Philipsburg and Marigot, where free-port shopping is the main pastime. Nightlife includes discos and casinos.

Nearby Islands

It's easy to include a visit to Anguilla, Saba, St. Kitts, or St. Barts. For Anguilla, take the boat from Marigot Harbor. Boats leave every half hour from 8 A.M. to 5:30 P.M. for the twenty-minute crossing.

For St. Barts, take the ferry from Pelican Marina at Simpson Bay or a large catamaran from several other locations.

Picturesque Saba is also nearby. Take the fifteen-minute flight from Juliana Airport or the ferry from the Pelican Marina at Simpson Bay.

BEACHES: Perfect white sand beaches line this island; it's just a matter of finding your favorite. Topless sunning is common; nude bathing at Orient Bay. Most hotels have their own beaches, which charge a small fee for nonguests. For most beaches on the Dutch side, like popular Mullet Bay, the dress code is "to stay covered."

DIVING: Ilet Pinel has good shallow diving, Green Kay has a barrier reef, and Flat Island has subsea geologic faults. Several dive operations offer reef, wreck, cave, night, and drift dives. Diving is done from boats as most sites are a distance offshore.

SPORTS: Equipment for snorkeling, waterskiing, parasailing, and windsurfing is readily available at hotels. Ask about lessons, as well. Golf, tennis, horseback riding, sailing, and deep-sea fishing are also available. Ask your hotel activity desk.

SHOPPING: Free-port shopping is one of this island's main attractions, and bargains abound. In Dutch Philipsburg, the Front Street shops are probably the best place to start. Good buys include Delftware, pipes, and Dutch cheese and chocolates, as well as imported crystal, china, linens, and liquors. In Marigot, on the French side, fashion items, cosmetics, French perfumes, porcelains, and housewares are the best buys. Shop comparatively; free port or not, merchants set their own prices. If you plan to buy something special, get an idea of prices at home before you travel.

FESTIVALS AND HOLIDAYS: Two national holidays are celebrated on both sides of the island with parades, parties, and fireworks—Dutch Coronation Day on 30 April and French Bastille Day on 14 July. In addition to other traditional holidays, St. Maarten's Trade Winds Regatta is held in spring, and Concordia Day is celebrated on 11 November.

FOOD: French wines and Dutch beers complement various dishes. Lobster and good fresh fish are easy to come by. Reservations are a good idea for dinner; lunches are more casual. You'll be able to find anything you have a craving for here, at any price. Shop around; you won't have to eat anywhere twice, unless you want to. Don't miss the French bakeries and the Dutch chocolates.

HOTELS: Hotels run the gamut here; the Dutch side alone has more than 4,000 rooms plus apartments. Check into airline packages; most of the larger resorts have them. A complete hotel list is available from the Tourist Board. Choose carefully and ask detailed questions; this is a sophisticated island, and you can as easily end up in a characterless high rise as a quaint seaside cottage. Book early; St. Maarten is often sold out in season. Most travel agents can help you reserve a room.

For More Information

ST. MARTIN
Office du Tourisme
Port de Marigot

97150 Saint Martin
telephone: (011) 590-87-57-21/23
fax: (011) 590-87-56-43

U.S.
St. Maarten Tourist Office
675 Third Avenue
New York, NY 10017
telephone: (212) 953-2084 or (800) 786-2278
fax: (212) 953-2145

French Government Tourist Office
610 Fifth Avenue
New York, NY 10020
telephone: (900) 990-0040 or (800) 786-2278
fax: (212) 247-6468

Marketing Challenges International
10 East 21st Street
New York, NY 10010
telephone: (212) 529-8484 or (800) 786-2278
fax: (212) 460-8287

St. Vincent and the Grenadines

AREA: 150 square miles, including more than 100 isles and cays.
POPULATION: 107,000.
CAPITAL CITY: Kingstown.
LANGUAGE: English.
RELIGION: Varied.
GOVERNMENT: Independent member of the British Commonwealth.
LOCATION: Windward Islands, 21 miles south of St. Lucia.

GETTING THERE: No direct air service; connect via Barbados, St. Lucia, Grenada, or Trinidad. Most hotels will help you book your connecting flight when you reserve your room.

CUSTOMS: U.S. and Canadian citizens need proof of citizenship and either a return or an ongoing ticket.

HEALTH: No special considerations; limited facilities—small hospitals and clinics.

CLOTHING: Informal tropical wear; minishorts and bathing suits are not allowed in town.

ELECTRICITY: 220–240 volts/50 cycles.

TIME ZONE: Atlantic standard time, one hour ahead of eastern standard time.

MONEY: Eastern Caribbean dollar; check in advance about credit cards.

TAX AND TIPS: 5 percent government tax, U.S. $8 airport departure tax; 10 percent service charge is added to hotel bills.

GETTING AROUND: Taxis, rental cars. Temporary driver's license available with valid license and a fee. Interisland air services and scheduled boats link the islands.

Overview

Deserted beaches and alluring blue waters are the big attractions on these lovely isles. More than 100 separate cays, islands, and isles makes up this chain. Major islands include Bequia, Mustique, Canouan, Mayreau, Union, and Petit St. Vincent. Lovely forests, plantations, rivers, and the volcanic peak Soufrière add dimension to St. Vincent's interior. Long a popular series of anchorages for Caribbean yachters, these islands offer visitors the best of sand, sea, and quiet.

History

Columbus landed on St. Vincent in 1498 and found in residence the Carib Indians, who had earlier taken the island from the peaceful Arawaks. The Caribs controlled the island until the late 1700s, when a few French colonists established settlements. The British took the island from the French in 1762; the French recaptured it in 1779. A treaty restored it to Britain in 1783, and the British spent the rest of the century deporting the Caribs.

St. Vincent was part of the Federation of the West Indies from 1958 to 1962. The island became independent from Britain on 27 October 1979.

Today, agriculture and related processing industries provide economic mainstays. Tourism is the fastest growing industry.

Things to See and Do

St. Vincent

This island is full of lovely vistas, freshwater streams, surf-beaten shores, deserted beaches, and acres of banana and coconut plantations. There are also lush forest and mineral springs to explore. A day's drive or a tour around the island will give you a delightful look at this world.

Kingstown: This bustling port, St. Vincent's capital, is full of color and boating activity. Don't miss the Saturday morning market, where local women bargain and sell produce. A stroll around town will give you a look at architecturally eclectic St. Mary's Church, a Kingstown landmark. Fort Charlotte, on the north side of town, commands a spectacular view of nearby waters (be forewarned: it's a steep climb).

Botanic Gardens: This 20-acre garden is the oldest botanical garden in the Western Hemisphere. It was started by Governor George Melville in 1765 and maintains an irresistible show of tropical plants and trees. The National Museum with its pre-Columbian artifacts is also on the grounds; open Wednesday mornings and Saturday afternoons.

The Soufrière: At 4,408 feet, St. Vincent's volcano on the northern part of the island is still rumbling, but it can be climbed by sturdy hikers. A reliable guide is a must for this one; your hotel or the Tourist Board will help you find one. Start your outing in Georgetown, where you can meet your guide and a jeep. This is an all-day climb (bring a hearty lunch) to be attempted only in good weather by those in good physical condition. Soufrière erupted in 1902 and killed 2,000 people. (This fact was lost to many since Mount Pelée's eruption the same year killed so many more.) Soufrière's most recent series of eruptions in 1979 caused a major evacuation and filled the Caribbean skies with ash.

Carib Petroglyphs: In the village of Layou; ask for "picture rock."

The Grenadines

These picturesque islands and islets, long enjoyed by yachters, stretch south from St. Vincent.

Bequia: Pronounced BECK-wee, this charming outpost, 9 miles south of St. Vincent, can be reached only by boat. Islanders are seafarers and boat builders of some reputation. Bequia is also one of the world's last whaling stations, where hand-hurled harpoons are used to kill whales (which, the Tourist Board quickly points out, is a rare event). The island also has some pleasant cafés and interesting souvenir shops. You may want to buy an accurate boat model from Sargeant's Model Boatshop as a memento of your visit. If you want an island tour, check with the Tourist Office near the dock for a recommended driver. Be sure to agree on the price in advance.

Mustique: Powdery white beaches and Princess Margaret's house are Mustique's claim to fame. If you're not staying in a private villa, the elegant Cotton House and the more moderately priced Firefly are your lodging choices on Mustique.

Canouan: This little isle has lovely beaches and good snorkeling. The Tamarind Beach Hotel and Yacht Club offers a number of rooms right on the beach.

Union Island: This mountainous island is a favorite with yachters. Its small airstrip provides a connection for launch service to Mayreau, Tobago Cays, Petit St. Vincent, and Palm islands.

Tobago Cays: These four uninhabited islets and the surrounding waters are a national marine park. They are great for camping, picnicking, and anchoring in protected harbors. Add this area to your list if you're going sailing.

Young Island, Palm Island, and Petit St. Vincent: On these private islands, most of the residents are resort guests. To get to Palm Island or Petit St. Vincent, fly to Union Island and meet the resort launch. Young Island is just off the south shore of St. Vincent.

SHOPPING: Local handicrafts such as boat models, batik clothing, carvings, and grass mats are offered at small shops throughout the islands. The local hot sauce, available at all groceries, is a popular souvenir.

FESTIVALS AND HOLIDAYS

St. Vincent and Grenadines Day, January.

Caricom Day, first Monday in July.

St. Vincent's Carnival, usually the last week in June.

Carnival Day, first Tuesday in July.

Emancipation Day, August Monday (first Monday in August).

Shops and businesses are closed on these and on traditional British holidays. Several regattas and boat races are held each year. Check with the Tourist Board for details.

FOOD: Caribbean and continental specialties with seafood are the main focus. Most dining is done at hotels. Several waterside restaurants offer a variety of simple dishes, including sandwiches. On Bequia, don't miss a meal of good island food at the Frangipani. Petit St. Vincent was mentioned in a recent *Gourmet* magazine article.

HOTELS: Hotels here are limited and tend to be exclusive and expensive. Many can be reached at toll-free numbers through your travel agent or the Tourist Office, which also can be reached toll free: (800) 729-1726.

For More Information

ST. VINCENT AND THE GRENADINES

St. Vincent and the Grenadines Tourist Office
Bay Street
P.O. Box 834, Kingstown
St. Vincent and the Grenadines
telephone: (809) 457-1502
fax: (809) 456-2610

St. Vincent and the Grenadines Hotel Association
E. T. Joshua Airport
P.O. Box 834, Arnos Vale
St. Vincent and the Grenadines
telephone: (809) 458-4379

U.S.

St. Vincent and the Grenadines Tourist Office
801 Second Avenue, 21st Floor
New York, NY 10017
telephone: (212) 687-4981 or (800) 729-1726
fax: (212) 949-5946

Trinidad and Tobago

AREA: Trinidad 1,846 miles; Tobago, 116 square miles.
POPULATION: Approximately 1.3 million.

CAPITAL CITY: Port-of-Spain, Trinidad.

LANGUAGE: English.

RELIGION: Mainly Roman Catholic, Protestant, and Hindu.

GOVERNMENT: Independent member of the British Commonwealth.

LOCATION: 9 miles from Venezuela.

GETTING THERE: Several major airlines fly into Port-of-Spain via Miami and San Juan. Interisland airlines and ferries link the two islands.

CUSTOMS: Passports and either a return or an ongoing ticket; visas necessary for stays over two months.

HEALTH: This is a very humid nation close to the South American mainland; outbreaks of yellow fever and other tropical diseases are not unknown.

CLOTHING: Standard tropical wear; keep beachwear on the beach. Visitors may want cocktail dresses or jackets and ties for hotel dining.

ELECTRICITY: 115 or 230 volts/60 cycles AC.

TIME ZONE: Atlantic standard time, one hour ahead of eastern standard time.

MONEY: Trinidadian dollar is the official currency, but U.S. dollars are accepted everywhere.

TAX AND TIPS: Airport departure tax U.S. $15; most hotels and restaurants add a 10 percent service charge to the bill.

GETTING AROUND: Taxis and rental cars are readily available. Public buses run frequently from Port-of-Spain to other cities.

Overview

Trinidad, only 8 miles from Venezuela, is the most southerly Caribbean island. With its rich oil and gas industry, it is also the most industrialized. Trinidad is the only Caribbean island that is not oceanic; it was once a part of South America, which has resulted in the diverse flora and fauna that have made the island popular with bird and animal watchers. There are fifteen official wildlife sanctuaries on Trinidad. From the spectacular scarlet ibis of Caroni Swamp to the monkeys, manatees, parrots, and four-eyed fish of Nariva Swamp, Trinidad is a great place to see a number of unique species. Since Trinidad is also the birthplace of both calypso and steel bands, it is also popular with music lovers. Port-of-Spain, the capital, is frenetic and full of life and cars. This is not the island to choose for seaside peace and quiet.

Tobago, on the other hand, is. These two islands contrast dramatically. Tobago is lined with dreamy white beaches and palms. Visitors often take in Trinidad's "wildlife" and then recuperate on tranquil Tobago. Tobago, with its offshore coral gardens and manta rays, offers some of the Caribbean's finest diving.

History

Columbus reached these islands in 1498. Cocoa and sugar plantations were established in the 1600s and 1700s with the benefits of African slave labor. Spanish land grants offered in the late 1700s attracted settlers of other nationalities, especially the French. The British captured Trinidad in 1797 and the island became a Crown Colony in 1802. Tobago was not acquired until 1814; it became a Crown Colony in 1877. The two islands became a single colony in 1889.

When the slaves were freed in 1833, the British imported large numbers of East Indians to work the plantations. More than 150,000 Hindus and Muslims from India came to Trinidad between 1845 and 1917. This influx has given Trinidad a multinational flavor that is still very apparent.

Oil and gas fields were discovered in the early 1970s, and oil revenues changed the country considerably. This nation, which became independent on 31 August 1962, now has one of the highest per capita incomes in the Caribbean.

Things to See and Do

Trinidad

Asa Wright Nature Center: Inveterate birders will want to make this an overnight to have both sunrise and sunset viewing hours. The 200-acre wildlife sanctuary, once part of an old cocoa and coffee plantation, offers guided nature walks and simple accommodations. It has 24 twin-bedded rooms and a restaurant; telephone: (809) 667-4655. Species on the property include exotic birds as well as the world's only accessible breeding colony of the nocturnal oilbird, or *guacharo.*

Caroni Bird Sanctuary: In the west coast mangrove swamp area about 7 miles south of Port-of-Spain, this sanctuary covers some 437 acres. The inner nesting area of the sanctuary is open only from May to October. Don't miss the heronries built by the little blue herons and streaked her-

TOBAGO

CARIBBEAN SEA

Speyside

Buccoo Reef
Pigeon Point

Scarborough

TRINIDAD

VENEZUELA

Las Cuevas Beach
Maracas Beach

Port of Spain
Caroni Bird Sanctuary

Nariva Swamp

La Brea

50 MI

50 KM

ons. Although many species make their homes here, the scarlet ibis is the most dramatic. Hundreds of these bright red birds come home to roost in the mangroves each evening and leave at dawn. The way to see this dramatic flocking is from the water. Several tour operators arrange this excursion. Boats usually leave the dock at 4:30 A.M. and 4:30 P.M. Plan about four hours for the excursion, and carry insect repellent. Reservations are a must.

Nariva Swamp: Across the island from the Caroni Bird Sanctuary, at Waller Field and the Agricultural Station, you may be able to spot Pied Water Tyrants, Red-breasted Blackbirds, and Blue-black Grassquits. The swamp also supports howler monkeys, alligators, anacondas, manatees, and macaws.

The Aripo Savannah and Aripo Range have at least seventy different bird species, including the Yellow-legged Thrush, which is found only above 2,000 feet.

The Tourist Office publishes several free color brochures detailing Trinidad's bird and animal life. Request their complete list of nature tour operators for options.

Emperor Valley Zoo: This zoo houses a collection of all the native animals including wild hogs, ocelots, monkeys, agoutis, pacas, and the cayman—a crocodile.

Blue Basin: In the Diego Martin Valley, some 10 miles out of Port-of-Spain, waterfalls cascade to a cold pool. Start at the basin trail and hike down for a swim (you'll need swimwear) and maybe a picnic. Wear sturdy shoes; the path is steep.

Trinidad has other many locales touted as tourist attractions, including 100-acre Pitch Lake, El Navanjo Tropical Gardens, Lopinot Historical Complex, Fort George, and bustling Port-of-Spain. Most visitors will want to spend at least half a day mingling with the masses in this busy capital. Walk, wander, plan a lunch out. The best place to start is probably Queen's Park Savannah. Be sure to include such architectural showpieces as the Roodal Residence and the Stollmeyer Castle. Don't forget the Royal Botanic Gardens. Narrow Frederick Street is the main shopping area. A bit of time spent in its diverse shops could yield the prize you're after.

BEACHES: Some of Trinidad's best are along the north coast. Maracas Bay has changing facilities and eating near its white sands. Las Cuevas Beach offers changing rooms, a snack bar, and a life guard. Farther on, Blanchisseuse Beach (no facilities) is lovely and usually not crowded. It's more than 30 miles to these beaches from the capital, but the drive offers wonders of its own. You may want to bring a picnic.

Tobago

Buccoo Reef: About a mile off Pigeon Point, this lovely reef attracts a crowd. Most hotels sell tickets for the reef and arrange for the short boat trip; times vary.

Tobago's Main Ridge: Established in 1776, the rain forest here is the oldest forest reserve in the Western Hemisphere. Just east of Scarborough, the island begins to rise to the ridge with its 2,100-foot summit. The deep valleys, waterfalls, and thick bamboo stands of this 14,000-acre preserve are full of wildlife and breathtaking views. Some visitors enjoy climbing or riding (sliding?) the more accessible waterfalls. Three-tiered Argyll Falls near Roxborough is a favorite. You can generally pick up an informal tour guide right on site. Other guide services can be arranged for those interested in nature walks or hiking to the ridge. Check with your hotel or one of the nature tour operators listed with the Tourism Office.

Bird of Paradise Sanctuary, Little Tobago: Long a nature reserve, this bird-watcher's paradise is best in early morning and late afternoon. There are many species of exotic birds on this 450-acre islet off Speyside. It's called Bird of Paradise after the forty-seven birds of paradise that were imported here in 1909. Unfortunately, their progeny perished in a hurricane in 1963. It is usually easy to get local fishermen to make the fifteen-minute boat trip to the island. They often include a guided tour and snack for a reasonable fee.

DIVING: Some of the best diving in the Caribbean can be found off the coast near Speyside, a picturesque fishing village. On the northeastern end of Tobago, Speyside's harbor, Tyrrel Bay, is protected by two islets, Goat and Little Tobago. These small islands are perhaps a mile offshore and are ringed with interesting outcrops, coves, and coral formations. However, as strong currents often run here, most of these dive sites are probably best suited for experienced divers. A number of qualified dive operators offer various dive options from Speyside and other bases. Dive Tobago at Pigeon Point is the island's oldest, most established dive operation. Man Friday Diving in Charlotteville is said to have a very personable dive operation.

BEACHES: Tobago has stunning views and sparkling sands, so head for the shore. You may want to try the well-known Pigeon Point on the northwest coast (lavatories and picnic tables); Man o' War Bay, a natural harbor with inviting sands on the south side; Store Bay; Turtle Beach; or Mount Irvine Bay. Or, you can drive up Main Ridge (the highest peak reaches 1,800 feet), look down on all these coves and beaches, and choose your own.

SHOPPING: For imported luxury items such as crystals, china, watches, and jewelry, try Stecher's in Port-of-Spain and on Tobago. Local crafts include miniature steel drums, carnival plaques, straw work, hand-crafted jewelry, and coconut shell items. Most visitors like to take home CDs or tapes of their favorite steel band and calypso tunes. Shops in the Frederick Street area of Trinidad have everything from Indian saris to leather goods and wood-carvings. There are also several good galleries in the Port-of-Spain area. Try Art Creators and Suppliers (Aldegonda Park).

FESTIVALS AND HOLIDAYS: Trinidad's Carnival is the Caribbean's biggest, with a week of calypso music, costume parades, and "jump-up" street dancing. The festivities turn Port-of-Spain into one big party from the Monday before Ash Wednesday to the following Tuesday night. Hotel reservations need to be made at least a year ahead for carnival time; prices may be double the usual rate.

FOOD: Trinidad offers lots of East Indian food such as *rotis* and curries, as well as Chinese, French, Spanish, and West Indian dishes. On Tobago, food is more of the Continental genre. Many of the hotels offer interesting dining.

HOTELS: Hotels in Port-of-Spain, Trinidad, run from expensive resorts to rustic guest houses. The north coast beaches are all at least a thirty-minute ride from Port-of-Spain; some hotels provide transportation. You might want to check on this in advance; cabs to the beach can get expensive. Consider spending the bulk of your holiday on Tobago if you're an avid beachgoer. Hotels there are slightly lower key and slightly less expensive.

Contact the Tourism Office (800-748-4224) for a complete list with prices, addresses, and booking agencies. Check the airlines for packages, which provide substantial savings in both winter and summer.

For More Information

TRINIDAD
Trinidad and Tobago Tourism Office
10-14 Phillipps Street
Port-of-Spain, Trinidad and Tobago
telephone: (809) 623-1932
fax: (809) 623-3848

U.S.
Trinidad and Tobago Tourism Office
7000 Boulevard East
Guttenberg, NJ 07093
telephone: (201) 662-3403 or (800) 748-4224
fax: (201) 869-7628

ENGLAND
Trinidad and Tobago Tourism Office
8a Hammersmith Broadway
London W6 7AL, England
telephone: (081) 741-4466
fax: (081) 741-1013

Turks and Caicos Islands

AREA: Between 166 and 193 square miles, depending on the source, including six principal islands and numerous small cays.

POPULATION: 15,500.

CAPITAL CITY: Cockburn Town, Grand Turk.

LANGUAGE: English.

RELIGION: Mainly Anglican, Protestant, and Roman Catholic.

GOVERNMENT: The islands are a stable British dependency that may become independent whenever they wish; headed by a crown-appointed governor and a partly elected state council.

LOCATION: 90 miles north of Haiti, about halfway between Miami and San Juan, and 30 sea miles south of the Bahamas' Mayaguana Island, forming the tail end of the Bahama archipelago.

GETTING THERE: Several airlines fly into the Turks and Caicos, usually via Miami or Nassau, Bahamas. The Club Med Turkoise on Provo runs its own charter flights out of New York and Miami.

CUSTOMS: Entering visitors from the U.S. and Canada do not need passports, only a birth certificate or voter's registration card for ID (a driver's license is not considered valid entry ID). Citizens of other countries need passports, but no visas are required. All visitors must have either return or ongoing tickets.

No spear guns are allowed on the islands; firearms are prohibited without a permit obtained in advance from the police department on Grand Turk. Visitors may bring one quart of liquor and either 200 cigarettes or 50 cigars or 8 ounces of tobacco duty free, plus personal items including cameras, film, and sports equipment as long as they are not for resale.

U.S. citizens may return with $100 worth of duty-free goods (at least forty-eight hours out of the country) and one quart of liquor. Canadians (also forty-eight hours out) may take back $25 Canadian worth of purchases; either two pounds of tobacco or 50 cigars or 200 cigarettes; and one imperial quart (40 ounces) of liquor. Canadians out of the country for twelve days get a $100 exemption.

HEALTH: No special precautions, but facilities for health care are minimal—a small hospital on Grand Turk; doctors on Grand Turk, South Caicos, and Provo; RNs on the other islands. No real pharmacies; take any medication you require.

CLOTHING: Informal beachwear for the most part; women may want a sarong or long pants for evening dining. Jackets and ties are not required by any establishments, but men and women both may want sweaters or light jackets for breezy evenings and outdoor dining. Be sure to bring hats and cover-ups; these islands are in the tropics and a sunburn can spoil a vacation. Note: bring all the sundries and cosmetic items you'll need. It's not uncommon for one of these small islands to be out of toothpaste or shampoo for several weeks. You'll also need to bring all your own reading material.

ELECTRICITY: 110 volts/60 cycles AC, as in the U.S.

TIME ZONE: Agrees with eastern standard time even during daylight saving time.

MONEY: U.S. dollar is legal tender. Don't count on using credit cards. Traveler's checks in U.S. dollars are preferred and are good anyplace that has enough change (generally, hotels, larger stores, and banks). There's a conversion charge for traveler's checks in currencies other than U.S. International banking facilities are on Grand Turk, South Caicos, and Provo; hours are Monday through Friday from 8:30 A.M. to 1 P.M. and 2 to 4:30 P.M.; closed Wednesday afternoons and weekends. Be sure to plan for weekend cash; lots of places run out of change.

TAX AND TIPS: Airport departure tax is $15 per person. There is a government bed tax of 7 percent on all hotel bills. Hotels also add a 10 to 15 percent service charge to the room rate; this includes anything charged to the room. Tip as in the U.S. for restaurant service.

GETTING AROUND: Most dependably on foot; some hotels provide bikes or know where you can rent them. Local people "stand by the road" (hitchhike). There really aren't very many places to go. A taxi tour will orient you and point out places of interest.

Taxis: Most hotels will call a cab for you and prices are set by law. A taxi of some sort will meet all incoming flights. Prepare to share; it might be crowded, but you could wait all day for another (in spite of promises for haste).

Car Rentals: Somewhat informal, to say the least. There are several agencies on Grand Turk and on Provo. There are also some local rentals available on Provo, Grand Turk, South Caicos, and North Caicos. Ask your hotel for the details, and make arrangements as soon as you arrive since vehicles are limited. Remember, it's left-hand drive in the British fashion.

Air Charters: You can hop from island to island on local air charters and small interisland air services. Book in advance and be there early; these flights are always crowded. Check at the airport or through your hotel desk.

Note: When traveling between islands, always carry a lunch or snacks; delays are the norm, snack bars aren't.

Overview

Once visitors are told that Turks and Caicos (pronounced Terks and CĀ-kōs) are "beyond the Bahamas, closer than the Caribbean," the next phrase will very likely include the world "uncommercialized." The fact is that these two small groups of islands are so uncommercialized, even words of commerce seem out of place. You can count on a few basic stores per island and an occasional front porch souvenir operation. What we're talking about here is sand—miles of it—and crystal blue waters like those that skirt the Bahamas, except that this far south the tides and currents are not as strong. There's no better place for snorkeling, scuba diving, sunbathing, or beachcombing than the Turks and Caicos Islands. The currents that brought Columbus still bring glass fishing floats from Portugal, unusual bottles, and the remains of pelagic animals.

There are better islands than these for comfort, easy airline connections, luxury resorts, service, food, and, without question, shopping. If these fall high on your vacation priority list, forget the back-to-nature beauty of Turks and Caicos. Life is simple and basic here. Because these are relatively low, dry islands, often with only 20 or so inches of rain a year, water is precious, and even hotel guests are asked to conserve. What the islands lack in lush foliage, however, they make up for in bird and sea life and quiet—blissful, soothing quiet. This is one place where your own footprints might be the only ones on the beach.

History

Some scholars believe that Columbus's first landfall was East Caicos and not San Salvador, Bahamas, a belief often called the Link Theory. When Columbus landed, he found a thriving community of Lucayan Indians living there and in the caves of Middle Caicos, which are now of archaeological interest.

The name "Caicos" may have come from Lucayan or may simply be another form of the Spanish *cayos*, for keys or islands. Most people believe that the Turks part of the name comes from the abundance of barreled Turkshead cactus, which are shaped like a Turkish fez topped with a red plumlike shape.

On his quest for the Fountain of Youth, Ponce de León stopped at Grand Turk in 1512, an uncontested date that marks the islands' official addition to the map.

The first permanent settlers were Bermudan salt rakers who set up housekeeping on Grank Turk in 1678. For the next seventy-odd years, these colonists were plagued with French and Spanish invasions, a Bahamian annexation attempt in 1700, and pirate raids (these islands were a favorite stomping ground of many of the infamous, including the female pirates Anne Bonny and Mary Read). So the colonists fled and returned and fought and rebuilt, continuing to tend the salinas, those shallow evaporating pools of seawater that are left to sun and time to yield dry salt.

American Loyalists settled on Caicos in 1787, establishing cotton and sisal plantations and slavery (which was abolished in 1834). In 1848 the Separation Act from the Bahamas was signed and the islands were governed by their own president and council until 1878, when they were annexed to Jamaica.

Jamaican independence in 1962 resulted in separate colony status for Turks and Caicos. That was also the year that astronaut John Glenn was debriefed at the NASA station on Grand Turk after his historic space circumnavigation.

Following the independence of the Bahamas in 1972, the islands received their own crown-appointed governor. In 1976, the first elections under the new constitution were held, which established the state ministerial government (some elected, some appointed officials) that runs the country today as a dependency of the United Kingdom. Independence is available to the islands whenever they desire it.

The 1980s saw some changes, particularly on Provo: the completion of the 9,000-foot runway at the jetport, and a new Club Med. Provo now has a casino, a golf course, and many resorts and private homes, making it the most developed of the Caicos Islands. All signs are that the quiet waters are stirring.

Things to See and Do

Natural Areas

Most of these cays and islands have relatively undisturbed flora and fauna that are not quite Antillean or completely Bahamian. Ospreys, or fish hawks, often perch on the sailboat masts in Third Turtle Cove, Provo. Turks and Caicos are one of the few places where even casual snorkelers may spot young hawksbill turtles sleeping among corals or sunning on the surface of the water. There are a number of bird and butterfly sanctuaries; these islands are home to several rare species, including the Erebus moth, which may have a 12-inch wingspan. The Turks and Caicos National Underwater Park is off Pine Cay. Nearby Fort George Cay is also a national park where iguanas are plentiful. The fort saw actual battles, and its five cannons, blown into the water by a storm, have become a dive attraction. Island flora includes the large-barreled turkshead cactus, prickly pear cactus, casuarina pines, and colorful seaside morning glories. These are dry islands and most of the standard tropical foliage is evident only in plantings around homes or hotels. Most islands have some mangroves, and beautiful shores line the cays and creeks. The byword is wander; it's safe. You'll find no dangerous wildlife—no poisonous snakes, no hostile people.

Grand Turk

The seat of government, with all the official buildings. Stroll the town to enjoy the quaint Bermudan architecture. A picturesque old lighthouse is on a remote part of the island (tours available by cab). If you want to pick up a few trinkets (don't overlook the beautiful postage stamps) or a tube of toothpaste, Grank Turk is the best place to do it. It's also a good place to initiate dive or fishing trips. Don't miss the Turks and Caicos Islands National Museum. Its main exhibit focuses on the Molasses Reef wreck, the oldest authenticated European shipwreck in the New World. The display features the remains of the ship's hull, its huge anchor, many tools of the era, and the world's largest collection of sixteenth-century wrought-iron breech-loading cannons. Other exhibits feature artifacts from early settlers.

Salt Cay

This 3½ square-mile cay is only 9 miles from Grand Turk and can be reached by sea or in five minutes by air. Balfour Town with its picturesque windmills and salinas (salt beds) has a history touched by whalers and salt rakers. The salinas are now a bird sanctuary, but the town is said to have changed little since it was first settled by Bermudans. Good snorkeling just offshore. The smallest of the populated islands in this chain, Salt Cay offers a marvelous vantage point for observing birds migrating through Columbus Passage during the winter months.

North Caicos

The more generous rainfall on this island helps support lusher vegetation. A favorite spot is Flamingo Pond, where the long-legged pink beauties fly in to roost. There is also a soft-shelled crab farm that visitors can tour.

Middle or Grand Caicos

Few people live on this island, the largest of the group and the least populated. Notable for its limestone caves (stalactites and stalagmites are reflected in salty pools); U.S. archaeologists have been visiting since 1977 to search the caves and ruins for Lucayan and Arawak Indian relics. No hotels or guest houses, only a government rest house for visitors. The island is reached by ferry from North Caicos; day trips are possible.

South Caicos

Lots of dive sites; a great natural harbor, Cockburn Harbor, is the center of the islands' lobster and conch export business. Site of the annual May regatta; quiet the rest of the year.

Pine Cay

A quiet, 800-acre cay with the Meridian Club (and its somewhat chic clientele) and about twenty private residences. Home of PRIDE (an association for the Protection of Reefs and Islands from Degradation and Exploitation), which runs a first-class dive operation and research center (they're working on the mariculture of the queen conch, among other things). Most of the area is protected; the National Underwater Park lies in these waters. Absolutely no live collecting. Hiking trails and nature walks. Fort George Cay with its iguanas is also a protected area and lies across the channel.

Provo (Providenciales)

The center of tourist development—a jetport, Club Med, and a number of luxury hotels. Provo now has a casino and a golf course. Most resorts have tennis courts, many with lights. Many rent water sports equipment as well. Diving and windsurfing are two of Provo's major draws. Visitors may enjoy visiting the plantation houses, Cheshire Hill and Richmond Hill. The Conch Farm and Island Sea Center is involved with conch mariculture, among other things. It raises the pearly pink mollusk to help prevents its depletion from the wild by providing an alternative commercial source. Different stages of conch development can be observed. A good gift shop features conch shell jewelry and books about marine life.

SWIMMING AND DIVING: Swimming, diving, beachcombing, and sunbathing top the list. These islands have 230 miles of beaches, some with gold sand, some with white. They're rimmed with crystal waters and barrier reefs. The combination of sand flats, shallow patch reefs, spectacular drop-offs, and romantic old wrecks (the proclaimed wreck of the *Pinta* lies in these waters) makes Turks and Caicos a diver's paradise. All the major islands have dive masters and well-thought-of dive outfits that offer certification, equipment rental, and dive trips. Most local divers are very protective when it comes to this superb reef area, and they follow the slogan of Pine Cay's PRIDE, "Take only pictures, leave only bubbles." Spear guns are illegal and not even allowed on the islands.

FISHING: Reef fishing for food fish is to be had almost anywhere; most hotels will cook your catch. Deep-sea fishing is available, but bonefish are the big sportfishing attraction here. The guides with good reputations include Julius Jennings on South Caicos, Dolphus Arthurs on Middle Caicos, and Bonefish Lem (Lemuel Stubbs) on Provo. Lem is also an excellent sailboat pilot if you're unsure of tricky reefs or entrances.

Boat rental is usually up to you and can be arranged through most hotels. Prices vary, starting at about $10 to $20 an hour for a small Boston whaler (four hours minimum) plus guide, gas, and lunch for all (you feed the guide), and up. It's also entirely possible to make a deal with a local fisherman who has his own boat. Ask around; these islands are small places where everyone knows everyone and where they are and probably what they're doing.

NIGHTLIFE: Aside from the casino on Provo, nightlife is quiet and generally centered around hotel bars. There are a couple of discos on Grand

Turk and some informal dancing on Provo. For the most part, plan to be self-sufficient.

SHOPPING: Stores close at 1 P.M. on Wednesdays; some are closed for a noon break as well. Offerings are limited but the careful shopper may find some pleasing artwork—straw, paintings, or sculpture, as well as handmade shell jewelry. The imported rum from the Dominican Republic and Haiti is often a good buy (no duty-free shops here). There is some local handiwork available. The handmade rag rugs are a real find. Beach wear and resort items are available in all hotel shops. On Provo, the Thursday market in Market Square is fun. Don't overlook the islands' beautiful postage stamps. Many of their commemorative issues are sought by stamp collectors throughout the world.

FOOD: Most restaurants are connected with hotels and inns and offer different island specialties, mostly seafood, in an informal setting. You may want to try whelk soup (made from large black and white sea snails and not unlike clam chowder) or one of the dishes made from local conch—chowder, salad, or fritters. Lobster dishes and fresh fish, often grouper, are usually on the menu. Please don't order the turtle steak that so many tourist places feel they must offer in spite of the animal's tenuous existence; sea turtles are endangered.

HOTELS: Aside from Club Med, the Ramada Turquoise Reef and the Royal Bay Resort and Villas on Provo, most of the accommodations on the Turks and Caicos are in fairly small hotels. Unfortunately, they are also rather pricey. Remember to figure in the government hotel tax of 7 percent and the 10 or 15 percent service charge (this is on everything charged to the room) when budgeting for your rooms. Dive packages often offer considerable savings on room rates. If air conditioning, phones, etc., are important to you, be sure to check availability in advance. Ask the Tourist Board for a complete listing. From the U.S., call (800) 441-4419.

GRAND TURK

Kittina Hotel: 43 rooms, including suites; built by Kit Fenimore himself of hand-quarried stone. Some rooms have balconies looking out on the sea, which is only a skip and a holler away; downstairs rooms open onto a courtyard. Dive shop, bar, and restaurant; five-minute walk into town. Expensive.

Salt Raker Inn: 12 units in a 150-year-old house. Across the road from the beach and a pleasant walk from downtown. Informal, with garden, pub, dining facilities, and a library for guests.

Turks Head Inn: 6 recently renovated rooms. Built of Canadian pine for a salt industry owner in the late 1860s. Notable for its lack of nails; all joints are pegged. Beach, pub, and dining room that's always busy on prime rib Fridays.

Ocean View: 10 double rooms with color TVs. On the beach between the airport and Kittina. Bar, dining room.

PROVO (PROVIDENCIALES)

Erebus at Latitude 22: on hillside overlooking Third Turtle Cove. Short walk to beach; two swimming pools, tennis courts, restaurant. Expensive.

Turtle Cove: 28 rooms and 2 suites overlooking the water and marina. Favorite of boaters and divers. Short walk to beach; pool, tennis courts, two restaurants on grounds.

Club Med Turkoise: about 200 rooms in one- and two-story clusters right on the beach. Complete resort, moderately priced inclusive package—airfare, water sports, food, and wine. No children under six. Through travel agents or Club Med: 40 West 57th Street, New York, NY 10019; telephone: (800) CLUB MED.

SALT CAY

Mount Pleasant Guesthouse: 5 rooms (3 with baths) in this 80-year-old home of James Morgan, who was in charge of salt production here for 25 years. Well known for wonderful home-cooked meals that could include your own catch. A favorite with divers.

Government Bungalows: 2 bungalows on lovely North Beach. Guests must provide their own food—bring staples with you; seafood may be purchased locally. Minimum 3-day stay at reasonable prices. Ask the Tourist Board on Grand Turk for help with arrangements.

NORTH CAICOS

Prospect of Whitby Resort: 26 rooms with everything (beach, boat rental, tennis, pool, dive equipment). Country club atmosphere. English pub. Bring clothes for dining in their stylish dining room. Expensive.

Ocean Beach Hotel: 10 rooms on the beach at Whitby. Tennis, pool, restaurant, and bar. Scuba and bonefishing available. Weekly rates. Two condos with kitchens.

SOUTH CAICOS

Admiral's Arms: 15 rooms with sea view. Dive packages make this inn popular with scuba groups. Pool, terrace, bar.

Harbour View: 12 basic rooms on the shore, mainly a simple base for fishermen and divers. Bar and island-type restaurant. Inexpensive. More information from Tourist Office.

PINE CAY

Meridian Club: 12 suites and some cottage rentals. Small, quiet, ecologically oriented island; nature walks, boat trips, PRIDE diving operation. Pool, bar, and restaurant with family-style meals. Expensive.

For More Information

TURKS AND CAICOS

Turks and Caicos Tourist Board
P.O. Box 218
Pond Street, Grand Turk
Turks and Caicos Islands
telephone: (800) 241-0824
fax: (809) 946-2733

U.S. Virgin Islands

AREA: About 75 small cays and rocks plus the three main islands of St. Croix (84 square miles), St. Thomas (32 square miles), and St. John (28 square miles).

POPULATION: Approximately 102,000.

CAPITAL CITY: Charlotte Amalie, St. Thomas.

LANGUAGE: English.

RELIGION: Varied.

GOVERNMENT: U.S. Territory with elected governor.

LOCATION: In the Leeward Islands, about 80 miles east of Puerto Rico.

GETTING THERE: Many major airlines fly directly to St. Thomas or St. Croix; others connect via San Juan. St. Thomas is a major cruise-ship port.

CUSTOMS: U.S. citizens need only proof of citizenship; other nationalities need the same documents they would to enter the U.S.

HEALTH: No special considerations; it's best to stick to bottled water, since local supplies are often questionable.

CLOTHING: Informal tropical wear. Shorts are okay in town; some hotels require jackets for men.

ELECTRICITY: 110 volts/60 cycles AC, as in the U.S.

TIME ZONE: Atlantic standard time, one hour ahead of eastern standard time.

MONEY: U.S. currency.

TAX AND TIPS: 7½ percent room tax. Many places add 10 to 15 percent service charge; check before you add a tip.

GETTING AROUND: Taxis, tours, regular jitney buses and taxi vans, rental cars, jeeps, and motor scooters. Valid U.S. driver's license required.

Overview

The U.S. Virgin Islands is a beautiful bit of U.S. territory in the Caribbean. The three main islands—St. Thomas, St.John, and St. Croix—are framed with lovely beaches but are distinctly different. Mountainous, busy St. Thomas is a major cruise-ship stop for free-port shopping. Nearby St. John is mostly U.S. national park, crisscrossed by hiking trails and bordered with world-famous sands. St. Croix, some 60 miles south of St. Thomas, is not as developed as St. Thomas or as sophisticated as St. John. The largest island of the group, St. Croix has the visual ease of rolling hills and historic towns; much of the island is still pastureland. The Salt River National Park, where Columbus first landed nearly 500 years ago, has an extensive mangrove stand and other shore habitats as well.

All three of the Virgin Islands make an easy vacation destination for U.S. citizens. They're American and modern enough to be convenient, yet exotic and foreign enough to satisfy the need for change. All have good diving and swimming and beautiful coral sand beaches as well as boating, tennis, and golf. They are an excellent vacation choice, especially for first-time Caribbean visitors.

UNITED STATES VIRGIN ISLANDS

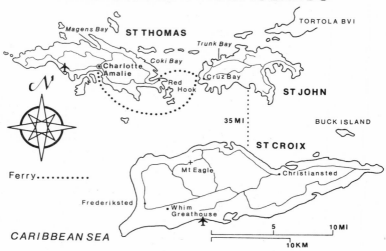

History

After Columbus landed in St. Croix on his second voyage in 1493, the Spaniards spent the 1500s exterminating the native Carib Indians. The first permanent settlement on St. Croix was established by the Danes in 1672. Denmark acquired St. John in 1716 and bought St. Croix from France in 1733.

The U.S. bought the islands from Denmark in 1917 for $25 million. In 1927, U.S. citizenship was granted to all Virgin Islanders. But it was not until 1968 that the islands elected their own governor. The St. John National Park was established in 1956. Leading industries include tourism, petroleum refining, and agriculture.

The unique beauty and historical architecture of the islands continue to be recognized. The Salt River area on St. Croix became a national park in 1993, the 500th anniversary of Columbus's landing. The towns of Charlotte Amalie, Christiansted, and Frederiksted are listed in the National Register of Historic Places. Buck Island Reef National Monument off St. Croix remains a favorite with visitors of all ages.

Note: The Virgin Islands are not without crime. It's best not to wander the streets after dark, especially the St. Thomas waterfront; the stroll from the yacht basin to town is inviting but unsafe. Take a taxi from your hotel to the restaurant in the evening. Watch your purse even in daytime. Also, avoid housing projects; they are not a good place for visitors day or night. With a little common sense, you're sure to have a pleasant sojourn.

Things to See and Do

St. Thomas

St. Thomas is a free port, as the busy stores lining the main streets of Charlotte Amalie attest. Many stores are located in restored Danish warehouses. You may want to visit historic Fort Christian, built by the Danes in 1671. It's massive and red—you can't miss it. The fort now contains the Virgin Islands Museum (open Monday through Friday from 8 A.M. to 5 P.M., Saturday from 1 to 5 P.M.; free). The Emancipation Garden, down the hill just off Main Street, is lined with lignum vitae trees. The dense, hard wood of these exotic trees was once used to carve idols; the tree itself continues to hold a place in Caribbean folklore. By walking through town to get to the Seven Arches Museum, a restored eighteenth-century Danish house with yellow ballast brick arches and a walled garden, you'll see a great deal of Charlotte Amalie's interesting architecture. The admission price includes a tropical drink.

For visitors interested in a more extended walking tour or more details about St. Thomas's historic buildings, ask the Division of Tourism for a copy of the "Historic District Guide."

Most tours of St. Thomas include a stop at the Mountain Top restaurant and bar, with its spectacular view and famous banana daiquiris. You can see all the way down to Drake's Passage, which separates the U.S. and British Virgin Islands.

Coral World: This aquarium and underwater observatory at Coki Beach is especially popular with nondivers who have never seen living corals. The complex contains pleasant restaurants, gift shops, a nature walk, and caged iguanas and mongooses, as well as changing rooms for beachgoers; admission charge.

St. Croix

Although St. Croix has taken a beating from hurricanes in recent years, the island seems to snap back with new buildings and new vitality. While the storms may have discouraged some plans for major resorts, they seem to have spawned a new appreciation for the island's natural resources. The St. Croix Environmental Association (SEA), with its small office in downtown Christiansted, has taken the lead in organizing guided nature hikes, as well as many other facets of environmental preservation, education, and appreciation. Visitors are encouraged to join one of their informative tours. Hikes include east end beaches, the rain forest at Caledonia, and Salt River National Park. Check with your hotel for more information or call SEA at 773-1989. About $20 for adults, less for children (not

Many buildings of Christiansted, St. Croix, U.S.V.I., a national historic site, retain an aura of earlier times. (Photo by Carrol Fleming.)

recommended for those under 6), members of SEA, and guests of participating hotels.

Other ways to get a closer look at St. Croix's natural treasures include rain forest horseback rides and mountain bike tours. Check with the Division of Tourism for details.

If you only do two things on St. Croix, snorkel Buck Island and visit Whim Plantation Great House. For those with more time, be sure to drive (or walk) the island's South Shore Road, where rolling pastures and abandoned mills skirt the open Atlantic.

Christiansted: St. Croix's main settlement, a U.S. national historic site, is a delightful harbor town with Old World charm and architecture. Pick up a free walking tour map at the Tourist Board in the Scale House on the harbor opposite the fort. Even if you don't take in all the sights, you may want to include Fort Christansvaern (the large yellow building) and the Steeple Building. As you wander, enjoy the many restored buildings and shops with their seventeenth- and eighteenth-century designs.

Frederiksted: St. Croix's second-largest town is historic Frederiksted, which shows its age more than much of restored Christiansted. Fort

Frederik, built in the eighteenth century, has been restored and is open daily. The small St. Croix Aquarium (across from the cruise-ship pier) is an interesting stop. Children are particularly taken with the "touch pond." Frederiksted is surrounded by some of the island's best beaches. The town is a good stop for lunch and for wandering.

When you drive from Christiansted to Frederiksted down Centerline Road (which is lined with mahogany trees), you'll pass a number of points of interest. Sunny Isle Shopping Center, with Woolworth's and other U.S. chain stores, is the main shopping area for locals. Farther on are Ville La Reine Shopping Center and the red-roofed University of the Virgin Islands. A bit farther on is St. George's Botanical Garden.

Head on to the *Whim Plantation Great House,* a must for everyone. Its huge tamarind trees, and sugar mill, and antique cook house, where visitors can buy johnnycakes cooked on a woodstove, give a vivid picture of life in another century. My daughter describes it as "olden days Disneyland on St. Croix." The admission charge helps support the Landmark Society (you may even want to join).

Mahogany Road: A good example of moist tropical forest that offers a shadowy respite from the heat of the day. You can include this on your Frederiksted circuit, as most tours do.

Creque Dam Road Area: This lovely tract with Spanish moss hanging from huge trees is a nice area for exploring. You might want to drive in and then wander on foot. Check the map for details or inquire at nearby Sprat Hall.

SALT RIVER NATIONAL PARK: This 912-acre park where Columbus landed in 1493 includes a rich estuary system lined with mangroves as well as prehistoric Indian sites. The bay and surrounding areas provide habitat for a rich population of plants and animals, including twenty-seven threatened or endangered species.

Buck Island Reef National Monument: Don't miss this chance "to swim in an aquarium," as many visitors describe their snorkel tours of this dazzling coral reef. Take a day boat from Christiansted Harbor or Green Cay Marina. Prices include snorkeling gear and instruction. Captain Francis Waters of *Diva,* out of Green Cay Marina, is a longtime resident, and his Buck Island charters, limited to six guests at a time, is always popular.

St. John

St. John is nearly all U.S. national park from sea to mountaintop. It has long been the destination of campers, hikers, and avid beachgoers. There's good snorkeling and diving off almost every shore. The National Park Service organizes several inshore night dives as well. The marked underwater trail at Trunk Bay has been damaged by heavy traffic, but its shallow waters and marked sea life make it good for beginners.

HIKING: Trails crisscross every habitat of this island. You'll want to carry a bathing suit with you on lots of them. Also, bring snacks and drinking water (there is none along the way); the park service suggests about a half gallon for each four hours of hiking time. Insect repellent and a hat are recommended. Be sure to pick up a good map before you go.

Several trails take considerably less than an hour, namely, Caneel Hill Spur Trail, Water Catchment Trail, Turtle Point, Francis Bay Trail, Anaberg Trail, Leinster Bay, and the Petroglyph Trail. Peace Hill Trail is only a ten-minute walk. Many of these short trails are easy walks that almost anyone can make; Anaberg is especially popular.

Other trails are more arduous, for which the park service offers a number of scheduled hikes with guides. Check at the Visitors' Center in Cruz Bay. The Reef Bay Trail, about 2½ miles long, is one of the most popular; it takes hikers through both moist and dry forest areas and passes a number of ruins. Get a complete trail list and map from the park Visitors' Center.

BEACHES: Magens Bay on St. Thomas is a frequent entry on the list of the world's ten most beautiful beaches; changing rooms and a snack bar. Other good beaches include Morningstar, Cowpet, Sapphire, and Brewer's Bay, near the University of the Virgin Islands. Many good beaches on St. Croix are in front of hotels, but all shorelines here are open to everyone, so go and enjoy. You might want to try the Buccaneer's beach (small charge), Divi St. Croix, or Sprat Hall. Other beauties around the island include Kramer Park (with facilities), Buck Island, Columbus Landing Point at Salt River, and Sandy Point in Frederiksted. St. John's shores are spectacular—each one has something different to offer. The extensive white sands of Trunk Bay, Caneel Bay, and Cinnamon Bay are world famous.

SHOPPING: Charlotte Amalie, St. Thomas, is one of the Caribbean's major free-port shopping areas. The Division of Tourism provides a map of the downtown area and suggestions of what to buy where. Continental and Little Switzerland (also in Christiansted) offer some of the best china and crystal. Try Boolchand's for cameras and linens, Cardow for jewelry. Browsing will turn up some local handicrafts, as well.

On St. Croix, Many Hands in Christiansted offers only locally made items and artwork. Many small shops and boutiques, as well as hotel gift shops, offer a complete selection of perfumes, jewelry, clothing, and souvenirs.

On St. John, Cruz Bay, Mongoose Junction, and Caneel Bay's gift shop may have the most interesting variety in the U.S.V.I.; they all seem to be striving for unique and handcrafted gifts.

FESTIVALS AND HOLIDAYS

Pre-Lenten Carnival varies by year. The big event on St. Thomas.

Annual Agriculture and Food Fair, Presidents' Day weekend in February. A unique event on St. Croix, like an old-fashioned country fair, Caribbean-style.

Summer Carnival, varies by year. Colorful festivities on St. John.

FOOD: Food ranges from Danish smorgasbord to McDonald's with Continental and West Indian specialties in between.

On St. Thomas, the Mafolie serves a good dinner with a spectacular view of the harbor. Pizza, Chinese food, and simpler fare are available along the waterfront; Sparky's is popular.

On St. Croix, the downtown hotels and restaurants offer a wide variety of seafood, steak, and West Indian dishes. The Hotel on the Cay (take the ferry at the wharf) makes a pleasant evening outing. The Comanche has long been popular with residents. Several north shore eateries offer creative cuisine right on the beach.

HOTELS: St. Thomas has hotels everywhere and one campground (see Camping for details). For beach hotels, try Bologna Beach, Pineapple Beach, or Mount Pleasant.

St. Croix doesn't have as many choices as St. Thomas, but there are a number of good ones. Beach hotels include Carambola, the Buccaneer, and the small Tamarind Reef.

St. John has refined Caneel Bay and the Virgin Grand in Cruz Bay as well as low-key guest houses and campsites (see Camping for a list).

Get a complete list of accommodations and prices from the Tourist Board. Ask about packages and off-season deals. From the U.S., call toll free; for St. Croix: (800) 524-2026; for St. Thomas / St. John: (800) 3GO-USVI.

For More Information

ST. CROIX

P.O. Box 4538

Christiansted, USVI 00822
telephone: (809) 773-0495
fax: (809) 778-9259

Custom House Building
Strand Street, Frederiksted, USVI 00840
telephone: (809) 772-0357

ST. JOHN
P.O. Box 200
Cruz Bay, USVI 00830
telephone: (809) 776-6450

ST. THOMAS
P.O. Box 6400
Charlotte Amalie, USVI 00840
telephone: (809) 774-8784
fax: (809) 774-4390

U.S.
Call 1–800–USVI–INFO or
225 Peachtree Street, NE, Suite 760
Atlanta, GA 30303
telephone: (404) 688-0906
fax: (404) 525-1102

500 North Michigan Avenue, Suite 2030
Chicago, IL 60611
telephone: (312) 670-8784
fax: (312) 670-8788/8789

2655 Le Jeune Road, Suite 907
Coral Gables, FL 33134
telephone: (305) 442-7200
fax: (305) 445-9044

3460 Wilshire Boulevard, Suite 412
Los Angeles, CA 90010
telephone: (213) 739-0138
fax: (213) 739-2005

1270 Avenue of the Americas, Suite 2108
New York, NY 10020

telephone: (212) 332-2222
fax: (212) 332-2223

900 17th Street N.W., Suite 500
Washington, DC 20006
telephone: (202) 293-3707
fax: (202) 785-2542

CANADA

The Mutual Group Centre
33 Bloor Street West
Suite 3120, Centre Tower
Toronto, Ontario M8X 2X3
Canada
telephone: (416) 233-1414
fax: (416) 233-9367

ENGLAND

2 Cinnamon Row, Plantation Wharf
York Place, London SW11 3TW
England
telephone: (071) 978-5262
fax: (071) 924-3171
telex: 27231

PUERTO RICO

1300 Ashford Avenue
Condado, Santurce
San Juan, Puerto Rico 00907
telephone: (809) 724-3816
fax: (809) 724-7223

Recommended Reading

There is a great deal of diverse information available on the Caribbean islands. Much of it is out of print, out of date, or simply inaccurate. Each island has its own selection of small press and self-published titles that will enrich a visit with their wealth of local detail. Check local shops on each island; often they are the only place to find these accounts. *Caribbean Travel and Life* magazine, available at most newsstands and by subscription, is a good course of current information on the area. Here is a list of additional sources.

Bacon, Peter R. *Flora and Fauna of the Caribbean*. Port-of-Spain, Trinidad: Key Caribbean Publications, 1978.

Blume, Helmut. *The Caribbean Islands*. London: Longman Group Ltd., 1968.

Bond, James. *Birds of the West Indies,* 3d ed. Boston: Houghton Mifflin Co., 1971.

Campbell, David G. *The Ephemeral Islands: A Natural History of the Bahamas*. London and Basingstoke: Macmillan Education Ltd. 1978.

Cracknell, Basil E. *Dominica*. Harrisburg, PA: Stackpole Books, 1973.

Fournet, Jacques. *Plants and Flowers of the Caribbean*. Papeete, Tahiti: Les Editions du Pacifique, 1977.

Greenberg, Idaz, and Jerry Greenberg. *Guide to Corals and Fishes of Florida, the Bahamas, and the Caribbean*. Miami: Seahawk Press.

Harman, Carter. *The West Indies*. New York: Life World Library, 1963.

Irish, George J. A. *Alliouagana Folk*. Plymouth, Montserrat: Jagpi Production, Harmony House, 1985.

Jadan, Doris. *A Guide to the Natural History of St. John*. St. John, U.S. Virgin Islands: V.I. Conservation Society, 1971.

Jones, Alick, and Nancy Sefton. *Marine Life in the Caribbean*. London and Basingstoke: Macmillan Caribbean, 1978.

Kaplan, Eugene H. *A Field Guide to Coral Reefs of the Caribbean and Florida*. Boston: Houghton Mifflin Co., 1982.

Lennox, G. W., and S. A. Seddon. *Flowers of the Caribbean: The Bahamas and Bermuda*. London and Basingstoke: Macmillan Caribbean, 1978.

Lewisohn, Florence. *The Romantic History of St. Croix*. St. Croix, U.S. Virgin Islands: St. Croix Landmarks Society, Inc.

Lewisohn, Walter, and Florence Lewisohn. *The Living Arts and Crafts of the West Indies*. Christiansted, St. Croix, U.S. Virgin Islands: Virgin Islands Council on the Arts, 1973.

Little, E. L., Jr., and R. O. Woodbury. *Trees of the Caribbean National Forest, Puerto Rico*. Rio Piedras, Puerto Rico: Institute of Tropical Forestry, 1976.

Mitchell, Carleton. *Isles of the Caribbees*. Washington, DC: National Geographic, 1966.

Morrison, Samuel Eliot, and Mauricio Obregón. *The Caribbean as Columbus Saw It*. Boston: Little, Brown and Co., 1964.

Naipal, V. S. *The Loss of El Dorado*. New York: Alfred A. Knopf, 1970.

Oakes, A. J., and James O. Butcher. *Poisonous and Injurious Plants of the Virgin Islands*. Kingshill, St. Croix, U.S. Virgin Islands: College of the Virgin Islands Cooperative Extension Service, 1962.

Olsen, Fred. *On the Trail of the Arawaks*. Norman: University of Oklahoma Press, 1974.

Petersen, Arona. *Herbs and Proverbs of the Virgin Islands*. Arona Petersen, Box 7455, St. Thomas, U.S. Virgin Islands 00801, 1974.

Raffaele, H. A. *A Guide to the Birds of Puerto Rico and the Virgin Islands*. San Juan: Fondo Educativo Interamericano, 1983.

Riley, Norman D. *Butterflies of the West Indies*. London: William Collins Sons & Co. Ltd., 1975.

Rivero, J. A. *The Amphibians and Reptiles of Puerto Rico*. Rio Piedras, Puerto Rico: Universidad de Puerto Rico, Editorial Universitaria, 1978.

Robinson, Alan. *Virgin Islands National Park: The Story Behind the Scenery*. Las Vegas: KC Publications, 1974.

Rodman, Selden. *The Caribbean*. New York: Hawthorn Books, Inc., 1968.

Slater, Mary. *Cooking the Caribbean Way*. London: Hamlyn Publishing Group Ltd., 1965.

Warmke, Germaine L., and R. Tucker Abbott. *Caribbean Seashells*. New York: Dover Publications, Inc., 1961.

Wauer, Roland H. *Virgin Islands Birdlife*. St. Croix: University of the Virgin Islands Cooperative Extension Service, 1988.

Williams, Eric. *From Columbus to Castro: The History of the Caribbean*. New York: Vintage Books, 1970.

Wood, Beryl. *Caribbean Fruits and Vegetables: Selected Recipes*. Longman Caribbean, 1973.

Permissions

The author is grateful for permission to reprint material from the following sources: *Herbs and Proverbs of the Virgin Islands* by Arona Petersen, St. Thomas, 1974. The following proverbs are used with her permission: "Time is longer than rope"; "Tis hurrystance ar kill yo"; "Take care is better than don't care"; "Put your ear to mango root, yo can hear crab laugh"; "Donkey say God make the world with hill and hallow, so when you climb the high hill, yo cud res' in the hallow."

Portions of the chapter on mangroves were taken from an article written for the OAS magazine, *Américas,* March–April 1983, pp. 9–12.

All or portions of the chapters on coral reefs, the rocky shore, and beachcombing are reprinted by permission of *Science 80* magazine / American Association for the Advancement of Science.

"The coral polyp: architect of the sea," *Science 80,* November, pp. 104–5; "Life and flotsam," *Science 81,* July–August, pp. 98–99.

Excerpt from a letter ("My Dear Herbie . . ."), which appears in Part 2 of this book, is used with permission of the Montserrat National Trust.

Special thanks to Erika J. Smilowitz, Ph.D., for her contribution, "Literature and Performance Poetry."

Index